SOCIAL JUSTICE IN A DIVERSE SOCIETY

Social Justice in a Diverse Society

Tom R. Tyler
University of California–Berkeley

Robert J. Boeckmann
Mills College

Heather J. Smith
Saint Mary's College

and Yuen J. Huo
Public Policy Institute of California

WestviewPress
A Division of HarperCollins*Publishers*

CALVIN T. RYAN LIBRARY
U. OF NEBRASKA AT KEARNEY

Published in 1997 in the United States of America by Westview Press, 5500 Central Avenue, Boulder, Colorado 80301-2877, and in the United Kingdom by Westview Press, 12 Hid's Copse Road, Cumnor Hill, Oxford OX2 9JJ

Typeset by Letra Libre

Library of Congress Cataloging-in-Publication Data
Social justice in a diverse society / Tom R. Tyler . . . [et al.].
    p. cm.
  Includes bibliographical references and index.
  ISBN 0-8133-3214-1.—ISBN 0-8133-3215-X (pbk.)
    1. Social justice. 2. Equality—United States. 3. United States—Social conditions.
  I. Tyler, Tom R.
HM216.S553 1997
303.3'72—dc21   96-49150
                                                                    CIP

10   9   8   7   6   5   4   3   2   1

CONTENTS

TABLES AND FIGURES

Part 1

INTRODUCTION

Issues of social justice have been an important part of social psychology since the explosion of psychological research that occurred during and after World War II. At that time, psychologists began to move away from earlier theories that paid little attention to people's subjective understanding of the world. As increasing attention was paid to people's thoughts about their social experiences, it was discovered that people are strongly affected by their assessments of what is just or fair in their dealings with others. This recognition has led to a broad range of studies exploring what people mean by justice and how it influences their thoughts, feelings, and behaviors.

1

The Psychology of Social Justice

Justice as a Philosophical or Theological Concern

Throughout history, the writings of philosophers, theologians, and social theorists as diverse as Aristotle, Kant, Marx, Plato, and Rawls have been shaped by efforts to define how individuals, groups, and societies should or ought to behave. Although diverse in many respects, all of these efforts have in common the argument that both people and societies should be governed by standards of conduct beyond simple deference to the possession of power and resources. The use of terms such as "right and wrong," "ethical and unethical," "moral and immoral," and "just and unjust" connotes that conduct ought to be influenced by justice criteria derived from logical analysis; the works of religious, political, or legal authorities; and many other sources. In other words, there is a widely shared belief that societies ought to be constructed in ways that reflect what is just, and social theorists have devoted considerable energy to defining what is just in objective terms.

Consider the work of Rawls (1971) on moral philosophy. Rawls argues that justice is the first virtue of social institutions. In other words, in designing social institutions, it is important that criteria of fairness be considered. Rawls suggests several such criteria. For example, he argues that principles of justice suggest that social allocation rules should not injure those within a society who are the most disadvantaged. This is an example of an objective normative principle. Rawls does not argue that everyone will necessarily agree with this principle, but he does suggest that it is the just or fair principle to use on philosophical grounds.

Another example of an objective normative statement of justice is the pastoral letter of the United States Catholic Bishops (1986) entitled "Economic Justice for All." This letter speaks to issues of social obligation in economic settings from the perspective of a "long tradition of thought and action on the moral dimensions of economic activity" (p. 410). For example, the bishops argue that "Every economic decision and institution must be judged in light of whether it protects or undermines the dignity of the human person" (p. 411). Why? Because, they say, human dignity develops from people's connection with God and should be served by economic institutions and practices. Again, these arguments depend on having an independent perspective—in this case, religious writing—from which to view social rules and institutions. Throughout history, religious authority has provided an important alternative perspective on social justice to the rules and norms articulated by political, legal, and managerial authorities (Kelman & Hamilton, 1989).

Justice as a Subjective Issue

Justice is not just a set of principles derived from objective sources, such as religious authorities. It is also an idea that exists within the minds of all individuals. This subjective sense of what is right or wrong is the focus of the psychology of justice. Unlike the objective principles of justice discussed earlier, subjective feelings about justice or injustice are not necessarily justified by reference to particular standards of authority. Our concern in exploring subjective justice is with understanding what people think is right and wrong, just or unjust, fair or unfair and with understanding how such judgments are justified by the people who hold them.

The primary argument made in this book is that it is important to pay attention to people's subjective judgments about what is just or fair. One reason is that justice matters to people within social groups. People's thoughts, feelings, and behaviors have been widely shown to be influenced by their judgments about the justice or injustice of their experiences. Hence, people's feelings about justice are an important basis of their reactions to others. This assumption has led social scientists to try to understand how people decide that justice has or has not occurred.

Because justice is important to individuals in organized groups, the deliberations and actions of social actors—that is, both leaders and followers in political, legal, religious, and business settings—are also shaped at least in part by the belief that moral ideals of rights and entitlements are distinct from the mere struggle for possession of power or resources. In other words, justice is not merely a concern of philosophers and social theorists. It is an important issue in interactions among people. Authorities in all types of societies and groups shape their actions to fit their judgments about what people will feel is just.

The United States Catholic Bishops' (1986) statement can be contrasted to a statement made at approximately the same time by the White House Office of Policy Information (H. C. Gordon & Keyes, 1983). This statement addresses the same subject addressed by the bishops—economic policy. And it invokes the same issues of justice and fairness. In fact, the report is entitled *Fairness II: An Executive Briefing Book*. In contrast to the bishops' statement, however, the White House statement is political in character. It attempts to tap into people's values about justice without presenting some objective philosophical or religious criteria for defining justice issues and concerns. The report assumes that how people react to proposed changes in aid to families, food stamps, and job training will depend upon their views about fairness.

Consider the specific example of proposed changes in programs for the poor (H. C. Gordon & Keyes, 1983, pp. 24–25). The policy book asks, "Why is it fair to make any cuts in programs for the poor?" (p. 24). Three reasons are given for why such cuts are fair: (1) many programs for the needy give money to people who are not needy; (2) the cuts will primarily deny benefits to those who do not deserve those benefits; and (3) the program changes influence inefficiencies and errors, not basic benefits. Further, the report asks, "What is fair about inflation" (p. 25) that hurts the disadvantaged? In other words, the report assumes that when people consider proposed changes, they will wonder if those changes are fair. It is based upon the assumption that people care about what is fair.

Understanding people's subjective judgments about fairness is different from determining objective standards of justice—either by reference to universal moral principles, as Rawls (1971) suggests, or by reference to people's relationship to God, as the United States Catholic Bishops (1986) suggest. The *psychological* study of social justice involves efforts at understanding the causes and consequences of subjective justice judgments.

The study of subjective justice also can be illustrated by efforts to examine how people feel about the philosophical principles of justice articulated by Rawls (1971). For example, political scientists have examined whether people actually feel that principles of justice, such as those articulated by Rawls, are fair or unfair (Frohlich & Oppenheimer, 1990). They do so by having people participate in groups that are governed by varying types of justice rules. The people who are in such groups are then given the opportunity to evaluate the rules they experience. Their evaluations usually reflect their subjective assessments of the justice of these rules—that is, what they think is fair or unfair.

Efforts to explore what people think is fair address a variety of questions that arise in studies of people's thoughts and behaviors in social settings. Why, for example, do people view unequal treatment as being fair in some cases and not in others? Why do people accept decisions they view as fair even if those decisions are costly or create disadvantages? How do people react to collective injustice? These questions cannot be answered using a single objective definition of justice. Instead, they require a psychological approach to justice.

What Is the Psychology of Social Justice About?

Social psychologists have long been interested in the bases of people's cognitions, attitudes, and behaviors in social interactions. Why does a concern about people's feelings and actions in social settings lead social psycho-logists to study social justice? They study it because people's feelings about what is just or unjust are found to have important social consequences.

Studies show that judgments about what is just, fair, or deserved (or about what one is entitled to receive) are at the heart of people's feelings, attitudes, and behaviors in their interactions with others. Perceptions of injustice are closely related to feelings of anger (Montada, 1994; P. Shaver, Schwartz, Kirson, & O'Connor, 1987) and envy (R. E. Smith, Parrott, Ozer & Moniz, 1994), to psychological depression (Hafer & Olson, 1993; I. Walker & Mann, 1987), to moral outrage (Montada, 1994), and to self-esteem (Koper, Van Knippenberg, Bouhuijs, Vermunt, & Wilke, 1993). Furthermore, judg-ments of fairness are related significantly to people's interpersonal per-ceptions (Lerner, 1981), political attitudes (Tyler, 1990; Tyler, Rasinski, & McGraw, 1985), and prejudice toward disadvantaged groups (Lipkus & Siegler, 1993; Pettigrew & Meertons, 1993).

People's behavior also is strongly linked to views about justice and injus-tice. A wide variety of studies have demonstrated links between justice judgments and positive behaviors such as willingness to accept third-party decisions (Lind, Kanfer, & Earley, 1990; Tyler, 1990), willingness to help the group (Moorman, 1991; Organ & Moorman, 1993), and willingness to empower group authorities (Tyler & Degoey, 1995). Conversely, other stud-ies have shown links between a lack of justice and sabotage, theft, vigilan-tism, and on a collective level, the willingness to rebel or protest (Green-berg, 1990a; Huggins, 1991; B. Moore, 1978; Muller & Jukam, 1983). In other words, how people feel and behave in social settings is strongly shaped by judgments about justice and injustice. This framework is shown in Figure 1.1.

Such justice judgments are of special interest to social psychologists because justice standards are a socially created reality. They have no external referent of the type associated with physical objects. Instead, they are cre-ated and maintained by individuals, groups, organizations, and societies. Justice judgments are central to such a social reality because they are the "grease" that allows groups to interact productively without conflict and social disintegration. Rawls (1971), taking a philosophical perspective, calls justice the "first virtue of social institutions." Behavioral scientists accord feelings about justice and injustice a central role in the ability of groups to maintain themselves.

The key argument is that judgments about justice mediate between objec-tive circumstances and people's reactions to particular events or issues. Con-sider a specific case, examined at length in Chapter 3. Pritchard, Dunnette, and Jorgenson (1972) hired workers to work in a fictitious factory. These workers were led to believe that they were either fairly paid, overpaid, or underpaid. Those who believed they were fairly paid were the most satis-

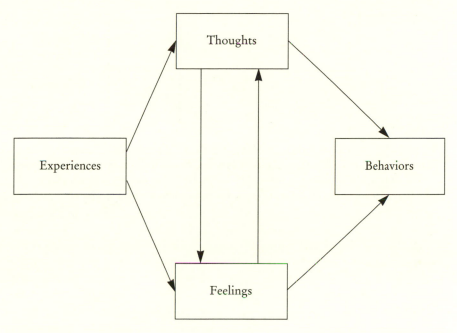

FIGURE 1.1   Overall conceptual model

fied. Other studies have shown that fairly paid workers are the most likely to stay on the job. In other words, workers' feelings and behaviors are shaped by what they think is fair.

Furthermore, studies have demonstrated that the impact of experiences is actually mediated by (i.e., flows through or is caused by) justice judgments. For example, Shultz, Schleifer, and Altman (1981) studied reactions to rule breakers. They demonstrated that there is no direct correlation between the characteristics of rule-breaking incidents and the magnitude of punishment responses following the rule breaking. Instead, as shown in Figure 1.2, it is the perceived injustice of a person's behavior that directly influences people's judgments of how severely the person should be punished, not whether the person actually caused the negative event.

A similar example is found in a recent study by Lind, Kulik, Ambrose, and de Vera Park (1993) of disputants' reactions to awards in federal courts. This study examines why people voluntarily accept the awards they receive in pretrial mediation sessions instead of going on to formal trials. The quality of the outcome has no direct effect on such decisions. Instead it is people's judgments of the fairness of the mediation procedure that is directly related to willingness to accept (see Figure 1.3). In other words,

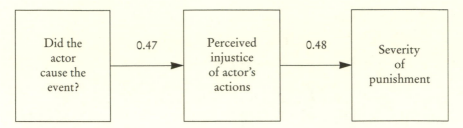

FIGURE 1.2   Reactions to rule breaking. SOURCE: "Judgments of Causation, Responsibility, and Punishment in Cases of Harm-Doing," by T. R. Shultz, M. Schleifer, and I. Altman, 1981, *Canadian Journal of Behavioural Science, 13,* 238–253. Copyright 1981 Canadian Psychological Association. Reprinted with permission.

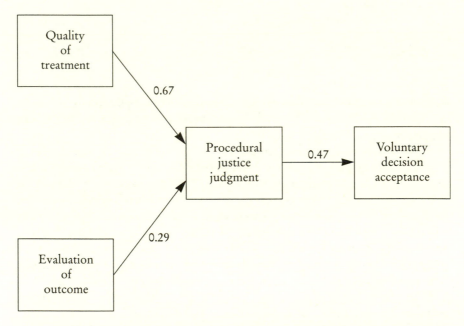

FIGURE 1.3   The effect of justice on willingness to accept dispute resolution decisions. SOURCE: "Individual and Corporate Dispute Resolution: Using Procedural Fairness as a Decision Heuristic," by E. A. Lind, C. T. Kulik, M. Ambrose, and M. V. de Vera Park, 1993, *Administrative Science Quarterly, 38,* 234. Copyright 1993 by Cornell University. Reprinted with permission.

they find that fairness mediates the relationship between decision favorability and the willingness to accept decisions.

Figures 1.2 and 1.3 are path analyses, which illustrate the causal relationship among a set of variables. The arrows presented show the influence that the variables on the left have on variables on the right. This direction of influence is indicated by the arrows and flows from antecedents to consequences. The absence of an arrow indicates no direct relationship. The value of a path analysis is that it can show influence that occurs through an intermediate variable (known as a mediating variable). For example, in Figure 1.2, judgments about an event's cause could potentially influence one's judgments about appropriate punishment either directly or by influencing one's judgments of moral responsibility. Although either type of influence is possible, the results presented in Figure 1.2 indicate that causal judgments have no direct effect on judgments about appropriate punishment. Instead, all of the influence of causal judgments flows through judgments about moral responsibility. Hence, judgments about causality only affect views about appropriate punishment to the degree that they shape judgments about moral responsibility.

Path diagrams also indicate the strength of the association between two variables. For example, in Figure 1.2, the numbers on the lines between variables indicate the strength of the association between two variables; higher numbers indicate greater influence. These numbers represent standardized coefficients (beta weights) adjusted to correct for differences in the scales used to measure different variables. Thus, the magnitude of different paths can be directly compared. The numbers range from zero (reflecting no association, as in the relationship between gender and the number of fingers a person has), to one (suggesting that one variable explains all of the variation in another, as in the relationship between gender and the ability to have children).

The examples given here focus on political and social issues. However, our concerns about social justice will be much broader. In many interpersonal situations, ranging from negotiating with parents to friends or lovers, people have been found to be very sensitive to issues of justice. Our goal is to consider the broad range of settings within which justice issues have been explored. As our review will show, this includes almost all settings in which people interact with one another, either as individuals or in groups.

Self-Interest, the Instrumental Model, and the Image of Human Nature

In addition to being important because it addresses central social psychological questions, social justice is important because its predictions are counterintuitive and contrary to the prevailing self-interest models that dominate the social sciences. The "rational" view of personal motivation that currently informs and influences much of social science and public policy assumes that people are motivated by self-interest, not by concerns about justice. Therefore, any departures from this rationality are both theoretically and socially important.

The dominance of the self-interest image of human nature within Western culture is striking. One example of this dominance is found in novels and films about situations in which people are stripped of their civilized facade by extreme circumstances, whether trapped together on a lifeboat, thrown together on a desert island, held captive in a prisoner-of-war camp, living in a post–nuclear war world, or any of a wide variety of similar situations of scarcity and conflict. In such situations, people often are depicted abandoning to some degree principles of justice and even compassion for others in a grim struggle in which the strongest survive.

Social justice research shows that people's feelings and beliefs are not consistent with the feelings that would be predicted by self-interest theories. For example, a self-interest model predicts that those who receive more compensation for their work will be more satisfied. However, this prediction is not borne out by the data. Instead, people's satisfaction is linked to whether they feel that they are receiving fair compensation. Those who believe that they are receiving fair compensation indicate greater satisfaction than those receiving higher levels of compensation that they perceive to be unfair (Walster, Walster, & Berscheid, 1978).

Social justice research on behavior also reflects departures from a self-interest or rational choice model. For example, people are willing to punish others who act unfairly, even at a personal cost to themselves. Furthermore, in situations of unequal power, self-interest models predict that people with greater power will use their power to achieve unequal gains. Research suggests that they do, but the research also suggests that they do not fully exploit their power advantages (Guth, Schmittberg, & Schwartze, 1982; Ochs & Roth, 1989). Instead, their behavior seems to reflect a concern for fairness. This failure of advantaged people to fully press their resource and power advantages is consistent with the suggestion that people care about justice (H. J. Smith & Tyler, 1996). This research suggests that people will support public policies that they believe are fair, even if these policies do not directly benefit them. Unfortunately, many policymakers assume a rational model and are unwilling to risk pursuing fair policies that they fear might cost them the support of important interest groups.

The Framework of Social Justice Research

Most social justice research deals with issues of allocation. As Leventhal (1980) notes, "All groups, organizations, and societies deal with the question of allocating rewards, punishments and resources" (p. 27). However, different theories approach this core issue from various perspectives. Early research on relative deprivation focuses on the negative consequences that follow from the absence of justice. In the United States, this research was inspired by concerns about economic inequality, political instability, and collective unrest that marked the 1940s and 1960s. Related research examines sabotage at work, criminal behavior, and self-destructive actions such as alcoholism and drug use. The focus of this research is on what society can lose when people feel unfairly treated. More recent justice theories—in particular, those underlying the study of procedural justice—focus on what can be gained when people feel fairly treated. This work developed out of concern over the circumstances in which disputants willingly accept the decisions of third parties. It also explores the willingness to obey rules, the antecedents of loyalty, and commitment to groups and organizations.

The Four Eras of Justice Research

The development of the field of social justice occurred in four waves of research stretching from 1945 to the present. The first wave of research involved relative deprivation. This research established the basic principle that satisfaction and dissatisfaction in the distribution of goods and services are linked to comparisons between what people have and what they feel they deserve. Relative deprivation ideas have figured prominently in efforts to understand and explain social unrest—riots, revolutions, and strikes.

The second wave of justice research involved the study of distributive justice—the fairness of outcome distributions. Outcomes have been broadly defined but typically involve goods and services, pay, and promotion. Distributive justice research demonstrates that people care about justice and shape their feelings and actions according to principles of what is fair and unfair. Distributive justice research—particularly the study of equity—began in response to widespread concerns about dissatisfaction with opportunities for pay and promotion in work settings (Adams, 1965). Equity theory proposes that people judge a situation to be fair if their ratio of inputs to outcomes is comparable to that of others (see Chapter 3). Work on equity theory was seen as providing an approach to compensation that would lead to greater satisfaction with the distribution of limited resources. In other words, it suggested an approach to allocating resources in situations in which authorities—whether managers, judges, or parents—could not give everyone what they wanted. Findings in this area have strongly supported equity theory. However, equity theory has not been as effective as was initially predicted as a mechanism for enhancing satisfaction in work settings for reasons that we will discuss.

The third wave of justice research involved the study of procedural justice—the fairness of different ways of resolving conflicts or making allocations. Like research on equity, the study of procedural justice was encouraged by concern over real-world problems. In particular, Thibaut and Walker (1975) focus on concerns within the legal system about the long-term effects of trials on the relationships among the parties to a dispute. They note the widespread feeling that trials are confrontational and contentious and as a consequence, the trials disrupt the social relationships among people who could have maintained long-term profitable exchange relationships. The researchers hope that using fair procedures to resolve disputes could make the outcomes of dispute resolution procedures more acceptable to all parties, particularly the losers. Hence, the idea of procedural justice, like earlier research on distributive justice, drew attention because of its promise as a way of creating more positive social dynamics in difficult situations in which not all parties can receive what they want and feel they deserve. Research findings on procedural justice also have strongly supported the importance of procedural justice as an idea; and the findings have suggested that using fair procedures can have an important positive influence on relationships among people who have conflicts.

The fourth wave of justice research reflects an emerging interest in retributive justice. Social psychologists recognize that an important aspect of social justice involves considering how people react to the breaking of social rules (Hogan & Emler, 1981; Vidmar & Miller, 1980)—that is, retributive justice. Retributive justice has been the least widely studied aspect of justice. Recently, however, there has been increasing attention to issues of attribution of responsibility for and responses to the breaking of social rules. In part, this increasing interest in retributive justice involves the increasing attention given to issues of rule breaking in American society. There is evidence that the American public has become increasingly concerned about rule breaking, especially in the context of the criminal justice system, and supports strong and punitive responses to the breaking of rules.

The Field of Social Justice

Research on social justice generally addresses five questions. The first is, Do judgments about justice and injustice shape people's feelings and attitudes? The most clear-cut evidence for the importance of justice concerns comes from investigations of what people think and feel. When people are asked to indicate their subjective reactions to their outcomes (for example, satisfaction or dissatisfaction) those reactions are found to be linked to judgments about whether the norms of justice have been violated, rather than to personal or group interests. This issue as it relates to relative deprivation, distributive justice, procedural justice, and retributive justice is addressed in Chapters 2, 3, 4, and 5, respectively.

The second question is, Which criteria do people use to determine whether justice has occurred? If people react to injustice, it is important to understand how they decide whether it has occurred. Justice research generally suggests that people are seldom at a loss when asked to make judgments about injustice—they know it when they see it! But how do they know it? The issue of criteria utilization as it relates to relative deprivation, distributive justice, procedural justice, and retributive justice also is addressed in Chapters 2, 3, 4, and 5, respectively.

The third question is, How do people respond behaviorally to justice or injustice once they decide it has occurred? Put another way, Will people acquiesce to injustice, will they choose individual remedies, or will they challenge the injustice collectively? The distinction between collective and individual reactions to injustice is particularly important for researchers interested in social movements. The recognition of collective injustice is proposed to motivate participation in social movements, collective protests, and political rebellions (Gurr, 1970; D. M. Taylor & Moghaddam, 1994). This question is considered in Chapters 6 and 7. Chapter 6 explores how people decide whether to respond to injustice either by creating a psychological justification or making a behavioral change. Chapter 7 considers the possible types of behavioral responses people can make to injustice and the rules that determine which type of response will be made.

The fourth question is, Why do people care about justice? Social psychologists discuss the social justice motive from two broad theoretical perspectives. The first is the theory of social exchange. This theory suggests that people are interested only in themselves in making their judgments and choices. Their concern about justice develops from a desire to maximize their own gains in interactions with others. The second theoretical perspective is based on social identification models. It argues that people use their social experiences to define and evaluate their social selves. Hence, justice is connected to people's feelings about the status of their group and to their social standing within that group, their self-worth, and their self-concepts. The psychology of justice is considered in Chapter 8.

The fifth question is, When do people care about justice? Some theories suggest that justice is a basic human motivation and will be present in all social interactions. Others argue that there is a range outside of which people do not care about issues of justice—that there is a limit to social justice concerns or, at least, that the strength of social justice concerns varies depending upon situational factors. Researchers have considered two situational factors: social roles and scarcity. This issue is considered in Chapters 9 and 10. Chapter 9 examines situational influences on justice concerns. Chapter 10 explores cultural differences in justice concerns.

2

RELATIVE DEPRIVATION

In this chapter, we consider *relative deprivation theory*, one of the major contributions of the social science research on American soldiers conducted during World War II (Stouffer, Suchman, DeVinney, Star, & Williams, 1949). In fact, it might be argued that the development of relative deprivation theory is one of the major postwar contributions of social psychology to our understanding of human behavior.

Stouffer and his colleagues (1949) developed the concept of relative deprivation to explain several unexpected relationships between soldiers' objective situations and their feelings of satisfaction. For example, highly promoted airmen were more dissatisfied with the promotion system than were the less frequently promoted military policemen. The researchers hypothesized that airmen compared their situation with the situation for other, more rapidly promoted air corps peers; they felt dissatisfied (or relatively deprived) because they were likely to know other people who were moving ahead of them. But military policemen compared their situations with those of other slowly promoted military police peers; the policemen felt satisfied because they were moving forward as rapidly as any of their colleagues. This research suggests that subjective satisfaction is not a simple reaction to the objective quality of a person's outcomes when dealing with others (Merton & Kitt, 1950). Instead, people evaluate the quality of their outcomes by comparing them with the outcomes of others. Implicit in such comparisons is a model of what they deserve relative to others. People use that model to decide how their outcomes ought to compare with those of others. Although not made explicit in this research, it is this emphasis on deserving and fairness that makes relative deprivation a justice theory.

Why Is Relative Deprivation Important?

Money and Happiness

The concept of relative deprivation is important within the social sciences because it offers social scientists an elegant way to explain apparent inconsistencies between the objective nature of people's experiences and their reactions to those experiences. One recurring inconsistency that relative deprivation models can explain is discrepancies between people's objective income and their feelings of satisfaction. For example, the objectively disadvantaged often are satisfied with receiving very low levels of social resources, but the objectively advantaged often are dissatisfied with very high levels of social resources. Empirical studies show very little relationship between one's objective standard of living and one's satisfaction with one's income. Strumpel (1976) suggests that "the objective standing of individuals in their socioeconomic environment has a limited influence upon their subjective perceptions of their economic well-being, and probably upon other aspects of their psychological well-being" (p. 126)—that is, how well-off people actually are has little to do with how they feel about how well-off they are or with their feelings about themselves. In particular, studies do not suggest that increasing objective income or raising one's standard of living to higher levels increases satisfaction with one's income or living standards (Myers, 1992). Not only can money not buy love, but also more money cannot guarantee happiness.

A similar inconsistency between objective and subjective judgments is found in studies exploring people's reactions to particular personal experiences. For example, studies of people's experiences with the civil and criminal justice system find very little relationship between people's objective gains or losses and their subjective satisfaction with the outcomes of their cases (Casper, Tyler, & Fisher, 1988; Lind, MacCoun, et al., 1990). The amount of money that people gain or lose in court or the length of time they receive in jail is, at best, a modest predictor of their satisfaction with their experience.

Why does more wealth (or better outcomes) not lead to greater happiness? One reason is that when judging their happiness, people compare their circumstances with others' circumstances rather than evaluating the absolute level of their wealth (Strumpel, 1976). Earning more money will not increase satisfaction if people believe that those with whom they compare themselves are earning more. For example, between 1952 and 1976, the average disposable income for a family of four steadily increased. By absolute standards, people should have felt better off. However, as the amount of disposable income increased, so did people's estimates of the smallest amount of money a family of four needed to get along for a week. In 1952, the median estimate was $50, but in 1976 the median estimate was $177 (see Frank, 1985, p. 32). The absolute amount of money people estimated they needed to get along increased $127, but the *relative* percentage of the average income for a family of four these dollar amounts represented stayed the same (approximately 40 percent; Frank, 1985). Since relative deprivation models suggest that people compare their outcomes to subjective standards when determining their satisfaction, it is not surprising that the absolute increase in disposable income did not increase satisfaction.

Collective Disorders

Relative deprivation theory can also explain the occurrence of collective protest and rebellion and who is motivated to participate in them. Empirical research shows that it is often the more advantaged members of disadvantaged groups who engage in collective action, not the most disadvantaged (Caplan & Paige, 1968; Gurin & Epps, 1975; Pettigrew, 1964). Although these people are not the most objectively deprived members of their group, they are the most likely members of their group to make subjective social comparisons with members of more advantaged groups. Therefore, they are more likely to know and feel angry about what they (and their group) are missing (Pettigrew, 1972; D. M. Taylor & Moghaddam, 1994). For example, survey evidence shows that women earn significantly less than men for the same work (Crosby, 1982; Major, 1994). One might expect that women employed in low-status occupations (who earn less money) resent this difference more than do women employed in high-status occupations (who earn more money). However, the opposite is true (Crosby, 1982). Crosby and her colleagues (Zanna, Crosby, & Loewenstein, 1987) argue that women in high-status occupations know more male colleagues, select male colleagues more often as comparisons, and consequently feel more deprived than women in low-status occupations.

Similarly, the era of urban riots that occurred in the United States during the 1960s followed a period of economic and political gain for the disadvantaged (the Civil Rights era), not a period of stable or decreased economic justice. Relative deprivation theorists argue that the experience of increased advantages provides the disadvantaged with new standards for comparisons and expectations that make them more sensitive to potential violations of those standards (Davies, 1962; Gurr, 1970). For example, the improvements in the situation of African Americans during the Civil Rights era led more members of that group into contact with white Americans. Once in contact with Whites, African Americans were more likely to compare themselves with that more advantaged group, leaving them feeling relatively deprived (Pettigrew, 1972).

Furthermore, following a period of improvement, people expect improvement to continue. Riots occur when the rate of improvement slows, creating a discrepancy between expectations and reality. When people expect to receive very little, they do not become dissatisfied if they receive very little. However, if they become accustomed to improvement, then receiving a constant or declining level of outcomes is upsetting because their expectations of what they deserve are violated. The relationship between relative deprivation and collective behavior is discussed in detail in Chapter 7.

Clarifying the Meaning of Relative Deprivation

Relative deprivation is a judgment that one is worse off compared to some standard; this judgment is linked, in turn, to feelings of anger and resentment. Contained within this definition are two important empirical requirements. First, measures of relative deprivation describe how people *feel* about particular comparisons (i.e., whether they feel angry; H. J. Smith, Pettigrew, & Vega, 1994). People may view some disadvantageous comparisons as reasonable or legitimate, so disadvantages do not lead to anger. Employees may recognize that they will never earn the salaries that managers do but may not feel especially angry about their fate. Second, measures of relative deprivation must be *comparative*. It is the comparative nature of the cognitive judgment, rather than the existence of feelings of anger and resentment, that distinguishes models of relative deprivation from the earlier frustration-aggression hypothesis (Dollard, Doob, Miller, Mowrer, & Sears, 1939).

Central to this definition of relative deprivation is the choice of comparison referent. People with the same objective outcome can potentially feel very happy or very angry, depending upon their comparison choice. For example, comparison choices can explain the unexpected tolerance of injustice by people who are unfairly disadvantaged (Major, 1994; Martin, 1986a, 1994; D. Moore, 1991). Members of disadvantaged groups are more likely to compare themselves with other members of the disadvantaged group or with their own experience and expectations than with members of an advantaged group (Major & Forcey, 1985; Major & Testa, 1988). Therefore, they may not think of themselves as disadvantaged. The same process can also explain why the advantaged may not view themselves as privileged. As illustrated in the baseball strike of 1994, million-dollar athletes often compare their situation with more fortunate teammates and wealthy team owners and feel mistreated, even though they are earning significantly more than minor-league players or the average fan.

Choice of Comparison Referent

The choice of a comparison standard is better described analytically as a series of choices (see Figure 2.1; Berger, Fisek, Norman, & Wagner, 1983; J. M. Levine & Moreland, 1987; I. Walker & Pettigrew, 1984). One set of choices involves possible dimensions of comparison. Many dimensions are possible, including physical attractiveness, athletic ability, intelligence, personality, accomplishments, and future potential. A second set of choices involves the target of the comparison. One basic choice presented in Figure 2.1 is whether to compare oneself as an individual or to think of oneself as a representative group member. Those making individual comparisons must decide whether to compare themselves with their own circumstances at other points in time or to compare themselves with other persons. If they compare themselves to their own circumstances at other points in time, they must choose time points. A person might compare himself or herself to a situation when younger or to an expected situation in the future. Those who compare themselves with others must decide with whom they want to make the comparison. Those who decide to make group comparisons must decide which of the groups to which they belong (e.g., women, Whites, teachers, the middle-aged) is the appropriate group for comparison. They then must decide whether to compare their group with an appropriate comparison group or to compare their group's present situation with either past or future circumstances.

Of course, it is unlikely that people explicitly consider each of these possibilities every time they evaluate their situations. People may have chronic preferences for particular sorts of comparisons, or the current context may make some comparisons more obvious and meaningful than others (Leach, Smith, & Garonzik, 1996; Turner et al., 1987; Oakes, Haslaam, & Turner, 1994). However, the variety of possible comparison choices reminds us that people are not simply prisoners of the objective world. Instead, as illustrated earlier, people create their subjective world through their choices of social comparison standards.

Comparisons with Oneself at Other Points in Time (Temporal Comparisons)

Different traditions of relative deprivation research focus on different types of comparisons. The tradition of relative deprivation research that has dominated political science is focused almost exclusively on people's comparisons with their own circumstances at different points in time (Davies, 1962; Feierabend, Feierabend, & Nesvold, 1969; Gurr, 1970; M. C. Taylor, 1982). For example, Gurr (1970) distinguishes among three different patterns of relative deprivation, each of which can create the necessary conditions for riots and rebellion (see Figure 2.2). The first pattern, *decremental deprivation*, describes the discrepancy that occurs when people's expectations remain constant but their capabilities to meet those expectations begin to fall. Current descriptions of downward mobility among the children of the middle class capture this pattern of relative deprivation. Given their parents' experience, people may feel they deserve to buy a house and own two cars on one income. However, they believe it is unlikely that their own level of income will afford the same lifestyle that their parents experienced.

A unique individual	Personal past experience
	Another person
	Future personal expectations
A representative group member	Group's past experience
	Another group
	Future group expectations

FIGURE 2.1   Choice of comparison target

The second pattern, *aspirational deprivation*, describes the discrepancy that occurs when people's capabilities remain constant but their expectations increase. For example, when more families in the immediate community started purchasing televisions, phones, and other modern conveniences, those without the same conveniences felt more relatively deprived (Bluhm, 1975). Their incomes and lifestyles remained the same before and after televisions and phones became common, but as others gained these items, people expected and felt they deserved the same lifestyle that their neighbors enjoyed.

The third pattern, *progressive deprivation*, describes the discrepancy that occurs when both expectations and capabilities increase but capabilities cannot keep pace with rising expectations. For example, dissatisfaction among urban Blacks in the United States during the 1960s increased even though their objective economic situation was improving. Researchers argue that objective economic changes could not keep pace with people's increased expectations. The J-curve theory proposed by Davies (1962) outlines a similar argument. Civil strife, revolutions, and political violence are more likely to occur if a prolonged period of economic growth is followed by a short-term economic reversal. Economic downturns, recessions, or increased

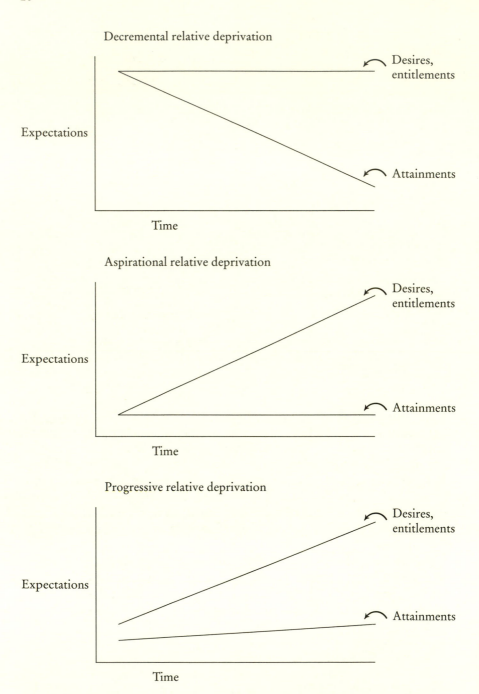

FIGURE 2.2   Three patterns of relative deprivation. SOURCE: *Why Men Rebel,* by T. R. Gurr. Copyright 1970 Princeton University Press. Reprinted by permission of T. R. Gurr.

scarcity in important resources can precipitate this pattern of relative deprivation (Lerner & Lerner, 1981). The sudden change in economic fortune violates people's expectations of continued economic improvement.

Psychological Evidence

The assumption supporting political science–oriented relative deprivation research is that people compare their current situations with either their past experiences or their future expectations. However, these individual experiences and expectations often are not measured directly. Instead, feelings of relative deprivation are inferred from aggregate objective indexes (e.g., the number of newspapers available in a particular nation-state or the literacy rate).

Consistent with the political science argument, when discrepancies between current conditions and both future expectations and past experiences are measured directly, they do influence people's emotional reactions to their current circumstances (Markus & Nuris, 1986). People may not react negatively to unfavorable objective conditions because they compare their present selves with past selves who were destitute or with future selves who are in even worse situations. However, if information from the environment challenges the probability of realizing a cherished possible self, people will react with anger and frustration.

The use of previous personal experience as an anchor for evaluating current events is dramatically illustrated by research on lottery winners and on victims of severe accidents (Brickman, Coates, & Janoff-Bulman, 1978). People with more extreme standards or previous experiences should react less extremely to mundane events. Brickman et al.'s (1978) study shows that people who have been lottery winners (and therefore have a high comparison standard, the day they won a million dollars) judge everyday events to be less satisfying. A converse study of the victims of severe accidents finds a more complex reverse pattern, but the study basically supports the argument that a severe negative experience makes everyday events more pleasant. In this study, accident victims remembered past everyday events as more pleasurable. The feelings generated by an event are linked to comparing that event against the standards set by other events.

Imagined Possibilities

The literature on temporal comparisons assumes that people use actual events as their source of comparison. However, the possibility of comparisons to a future self, discussed by Markus and Nuris (1986), points to the more general possibility that people will make self-comparisons using imagined events or counterfactuals (i.e., events that might have occurred; Kahneman and Miller, 1986). For example, people have been found to be more upset when they imagine racing to the airport and missing their airplane by five minutes than racing to the airport and missing their airplane by thirty minutes. Why? Because it is easier to imagine ways to have caught the airplane that was missed by only five minutes (e.g., "If only I had *not* stopped to drop off my cleaning!").

People also may compare themselves with internal standards of what they "ought" to have obtained at various points in their lives. Helson (1964) refers to such standards as social clocks. She argues that people have beliefs about the age at which they should have married, should have had children, and/or should have been finished with their education and holding a "real" job. Their feelings of satisfaction and dissatisfaction are shaped by their situation compared to those standards. Hence, some people believe that they should have both personal and professional success quickly (e.g., marriage, family, and a career). Success in one of these arenas, although it might make many people happy, would lead someone with a different social clock to feel deprived relative to their sense of where they ought to be at age thirty-six.

Of course, imagined possibilities or internal standards (i.e., social clocks) do not necessarily involve feelings of entitlement. The fact that a person might have expected to be married with children by age thirty-six does not mean that the person feels entitled to be married. Mere dissatisfaction or frustration does not necessarily amount to feelings of injustice. As a result, these studies provide important insights into the relative and subjective character of happiness and explain deviations from rational/economic models, but they fall short of addressing feelings of injustice. The key variable missing in this research is the mediating moral judgment that the state with which one is unhappy is unfair, undeserved, or a violation of one's entitlements. Models that incorporate judgments about both the morality underlying one's state and the social comparisons used to construct this judgment are true social-justice models.

One relative deprivation model that includes both imagined possibilities and judgments of deservedness is referent cognitions theory (Folger, 1986, 1987). The premise of referent cognitions theory is that feelings of deprivation are the product of the stories people tell themselves about what might have been—that is, of imagined possibilities. Folger (1987) argues that imagining a more satisfying alternative can create feelings of resentment if people believe that (1) current outcomes are not clearly justified and (2) the likelihood that the situation will change is relatively low. Referent cognitions theory suggests that people are influenced by their knowledge of what might have been under other circumstances. Consequently, what might have been shapes their reactions to what is.

Results from laboratory studies in which the likelihood of winning a prize, the justification for changing the rules for winning the prize, and the likelihood of winning the prize under the previous set of rules are each independently manipulated provide evidence for the referent cognitions model (Ambrose, Harland, & Kulik, 1991; Folger, 1986, 1987; Folger, Rosenfield & Robinson, 1983; Folger, Rosenfield, Rheame, & Martin, 1983). In a typical experiment, participants compete for prizes, but after the practice task and before the real competition, the experimenter announces a change in the scoring rule. In the high-outcome referent experimental condition, the experimenter tells the participants after the real competition that they would have won the prize if the old scoring rule had been used. In the low-outcome referent experimental condition, the experimenter tells the participants that they would have lost in either case. In the high-justification experimental condition, the researcher gives a long explanation as to why the new scoring rule is fairer than the old rule, but in the low-justification experimental condition, the experimenter gives no explanation. As predicted, participants are most upset when they can imagine winning under the old rule and no reason is given for the rule change.

Comparisons with Other People

In contrast to the political science emphasis on self-comparisons across time, most social psychology research beginning with Stouffer et al. (1949) focuses on comparisons with other people. This emphasis on other people and groups as sources of comparison information links relative deprivation models to a family of self-evaluation theories, all of which build on similar premises about the social nature of the comparison process (Pettigrew, 1967). Although studies on social comparison (Suls & Wills, 1991), reference-group theory (Hyman & Singer, 1968), expectation-states theory (Berger et al., 1983), and aspiration levels (Lewin, Dembo, Festinger & Sears, 1944) are not explicitly linked to judgments about justice, they share with relative-deprivation models an emphasis on using comparisons with others to evaluate one's current situation.

A central question for self-evaluation theories is, With whom will people compare themselves? Festinger's (1954) social comparison theory proposes that people prefer upward-similar comparisons, evaluating their own situations by comparing them with the situations of people who are like them but in slightly better situations (Martin, 1981). Research supports the notion that people prefer to make upward-similar comparisons when they are seeking to evaluate their outcomes (Major, 1994; Suls & Wills, 1991). However, other research suggests that people do not always limit themselves to comparisons with others like themselves (Martin, 1981).

Current approaches argue that comparison choices are partly the product of availability (e.g., J. M. Levine & Moreland, 1987; Wood, 1989). For example, social networks and contexts can prevent or force particular comparison choices (Gartrell, 1987; J. C. Masters & Smith, 1987; Olson, Herman, &

Zanna, 1986; Suls & Wills, 1991). Historically, one of the major factors shaping social comparisons has been residential segregation. Because members of different ethnic and social classes have traditionally lived in different neighborhoods, any tendency of workers to compare themselves with managers is lessened. A worker is not likely, for example, to look across the street and see his or her boss driving a BMW, because the boss usually lives in another part of town. Similarly, because people tend to become friends with those who live and work around them, most friendships are with others similar to themselves (Gartrell, 1987). Conversations with friends are a major source of information about relative outcomes, so people are likely to feel that most others live on a very similar level. For example, in the middle of the Great Depression, J. P. Morgan, a rich New York banker, estimated that one-third of the U.S. population had servants (Lane, 1993). His estimate was probably based on the experiences of his friends.

The immediate social context can mean that socially dissimilar others, particularly if they are in the majority, will be chosen as comparisons rather than distant but more socially similar others (Martin, 1981; Singer, 1981). When members of a disadvantaged group work or live primarily with advantaged group members, they are more likely to identify with their particular disadvantaged group (Lau, 1989). However, when they make social comparisons, they are more likely to choose an advantaged group member whose situation is similar to their own (Major, 1994; Zanna et al., 1987). Compared to a minority employee who works mostly with minority employees, a minority employee who works with mostly majority employees probably is more likely to notice who is not in the country club or who is living where.

Companies are aware of the fact that the immediate social environment can limit the social comparisons that people will use to evaluate their outcomes. As an example, college campus recruiters offer college graduates from women's colleges significantly lower starting salaries than equally qualified women at coed colleges. They assume that women at women's colleges do not have the same access to information about the range of starting salaries as women at coed colleges. In particular, the companies believe that the women at women's colleges lack information about the starting salaries of men (Belleveau, 1995). Furthermore, according to Belleveau (1995), companies assume that if women had access to information about men's salaries, as do men, they would find their offers low compared to the offers given to men. These assumptions are supported by research into salaries at various universities. For example, salaries for biochemistry professors are much higher at the University of Michigan than they are at Cornell University (Frank, 1985). Unlike Cornell University, the University of Michigan Medical School is located right next to the Biochemistry Department. Therefore, biochemists often interact with highly paid medical school professors and are assumed to know how highly paid their medical school colleagues are. Therefore, they are paid higher salaries. In contrast, biochemists at Cornell University do not have the same opportunity for interaction and, therefore, should be less likely to know about the high medical school salaries and want higher salaries of their own.

Although the social context influences the salience or availability of different comparison choices, it does not determine comparison choices. Personal motivations also influence people's assessments of the desirability of making those comparisons (J. M. Levine & Moreland, 1987). Desirability, then, influences the comparisons that people make. For example, the lack of relationship between wealth and happiness is linked to people's tendency to shift their social comparisons as they become more affluent. Before an employee receives a big raise, comparing her situation with that of the company vice president does not seem relevant, but after the raise, the same comparison may seem quite reasonable (Lane, 1993). Of course, this new comparison choice may contribute to feelings of dissatisfaction. However, people can combat this tendency to chose new (wealthier) comparisons by focusing on comparisons with themselves over time. For example, people can continue to compare their economic situation to the poverty of their childhood. In this case, their increasing affluence will lead to greater satisfaction with their economic situation.

Comparison choices can be motivated by the desire for self-evaluation, self-improvement, or self-deprivation (J. M. Levine & Moreland, 1987; Wood, 1989). In particular, people often prefer to make downward comparisons to enhance or protect their feelings of self-worth rather than make upward comparisons that can lead to feelings of deprivation (S. E. Taylor & Lobel, 1989; Wills, 1991; Wood, 1989). This preference for downward comparisons can explain why many members of disadvantaged groups report low levels of deprivation. Instead of comparing their situation upward to the situation of a more privileged group, they compare downward with other disadvantaged group members who are in worse shape (D. Moore, 1991; H. J. Smith, Spears, & Oyen, 1994). For example, Israeli women employed in nontraditional occupations earn higher pay than women in traditional occupations but lower pay than men in the same occupations. These women prefer comparisons with other working women in traditional occupations over comparisons with working men in their own professions (D. Moore, 1991). Similarly, research on married couples shows that married women prefer referential comparisons with other married women that support feelings of relative advantage rather than relational comparisons with their male partners that provide evidence of relative disadvantage (VanYperen & Buunk, 1994). In contrast to potentially painful upward comparisons, these downward comparisons can protect or enhance feelings of self-worth.

The ability to choose their comparison others allows people to feel good about their situation even when, by objective standards, it is quite poor.

Consider the Japanese survivors of the Kobe earthquake of 1995. Reporters found that many seemed happy, and they were laughing and joking with friends. Why? One reason is that they focused on ways in which they were better off than others: "We can laugh and smile. After all, we know that lots of folks in this area really are suffering with worse problems. Some people down the street lost their youngest child. Over there, a young couple was killed. But my family members, we're all safe." Furthermore, they focused on what they had gained—recognition of their caring for each other—instead of what they had lost: "When my sons came to look for me, they were in tears to find that their father was fine. They were so happy! I knew that I loved my sons and that they loved me" (Kristof, 1995).

Comparison choices are not linked only to people's feelings. Social comparisons also shape people's effectiveness in the social world. For example, studies show that achievement is linked to the effective use of social comparisons. Successful achievement develops from comparisons with similar others who are superior on the dimension under evaluation (Wood & Taylor, 1991). The resulting feeling of relative inferiority motivates personal growth. In contrast, downward comparisons with similar others are more comforting, but they do not motivate achievement because the person making the comparison is already superior to the comparison choice. Given the importance of social comparison choices to happiness and adaptive behavior, it is not surprising that helping people make more appropriate social comparison choices is an important part of therapeutic procedures (Affleck, Tennen, Pfiffer & Fifield, 1987).

A consideration of both the availability and attractiveness of different comparison choices enables researchers to understand counterintuitive reactions to changes in status. For example, a colleague recently traded in his Toyota Tercel for a Volvo 240. Although he expected to receive increased social status by owning a much more prestigious car, that effect did not occur. Instead, he found that he had entered a new social comparison group—Volvo owners. In that group, he was actually a low-status member since many other Volvo owners owned the more expensive Volvo 740. Hence, an increase in the absolute value of the car owned did not translate into feelings of high social status, happiness, and personal satisfaction because he had left his old reference group of Toyota owners for a new reference group of Volvo owners. Of course, one solution to this problem is to try to always occupy the highest status position within a particular reference group. But who knows with whom the owners of Volvo 740s compare themselves?

Individual Versus Group Relative Deprivation

One of the most important conceptual distinctions in relative-deprivation theory, originally introduced by Runciman (1966), is between *individual egoistic deprivation*, produced by interpersonal comparisons, and *group-based fraternal deprivation*, produced by intergroup comparisons. People might decide, for example, that they are personally deprived and/or that a social group to which they belong is deprived because of shared group characteristics like gender, racial/ethnic background, or age.

Unfortunately, researchers often ignore or overlook the distinction between individual and group relative deprivation (I. Walker & Pettigrew, 1984). For example, many researchers investigating political attitudes assess individual but not group relative deprivation (e.g., Herring, 1985; Issac, Mutran, & Stryker, 1980; N. E. Muller, 1980). This neglect of Runciman's (1966) original distinction leads some reviewers to dismiss relative deprivation as an explanation of collective behavior (Finkel & Rule, 1987; Gurney & Tierney, 1982; Snyder & Tilly, 1972). In fact, however, collective (e.g., fraternal) judgments are found to have two consequences that either are not found or are weaker with individual judgments.

First, some evidence suggests that people are more likely to acknowledge the existence of injustice at the collective or group level (see Chapter 6). Studies suggest that victims are not likely to acknowledge personal victimization but are more willing to recognize group victimization. Crosby (1982), for example, found that underpaid working women recognized that women as a group were underpaid but did not recognize that they personally were underpaid. Hence, people are more likely to acknowledge injustice when they interpret their experiences in group-based terms.

Second, people are more likely to engage in political protests and active attempts to change the social system when they interpret their experiences in group-based terms (Hafer & Olson, 1993; Pettigrew, 1964, 1967; H. J. Smith, Pettigrew, & Vega, 1994; Vanneman and Pettigrew, 1972; Walker and Mann, 1987; see Chapter 7). A variety of research investigations suggest that feelings of group relative deprivation rather than individual relative deprivation promote people's support for participation in collective protest (Dion, 1986; Dube & Guimond, 1986; Hafer & Olson, 1993; I. Walker & Mann, 1987). In contrast, feelings of individual relative deprivation (and not group relative deprivation) are associated with psychological depression and symptoms of physical stress (Hafer & Olson, 1993; Parker & Kleiner, 1966; I. Walker & Mann, 1987).

These striking differences in the reactions associated with individual and group relative deprivation suggest that it is important to determine when people are more likely to make interpersonal or intergroup comparisons. Social identity theory (Tajfel & Turner, 1986) helps us to understand Runciman's (1966) model by discussing how people decide when to think of themselves as individuals and when to think of themselves as members of groups. Consequently, the theory helps us to understand when people will make interpersonal comparisons and when they will make intergroup comparisons (Abrams, 1990; Ellemers, 1993; Hogg & Abrams, 1988; Kawakami & Dion, 1993; H. J. Smith, Spears, & Oyen, 1994; I. Walker & Pettigrew, 1984). According to social-identity theory, two types of identity contribute to the self-concept: (1) *personal identity*, or the unique or idio-syncratic aspects of the individual, and (2) *social identity*, or the membership groups and social categories with which individuals identify. People are simultaneously individuals and group members and must decide the degree to which they choose to define themselves in both ways.

The manner in which people define themselves is important because it shapes the way people interpret and react to their social experiences. Different self-definitions should drive different personal and group-level comparisons. If personal identity is salient, people are more likely to make the interpersonal comparisons between themselves and others that can lead to feelings of individual relative deprivation. If group membership is salient, people are more likely to make the intergroup comparisons between their membership group and other groups that can lead to feelings of group rela-tive deprivation. In fact, members of disadvantaged groups who report identifying more closely with their disadvantaged groups report greater frustration and resentment with group-level inequities than do members who identify less closely with their disadvantaged groups (Abrams, 1990; Gurin & Townsend, 1986; Tougas & Veilleux, 1988). A social identity framework suggests that the most important distinction between group and individual relative deprivation is not the comparison target but whether people think of themselves as group members or as isolated individuals.

Initial descriptions of social identity theory proposed that group mem-bers prefer downward comparisons—comparisons that showed that their group was better off than other groups (Tajfel & Turner, 1986). Just as inter-personal downward comparisons are assumed to enhance or protect self-esteem, intergroup downward comparisons also are assumed to contribute to feelings of self-worth. However, more recent discussions of social iden-tity theory recognize that group members make intergroup comparisons for a variety of reasons, just as recent discussions of interpersonal comparison research describe a variety of different types of interpersonal comparisons (Hogg & Abrams, 1993; Leach et al., 1996; D. M. Taylor, Moghaddam, & Bellerose, 1989). Hence, social identity theorists acknowledge that people sometimes will make the upward social comparisons that Festinger (1954) originally described.

Identification with particular social groups or categories also suggests a psychological mechanism for explaining how individual perceptions of deprivation form the shared discontent that prompts collective protest (Abrams, 1990; Dube & Guimond, 1986; Kawakami & Dion, 1993). Dif-ferent people who share the same group membership will be sensitive to the same justice norms and, more important, to violations of those norms

(Reicher, 1987; Turner, 1991). For example, participants in one collective action, the St. Paul's riots in Bristol, identified strongly with the local community and interpreted a police raid on a local community tavern as a violation of the community's rights. However, nonparticipants who were not identified with the community did not share the same interpretation of the event (Potter & Reicher, 1987; Reicher, 1987). Recent experimental evidence also shows that people are more likely to behave collectively when a shared disadvantaged group membership becomes important (Lalonde & Silverman, 1994). Similarly, identification with a shared community and unambiguous beliefs that the target had violated community safety and local social norms mark examples of spontaneous vigilante behavior (Shotland, 1976).

Recognizing the importance of interpreting experience moves social psychology away from models of human feeling that link subjective feelings closely to objective conditions (see, e.g., Dollard et al., 1939). This recognition anticipated the more complex cognitive models of subjective judgments about social interaction that developed later in the context of theories of social cognition (S. T. Fiske & Taylor, 1991). The concept of relative deprivation reflects a change in the image of the social perceiver that makes theories about the origins of social feelings and behaviors more consistent with emerging cognitive models of cognition, judgment, and decisionmaking.

The importance of interpreting experience also highlights the potential importance of social influences on the individual. Because people's reactions to their experiences are not rooted in the objective quality of those experiences, people can be influenced by the social context within which they live. That context influences people's choices of comparisons to others, their definition of their identity as individual or group based, and their evaluations of how much importance to place on possessing various types of material or nonmaterial resources. Through social institutions such as mass communication and through the cultural socialization process, society can encourage people to structure and interpret their experiences in particular ways. Those interpretations can, for example, lead individuals to accept objective deprivations without dissatisfaction or to feel dissatisfied amid abundance. The social construction of reality has an important social influence on the cognitive processing of outcomes.

An example of social influence on the interpretation of experience is provided by the extreme individualism of American society. In some European societies, group memberships are salient and fraternal deprivation is a frequently made social justice judgment. However, American society traditionally has encouraged people to accept personal responsibility for successes and failures (as do the English and German societies), unlike societies such as Sweden. For example, Swedish factory workers are significantly more likely to express feelings of group deprivation than English workers, even though the wage differences between workers and management in the two countries are approximately the same (Scase, 1974). Thus, an individualistic social context discourages interpreting personal experiences in group-based terms. Consequently, people in these contexts emphasize individual-level reactions to deprivation, including positive behaviors such as working harder and getting more education and negative behaviors such as drug use and alcoholism.

Interestingly, the American social context itself appears to be changing with the increasing emergence of ethnic-, gender-, and class-based self-identifications (Rose, 1993). This increasing group-based identification should lead to a greater tendency for Americans to interpret their experiences in fraternal terms. That change in the interpretation of experience should, in turn, lead to greater group-based behavior, including both heightened political activity and a greater likelihood of collective disturbances.

Conceptualizing Social Identities

The introduction of social identities as an antecedent for experiencing group relative deprivation raises two issues. First, is identification only a *cause* of social comparisons? Identification with particular groups or social categories may also be a *consequence*, rather than an antecedent, of disadvantageous intergroup comparisons (Petta & Walker, 1992). When women learn that their average earnings are significantly less than men, they increase their identification with women as a group.

Second, if viewing oneself as a group member promotes intergroup comparisons, it is critical to determine what makes particular group memberships salient or important. Researchers have suggested that the same factors that promote particular comparison choices (e.g., availability and attractiveness) also make particular group memberships salient (Oakes, Haslam, & Turner, 1994). Alternatively, it may be the character of interpersonal relations between group members (fostering a sense of belonging or exclusion/alienation) or the structure of intergroup relations (as Augoustinos & Walker [1995] suggest) that shapes the salience of group membership. Investigating what makes particular group memberships and comparisons salient and attractive is a key issue for future research.

This second question is related to a broader difficulty for relative deprivation theory. Ideally, relative deprivation models should be able to predict with whom people will compare themselves. Unfortunately, relative deprivation theory is unable to specify in advance who the comparison referent will be (Pettigrew, 1978; D. M. Taylor & Moghaddam, 1994). Some researchers have suggested that when particular social identities become salient or important, the number of potential group comparisons is more limited than the number of interpersonal comparisons (e.g., workers most likely will compare themselves with managers; Pettigrew, 1978). However, when respondents select group targets for comparisons in response to self-enhancement, self-deprivation, or self-evaluation of their own group's position, they select a wide variety of different groups (D. M. Taylor, Moghaddam, & Bellerose, 1989).

This post hoc quality is a major limitation of relative-deprivation theory (Taylor and Moghaddam, 1994). Researchers often try to solve this problem by selecting particular comparison choices to present to research participants before measuring their attitudes and behavior, rather than allowing people to chose their comparisons freely. Another approach has been to measure feelings of deprivation and comparison choices after people have already behaved. However, social scientists typically evaluate the worth of a theory by its ability to make predictions before behavior has occurred. Therefore, the post hoc quality of relative deprivation predictions is the model's greatest weakness.

Multiple Sources of Comparison Information

Although most empirical research has focused on a single source of comparison information (see Figure 2.1), a variety of possible sources of comparison information have been identified. It is likely that in natural settings, people use more than one source of comparison information. For example, people's satisfaction and sense of injustice reflect (1) the difference between their current outcomes and their past or expected future outcomes (a self- or intrapersonal comparison) and (2) the difference between their current outcomes and other people's outcomes (a social or interpersonal comparison; Loewenstein, Thompson, & Bazerman, 1989; Messe & Watts, 1983; Messick & Sentis, 1985; O'Malley, 1983).

Research also suggests that the degree to which people use various types of comparison information depends on the social context. For example, judgments that one is receiving less than others are especially unsettling when these outcomes already violate expectations of what is fair (Messe & Watts, 1983). Other research suggests that when one experiences gains, the outcomes of other persons are important determinants of fairness judgments. However, when one experiences a loss, the outcomes of others have little impact on fairness assessments (de Dreu, Lualhati, & McCusker, 1994).

The potent combination of expectations and social comparisons is illustrated by recent survey evidence in South Africa. This evidence shows that white South Africans are the most resistant to residential desegregation if they believe that their personal economic situation will be poorer than that of Blacks *in the future* (Van Dyk's 1988 study as cited in Foster, 1991a). Note that this research combines intrapersonal comparisons with comparisons to other groups rather than individuals, a possibility outlined in Figure

2.1. An important goal for future research is to test all the comparison possibilities outlined in Figure 2.1.

The comparison literature also suggests the importance of distinguishing between the antecedents of satisfaction and of judgments about fairness. Although fairness and satisfaction typically are found to be related, the two ideas are not the same. For example, social-comparison information appears more closely related to perceptions of fairness than to satisfaction (Austin, McGinn, & Susmilch, 1978; Messe & Watts, 1983). Satisfaction, though, appears more closely related to absolute levels of rewards (Messe & Watts, 1983) and prior expectations (determined by previous personal experience, Austin et al., 1978). This finding supports the argument that fairness is a socially constructed judgment, whereas satisfaction is more personally grounded (Messe & Watts, 1983). In other words, satisfaction is the product of people's general feelings or personal dispositions, but fairness is a cognitive appraisal of the situation (Organ & Moorman, 1993). Fairness is a social judgment that is constructed and negotiated between people.

Cognitive Antecedents of Relative Deprivation

Besides comparison choices, researchers have investigated a variety of other psychological antecedents to feelings of deprivation or resentment and anger. For example, Olson and his colleagues (Hafer & Olson, 1989; Olson, 1986; Olson, Hafer, Couzens, & Kramins, 1990) investigate the influence that people's perceptions of their own qualifications, their beliefs that the world is just, and their self-presentation motives have on feelings of resentment. The most complex model of individual relative deprivation (Crosby, 1976) proposes that relative deprivation should be interpreted as an emotional psychological state produced by five factors. To feel deprived, people who lack some object or opportunity must (1) want it, (2) feel entitled to it, (3) perceive that someone else has it, (4) think that it is feasible to attain it, and (5) refuse to accept personal responsibility for their lack of it. More recent research supports a more parsimonious model of the antecedents of relative deprivation, which includes three antecedents of feelings of deprivation: (1) wanting a particular object, (2) not having it, and (3) feeling entitled to the object (Crosby, 1982, 1984; Olson, Roese, Meen, & Robertson, 1994). In turn, social comparison choices, feasibility, and personal responsibility are assumed to shape desire and judgments of entitlement (Crosby, Muehrer, & Loewenstein, 1986).

One undeveloped implication of the three-factor model outlined above is the suggestion that two sets of cognitions are important for understanding relative deprivation. The first set of cognitions—attributions of entitlement and personal responsibility—constitutes important antecedents for feeling that one has been deprived of a deserved outcome. The second set of cognitions—analysis of costs and benefits, feasibility of change, and feelings of shared support—moderates whether feelings of deprivation motivate behavioral responses. In other words, people are first influenced by their judgments about an event. For example, they may not feel dissatisfied with deprivations if they feel personally responsible for their fate. Second, if people feel deprived of a deserved outcome, whether they will react behaviorally and what form that reaction will take are influenced by their judgments about the situation. People are less likely to act on their feelings if they think their actions are personally dangerous and/or will not lead to favorable change. Similarly, self-presentation concerns encourage people to express or hide their feelings of resentment or frustration depending upon the audience (Olson et al., 1994).

Although more explicitly cognitive than the three-factor model proposed by Crosby and her colleagues (Crosby et al., 1986), the referent-cognitions model (Folger, 1987) described earlier emphasizes similar antecedent conditions. Olson and Hafer (1994) suggest that the concept of wanting is implicit in the suggestion that individuals must be able to imagine better alternative situations, the first requirement outlined in the referent cognitions model. The second requirement—that people must believe that it is unlikely the situation will improve—is similar to the concept of future feasibility. Finally, the third requirement—that the current outcomes must be viewed as unjustified—is conceptually similar to entitlement.

One inconsistency in the models outlined is the role of feasibility. In some theories, feasibility influences what a person feels entitled to have (Crosby, 1982; Folger, 1987). Folger (1987) argues that imagining a more satisfying alternative only creates feelings of resentment if the likelihood that people will receive that outcome is low (low feasibility). If people feel that they deserve something and are unlikely to receive it under current circumstances, they become angry. In other words, low feasibility leads to high anger.

Other researchers suggest that feasibility influences both anger and judgments about what actions to take (Ellemers, 1993). People become angry about not having something if they feel that it is not feasible for them to obtain it; again, low feasibility leads to high anger. The less feasible obtaining desired outcomes seems, the more angry people become. However, people do not take action unless they think they can change the nature of the world; low feasibility leads to low action. Therefore, in Figure 2.3, feasibility is shown as modifying both feelings and action in the overall model.

This more elaborate model suggests the possibility of a group of people who feel anger but take no action. Angry feelings may accumulate over time. People will then act with surprising intensity or resolve when an opportunity for change appears. For example, many workers feel angry about various slights or unfairness they have experienced at work. These

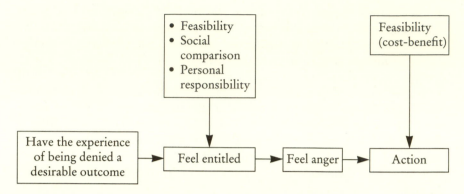

FIGURE 2.3   The sequence of reactions to possible injustice

feelings can lead to quick and decisive action when those workers are presented with the possibility of taking an alternative job.

Advantaged Groups

An important but sometimes overlooked implication of all relative-deprivation models is that feelings of relative deprivation are not limited to members of objectively disadvantaged groups. Advantaged group members can feel threatened by up-and-coming disadvantaged groups (Vanneman & Pettigrew, 1972; Veilleux & Tougas, 1989; I. Walker & Pettigrew, 1984). For example, the feeling that one's own group is being unfairly surpassed and ignored is significantly related to white voters' opposition to minority political candidates (Pettigrew, 1985; Vanneman & Pettigrew, 1972). Opposition to affirmative action policies and participation in socially conservative or reactionary movements also are linked to similar feelings of group deprivation (Klandermans, 1989; Lea, Smith, & Tyler, 1995; Veilleux & Tougas, 1989). In fact, Williams (1975) proposes that the narrowing of a gap between oneself or one's group and a lower-status person or group will have a greater impact on behaviors and attitudes than a widening gap between oneself or one's group and a higher-status person or group. For example, toolroom workers in an aircraft engineering factory preferred to prevent a decrease in the wage gap between themselves and two other less prestigious work groups who earned less, even though this requirement meant they sacrificed an absolute wage gain for themselves (R. J. Brown, 1978). This result may reflect the greater psychological impact of a loss compared to a missed opportunity for gain (Brewer & Kramer, 1986; Crosby, 1984; Kahneman & Tversky, 1973).

Alternatively, people may tend to know more information about lower- and equal-status others than they do about higher-status others (Gartrell, 1987). Therefore, they are more likely to know about changes in the situations of lower- and equal-status others than changes for higher-status others. Of course, this is not meant to suggest that people do not pay more attention to or process information more carefully about higher-status or more powerful others (e.g., S. T. Fiske, 1995). It means that structural variables (e.g., pay secrecy) prevent them from learning key information. In general, the advantaged are better able to conceal their advantage. For example, upper-class neighborhoods can have locked gates that literally make social comparisons impossible, or the neighborhoods simply may be so geographically inaccessible that people do not typically see them.

Problems for the Future

One of the more striking trends in American society is the growing divergence between the rich and the poor. This disparity can be shown in several ways. First, consider the average annual income of each quartile of the population (Bernstein, 1994). This is shown in Figure 2.4. In addition, consider the change in incomes for different income groups from 1970 to 1990 that shows that this inequity is increasing (Klugman, 1994, p. 25). Klugman (1994) writes, "The growth in inequality is startling. While the incomes of the top 1 percent of families doubled, that of the bottom fifth of families fell by 10 percent. . . . [These changes show] a simultaneous growth in wealth and poverty unprecedented in the twentieth century" (p. 24).

Will this divergence in incomes lead to social unrest? The models outlined suggest that the impact of this divergence will depend upon how people understand it. If people think in group terms, there should be social unrest. If they think in individual terms, there should not be unrest. It is how people interpret this social change that determines its social consequences.

Consider a concrete implication of the argument that the way people frame differences is a key antecedent to their reaction to those differences. The United States has never had strong Communist or Socialist political parties, whose ideologies are strongly based on class distinctions, because Americans do not typically react strongly to class distinctions. Instead, most Americans think of themselves as middle class. Consequently, it seems unlikely that the growing disparity between the rich and the poor will be conceptualized in group terms and serve as the basis of political movements or collective actions. It would seem very strange to see a riot of the poor because William Gates (the CEO of Microsoft Corporation) has made another billion dollars or because the richest 0.5 percent of the American population now have 31 percent of the net wealth in America (Thurow, 1995).

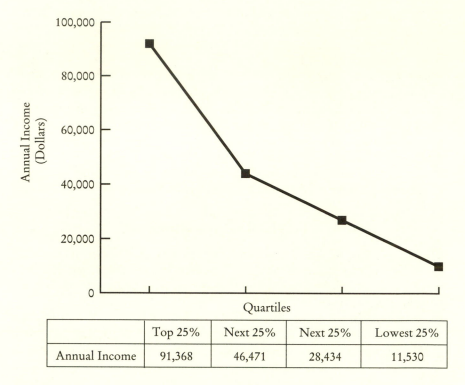

	Top 25%	Next 25%	Next 25%	Lowest 25%
Annual Income	91,368	46,471	28,434	11,530

FIGURE 2.4   Average annual income of U.S. families in 1992.

However, race and racial divisions have always been central to American thinking (see Myrdal, 1944). Furthermore, there is evidence that ethnic and racial groups are becoming increasingly important within the United States (Rose, 1993). Thus, it seems very likely that racial or ethnic groupings will serve as a basis for political movements and collective actions, such as riots. The recent Los Angeles riots that developed out of police mistreatment of minorities are a natural extension of a long history of troubled race relations in the United States. Furthermore, current social trends toward increasing self-conceptualization in racial or ethnic group terms seem likely to exacerbate, rather than alleviate, racial tensions (Rose, 1993).

Interestingly, the net worth of married couples is dramatically different for different ethnic groups in the United States (see Figure 2.5). When income data are presented in a way that highlights ethnic disparities, we predict that most people will believe that the income distribution is unjust. In

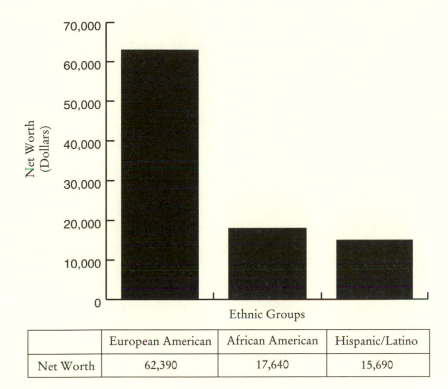

	European American	African American	Hispanic/Latino
Net Worth	62,390	17,640	15,690

FIGURE 2.5   Married couples' 1988 household net worth by ethnicity (U.S. Department of Labor).

other words, people will accept the idea that ethnic group differences are "unfair" more easily than the idea that class differences are "unfair."

The Hedonic Treadmill

The research outlined in this chapter is based upon the assumption that events have a constant evaluative value—that is, that experiencing good things remains equally good over time and experiencing bad things remains equally bad over time. However, some theorists have suggested that the value people place upon a particular outcome changes over time. In particular, it is argued that people habituate to their current situation. For example, a comparison of the future-happiness estimates of lottery winners and the victims of severe accidents reveals no differences in happiness, suggesting that the happiness associated with winning a large amount of money wears off over time (Brickman et al., 1978). This habituation model suggests that the aspirational and progressive patterns of relative deprivation described by Gurr (1970) are quite common. People become accustomed to the level of gains they have achieved; therefore, those gains are less psychologically rewarding. Hence, what initially is exciting becomes everyday and mundane.

Consider the case of one of the authors of this book, who moved from Chicago to San Francisco. During his first December in San Francisco, he was thrilled not to be standing knee-deep in snow and vowed never to forget how wonderful the change in weather was. Now, five years later, he joins other Northern Californians in complaining when there is too much rain. Over time, he has habituated to the wonderful climate in San Francisco, and it has become less of a psychologically satisfying part of life. Similarly, people react to salary increases with initial excitement, followed by habituation and a desire for further increases.

The idea of habituation leads to the *hedonic-treadmill* model. The hedonic-treadmill model described by Brickman and Campbell (1971) argues that people adjust to the status quo and no longer find it fulfilling. According to these authors, interpersonal comparisons suffer from a pernicious ratchet effect, with ever greater levels of outcomes required to maintain a constant level of psychological satisfaction. In other words, expectations continue to rise even if outcomes do not.

The idea of habituation is distinct from the idea of comparison standards as defined in relative deprivation models. Habituation refers to how people's reactions to the same standards change over time, but relative deprivation models assume that change occurs because the comparison standard has changed. The implications of each model can be illustrated by considering how people might react to a steady-state economy.

It has been argued in ecological terms that the depletion of natural resources and the problems of pollution and waste management make the development of steady-state economies inevitable. Such a steady-state society is "one that has achieved a basic, long-term balance between the dreams of a population and the environment that supplies its wants. Implicit in this definition are the preservation of a healthy biosphere, the careful husbanding of resources, self-imposed limitations on consumption, long-term goals to guide short-term choices, and a general attitude of trusteeship toward future generations" (Ophuls, 1977, p. 13). Recognition of this future has led to calls for developing both a politics of the steady state (Ophuls, 1977) and ecologically sustainable business organizations (Gladwin, Kennelly, & Krause, 1995). Gladwin, Kennelly, and Krause (1995) suggest that discussions about the "fair distribution of resources and property rights, both within and between generations, is a central dimension of nearly all conceptions of sustainable development" (p. 879).

In contrast to the ever expanding U.S. economy enjoyed by previous generations, a steady-state economy creates a very different set of economic expectations and reality. The traditional American assumption (illustrated by the ad shown in Figure 2.6) has been that each generation will do better economically than the generation before it, as the economy expands (Longworth & Stein, 1995).

If the economic situation fails to meet people's expectations, relative-deprivation models predict that people will feel resentful and more likely to protest, just as African Americans rioted at the end of the Civil Rights era. In fact, when objective economic projections are compared with expectations, three groups can be distinguished: the traditional middle class, the cheated class, and the anxious class (Longworth & Stein, 1995). The traditional middle class, people in their 50s and 60s, expected to live a middle-class life, and their expectations were confirmed—they did live a middle-class life (see Table 2.1). The cheated class, the Vietnam generation, expected to follow their parents and live a middle-class life, but they did not have the opportunity to do so. Finally, there is the anxious class, students currently in school. This generation expects to do no better than their parents and is anxious about the possibility that they will not do as well. Which generation should feel the most relative deprivation? According to the theory of relative deprivation, it is the cheated generation. Young people, who actually face an objectively bleaker future, should feel less discontent since their expectations have never been as high. This suggests that future generations will accept a steady-state economy without discontent.

The habituation model paints a more disturbing picture of the future. It suggests that people are inevitably dissatisfied with the level of achievement or resources that they attain; they want more, regardless of their initial expectations or social comparisons. This model suggests that people will inevitably feel frustrated with a steady-state life and will want to make gains. Hence, the hedonic-treadmill model suggests that social conflict will be inevitable and prolonged in groups faced with a fixed or shrinking slice of the economic pie. Given the many signs that ecological realities are forcing societies like our own into an economic steady state, this psychological model of the person is troubling. It suggests that people are psychologically unsuited to live in a steady-state world.

· It is also possible that not all resources have the habituating characteristics suggested by the hedonic-treadmill model. Lane (1993) argues that although people may habituate to material possessions and income, they do not habituate to friends and family. In other words, our exciting new friends do not inevitably become boring, and we can feel as excited about our marriage after ten years as we did when it occurred. If habituation only occurs in some areas of life, then a shift away from materialism is one approach to living in a steady-state world. A move toward a postmaterialist world in

FIGURE 2.6   Expectations for heightened income.
SOURCE: Teachers Insurance and Annuity Associa-
tion/College Retirement Equities Fund. Copyright
1995 Abe Selzer. Reprinted with permission.

which people focus on relationships and family rather than money should
increase the likelihood of widespread happiness.

Although appealing, Lane's (1993) suggestion may be overoptimistic.
Berscheid (1983) suggests that close relationships also follow a habituation
pattern. That is why a compliment from a stranger evokes a stronger emotional response than the same compliment from a longtime romantic partner. She argues that long-term partnerships become flat emotionally because
people have habituated to the benefits they gain from their partners.

The traditional American solution to the problem of giving more to each
generation is to increase absolute wealth. Thus, each generation does better
than the past generation because the overall size of the economy is growing.
This idea of moving ahead of prior generations becomes a standard against
which people judge themselves. In a steady-state world, gains can still be
achieved, but only at the expense of others. Therefore, issues of redistribution

TABLE 2.1   Generational Relative Deprivation Effects

Class Status	Expectation	Achievement
Traditional middle class	High	High
Cheated middle class	High	Low
Anxious middle class	Low	Low

become more central, with people contending against each other for resources. In other words, people will increasingly think of "doing better" as "doing better than their peers" rather than "having more than the past generation." A change in the nature of society (the inability to create new wealth) will lead to a change in the way people define their well-being. Consider the difference between American history and European history. In the United States, people have been able to move to the frontier to claim new land and new resources. They could always do better for themselves without having to directly confront other European Americans who already occupied land and controlled resources. With the decline of the frontier, people increasingly have been required to compete for a finite pool of existing resources, as Europeans have for centuries. Does this change in American society mean that discontent is inevitable? Not necessarily. By shifting their comparisons to a similarly situated cohort of peers (as opposed to the situation of previous generations), young people should feel less decremental deprivation. However, the shift to comparisons with others increases the possibility of conflict among members of the same generation. Hence, it is not clear that this shift will lead to decreasing social conflict. Combined with the already outlined development of a group based fraternal thinking about experiences, it may lead to heightened social conflict structured about the entitlement of varying groups.

The Missing Piece

Most relative deprivation theories seem clearly linked to ideas that are justice based. Although the relative deprivation theories outlined use a variety of terms, including "deserving," "entitlement," and "justified" or "unjustified" outcome, all of these terms refer to the core idea that a moral or justice-based rule has been violated. These approaches to relative deprivation jointly view unhappiness as developing out of a feeling of moral wrong in which people have not received some outcome that they ought to have received. As noted in Chapter 1, they view grievances and perceived discrepancies in outcomes as having an effect through their influence on judgments about justice and injustice.

However, theories of relative deprivation are often incomplete as justice theories. These models typically assume people are concerned about depri-

vation relative to some standard, but the models often do not demonstrate
that such deprivation is specifically linked to issues of justice. The failure to
show that entitlement mediates between people's perceptions of the situation and their reactions means that relative deprivation models are not
clearly different from a variety of other psychological theories that argue
that people's hedonic reactions to their experiences do not occur in the
abstract. Instead, these reactions occur through the comparison of experiences to reference points (e.g., anchoring and adjustment, see Kahneman &
Tversky, 1982; prospect theory, see Kahneman, 1992; norm theory, see
Kahneman & Miller, 1986). However, judgments of justice or injustice are
not assumed to mediate those reactions. For example, Helson's (1964) adaptation-level theory links dissatisfaction to discrepancies between obtained
and desired states without including mediating judgments of fairness. As the
interviews with lottery winners and accident victims described earlier illustrate, people react to current events based on the level of satisfaction to
which they are accustomed because of their prior history (Brickman et al.,
1978). However, there is no suggestion that people feel that having an ordinary day (e.g., a day in which they do not win the lottery) is unfair, simply
that it is unsatisfactory. Mere dissatisfaction, envy, or frustration does not
necessarily amount to feelings of injustice. As a result, these studies provide
important insights into the relative and subjective character of happiness
and explain deviation from rational/economic models. However, the studies
fall short of demonstrating that they are addressing feelings of injustice.

Because these models fail to identify judgments about justice as mediators
of reactions to experience, they are not justice theories. In contrast, most
versions of relative deprivation theory regard judgments of entitlement or
deservedness as central mediators (Crosby, 1984). These theories are justice
theories. These models frame the issue addressed by all subsequent theories
of justice. People compare their situations with other possibilities using
some principle that describes what ought to be. The next step is to define the
principles that people use to determine what ought to be.

Part 2

Is Justice Important to People's Feelings and Attitudes?

The first issue to be addressed is the degree to which people's feelings and attitudes are shaped by justice judgments. Our concern is with the degree to which people are affected by experiences of injustice. Unless there is evidence that people's subjective reactions to their experiences are actually influenced by assessments of justice or injustice, justice models are of little social importance. The second issue to be addressed is the meaning of justice. If we know that people care about justice, we cannot predict their behavior unless we also know how they define justice. Hence, we need to identify the criteria that people employ in judging the fairness of outcomes, procedures, and punishments.

Three bodies of justice theory seek to examine the influence of judgments about justice and injustice on feelings and attitudes: distributive justice, procedural justice, and retributive justice. Chapter 3 explores issues of distributive justice. Chapter 4 considers issues of procedural justice. Finally, Chapter 5 explores retributive justice concerns.

3

Distributive Justice

We have already noted that relative deprivation theories are incomplete because they do not clearly articulate that justice judgments mediate the impact of subjective comparisons on feelings and actions. They also are incomplete for a second reason: They do not explain how people know whether something is deserved. For example, William Gates makes vastly more money than most other Americans. But when people compare their income to his income, do they view the difference as unfair? Without knowing what principle people use to make comparisons, it is impossible to say whether a discrepancy will lead people to feel that their own income is undeservedly low.

Do people believe that everyone should receive equal outcomes, for example, or that discrepancies are justified by differences in effort, ability, or need? The relative deprivation models do not answer this question. Instead, they make entitlement a precondition for the occurrence of relative deprivation. In contrast to the relative deprivation approach of beginning with judgments of deservedness, determining which principle of justice people use to make deservedness judgments is a central concern for distributive, procedural, and retributive justice literatures.

An important advance in theories of social justice is the development of models of distributive justice. These models seek both to show that justice matters and to identify the principles underlying people's judgments that their outcomes are or are not fair (Walster, Berscheid & Walster, 1973; Walster & Walster, 1975; Walster et al., 1978). Of course, these theories build on relative deprivation theory by assuming that people are making a comparison with others using some principle of justice or deservedness.

Equity Theory

The first model of distributive justice is equity theory (Adams, 1965). It originally developed in the context of work organizations to explain workers' reactions to their wages. Businesses became concerned when they found evidence of widespread unhappiness with wages and promotions in work settings. Distributive-justice theories held out the possibility that such discontent could be lessened if pay and promotions were allocated in ways that workers viewed as fair. Thus, equity theory sought to identify and articulate a model of outcome fairness in work settings.

Equity theory subsequently developed into a general theory of justice used to explain all social interactions, ranging from the allocation of pay to romantic relationships (see Walster et al., 1978). First, equity theory hypothesizes that both satisfaction and behavior are linked not to objective outcome levels but to outcomes received relative to those judged to be equitable. Second, it articulates a criterion against which individuals are suggested to judge the equity of their wages.

The basic justice principle underlying equity theory is a balance between contributions and rewards. For example, if there are several workers in a company, they perceive their salaries as being fair if the salaries are in proportion to the relative contributions those workers make to the company. In its simplest form, the theory would hold that a person who works four hours should be paid twice as much as a person who works two hours.

Equity theory argues that people will feel upset when they do not receive equitable outcomes. This emotional reaction, whether guilt over receiving too much or anger over receiving too little, leads to efforts to restore a fair balance between inputs and outcomes. Interestingly, research has directly documented the emotional nature of this response using measures of psychological arousal. Markovsky (1988) used skin-conductance measures to demonstrate that both overpaid and underpaid subjects reacted physiologically to inequity. His findings are shown in Figure 3.1.

Equity theory identifies two groups of people who should feel upset: those who are underbenefited and those who are overbenefited. Of these two groups, the overbenefited group is especially interesting. Equity theory suggests that those who receive too much relative to norms of equity should feel less satisfied than those who receive a lesser but fair level of rewards. It is not surprising that underbenefited people feel angry, since this is predicted by both justice theories and theories of self-interest. However, overbenefited people are predicted to be dissatisfied by justice theories but predicted to be highly satisfied by self-interest theories. Those people whose rewards and contributions are not consistent are predicted to feel psychological distress, either guilt if they have too much or anger if they have too little. They are also predicted to engage in behaviors designed to restore equity.

A number of studies have supported equity theory by showing that people become upset if they are over- or underpaid. Studies typically present workers with a wage that they are told is overpayment, underpayment, or fair payment for some type of work. The studies demonstrate that people feel most satisfied with fair pay. This extensive literature has had an important role in demonstrating the importance of justice judgments on

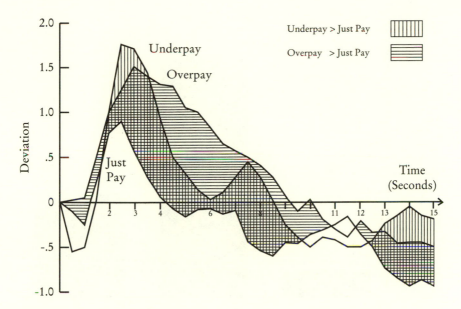

FIGURE 3.1   Emotional arousal provoked by injustice. SOURCE: "Injustice and Arousal," by B. Markovsky, 1988, *Social Justice Research, 2,* 229. Copyright 1988 Plenum Publishing Corp. Reproduced with permission.

people's attitudes and behaviors (see Adams, 1965; Berkowitz & Walster, 1976; Walster et al., 1978 for reviews; see Adams & Freedman, 1976, for a list of studies).

Consider as an example a study conducted by Pritchard et al. (1972). They hired workers for a fictitious factory through a job ad. When the workers arrived, they were told one of three things. In the fairly paid condition, they were told that they would be paid the advertised amount—the fair wage. In the unfairly overpaid condition, they were told that there was an error in the newspaper ad and the job should pay less than advertised. However, for legal reasons, they would receive the advertised but unfairly high salary in the ad. Conversely, the unfairly underpaid workers were told that the job was advertised erroneously at an unfairly low wage and that they would receive the lower amount.

The results show that as predicted by equity theory, fairly paid people are more satisfied with their wages than either under- or overpaid people. In addition, however, the findings indicate some evidence of self-interest: The unfairly overpaid are less dissatisfied than the unfairly underpaid. The findings are shown in Figure 3.2. How people feel is shaped by the relationship of what they receive to what they view as fair.

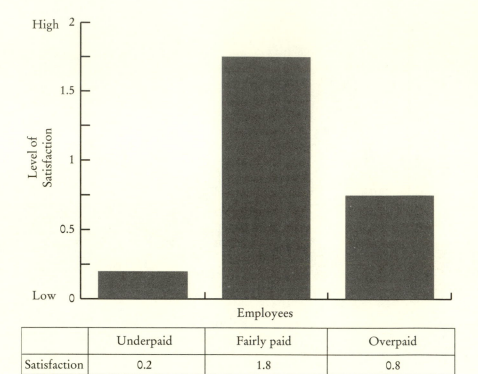

	Underpaid	Fairly paid	Overpaid
Satisfaction	0.2	1.8	0.8

FIGURE 3.2   Satisfaction with fair and unfair pay. SOURCE: "Effects of Perceptions of Equity and Inequity on Worker Performance and Satisfaction," by R. D. Pritchard, M. D. Dunnette, and D. O. Jorgenson, 1972, *Journal of Applied Psychology, 56,* 75–94. Copyright 1972 by American Psychological Association. Reprinted by permission of Robert D. Pritchard.

Other studies suggest that unfairly paid workers adjust their level of effort and productivity to restore equity. Greenberg (1988), for example, took advantage of an office reorganization to assign workers to offices of higher, equal, or lower status than their organizational position merited. Workers responded to this change by changing their job performance to match the level of their new office: Those in higher-status offices worked more and those in lower-status offices worked less (see Figure 3.3). Another study showed that those who felt unfairly underpaid tried to restore equity by stealing (Greenberg, 1990a). Thus, perceptions of equity shape what people do within their work organizations. In addition, people leave situations characterized by inequity. They prefer to be in settings in which wages are more fairly distributed, even if being in those situations leads them to receive fewer resources (Schmitt & Marwell, 1972).

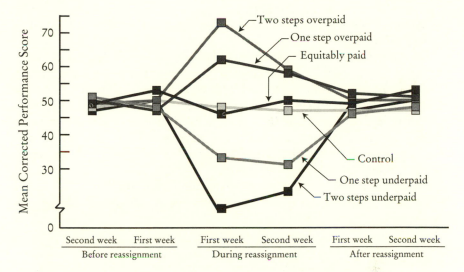

FIGURE 3.3 Mean job performance for each payment group over time. SOURCE: "Equity and Workplace Status: A Field Experiment," by J. Greenberg, 1988, *Journal of Applied Psychology, 73,* 610. Copyright 1988 American Psychological Association. Adapted with permission.

As has been noted, the many equity studies showing that people's feelings and behaviors in work settings are affected in ways that can be predicted by equity theory are an important demonstration of the power of social-justice judgments (Greenberg, 1982, 1990a; Walster et al., 1978).

In addition, the principles of equity theory help to explain behavior that appears confusing from a relative deprivation perspective. In studies of relative deprivation, it was noted that secretaries seemed more troubled by minor discrepancies in income vis-à-vis other secretaries than they were by major discrepancies in income vis-à-vis managers. This finding was linked to the social comparisons made by secretaries, who view other secretaries as more suitable for comparison. However, equity theory provides another possible explanation: Secretaries view managers as being more highly trained or as making more important contributions to the organization, so their higher incomes are justified. When secretaries compare themselves with managers, they see their inputs as different, so equity is not determined by discrepancies in pay.

Although these patterns of results are consistent with equity-theory predictions, the studies outlined typically do not directly measure people's judgments about fairness and unfairness. Hence, it is possible that people are acting out of motives besides fairness. One possible motive is the desire to present oneself in a socially desirable way. To show that this is not the case, studies have demonstrated that people change their behavior even when productivity is private, and what they produce cannot be connected to individual workers.

However, there are other possible explanations for equity effects. It might be, for example, that telling workers that they are unfairly overpaid damages their self-esteem, so they work harder to try to restore their positive feelings about themselves. Conversely, telling workers that they are unfairly over-paid may lead them to think they deserve higher wages, leading them to be more likely to leave their jobs for better paying ones. In other words, the findings reported could be mediated by other psychological processes besides feelings of unfairness. Because support for equity theory is inferred from the pattern of satisfaction and behavior across conditions, it is never possible to completely eliminate such alternative explanations for the effects observed.

The Scope of Equity Effects

Equity theorists have argued that equity principles apply broadly. For example, the general principles of equity theory have been used as a frame-work for investigating the giving and accepting of resources in close, inti-mate, ongoing social relationships, including close friendships, romantic relationships, and marriages (see Hatfield & Traupmann, 1981; Hatfield, Utne, & Traupmann, 1979). Satisfaction in relationships has been predicted using (1) global equity measures based on inputs and outcomes (Davidson, 1984; Hatfield, Traupmann, Sprecher, Utne, & Hay, 1985; Rachlin, 1987; Snell & Belk, 1985), (2) specific measures of self-disclosure (Davidson, Bals-wick & Halverson, 1983), (3) physical attractiveness (McKillip & Riedel, 1983), (4) the division of household chores (Steil & Turetsky, 1987), and (5) relative power in the relationship (Mirowsky, 1985). People who report more equitable romantic relationships indicate feeling more confident that they will stay together, feeling more content in their lives and satisfied with the relationships, and feeling more commitment to their relationships. Fur-thermore, people who report equity in their relationships are more likely to stay together and are also less likely to report extramarital affairs (Clark & Chrisman, 1994).

An example of research findings confirming the basic equity theory pat-tern is a study by VanYperen and Buunk (1994). Members of couples were asked about the frequency with which interactions with their spouses were equitable. The findings, shown in Figure 3.4, support the basic equity theory prediction. Members of couples who view interactions as equi-table—that is, those who think that what he or she gets out of the relation-ship relative to what they contribute is equal to the same ratio of his or her spouse—are more likely to indicate satisfaction with the marriage.

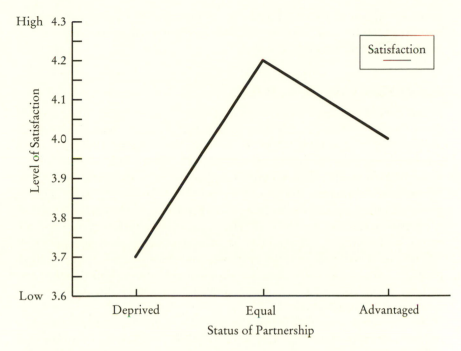

FIGURE 3.4   Satisfaction with relationship and comparisons to partner. SOURCE: "Social Comparison and Social Exchange in Marital Relationships," by N. W. VanYperen and B. P. Buunk, 1994, in *Entitlement and the Affectionate Bond: Justice in Close Relationships,* M. J. Lerner and G. Mikula (Eds.), New York: Plenum Press. Copyright 1994 Plenum Publishing Corp. Reprinted with permission.

Although research findings support the use of an equity-theory framework for understanding romantic relationships, there are also findings suggesting that equity may not completely account for people's feelings and actions in the context of interpersonal relationships. As couples become closer, they increasingly feel that keeping track of their relative inputs is inappropriate. People adopt a long-term framework for their relationship and do not seek to balance inputs and outputs in the short term. Furthermore, people increasingly focus on equality and need as principles of allocation. For example, parents deal with their children based upon need because children are seldom able to make equitable inputs into the family. Equity research also demonstrates that other measures besides equity are related to feelings of satisfaction, suggesting that people are not completely equity oriented (Hays, 1985; Steil, 1994). Therefore, although supporting the applicability of an equity-theory framework, research findings in this area also suggest that such a framework is inadequate as a complete explanation for feelings and behavior in close interpersonal relationships (Van-Yperen & Buunk, 1994).

Equity Theory and Public Policy

Equity theory also can be used as a framework for explaining public opposition to redistributive policies such as affirmative action (Nacoste, 1990; D. M. Taylor & Moghaddam, 1994). Taylor and Moghaddam (1994) argue that public conceptions of appropriate inputs into equity judgments focus on individual effort and skills, not group memberships, with people using those factors when evaluating the fairness of pay distributions. By bringing such group membership judgments (e.g., race, gender) into the equity equation, principles of fairness are violated. They argue that a different conceptualization of the issue of redistribution is necessary for promoting support for affirmative-action policies—for example, considering as an input the effort people have made to overcome hardships in their lives. This conceptualization is more consistent with views about equity and might, consequently, be more publicly acceptable.

An alternative argument is that because U.S. society is highly focused on individual responsibility, people tend to think of inputs and outcomes in individual terms. One possible type of change is to create a fraternal version of equity theory in which people think about inputs and outcomes on the group level. Affirmative-action policies, for example, can be interpreted as achieving equity at the collective or group level.

The application of equity theory to policymaking highlights the important role of societal and/or cultural rules in specifying appropriate or inappropriate inputs. For example, in Indian society, one's caste (e.g., the status of one's group memberships) would be considered an individual input into one's value at work. A recent letter in support of an Indian student's application for admission to graduate school, for example, suggested in part that the student should be admitted because he came from a good family.

Even in the United States, group memberships are sometimes considered a legitimate input into individual equity decisions. As examples, the children of graduates from a particular college (legacies) are given preference in admissions, veterans are given preference in hiring for government jobs (bonus points), and national citizenship is used as a criterion for access to public education and health care.

There also are other possible modifications in the way individual equity is conceptualized. Most Americans think of worth as being linked to market value. So the fair salary, they believe, is what employers are willing to pay someone to do a job. Those who are worth more (because others will hire them to do other things for more money) deserve to be paid more. Given this ideology, people oppose comparable-worth policies that try to link salary to the actual value of the work being done. Interestingly, however, defining worth in terms of the actual value of what one produces, not one's market value, is contained in the classic writings of Adam Smith (Mahoney, 1987).

Support for policies that restrict the operation of individual-level equity principles.   Research supports the argument that perceived injustice motivates people to consider changing their support for the application of individual-level equity principles. For example, although people generally oppose affirmative-action programs, studies suggest that when people feel that economic opportunities are unfairly distributed, they are more willing to support policies designed to redistribute resources (H. J. Smith & Tyler, 1996).

Interestingly, although judgments that economic opportunities are unfairly distributed contribute to the willingness to support compensatory policies such as antidiscrimination laws and affirmative action, such judgments are not the primary antecedent of policy support. Lea et al. (1995) compare the influence of three factors shaping support for affirmative action: respondent characteristics (e.g., age, race, ideology), judgments about the unfairness of current racial disparities in economic opportunities, and judgments about the fairness of compensatory policies. In their study, both respondent characteristics (explaining 11 percent of the variance) and judgments about the magnitude of current distributive injustices (explaining 8 percent of the variance) influenced policy support. However, the primary antecedent of support for or opposition to compensatory policies was judgments about the fairness of the proposed policies designed to remedy the situation (explaining 30 percent of the variance).

These findings suggest that the specifics of a program designed to remedy a distributive injustice (fairness of the remedial process) have a large impact on people's willingness to support remedies. An example of how the manner in which a policy is framed influences reactions to that policy is provided by the findings of Kravitz and Platania (1993). Their research, summarized in Table 3.1, indicates that support for affirmative action varies dramatically depending upon how the policy is presented.

Consider the current American health care crisis. One position that might be taken is that if the problem is large, then many policies might be acceptable because it is so important to solve the problem. However, people do not seem to be taking that perspective. Instead, they are focusing on the proximal characteristics of the remedy rather than on the more distal characteristics related to the importance of the problem (Lea et al., 1995).

This finding would seem to be discouraging because it suggests that people who regard the problem as large will not necessarily support policies to solve it. However, the same finding suggests that the many people who

TABLE 3.1   Support for Varying Kinds of Implementation of Affirmative Action

Type of Implementation	Support
Group-merit	1.83
Merit-group	2.35
Required	2.58
Quotas	2.74
Training	4.13

Higher numbers indicate greater support.

SOURCE: "Attitudes and Beliefs about Affirmative Action: Effects of Target and of Respondent Sex and Ethnicity," by D. Kravitz and J. Platania, 1993, *Journal of Applied Psychology, 78,* 931. Copyright 1993 American Psychological Association. Adapted with permission.

do not see the problem as serious will nonetheless support policies to solve it if the procedures used to implement those policies seem fair. Issues of procedural fairness—the fairness of the policies implementing changes—will be considered in the next chapter.

Problems with Equity Research

As studied by psychologists, equity is a psychological assessment that people make about their own work rewards and contributions relative to others. Thus, equity or inequity is in the eye of the beholder. Furthermore, equity judgments are not necessarily linked to objective factors in the same way for all people. If there are fifteen people sitting around a table watching the same interaction, there can be fifteen different views about the value of the inputs and outcomes involved—fifteen different views about the degree of equity or inequity in the same transaction.

There are a number of problems that arise when issues of equity are studied. First, as suggested above, how inputs and outcomes are defined is subjective and often controversial. People involved in particular social interactions may not agree in their judgments about what constitutes a contribution or a reward. They also may disagree about how much of a contribution each person is making and/or what level of rewards people are receiving.

In studies of equity, the problems outlined above are usually minimized by creating artificial situations in which (1) there are only limited types of contributions to be considered, (2) there are clear and generally accepted rules about appropriate rewards, and (3) rewards and contributions are easily quantifiable, as is true when exchanges are dominated by piece work and money. In addition, researchers sometimes tell people that their rewards are fair or unfair, as opposed to hoping that they will make this judgment naturally when presented with objectively unfair distributions.

An interesting example of the effort to quantify inputs and outcomes is a study of a difficult problem that arises in divorce cases—how to quantify people's contributions to a marriage. Eisner and Zimmerman (1989) studied this problem in the context of divorcing couples. In the cases studied, spouses had provided financial support for their professional partners while those partners were students. The study found that (1) the amount of financial support provided, (2) the degree of personal sacrifice (i.e. giving up one's own career), (3) the amount of money available/length of the marriage, and (4) relative earning capabilities all influenced the amount of support people felt the spouse should receive.

Self-serving biases.   One of the major problems confronting equity theory is the finding of self-serving biases—that is, people tend to exaggerate their personal contributions to collective efforts, leading to inevitable and widespread conflicts (Schlenker & Miller, 1977). In other words, if members of work groups are asked to estimate the percentage of their contribution to a successful project, or if husbands and wives are asked to estimate the percentage of their contribution to housework, the sum of those estimates will exceed 100 percent.

Self-serving biases have been found in a variety of settings. Lerner, Somers, Reid, Chiriboga, and Tierney (1991), for example, examined the fairness judgments of siblings sharing care of their parents. In their study, each sibling saw himself or herself as contributing more than the other(s) and as being less appreciated than he or she should be. Furthermore, this pattern became stronger the more needy the parents were. What lessened such self-serving judgments? In this case, it was respect for the other sibling(s) involved.

On a more general level, Messick, Bloom, Boldizar, and Samuelson (1985) found evidence of a general self-serving tendency in people's views about themselves relative to others. People in their study saw themselves as more likely to engage in fair behaviors and less likely to engage in unfair behaviors than were others. In addition, although people admitted that they were likely to engage in unfair actions (e.g., being rude or inconsiderate), they thought that others were more likely to engage in more serious unfair actions (e.g., cheating, lying, stealing).

The finding that there are self-serving biases in judgments about people's inputs and outcomes relative to others helps us to understand why equity theory was not more effective as a model for ending discontent over pay and promotion. For example, although workers want fair outcomes for their inputs, they exaggerate the value of their own inputs and minimize the value of the inputs of other workers. Much of the initial excitement about the promise of equity theory stemmed from the possibility of dealing with widespread dissatisfaction over compensation found in work settings. It was believed that people would accept compensation more willingly if they understood that it was the result of fair allocations (e.g., the use of equity). However, more recent research on self-serving biases in justice judgments suggests that this hope did not take into account people's tendencies to exaggerate both their personal fairness and their contributions to group efforts (S. E. Taylor & Brown, 1988; Tyler & Hastie, 1991).

An example of the difficulties created by egocentric views of fairness is provided by a recent study of negotiation (Thompson & Loewenstein, 1992). In the study, subjects engaged in a negotiation in which it was to the advantage of both parties to reach an agreement. The study showed that negotiators who viewed the fairness of outcomes from an egocentric perspective were less likely to be able to reach mutually advantageous solutions. These negotiators were also found to recall more information from bargaining that was favorable to themselves, supporting their egocentric views. As this study demonstrates, "Egocentric interpretations of fairness hinder conflict resolution because people are reluctant to agree to what they perceive to be an inequitable settlement" (Thompson & Loewenstein, 1992, p. 176).

The Criteria Used to Evaluate Distributive Justice

The previous section demonstrates that distributive fairness judgments have a widespread and substantial influence on people's thoughts, judgments, and feelings in social settings. The next question of concern is how people know whether distributive justice has occurred.

One of the most striking findings of social justice research is that people are seldom at a loss when asked whether an allocation, a procedure, or a punishment is fair. People have moral frameworks that allow them to make justice judgments. Furthermore, those frameworks are fairly extensive. Studies suggest that people consider seven or eight distinct criteria when evaluating the fairness of a procedure, that a variety of issues are considered when making punishment decisions, and that people make trade-offs between several principles of distributive justice when determining fair pay within organizational settings.

Moreover, principles of distributive justice are situationally based. People do not simply apply general principles of justice to all settings. Instead, they have situational frameworks that indicate that different principles of justice matter in different settings. Through such frameworks, people are able to determine the appropriate principles of justice to apply within a given situation.

Equity Theory

As criteria for determining entitlement, equity theory emphasizes (1) the centrality of judgments about justice or deservedness to people's reactions to the outcomes they receive from others and (2) the evaluation of relative contributions. Equity theory is an important advance beyond relative deprivation since it specifies a justice rule. However, in proposing that social behavior is driven by justice concerns and in specifying the sole criteria used to assess justice, it confounds two issues: whether justice matters and the criteria that people use to define justice.

In an important qualification of equity theory, Deutsch (1975) distinguishes these two questions. He suggests that people might evaluate their outcomes using judgments of justice or deservedness but that they might use a variety of different principles besides equity to define deservedness. Consider a typical situation in a work setting: two workers making widgets. One worker makes ten widgets, the other twenty widgets. At the end of the work session, each worker is paid ten dollars. According to equity theory, this demonstrates a lack of concern with justice principles because the outcome is not consistent with equity principles. However, Deutsch argues that the supervisor still might be motivated by fairness but applying a different justice standard. For example, people might believe that an equal division of the money is fair.

Deutsch (1975) emphasizes two additional principles: equality and need. Subsequent research has suggested that under varying circumstances, people use a wide variety of principles of distributive justice, including equity, equality, need, and many others (Lerner, 1977; Leventhal, 1980; Reis, 1986, 1987; Schwinger, 1986). The key point is that there are many standards of fairness against which outcomes might be compared. We cannot know whether people are motivated out of a concern for justice unless we know which principle they are using.

The identification of multiple distributive justice principles raises the question of how people choose among different justice principles. Deutsch (1975) links such choices to the goals that people are pursuing within the particular interaction. Deutsch identifies three such goals. If people are pursuing economic productivity as a goal, they should use equity as a principle of justice. If they are trying to foster enjoyable and harmonious social relationships, they should use equality as their principle of justice. Finally, to foster personal development and personal welfare, people should use need as their principle of social justice. In other words, the goals people are pursuing should determine the principles of justice they apply.

Barrett-Howard and Tyler (1986) directly test Deutsch's (1975) suggestion by exploring the relationship between goals and principles of justice. They find, as Deutsch predicts, that people who view productivity as a goal are more likely to use equity as a justice standard. Similarly, those who view harmony and welfare as a goal are more likely to use equality and need as justice standards.

An additional issue raised by Deutsch (1975) is which principles ought to govern distributions. Deutsch raises this more normative question in his discussion of various possible principles of justice, but he does not develop a model for exploring it. Political scientists such as Lane (1981) have addressed it in more detail. The problem with addressing this question from a psychological perspective is that it is not a psychological question. Psychologists typically examine the subjective reactions people have to experiences. But as Lane notes, philosophers and other social theorists have not always viewed subjective reactions as key to objective justice. For example, is a good society one in which people are happy? It is important to recognize that the study of subjective reactions occurs within a larger framework of justice issues that include objective questions beyond people's feelings (see Chapter 1). However, these objective issues are difficult to address from a psychological perspective.

Interdependence

Deutsch (1982) further proposes that the nature of the interdependence underlying the relationship between people influences the choice of justice criteria. Deutsch proposes a typology of relationships varying along four dimensions: cooperative versus competitive, equal versus unequal power, task versus socioemotional, and formal versus informal. He hypothesizes that variations along these dimensions shape the cognitive, motivational, and moral orientations of the people within them. Barrett-Howard and Tyler (1986) support this prediction by showing that the nature of the relationship shapes both the goals that people pursue within that relationship and the principles of distributive justice they use. These principles and goals and similar models by several other researchers are shown in Table 3.2.

Also consistent with Deutsch's (1982) argument, a multidimensional scaling analysis of situations people viewed as unfair revealed that the primary ordering dimension was the nature of the social relationship among the parties involved (Mikula, Petri & Tanzer, 1990). Research suggests that the type of relationship between people determines the extent to which both need and merit will be important to the allocation of rewards (Lamm & Keyser, 1978). Similarly, in their research, Clark and Mills (Clark, 1984; Clark, Mills & Powell, 1986) distinguish between two different types of interpersonal relationships. In exchange relationships, benefits are given with the expectation of immediate repayment in kind, but in communal relationships, benefits are given based on the other person's needs. In other words, the structure of the relationship determines the principles of justice that people will use within that relationship.

A. P. Fiske (1991, 1992) also makes the argument that social relationships influence justice concerns. Fiske differentiates among four elementary forms of social relationships: communal sharing, authority ranking, equality matching, and market pricing. He argues that each form of

TABLE 3.2   Factors Associated with Different Distributive-Justice Principles

Justice Rule Allocation	Interaction Goal (Deutsch, 1975)	Form of Relationship (Fiske, 1992)	Political Orientation (Skitka & Tetlock, 1992)	Resource Being Exchanged (Foa & Foa, 1976)
Equity	Economic productivity	Exchange/authority ranking	Conservative	Money Goods
Equality	Social harmony	Equality matching	Liberal	Information Status
Need	Personal development/ individual welfare	Communal sharing	Liberal	Love

sociality has a characteristic model of distributive justice. In communal-sharing relationships, individuals use resources as needed. In authority-ranking relationships, equity governs resource distributions, with hierarchical position defining inputs. In equality-matching relationships, equality governs resource distributions. And in market-pricing relationships, equity again governs resource distributions, with productivity or market value defining inputs.

Social Values

People are influenced not only by their particular goals in social interactions but also by their general social orientations—that is, by the values they hold (Rasinski, 1987). For example, conservatives evaluate equity as fairer than do liberals, who evaluate equality as fairer (Rasinski, 1987; Skitka & Tetlock, 1992). Personal values often reflect generally held ideologies, with conservatives generally supporting proportionality (equity) and liberals generally supporting egalitarianism (equality).

Furthermore, preferences for particular distributive-justice principles support particular sorts of economic and political relationships (Augoustinos & Walker, 1995; Jost & Banaji, 1994). They also lead to support for particular political candidates. In his study, Rasinski (1987) found that both liberals and conservatives reacted to public policies and to particular political candidates in justice terms. However, the meaning of justice differed between the two groups. Conservatives thought that Walter Mondale, the Democratic Party presidential nominee during the 1984 elections, was both distributively and procedurally unfair. Distributively, he supported redistribution to the poor (i.e., he was too egalitarian), and procedurally, he gave too much attention to special interests. Liberals thought that Ronald Reagan, the Republican Party presidential nominee, was both distributively and procedurally unfair. Distributively, he supported redistribution to the rich (i.e., he was too proportional), and procedurally, he was too autocratic. Both groups acted on their justice judgments by supporting the fairer candidate. However, since they defined justice differently, supporting the fairer candidate led liberals to support Mondale and conservatives to support Reagan.

Interestingly, there is also evidence to suggest that people's allocation behaviors are influenced by their beliefs about the social orientation of the recipient. In a study in which subjects played the roles of supervisors in a business context (Messe, Hymes & MacCoun, 1986), usage of equity as a distributive rule was moderated by the gender of the worker. Supervisors were more likely to adhere to the equity rule when allocating payment to male workers versus female workers. It is argued that the equity norm is more salient among men and that egalitarianism is more salient among women. Consequently, supervisors took into account these prior beliefs and adjusted their allocation behavior to accommodate the norms relevant to workers of each gender.

At a broader level, Sampson (1975) argues that the principles of distributive justice used shape the social climate. Equity values encourage and legitimate individual competition and personal advancement at the expense of cooperation, communion, and equality. In contrast, the use of equality encourages cooperation, communion, and equality, possibly at the cost of the benefits of competition.

Resource Typologies

As illustrated by the equity research on close relationships described earlier, distributive justice is not limited to the exchange of material goods. One example of a typology of resources is the work of Foa and colleagues. Resource theory (U. G. Foa, Converse, Tornblom, & Foa, 1993; E. B. Foa & Foa, 1976) suggests there are a limited number of basic resources that are exchanged in a give-and-take fashion in all social interactions. Specifically, resources exchanged in social interactions are classified into six classes: money, goods, services, love, status, and information. These resources can be ordered with respect to two orthogonal dimensions: particularism and concreteness. Particularism refers to the extent to which it matters with whom you exchange the resource. The concreteness dimension ranges from low concreteness (intangible or symbolic) to high concreteness. Some resources, such as status, are rather intangible or symbolic, whereas other resources, such as goods, are very concrete. This typology is shown in Figure 3.5.

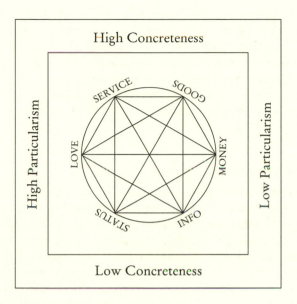

FIGURE 3.5 The Foa and Foa resource typology. SOURCE: *Resource Theory: Explorations and Applications*, p. 11, U. G. Foa, J. Converse, Jr., K. Y. Tornblom, and E. B. Foa (Eds.), 1993, San Diego: Academic Press, Inc. Copyright 1993 Academic Press, Inc. Reproduced with permission.

The resource theory typology is important to equity theory and distributive justice research for several reasons. First, resource theory suggests that the principle of exchange used will be a function of the nature of the resource exchanged. For example, money and goods are likely to be exchanged according to the principle of equity, whereas love may be exchanged on the basis of need.

Second, the theory proposes that resources will tend to be exchanged for similar kinds of resources. People find it appropriate to exchange love for love but find it abhorrent to exchange love for money. By extension, when an inequity or distributive injustice is created, people prefer to be compensated in kind. The lack of respect shown by a canceled dinner date is better restored by a sincere apology than by an effort to give the injured person fifty dollars.

Third, equity theory assumes that the inputs and outcomes used in assessing the equity of a situation conform to particular quantitative properties (Walster et al., 1978). Resource theory points out that some resources can be given without depletion. For example, it is possible to give information without a loss of information to oneself.

As a general point, resource theory notes that unfair exchanges or distributions of material goods are only one form of injustice. More important, other research indicates that a focus on this form of resource fails to capture much of the phenomenon of injustice. For example, when people are asked to describe their personal experiences with injustice, they do not describe issues of unfair payment or unfair distributions of material goods (Mikula, 1986). In fact, only approximately 4 percent of the incidents mentioned fit into this category.

Reciprocal Causation

This analysis has presented the structure of relationships as shaping the choice of justice principles used. However, Deutsch (1975) recognizes that the structure of influence over time is bidirectional. Deutsch's "crude hypothesis of social relations" (p. 147) asserts that a reciprocal causal connection exists between the type of relationship, the relevant goals, and the relevant justice principle. In other words, people use allocation principles as cues to the nature of social relationship, and vice versa. If two people use an equality rule to divide costs or rewards, observers evaluate the relationship as being closer than one in which two people use an equity rule (Greenberg, 1983). Hence, people signal their views about their relationships through their choice of justice principles, and those choices influence the nature of those future relationships. If a person on a date, for example, chooses to suggest using the principle of equality instead of the principle of equity to divide the dinner check, that choice leads the partner to think the relationship is closer and more personal. This perception leads to behaviors that make the relationship even more personal and closer. Conversely, the use of equity would encourage more social distance, leading others to respond by becoming more distant. Thus, people define and create the nature of their relationships with others through their choices of justice principles. This reasoning also extends to expectations for relationships. When one anticipates having a close relationship with another person, one does not attend to equity concerns in exchanges. Conversely, exchanges with a person expected to remain a stranger are closely monitored for inputs to maintain equity (Clark, Mills & Corcoran, 1989).

Trade-Offs

Perhaps the most interesting idea to emerge from the distributive justice literature is the possibility of trade-offs different justice principles (Okun, 1975). For example, it is argued that there is a trade-off between the use of equity and equality. The assumption is that equity promotes productivity but harms social harmony. The use of equality, though, is suggested to promote social harmony at the expense of productivity. Consequently, a balance between these objectives, leading to a balance between principles of justice, must be settled upon.

Three methods of balancing trade-offs have been identified (see Figure 3.6). One is to use a hybrid rule that mixes the use of equity and equality in allocating a resource such as money. For example, a company gives all employees a 3 percent raise, then adds an additional 2 percent for the most productive employees. This trade-off occurs within one class of resources.

A second method of balancing is to distribute some resources and rewards based upon principles of merit and equity and other resources and rewards based upon principles of need and equality. Pay and monetary benefits in organizations can be determined by merit (or tenure), whereas socioemotional benefits can be determined by need or equality (Martin & Harder, 1994). For example, employees all receive the same size office or are invited to the Christmas party, but higher-productivity employees are paid more. Combining justice principles within the same context but for different classes of resources offers another reason why large pay inequities may be tolerated (Martin & Harder, 1994).

A third method is to focus on procedural concerns when seeking to enhance harmony, leaving distributive-justice norms free to be shaped in ways that enhance productivity (Tyler, 1991; Tyler & Belliveau, 1996). This suggestion draws on findings of the procedural justice literature that will be discussed in the next chapter.

Research has not compared the relative effectiveness of these different approaches to dealing with issues of making trade-offs. Therefore, it is unclear which is most effective. The first method has the advantage of using the common metric of money, whereas the second method has the advantage of using interpersonal resources (perhaps more easily attainable and less costly) to promote social harmony. For example, a vice president can easily be made an executive vice president and given a gold watch, a large wall plaque, and/or a private parking space. However, it might be much more difficult for the company to give a huge financial raise. The third method has the advantage of building on the powerful influence that procedures have on commitment and loyalty (see the next chapter). Hence, all are plausible candidates for approaches to handling the trade-off between equity and equality.

Deutsch (1985, 1987) addresses the issue of trade-offs in a different way. He questions the assumption that trade-offs occur by examining whether the use of equity is especially likely to promote productivity. He presents experimental data suggesting that equality is often as effective as equity in promoting productivity. He suggests that outside of situations of minimal interdependence, the negative effects of equity on social harmony offset any productivity gains from the use of equity. Most of the settings used in experimental research

1. **Use hybrid rules**

   Distribute the same resource partially in response to each rule. For example, pay all workers the same base salary with a bonus for productivity.

2. **Balance among the resources**

   Distribute one resource equitably and another equally. For example, give all workers equal health care, but give managers larger offices.

3. **Balance procedures and outcomes**

   Use fair procedures to enhance social harmony. Use pay distributions to encourage productivity.

FIGURE 3.6   Balancing trade-offs

involve situations of minimal interdependence: for example, workers individually making widgets or students individually working to get high grades. However, most real-world work settings involve long-term relationships and work teams. In such settings of high interdependence, negative effects on social harmony are quite costly.

If Deutsch (1985, 1987) is correct, in most real work settings, there is no necessary trade-off between the goal of productivity and the use of equality as a reward principle. Thus, there may be no need to balance equity and equality. However, true economic cooperation and equality may be difficult to achieve. For example, in school districts in which both administrators and low-income parents are equally represented on school boards, administrators' opinions still influence board decisions more than the opinions of low-income parents (Vanderslice, 1994). Further, economic cooperatives that cannot in principle recognize differences in skills and commitment often lose their most productive and skilled employees. For example, in a construction cooperative in which everyone earned relatively low wages and completed a variety of tasks, it took longer to complete single jobs. People learned the necessary construction skills and immediately left for better-paying jobs. As one worker reported, "It is difficult to feel empowered when you're not earning much in a culture that judges value by the size of your paycheck" (quoted in Vanderslice, 1995, p. 191).

One reason that equity may not always be linked to heightened productivity is that equity can be defined in various ways, with organizations often adopting equity-based approaches that are less effective in promoting productivity. Deutsch (1975) suggests that equity might enhance productivity if it is defined as giving resources to those most able to use them in the future. However, equity is often defined as a reward for past achievements. Older workers command high salaries because they were once productive, and formerly productive scientists receive large grants. Hence, there are more or less productive ways to allocate compensation within the general framework of equity. On a societal level, retiring workers receive rewards for work they have already performed via pensions and social security, whereas investments in educating the young (linked to increases in future productivity) are low.

However, current discussions about health care rationing increasingly argue that medical benefits should go to those with the greatest likelihood of making future contributions to society (efficiency). This means that people can work for many years, lead useful and productive lives, make many social contributions—raise a family, create new products, and so forth—only to be denied medical care when they are old and most in need. In contrast, the young, who have not yet made any contributions to society, receive first priority for medical care. These issues illustrate the tension between individual-level justice and justice from the perspective of society.

Micro Versus Macro Distributive Justice

Concern about justice from the perspective of society raises the issue of the criteria used to define justice. One aspect of this issue involves the level at which the judgment is being made. This subtle but important distinction was first outlined by Brickman, Folger, Goode, and Schul (1981). They distinguish between microjustice judgments of the fairness of rewards for single individuals (or groups) and macrojustice judgments of the fairness of rewards for entire societies. Judgments of macrojustice reflect assessments about the overall distribution of rewards or the overall procedures of a society.

A key difference between these two types of judgments is the relative self-involvement of the person making the judgment. When people judge fairness as a single individual or group representative, they are extremely aware of how these judgments affect them personally. When people judge the overall fairness of an aggregate distribution, the personal consequences may be less relevant.

The discussion of micro- and macrojustice has grown more complex as social psychologists have recognized the important role that group memberships play in self-definitions. Microjustice traditionally has been focused on individual-level concerns—for example, a worker's desire to receive fair pay. Macrojustice, as articulated by Brickman et al. (1981), is concerned with justice on a societal level. However, there is an intermediate form of justice that is inadequately examined: people's concerns that their groups receive appropriate treatment and resources. Despite the recognition of the importance of fraternal deprivation judgments, group-based justice has received inadequate attention. In particular, it is not clear whether group-based judgments ought to be considered as microjustice or as macrojustice.

The difference between microjustice and macrojustice as it relates to group membership is illustrated in Figure 3.7. A macrojustice evaluation of the distribution of income represented in this graph would be based on a consideration of all the different data points. In macro terms, as the level of education increases, the level of income also increases. The key macrojustice question is whether the shape of the distribution is fair or unfair. In contrast, a microjustice evaluation would focus on a single data point, point X, for example. At this point, a relatively higher level of education is associated with a relatively low level of income (perhaps this person is a graduate student!). The key microjustice question is whether the amount of income for this particular point is fair or not.

With these two questions in mind, we can consider the role of group membership. For example, think of yourself as a psychologist and imagine that the graph in Figure 3.7 represents the distribution of income for all psychologists. In this case, we expect that increasing the salience of one's membership in the group, psychologists, will promote a macrojustice focus. People will be concerned with how income is distributed across all group members. Now imagine that point X in Figure 3.7 represents the income for the average psychologist, point Y represents the income for the average economist, and point Z represents the income for the average lawyer. Now we expect that increasing the salience of one's membership in the group, psychologists, will actually promote a microjustice focus with groups, rather than individuals, being the focus of self-interest. People will be concerned with whether their group (compared with other groups) is getting the right amount of income.

As social order has been conceptualized in the past, society has encouraged citizens to frame their outcome judgments in individual terms, rather than on a group level (Azzi, 1994; Major, 1994). Deprivations interpreted in group terms, after all, are more likely to lead to collective unrest. Thus, social instability seems a likely prediction for the future if people increasingly frame entitlement concerns in group-based terms. However, new forms of social order may emerge that are linked to mosaic frameworks that give greater salience to groups and group entitlements, just as current frameworks recognize that different individuals have different interests and goals.

The distinction between individual and group justice concerns highlights an important contribution of social justice to the field of social psychology.

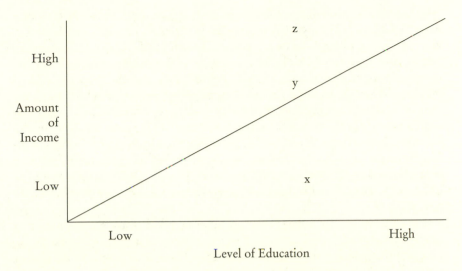

FIGURE 3.7   The distinction between microjustice and macrojustice

Reflecting the individualistic nature of American culture, early work on social justice has been strongly individual in character. However, the important early distinction between egoistic and fraternal deprivation (by the European author Runciman, 1966) foreshadowed an important emerging issue within the field of justice. Theories of justice must accommodate group-based justice models, since the development of multilevel justice models appears inevitable with the development of multicultural societies.

In fact, despite the limits of the current literature, justice theories and research have been infused with the social identity perspective on the individual more than most areas of social psychology (Ellemers, 1993; D. M. Taylor & Moghaddam, 1994). That perspective emphasizes that people's identities are shaped both by unique individual qualities and by memberships in important groups and social categories (social identities). The justice literature demonstrates that social identities have important social implications. If people define themselves in group terms, they are more likely to interpret their experiences in group terms, more likely to feel group deprivation, and more likely to engage in collective actions.

Macrojustice and Social Policy

The idea of macrojustice is important from a social policy perspective. Many social policies that are judged to be unfair in microjustice terms are fair when evaluated from the perspective of macrojustice. For example, comparable worth, affirmative action, and universal health care are all policies that are fair from the perspective of at least some principles of macrojustice. In fact, a typology of policies can be created in which policies are viewed by most people as fair at either or both levels. Consider the issues outlined in Figure 3.8. An issue that might be considered fair at both the micro and the macro levels is the use of a lottery to allocate benefits and/or burdens. Whether deciding who to draft into the army or to whom to give a kidney, people generally regard lotteries as a fair approach to allocation. An issue that might be viewed as fair on the macro level but not fair on the micro level is triage. Conversely, allowing people to decide whether to smoke might be viewed as fair on a micro level but likely to be unfair on a macro level as society copes with health care costs. Police taking bribes is likely to be considered unfair from both the micro- and the macro-justice perspectives.

The observation that many real-world social policies are seen as unfair in microjustice terms but not in terms of macrojustice suggests that macrojustice has an important societal role. If these policies were simply evaluated in micro-level terms, there would be no reason to enact them. Before considering this issue, however, we need to define the principles that allow people to make macrojustice judgments.

It is important to recognize that the way justice rules are conceptualized is not just an abstract issue; it has practical implications for who is helped or hurt by social policies. Consider the case of affirmative action. By defining affirmative action in group terms, the policy identified individuals who might benefit—the members of disadvantaged groups. But European Americans from poor and disadvantaged backgrounds who might have been entitled to benefits as individuals were excluded.

An alternative conceptualization of affirmative action as helping needy individuals would have included needy, deserving European Americans as well. For example, many recent immigrants from the former Soviet Union are new American citizens who are struggling to succeed in American society. However, they are not considered eligible for affirmative action, since they are not members of "disadvantaged" groups. Although European Americans may be advantaged as a group, there are individuals within that group who are not advantaged if judged as individuals.

Conversely, it could be argued that the individual conceptualization of affirmative action fails to consider the stigma of certain group memberships (for example, the effects of racism in American society). Many would argue that being poor and White is not the same as being poor and African American. In particular, there have been institutional barriers designed to prevent poor minorities from succeeding (such as barriers to living in integrated housing) that have not been applied to Whites (see Duster, 1995).

Conceptualizing affirmative action as group based has also led the program to be most beneficial to the members of disadvantaged groups who are

		Microjustice	
		Fair	Unfair
Macro-justice	Fair	The lottery for choosing who is drafted in to the army.	Triage (choosing who to save based upon likelihood of survival, not cause of injury).
	Unfair	Letting people decide whether to smoke, wear seat belts, wear motorcycle helmets.	Police officers taking bribes to fix tickets.

FIGURE 3.8   Microjustice and macrojustice

least disadvantaged. For example, affirmative-action programs have helped the African American middle class more than poor African Americans. Why? Because employers can hire any member of the group to meet their affirmative-action criteria (i.e., to behave fairly). Naturally, there is pressure to hire the most advantaged and qualified members of disadvantaged groups. For example, in admitting graduate students, committees often receive applications from "disadvantaged" minority students whose parents are doctors or lawyers, who have grown up in upper-middle-class communities, and who have attended schools such as Harvard or Yale. Yet these applications receive preferential admission under group-based justice criteria. Similarly, women, the most highly educated "disadvantaged" group, have benefited from affirmative-action programs more than African Americans have.

In contrast, a program based on individual justice would provide the most benefits to those who are most in need of those benefits—the individuals who have personally experienced disadvantage. This would, however, change the focus of affirmative-action programs from justice for groups to justice for individuals.

Principles of Macrojustice

What are principles of macrojustice? Brickman and his colleagues (1981) give three examples of macrojustice principles in the arena of distributive justice. The minimum principle suggests that the range between the least well-off and the most well-off in society should be small. The average principle suggests that there should be a balance between the proportion of social resources used in different ways. For example, if society values education and defense equally, the budget for defense should not be three times as great as the budget for education. Finally, the subgroup principle suggests that there should be a balance between the resources/opportunities given to different groups in society.

Interestingly, the macrojustice examples given by Brickman and his colleagues (1981) do not specify any clear justice principle beyond balance—balance between the poor and the wealthy, between allocation priorities, and between subgroups. They do not indicate how balance is judged to be fair or unfair. This lack of specification suggests that an important area for future research is the specification of macrojustice rules.

Empirical Research

The one empirical finding in this area is that a tension exists between microjustice and macrojustice principles of distributive justice. When people are asked about microjustice principles for distributing economic outcomes, they typically support differences based on differences in ability and effort (i.e., equity). However, when people are shown aggregate distributions of outcomes for societies functioning on these microjustice principles, they often judge those aggregate distributions to be unfair. Studies suggest that people typically modify such distributions by increasing resources to those with the least and decreasing resources to those with the most (Hermkens & van Kreveld, 1992; Mitchell, Tetlock, Mellers, & Ordonez, 1993; Ordonez & Mellers, 1993). These modifications are examples of the minimal-distance principle of balance.

It would be interesting to extend this analysis to the issue of subgroup balance. This question arises directly in such policies as affirmative action. We have already presented the mean net worth of households of varying ethnic groups in the United States (see Figure 2.5). Clearly, there are differences. Do these differences indicate a lack of balance between subgroups? This is a subjective issue that can only be addressed by interviewing samples of people. Such interviews would indicate whether there is also a tension similar to the one already outlined about the overall distribution of wealth—that is, the tension between existing group differences in wealth and people's conceptions of macrofairness. Are differences in income more psychologically compelling if framed in ethnic group terms?

Situational Influences

The degree of tension between microjustice and macrojustice varies with the situation. Several explanations might potentially underlie observed micro/macro tensions. One type of explanation is cognitive. People may have different information or consider different issues when making justice judgments on the two levels. For example, people may consider aggregate or base-rate data on the macro level, whereas they may often minimize attention to base rates when making micro-level judgments. Conversely, people may minimize attention to individuating information when making macro-level judgments. For example, people may not consider the long hours of work and years in school that lead to the high levels of income represented in aggregate distributions. Further, people may have incorrect assumptions about the objective relationship between micro and macro distributions, misunderstanding the true role of ability, effort, and so forth, in creating aggregate distributions of income. Finally, people may have greater personal experience making micro-level judgments, such as dividing resources with a friend, than with making macro-level policy decisions. Hence, they may rely more on personal experience in one case than in the other.

There are also motivational explanations for micro/macro differences. In making micro-level judgments, people are motivated to do what is fair for particular people. In making macro-level judgments, people are concerned with what a just society should look like. Similarly, on the micro level, people are motivated by the goal of interpersonal harmony, whereas macro-level motivations are directed at aggregate social harmony.

Finally, self-interest may differ on the micro and macro levels. On the micro level, people may be concerned about maximizing their personal self-interest and their exchange relations with particular others. Their preferences may be strongly affected by the desire to be free to pursue personal gain. On the macro level, people may be concerned about larger societal constraints on freedom of action. For example, the minimum-difference principle restricts the ability of the wealthy to amass large sums of wealth. Within organizations, individuals typically strive to maximize their personal compensation, but organizations have to worry about the macro-level implications of large differences between the salaries of workers and CEOs (Sheppard, Lewicki, & Minton, 1992).

It is also important to consider which situational factors influence the balance between the attention given to micro- and macro-level justice issues when making overall justice judgments. Several factors have been suggested to encourage people to focus on macro-level issues. First, people are more likely to make macro-level judgments about issues that they believe are beyond a single individual's control. When a person is viewed as able to control a problem and hence as responsible for the problem, they are judged in micro-level terms. When a problem is beyond personal responsibility, it is judged in macro-level terms. For example, welfare is viewed as appropriate for those who are not responsible for their plight (e.g., not lazy) and not appropriate for those who are responsible (a microjustice judgment). However, allocating support for the elderly or handicapped, who are generally not viewed as responsible for their situation, is generally framed in macrojustice terms. A macrojustice perspective is more likely to occur when the problems involved are universal within the society. Universal aspects of life, like getting old, typically are not evaluated in terms of a person's responsibility. Even within these general categories, however, people make distinctions. For example, being born handicapped is different than being handicapped because of a motorcycle accident in which a person was not wearing a helmet, just as having bone cancer is not the same as having lung cancer because of lifelong smoking.

Some health care policies consider judgments about individuals' responsibility for their plight when allocating benefits. An example is denying persons an organ transplant or other expensive health care procedures because they are overweight, smoke, or are otherwise contributing to their own health problems. A hospital, for example, would treat a person who has skin cancer before they would treat someone with lung cancer if the lung cancer had been "caused" by the individual's smoking behavior. Such microjustice might or might not correspond to the macro goals. It might correspond to the macrojustice goal of efficiency by encouraging responsible health behavior. However, it might conflict with macrojustice goals of efficiency if treatment is not allocated in relationship to the likelihood of success. Just because one has caused one's own problem, for example, does not mean that one is less likely to survive and make further social contributions than people not responsible for their problems. Extending this principle even further, we might say that a great scientist should be forgiven an occasional murder so that he/she can continue to work and make valuable contributions to society. Although this might seem far-fetched, the United States readily forgave German scientists investigated for war crimes they might have committed while working for Germany during World War II in order to put them into productive labor in the American military.

Second, the social context influences the relative importance of macrojustice. People think in macro terms when rules are being formulated and societies created or changed. The centrality of macro-level issues promotes consideration of macrojustice. Further, people may find themselves placed within roles that encourage macro thinking, such as an allocator of resources or a leader. Such people are accountable to society for their actions and must consider justice principles that legitimize their actions. This may explain the allocator/recipient differences in justice that will be discussed in Chapter 9.

Third, allocators of resources may emphasize macro-level judgments during periods of scarcity (also see Chapter 9). If resources are sufficiently abundant, little effort is made to distinguish between recipients (Greenberg, 1981), and equality principles may be used to allocate the resource (Skitka & Tetlock, 1992). However, society often faces the difficult situation of allocating scarce resources. In such instances, allocators may use a variety of principles to allocate resources. However, the efficiency principle—which gives resources to people who do or can do the most to help society—often emerges as an important principle for allocating scarce resources (Greenberg, 1981; Skitka & Tetlock, 1992). Consider the example of triage (choosing who to treat first in a medical emergency). In such a situation, doctors typically help first the wounded who are most likely to survive, irrespective of whether they became wounded attacking the enemy, throwing themselves on a grenade to save their buddies, or running away from the battle. Although evaluations of efficiency require reference to individual characteristics (in the triage case, the likelihood of survival), the use of this principle is aimed at maximizing the aggregate or macrojustice of the distribution (Elster, 1992), not providing individual-level justice.

Fourth, the arena involved may be important. Brickman et al. (1981) argue that people think of economic situations in microjustice terms but think of political situations in macrojustice terms. As they note, "Microjustice refers more easily to the economic domain and macrojustice to the political domain" (p. 181). Why? Brickman et al. continue, "Microjustice principles may appear to apply more easily to informal or decentralized groups, while macrojustice requires some form of centralized authority. Macrojustice, because it requires some consciousness of a collective whole, may appear more easily associated with cooperation, group spirit, and the production of public goods, and microjustice may be more associated with competition, selfishness, and private goods" (p. 181).

The Domain of Distributive Injustice Concerns

Because of the extensive body of research developed under the rubric of equity theory, discussions about distributive justice often focus on questions of pay and promotion in work settings. As has been noted, such settings are ideal from a research perspective because rewards and contributions are easier to identify and quantify in work settings than in more complex settings. However, distributive-justice researchers question whether this choice of arenas captures all of people's typical distributive-justice concerns.

Messick et al. (1985) asked subjects to think about fair and unfair acts in dealings with other people. They found that respondents "do not think of allocative behaviors of the sort that are common in social psychology experiments. None of the eighty behaviors that we sampled had to do with payments for work accomplished, the prototypical task used to study equity and fairness. The majority of acts had to do with interpersonal considerations and politeness" (p. 499).

Even studies of managers suggest that most of the work conflicts they deal with involve issues other than pay and performance (Lissak & Sheppard, 1983; Sheppard & Lewicki, 1987). For example, Sheppard and Lewicki (1987) had managers describe recent management conflicts in which they had been involved. Of 747 conflicts mentioned, fifty-eight (8 percent) were about reward allocation. These studies suggest that many of the concerns about distributive justice that are mentioned are not about questions of pay. Hence, the focus on pay issues has missed many other aspects of distributive injustice. More important, many of the examples people describe concern questions of procedure. These authors (Lissak & Sheppard, 1983; Sheppard & Lewicki, 1987) suggest that a broader justice focus is needed that also includes attention to how decisions are made. These issues will be addressed in the next chapter.

4

PROCEDURAL JUSTICE

Thus far, our discussions of justice have assumed that people basically are concerned about the outcomes they receive from others and compare their own outcomes with those of others using principles of distributive justice. Such a view flows easily from the social exchange model that dominates the social psychology of groups. That model suggests that people evaluate their own outcomes by comparing them with the outcomes of others, as described in relative deprivation theory. It also suggests that they determine how to behave by considering the potential personal gain or loss in various actions (see Thibaut & Kelley, 1959).

During the 1970s, several social-justice researchers raised questions about the completeness of outcome-oriented justice models. Leventhal (1980; Leventhal, Karuza, & Fry, 1980) elaborated a justice framework that incorporated both distributive and procedural criteria in an effort to expand the justice framework provided by equity theory. The expanded model recognizes that people are concerned about how decisions are made as well as about what those decisions are.

Thibaut and Walker (1975) similarly differentiate feelings of distributive and procedural justice concerns, drawing on the legal literature that distinguishes between substantive and procedural justice. In doing so, they seek objective criteria for identifying each type of justice. Thibaut and Walker's model of procedural justice is also rooted in equity theory. Thibaut and Walker (1978) suggest that people view fair procedures as a mechanism through which to obtain equitable outcomes—which is the goal in cases of conflict of interest.

Thibaut and Walker (1978) distinguish conflicts of interest from truth conflicts. If, for example, a group of people are lost in the woods, they have a common interest in finding their way out (finding truth). Thibaut and Walker argue that in such a situation, the psychology of procedural preference is different. Thibaut and Walker suggest that in truth conflicts, people are not primarily interested in obtaining fair outcomes. Instead, they are interested in obtaining the correct answer. In such situations, people prefer more autocratic procedures.

These procedural justice theories recognize that people are concerned with the process through which outcomes are distributed in groups. In addition to evaluating the fairness of outcomes, people evaluate the fairness of the procedures by which those outcomes are determined. Such fairness judgments have been labeled "judgments of procedural justice." The interesting implication of procedural justice theories is that people are willing to accept and view as fair outcomes that they regard as unfavorable because of the process through which those outcomes were derived. For example, one may think that losing one's property to another is unfair if the property is taken at gunpoint, but one may think that losing the same property is fairer if a jury in a civil trial decides that the property rightly belongs to another person.

Like equity theory, the argument of procedural justice theory initially encountered skepticism. Given the instrumental orientation of social-psychological models of the person (see Chapter 1; Thibaut & Kelley, 1959) that view people as wanting to maximize the resources they gain in interactions with others, the procedural justice argument is counterintuitive. It is difficult to believe that people will find a negative or undesirable outcome more acceptable simply because of the manner in which it was arrived.

This skepticism accords well with the attitude of judges and managers, who typically think that people respond to the favorableness of decisions, not to the procedure used to make them. Further, when people are interviewed about what they want from dispute resolution procedures, they typically indicate that they want to win and evaluate their experiences in terms of how much they gain or lose. In fact, studies relying on people's own views about themselves suggest that people tend to see themselves as focused on gains or losses (D. T. Miller & Ratner, in press). However, psychologists caution that people are often unaware of the basis of their own behavior (Greenwald & Benaji, 1995; Nisbett & Wilson, 1977).

Procedural Justice Research

Although many justice researchers had noted the potential importance of procedural issues (see Leventhal, 1976, 1980), Thibaut and Walker (1975) developed the first systematic psychological research program to try to demonstrate the importance of procedural justice as a distinct social justice concern. They hypothesized that people's evaluations of the fairness of decisionmaking procedures have an influence on their reactions to the outcomes of those procedures that is distinct from their reactions to outcomes themselves.

Thibaut and Walker (1975) looked for such procedural justice effects in a series of studies comparing the adversarial and the inquisitorial procedures for dispute resolution. Both systems have many variations, but each has some core characteristics. The adversary system that is familiar to most Americans from television shows such as *Perry Mason* or *LA Law* (as well as events such as the O. J. Simpson trial, a recent, highly publicized jury trial of a famous black athlete accused of killing his wife) is the legal system used in the United States. In it, each party has an attorney who argues on its behalf. The judge is a neutral referee, and either the judge or a jury makes decisions of guilt or innocence and decides on appropriate penalties and/or damage awards. The inquisitorial system that is used in European courts differs primarily because it gives the parties to a dispute less control over the presentation of evidence. For example, in many such courts, there is one attorney, who works for the court system. That attorney investigates the case, talking to all parties, and then delivers a report in court to the judge. The judge then asks questions of the attorney, the witnesses, and/or the parties to the dispute. The judge and/or a jury make(s) decisions of guilt or innocence and decide(s) on appropriate penalties and/or damage awards.

Thibaut and Walker's (1975) research addresses three psychological issues in the context of third-party efforts at dispute resolution. Those issues are (1) when and why people go to third parties, (2) what procedures are more objectively fair, and (3) what procedures are more subjectively fair.

Choosing to Go to Third Parties

The first issue includes (1) when people are willing to go to third parties and (2) how people choose the type of third-party procedure (e.g., mediation, arbitration, trial) they prefer to use in resolving their dispute. Thibaut and Walker's (1975) work demonstrates that people are reluctant to take disputes to third-party authorities and do so primarily when they are unable to resolve those disputes through negotiation.

The finding that people are reluctant to go to third parties is consistent with the general finding that people are reluctant to take their problems to others. From the perspective articulated by Thibaut and Walker (1975), this reluctance flows from the desire to maintain personal control, because maintaining it is the best way to maximize one's own outcomes. When people go to third parties, they must give up some control, and people are reluctant to do so. However, Thibaut and Walker demonstrate that people do give up control when they feel that it is necessary to do so in order to resolve a dispute. For example, when it is urgent that a dispute be resolved or when the interests of the parties are more divergent (and settlement by bargaining is therefore less likely), people are more likely to give control to third parties.

The finding that people seek outside authority when they feel that such authority will help to resolve conflicts more effectively is also demonstrated by other social-psychological research. For example, Messick and colleagues

(1983) studied people's responses to community problems in allocating collective resources. In their study, when some members of the community were overusing collective resources, other members of the community were more willing to vote to create an autocratic authority responsible for allocating resources to all community members. Similarly, Thibaut and Faucheux (1965) found that the possibility that a mutually beneficial exchange relationship would collapse due to structural instabilities (with one party having greater power and the other party having attractive alternatives to staying in the relationship) lead group members to develop and follow rules for the allocation of resources.

Thibaut and Walker's (1975) research further demonstrates that procedural fairness judgments have an important influence on procedural choices. People choose the procedures that they would like to use to resolve their disputes in large part through assessments of procedural fairness. In other words, people do not simply choose the procedure that they think will allow them to win. They are actually interested in finding a procedure that they think will be fair and will yield a fair outcome.

In the case of trial procedures of the type studied by Thibaut and Walker (1975), it is often assumed that the key issue is the ability of procedures to produce accurate verdicts. However, a study of Americans by Austin and Tobiasen (1985) suggests a more complex picture. Tobiasen and Austin presented subjects with brief descriptions of cases handled via the adversary and inquisitorial procedures and found that subjects rated the adversary procedure as fairer and more accurate. The study found that under these conditions, subjects preferred the adversary system. This finding seems natural since when they have very little information, American subjects regard the adversary system as producing both more accurate and fairer decisions. However, when given longer transcripts of the two procedures, subjects rated the inquisitorial procedure as producing more accurate decisions. However, they still viewed the adversary procedure as fairer. Hence, when given greater information, American subjects judged that the same procedure did not lead to both desirable goals: accurate verdicts and fair verdicts. Faced with this conflict, subjects rated the adversary procedure to be more desirable. This suggests that there is something more to desirability and judgments of fairness than simply the belief that a procedure leads to accurate outcomes.

The Objective Fairness of Procedures

The second issue is the objective fairness of different dispute resolution procedures. The 1975 work of Thibaut and Walker concludes that adversary legal procedures are objectively fairer than those used in the inquisitorial system on several dimensions, including favoring the disadvantaged party in evidence collection (seeking and transmitting facts) and eliminating pretrial bias (combating external bias). However, their 1978 work presents a somewhat different picture of the adversary and inquisitorial procedures. In the later work, they argue that the adversary procedure is less likely to result in truth than is the inquisitorial system. Thus, the objective merits of the two systems ultimately depend on the objective criteria against which they are evaluated. For example, is it better or worse to favor the disadvantaged party?

Ultimately, decisions about what type of errors to allow and what type of errors to minimize are social-value judgments. For example, America has traditionally set a high threshold for conviction, feeling that it is better for ten guilty people to go free than for one innocent person to be convicted. One structural feature ensuring such a high threshold is the requirement for unanimous jury decisions. Recently, however, there have been social movements to lower this high threshold in order to make convictions more likely. Such decisions invoke social judgments about the values a society should follow and are not psychological judgments. For example, during the Cultural Revolution in China, one government official said that "wrongly killing 100 is better than letting one guilty one escape" (quoted in Terrill, 1996, p. 25).

Although not directly psychological, Thibaut and Walker's (1975, 1978) efforts to examine the objective qualities of procedures develop from a long-standing tradition of examining the objective consequences of procedures that begins in the classic studies of Lewin. For example, Lewin, Lippitt, and White (1939) examine the characteristics of groups that are governed by three types of social climates: autocratic, democratic, and laissez-faire. These climates or procedures of group decisionmaking influenced the nature of task performance, the socioemotional climate, and whether the group's behavior changed when the leader was either present or absent. This study represents an early demonstration that objective variations in the nature of group decisionmaking procedures influence the behavior and attitudes of group members. More recent efforts to study the influence of the objective character of groups include studies of the effect of elected and appointed leaders (Hollander, 1985) and studies of the effect of variations in the structure of the jury (Davis, 1980).

Subjective Reactions to Procedures

The third issue Thibaut and Walker (1975) consider is the subjective reactions of people who have experienced various types of procedures. Their work suggests that these reactions are independently influenced by procedural fairness judgments (L. Walker, LaTour, Lind & Thibaut, 1974). In experimental research that manipulated guilt, trial outcome, and trial procedure in various combinations, people were found to be more satisfied if they experienced a fairer trial procedure, regardless of trial outcome.

Overall, people rated their satisfaction to be 5.94 when they had adversary trials and only 3.91 when they had inquisitorial trials (with high scores indicating greater satisfaction). The mean level of satisfaction with procedures in each of the conditions is shown in Table 4.1. Consider the most dramatic case: people who were actually innocent but were found guilty. If those people had an adversary trial, their average satisfaction was 4.13. If they had an inquisitorial trial, their average satisfaction was 1.13. Therefore, the adversary system can deliver negative and in this case, undeserved outcomes with less dissatisfaction. Conversely, people who were innocent and who were vindicated were more satisfied if they had been vindicated via the adversary system (mean satisfaction 7.57 as compared with 4.78 for the inquisitorial system).

Thibaut and Walker's (1975) work provides several types of evidence suggesting that the preference for the adversary system is a basic human characteristic. First, people prefer the adversary system when they are behind the veil of ignorance (Rawls, 1971) and do not know what position in a dispute they will occupy. Second, observers who have no stake in particular cases rate the adversary system as the fairest way to resolve them. Finally, people in cultures that do not have the adversary system (e.g., France and Germany) rate it to be fairer than the inquisitorial system.

Implications for Future Procedural Justice Research

Thibaut and Walker's (1975) research compares the adversary and the inquisitorial legal systems. This framing of the study of procedural justice has influenced in several important ways the issues addressed in their own and others' research on procedural justice. First, they focus on formal characteristics of procedures, as opposed to informal aspects of the procedure (Tyler & Bies, 1990). The adversary system of legal procedure specifies a formal structure for a procedure (e.g., people have their own lawyers and so on), but it is implemented differently by particular judges and lawyers.

Further, their work focuses heavily on people who are personally involved in disputes (although some studies had observers) and on particular disputes. People are not asked abstract questions about justice (e.g., who should have a kidney?). This focus on cases reflects the legal-system background within which Thibaut and Walker (1975) framed the procedural problems they studied.

Third, people are asked about the fairness of procedures in ways that discourage them from making judgments about the fundamental fairness of institutionalized procedures. In the context of a jury trial, for example, asking people to evaluate the fairness of their trial leads them to consider

TABLE 4.1   Procedural Satisfaction Following Adversary and Inquisitorial Trials

Type of Procedure	Actually	Found	Average Satisfaction
Adversary	Innocent	Innocent	7.57
		Guilty	4.13
	Guilty	Innocent	7.75
		Guilty	4.29
		Average	5.94
Inquisitorial	Innocent	Innocent	4.78
		Guilty	1.13
	Guilty	Innocent	6.11
		Guilty	3.63
		Average	3.91

Higher numbers indicate greater satisfaction.

SOURCE: *Procedural Justice: A Psychological Analysis* by J. Thibaut and L. Walker, 1978, Hillsdale, NJ: Lawrence Earlbaum, 75. Copyright 1978 Lawrence Earlbaum. Adapted with permission.

whether the trial procedures are enacted justly. However, people might also be asked whether it is fair to make decisions about innocence or guilt using a jury trial.

The way Thibaut and Walker (1975) framed procedural justice research enabled researchers to conduct a number of procedural justice studies because it clearly specified a series of procedural questions that could be addressed empirically. However, their work also constrained the types of questions considered. Many potential procedural-justice issues were not examined.

As the field of procedural justice research has evolved, concern over procedural preferences and over the objective quality of procedures has become less central. Most research has focused on the subjective consequences of experiencing procedures judged to be fair or unfair. Further, the formal structural approach of Thibaut and Walker (1975) has gradually evolved into a wider study of informal procedures (such as those found in business settings), the enactment of procedures (such as jury deliberations in a particular case, as opposed to the size and verdict rule used by juries), and interpersonal aspects of interactions (such as politeness and respect).

It is also interesting to note that whereas distributive justice research focuses attention on what is lost when people feel that they are receiving unfair outcomes, the procedural justice approach of Thibaut and Walker (1975) focuses on what is gained when people feel fairly treated. Consider the attitudes and behaviors that are the focus of relative deprivation and distributive justice research. These bodies of research, especially the literature on relative deprivation, focus on anger and on socially destructive behaviors such as sabotage, malingering, riots, work slowdowns, theft, drug use, and alcoholism. In contrast, Thibaut and Walker focus on the more hopeful perspective of what might be gained through using fair procedures to settle conflicts. Thus, the procedural literature focuses on developing and maintaining social relationships and on favorable views about legal authorities and legal institutions. It also focuses on gaining voluntary acceptance of decisions, voluntary compliance with legal rules, and the willingness to proactively help society and social authorities.

Research Findings

Since the publication of Thibaut and Walker's book (1975) *Procedural Justice,* a substantial body of research has been conducted on the subjective consequences of experiencing procedures of varying fairness. Studies demonstrate that people react to the fairness of procedures in a wide variety of settings, including legal trial procedures (LaTour, 1978; Lind, Kurtz, Musante, Walker, & Thibaut, 1980), plea bargaining and mediation (Adler, Hensler, & Nelson, 1983; Casper, Tyler & Fisher, 1988; Houlden, 1980; Lind et al., 1989; MacCoun, Lind, Hensler, Bryant, & Ebener, 1988), administrative hearings (Brisbin & Hunter, 1992), and police-citizen interactions (Tyler, 1988, 1990; Tyler & Folger, 1980). Procedural justice effects also have been found in organizational (Folger & Greenberg, 1985; Greenberg, 1987a, 1987b, 1990a; Greenberg & Folger, 1983; Sheppard et al., 1992), interpersonal (Barrett-Howard & Tyler, 1986; Senchak & Reis, 1988), political (Tyler, Rasinski, & McGraw, 1985), and educational (Tyler & Caine, 1981) settings (see Lind & Tyler, 1988, for a review).

These empirical findings confirm the importance that legal scholars attach to evaluating trials by procedural criteria (see Thibaut and Walker, 1975), in addition to evaluations of outcomes. Legal rules always have had as a goal the attainment of outcome fairness (substantive justice). The law dictates the use of particular types of procedures designed to produce fair outcomes. Hence, procedural justice exists to further the goal of substantive justice. In addition, legal scholars recognize that using fair procedures enhances the dignity of the individual as well as the individual's commitment to the law (Mashaw, 1985).

Interestingly, initial reactions to Thibaut and Walker's (1975) work were somewhat skeptical, given legal scholars' doubts about the laboratory experimental approach used in the work and the fact that real outcomes were not at stake (Hayden & Anderson, 1979). Subsequent research has demonstrated strong procedural justice effects in real world settings both when people's liberties are at stake (Casper et al., 1988; Tyler, Casper, & Fisher,

1989) and when substantial sums of money are involved (Lind, Kulik, Ambrose, & de Vera Park, 1993). Casper et al. (1988) found that people on trial for felonies, whose sentences ranged up to twenty years in prison, were sensitive to the fairness of the procedure used to decide their cases. Lind et al. (1993) studied people pursuing grievances in federal court. Following pretrial mediation, they needed to decide whether to accept mediation awards or go on to have a formal trial. The researchers found that the willingness to accept mediation decisions was strongly predicted by procedural justice judgments about the way those decisions were made (see Figure 1.3).

Subsequent writers in management also have identified strong procedural influences on performance appraisal (Folger, Konovsky, & Cropanzano, 1992; Greenberg, 1986), pay decisions (Miceli, 1993), employee selection (Guilland, 1993), workplace grievance procedures (Feuille & Delaney, 1992; H. E. Gordon & Fryxell, 1993; Pavlak, Clark, & Gallagher, 1992), and corporate acquisitions (Citera & Rentsch, 1993). The empirical findings of procedural justice research in management settings, therefore, confirm the insights of legal scholars: Procedural issues have an important independent influence on people's reactions to organizational decisions. For example, Greenberg (1987a) varied procedural and outcome fairness in a pay-for-performance task and demonstrated that procedural unfairness independently influenced workers' reactions to their outcomes. Further, procedures and outcomes interacted: Workers were most likely to take action when they received low outcomes via an unfair procedure.

This research shows that both distributive and procedural justice significantly affect personal satisfaction with outcomes received from third parties. However, people's evaluations of group authorities, institutions, and rules have been found to be influenced primarily by procedural-justice judgments. This is found in studies of legal (Tyler, 1984, 1990, 1994b), political (Tyler & Caine, 1981; Tyler, Rasinski, & McGraw, 1985), and managerial (Alexander & Ruderman, 1987; Folger & Konovsky, 1989) authorities. For example, in Casper et al.'s (1988) study, both distributive and procedural injustice influenced satisfaction with case dispositions among felons, but only procedural justice judgments influenced the impact of the experience on views about legal authorities (Tyler, Casper, & Fisher, 1989). Similarly, in Greenberg's (1987a) study, workers were more likely to take action against procedural injustice if they felt that the injustice represented an organizational policy. Studies also suggest that procedural justice enhances feelings of loyalty and willingness to help organizations (Konovsky & Cropanzano, 1991; McFarlin & Sweeney, 1992; Sweeney & McFarlin, 1993).

The findings outlined suggest that procedural concerns are especially important when people's interactions have implications for their social connections to organizational authorities. This suggestion is supported by other studies that differentiate among different types of reactions to experiences. Personal judgments such as job and pay satisfaction (and subsequent intentions to leave an organization) have a strong distributive justice component, whereas organizational judgments such as commitment to one's work organization are more strongly procedural in nature (Alexander & Ruderman, 1987; McFarlin & Sweeney, 1992; Sweeney & McFarlin, 1993). Similarly, personal decisions such as whether to return an unsatisfactory purchase (Clemmer, 1993) or how to deal with a parking ticket (Conlon, 1993) are evaluated in more strongly distributive terms. Further, evaluations of commitment to one's organization or reactions to overall organizational rules are more procedurally based than are reactions to a particular decision made by management (Tyler & Lind, 1992).

Although most procedural justice studies explore hierarchical settings, a direct comparison between hierarchical relationships and peer relationships suggests that procedural justice is equally important in both (Barrett-Howard & Tyler, 1986). However, the importance of distributive justice increases as the setting becomes more hierarchical.

Social Policy Support

Procedural-justice judgments also have been demonstrated to have an important influence on people's reactions to social policies. In fact, research suggests that when deciding whether to support social policies, people focus more strongly on their evaluations of the procedural justice of social policies than on the degree of the distributive injustices that those policies are designed to correct (Lea et al., 1995). This suggests that policymakers can shape reactions to public policies by framing those policies in ways in which they will be viewed as procedurally fair or unfair (Nacoste, 1990). For both beneficiaries and nonbeneficiaries of affirmative-action policies, perceptions of policy fairness influence emotional reactions, expectations about how one's performance will be evaluated, and feelings of personal confidence (Nacoste, 1989, 1990, 1992, 1993).

A Broader Procedural Justice Framework

Although the procedural justice framework of Thibaut and Walker (1975) has been the most influential, it does not define the concept of procedural justice broadly. Leventhal (1980) takes a broader theoretical approach but does not test his ideas through empirical research.

Leventhal (1980) outlines structural components that every procedure must have. These structural elements of procedures include (1) allocation of the responsibility for the selection of agents, (2) allocation of the responsibility for setting ground rules, (3) processes for gathering information, (4) processes for using information to make decisions, (5) processes for handling appeals and for other such safeguards, and (6) mechanisms for considering and implementing changes.

Leventhal (1980) also explores what influences the balance between distributive and procedural concerns. He suggests that under normal circumstances, distributive justice is more important than procedural justice. This prediction has not been supported by research (Barrett-Howard & Tyler, 1986; see Table 4.2). The findings of Barrett-Howard and Tyler also support the suggestion that the situation affects the importance of justice. Procedural justice matters in situations of moderate social connections. In situations of minimal social connections, people do not care whether the relationship is maintained. In situations of strong social connections, interpersonal and social bonds hold the relationship together. In intermediate situations, however, procedural justice is important.

Like Thibaut and Walker (1975), Leventhal (1980) makes the distinction between objective and subjective concerns. Leventhal distinguishes between structural components of a procedure—for example, what type of appeals mechanisms it contains (an objective issue)—and the justice rules that are used to evaluate whether a procedure is fair (a subjective issue). The subjective issue of justice rules receives the greatest attention in subsequent studies (Barrett-Howard & Tyler, 1986; Tyler, 1988).

The emphasis on justice rules, not structural components, also reflects the procedural justice research focus on the person rather than on entire institutions or societies. Research has been concerned with how people experience existing procedures, rather than with which structural issues must be considered when designing procedural systems. In this respect, procedural justice research has generally been reactive rather than proactive (Greenberg, 1987b). This reactive framing follows the framing of equity theory research that has generally been concerned with how people deal with experiencing fair or unfair outcome distributions.

Legitimacy

For people to react to authorities based on fairness, they must trust the motives of the authorities with whom they are dealing. Today, people's dealings with the legal system occur against the backdrop of fifty years of declining legitimacy for legal and political authorities. People are less willing to trust political and legal authorities than in the past. This has led to a number of negative consequences, including less willingness to accept judicial decisions and less willingness to comply with the law. Juries have been more willing to acquit those citizens who take the law into their own hands (Robinson & Darley, 1995). Further, there have been efforts such as passing determinant-sentencing laws to restrict the discretion of legal authorities (Tyler & Boeckmann, in press).

TABLE 4.2   Importance of Decision Criteria in Allocations of Resources

Decision Criteria	*Importance*
Procedural justice	4.59
Distributive justice	4.47
Speed of decisionmaking	2.33
Factuality of decisions	3.65
Animosity reduction	4.25
Feasibility of implementation	4.20

Higher numbers indicate greater importance.

SOURCE: "Procedural Justice as a Criterion in Allocation Decisions," by E. Barret-Howard and T. R. Tyler, 1986, *Journal of Personality and Social Psychology, 50,* 299. Copyright 1986 American Psychological Association. Adapted with permission.

   In the context of a particular case, negative prior views about authorities in general matter in two ways. First, as noted previously, people are more willing to focus on procedural issues, not outcomes, if they have positive views about authorities. Thus, the willingness to use fairness judgments depends on prior trust and legitimacy. (For a more detailed discussion of these issues, see Chapter 7.)

   Second, prior views shape the interpretation of experiences. Those who view authorities as fair are more likely to interpret their actions as fair. In other words, authorities benefit from the prior trust and loyalty of those with whom they deal. Since people interpret their experiences through their prior frameworks and beliefs, those who regard the authority with whom they are dealing as legitimate are more likely to interpret their actions as just.

   It is also interesting to note, however, that when those with favorable views feel unfairly treated, they change their attitudes about the outcomes more than other people (Brockner, Tyler, & Cooper-Schneider, 1992). In other words, prior legitimacy is a double-edged sword: It helps authorities by facilitating a favorable interpretation of actions, but it leads loyal people who feel betrayed to react more negatively than others.

Procedure and the Effective Functioning of Society

We already have noted that the original impetus for distributive justice research was broad dissatisfaction with pay and promotion in work settings. It was hoped that distributing rewards fairly would alleviate such dissatisfaction. However, problems of defining fairness and the existence of self-serving judgments about fairness led distributive justice research to be less effective than initially hoped as a way to lessen dissatisfaction. Procedural justice also became important because of a social problem—difficulties in resolving conflicts between individuals. This problem was widely noted in the legal system because people often take difficult cases to legal authorities for resolution. The findings outlined suggest that using fair procedural mechanisms is more effective than reaching favorable outcomes. To a considerable degree, people defer to the fairness of procedures and accept outcomes because those outcomes are arrived at through fair procedures.

As noted earlier, American society is facing the problem of scarcity and economic stagnation. Because the American economic pie is unlikely to continue growing (at least at the rate experienced in the past), conflicts over allocating existing resources are likely to intensify. Procedural justice suggests a strategy for dealing with such problems, so procedural mechanisms provide hope in an era of scarcity. As Thibaut and Walker (1975) note:

> One prediction that can be advanced with sure confidence is that human life on this planet faces a steady increase in the potential for interpersonal and intergroup conflict. The rising expectations of a continuously more numerous population in competition for control over rapidly diminishing resources create the conditions for an increasingly dangerous existence. It seems clear that the quality of future human life is likely to be importantly determined by the effectiveness with which disputes can be managed, moderated, or resolved. Procedures or methods that may be put to this task of conflict resolution therefore claim our attention. (p. 1)

One threat to the viability of a procedural justice strategy is the low legitimacy of government and other authorities. Procedural justice strategies emphasize using fair procedures to allocate resources. Such procedural mechanisms are heavily dependent on trust in others, either other parties to the dispute and/or third-party authorities. As Americans have become increasingly distrustful of both other people and third-party authorities, the issue of whether procedures can bridge differences in views has become increasingly important.

Procedural Justice Criteria

As was the case in studying distributive justice, it is important to distinguish between two issues in studying procedural justice: whether procedural justice matters and the criteria that people use to evaluate the fairness of procedures. Thibaut and Walker (1975) argue that the key procedural characteristic shaping people's views about the fairness of procedures is the distribution of control between disputants and the third-party decisionmaker. Thibaut and Walker distinguish between two types of control: process control and decision control. Process control refers to the extent and nature of a disputant's control over the presentation of evidence. Decision control refers to the extent and nature of a disputant's control over the actual decisions made.

Thibaut and Walker (1975) assume that disputants are primarily concerned with the problem or dispute that brings them to a third-party authority. Judgments of the fairness of various dispute-resolution procedures are based on instrumental concerns in the sense that disputants are thought to view procedures as means to the end of improving the fairness or equity of their outcomes. Thibaut and Walker do not devote much attention to disputants' concerns about their long-term relationship with authorities. Implicit in their model is the assumption that disputants by and large view their experience with the judge and the court system as a one-shot encounter.

These assumptions lead to the view that disputants are concerned about control in the immediate situation when they evaluate procedures. They want control because they see it as a way to attain the outcomes they desire. This model links procedural desirability to previously outlined ideas about equity. Because equity models link what people receive to what they contribute, procedures need to provide disputants with opportunities to present information about their contributions. Process control is important because it assures people that the third party receives their information on contributions and preferred outcomes; this, in turn, allows the third party to use equity rules to resolve the dispute fairly (Thibaut & Walker, 1978).

Much of the research conducted on procedural justice focuses on the effects that procedural variations in opportunities for process control have on people's feelings about their control within those procedures (their sense of having a voice; Folger, 1977). A large number of studies support the suggestion that the distribution of control influences assessments of procedural justice; procedures with greater process control are judged to be fairer (Folger, 1977; Kanfer, Sawyer, Earley, & Lind, 1987; LaTour, 1978; Lind et al., 1980; Lind, Lissak, & Conlon, 1983; Tyler, 1987; Tyler, Rasinski, & Spodick, 1985; L. Walker et al., 1974). For example, Kanfer et al. (1987) had subjects in a laboratory experiment perform a task that involved generating a list of innovative names for some common household products; then the names were evaluated by a supervisor who dispensed rewards. In the high-process control condition, subjects not only gave names but also gave explanations of how they came up with the names. This resulted in both higher procedural-justice ratings and higher ratings of the supervisor, even though the rewards given by the supervisor were the same in both the high- and the low-control experimental conditions.

Studies on control suggest that procedures that give people control lead them to feel more fairly treated. Crime suspects feel more fairly treated if they are allowed to speak about how they should be treated. Victims and their families also feel more fairly treated if they can speak about how a criminal should be sentenced. Workers feel more fairly treated if they can present evidence about their contributions before pay and promotion decisions. And students feel more fairly treated if they have greater opportunities to present evidence of their abilities before grades are determined. Consider one example—child custody hearings (Emery, Matthews, & Kitzmann, 1994; Kitzmann & Emery, 1993). In such situations, mothers typically win (90 percent of the time in this study). However, fathers feel more satisfied with the hearings if the court allows them to present their cases and speak about their wishes, even in situations in which they do not win custody (Emery et al., 1994; Kitzmann & Emery, 1993).

Conversely, failures to provide opportunities for participant input lead to discontent. Consider the 1994 French public-sector worker's strike. The workers struck against proposed cuts in benefits. But, as Cohn-Bendit (1995) suggests, they also opposed their lack of voice in designing the proposed cuts. He wrote, "In America, before major changes in anything there are Congressional hearings, public debates between Congress and the President, and a whole process of public discussion that is completely absent in France. [Here] the government comes up in private with a plan, throws it onto the table and tells everybody it has to be accepted. The natural reaction is to reject it instead" (Whitney, 1995).

On a more mundane level, consider the thirty-two residents of a University of California, Berkeley, cooperative dormitory who were told to leave it for unruly behavior. Students simply received notices instructing them to leave the dormitory, and there was no due process. The dorm administrator who made the decisions said, "It was more important to have an efficient process than to have a long drawn-out affair and discuss everyone's feelings. The board was more concerned about being efficient than being fair." The result, according to a reporter's account: "The notices caused a 'near riot' at the co-op." Initially, "someone burned all of the notices the central office had sent." Then, "angry residents threw bricks and toilets through house windows and ignited an M-80 explosive" (Franklin, 1995).

Consider, in contrast, the way Jamie Gorelick, the deputy attorney general of the United States, handled the difficult issue of creating a policy that integrated gays into the American military. The new policy had been set before Gorelick was hired. The problem she faced was to gain acceptance from the military. Gorelick "decided to discuss the policy as broadly as possible and have a very open process even if it meant taking much longer than the secretary [of defense] would have liked" (Masters, 1995, p. 10). Although regulations were due in September 1995, they were not ready for implementation until December of that year. However, by creating a process in which all parties were allowed to discuss the issues, she created regulations that were accepted. "Nobody was that happy with [the regulations], but the issue's just gone away. That's a brilliant stroke" (Masters, 1995, p. 10).

In contrast to what the Thibaut and Walker (1975) model predicts, however, process control has been shown to be more central to feelings of fairness than is decision control. For example, Lind, Kanfer, and Earley (1990) gave people the opportunity to present evidence after a decision had already been made and found that feelings of procedural justice were nonetheless enhanced. Tyler (1987) similarly demonstrates that people value the opportunity to speak even when they think they are having little or no influence on the decisionmaker. People's desire to have voice or process control is not simply instrumental. They also value the opportunity to speak for other reasons.

The Meaning of Fairness in Procedures—Issues of Control

Control research makes clear that it is important to understand why people regard particular procedures as fair. Consider the courtroom trial. What is it about a trial that leads viewers to evaluate it as fair or unfair? One possibility is control over evidence presentation. That control is given to the lawyers representing each side of the case. However, control is a complex concept and has many dimensions. One dimension is what evidence is allowed into the court. Another is how the evidence is presented. Each of these issues has a structural form (e.g., adversary attorneys) and a particular enactment within a given procedure (e.g., Johnny Cochran versus Marcia Clark during the O. J. Simpson trial). People may also be affected by other dimensions such as who makes the decision (e.g., the jury). In order to understand how to build and sustain confidence in the courts, it is necessary to understand why people evaluate procedures to be fair or unfair (whether those procedures pertain to the O. J. Simpson trial or to a teacher grading students).

Beyond Control

Although the Thibaut and Walker (1975) control model has been important in generating research, it has had the restrictive consequence of focusing discussions about the criteria of procedural justice on only control issues. Leventhal (1980) suggests a broader framework for evaluating the justice of procedures. His framework distinguishes six justice rules (see Table 4.3). *Consistency* refers to consistency across people and over time. For example, the same issues should be considered when making promotion decisions for different employees. *Bias suppression* involves avoiding self-interest or ideological preconceptions (i.e., personal biases). For example, judges should withdraw from cases that influence their personal financial well-being.

TABLE 4.3   Leventhal's (1980) Criteria of Procedural Justice

Criterion	Description
Consistency	Equal treatment across persons and over time.
Bias suppression	Avoiding self-interest or ideological preconceptions.
Accuracy	Using good, accurate information and informed opinions.
Correctability	Opportunities for review.
Representativeness	Everyone is involved in decisionmaking.
Ethicality	Compatible with fundamental moral and ethical values.

Accuracy involves using good, accurate information and informed opinions. *Correctability* involves providing opportunities to have other authorities modify or reverse decisions (i.e., appeals mechanisms). *Representativeness* involves considering everyone's concerns, values, and outlook during all phases of the process. This criterion is similar to Thibaut and Walker's (1975) conception of control. Finally, *ethicality* involves compatibility with fundamental moral and ethical values. For example, torture is not used in trials irrespective of whether it produces reliable information.

Several studies find experimental support for the importance of the six justice rules in the Leventhal (1980) model (Fry & Cheney, 1981; Fry & Leventhal, 1979). In a broader test, Barrett-Howard and Tyler (1986) presented undergraduates with scenarios describing allocation situations. The situations varied along the four basic dimensions of interpersonal relationships (see Deutsch, 1982; Wish, Deutsch, & Kaplan, 1976; Wish & Kaplan, 1977). They found, after averaging across situational variations, that four criteria were especially important in shaping procedural justice judgments: consistency across people, ethicality, bias suppression, and accuracy. Interestingly, all four of these criteria were more important than the representativeness criterion (ranked fifth) that included the control judgments central to Thibaut and Walker's (1975) theory.

Thibaut and Walker (1975) also find that the importance of procedural and distributive justice, although generally high, varies in importance across situations, both in absolute terms and relative to the influence of factors other than fairness. Replicating this finding in a real-world setting, Lissak and Sheppard (1983) find that procedural justice is the primary criterion for evaluating procedures in a legal setting but not in a managerial setting.

Interestingly, Barrett-Howard and Tyler (1986) find that people link different procedural criteria to the attainment of different social goals. They judge accuracy in decisionmaking as central to productivity, whereas the attainment of social welfare and harmony is linked to bias suppression and ethicality. Consistency of treatment across people is linked to both maximizing productivity and maximizing social harmony and welfare.

Tyler (1988) examines the influence of Leventhal's (1980) criteria and other factors on people's evaluations of legal procedures in a natural setting—people's actual experiences with legal authorities. He finds that people have complex procedural models. In his study, seven aspects of procedures independently influenced people's judgments about the fairness of procedures: six of Leventhal's rules (ethicality, opportunities for representation, bias, honesty, decision accuracy, and correctability of decisions) plus the trustworthiness of the authority. A replication of this study in a managerial setting found that six aspects of procedures made independent contributions to employees' procedural fairness judgments when dealing with their supervisors: five of Leventhal's rules (ethicality, representativeness, bias, honesty, and consistency) and trustworthiness (Tyler, 1994a; Tyler & Lind, 1992). The results of these two studies are shown in Table 4.4.

Other studies also find that people distinguish and consider a number of procedural dimensions (Lissak & Sheppard, 1983; Sheppard & Lewicki, 1987). These findings validate Leventhal's (1980) argument that procedural-justice judgments are multifaceted. People are sophisticated ethical reasoners who consider a variety of issues when forming justice judgments.

Interestingly, people's ratings of the importance of differing criteria are found to vary depending on the nature of the situation (see Barrett-Howard & Tyler, 1986; Rasinski, 1992; Tyler, 1988). These findings, therefore, suggest that there is no universally fair or unfair procedure. For example, Tyler (1988) finds that control is important in disputes (conflicts of interest) but not important in problem-solving situations (truth conflicts).

However, within a given situation, people of differing backgrounds (age, ethnicity, and so forth) agree about the criteria for procedural fairness. This suggests that there is considerable consensus among Americans about what constitutes a fair procedure within a particular setting, just as the previous chapter suggested that there is considerable consensus about what constitutes distributive fairness within a particular setting.

People's use of different criteria also varies depending upon their experience and/or the information that they have available. For example, Barrett-Howard and Tyler (1986) find that consistency across people is very important, whereas Tyler (1988) finds little influence of consistency. It may be that the citizens studied by Tyler had little experience with the criminal justice system and were unlikely to have friends who had had similar experiences. Hence, they would not have other experiences with which to compare their own. Consistent with this argument, Casper et al. (1988) find that criminals who do know more about the criminal justice system and other people's sentences use consistency when evaluating their sentences. Similarly, the Barrett-Howard and Tyler scenarios, in contrast, examined inter-

TABLE 4.4   Antecedents of Fairness in Legal and Managerial Settings

	Setting	
Criterion	Law	Management
Representativeness (control)	0.17***	0.21***
Consistency	0.04	0.08*
Correctability	0.14***	0.04
Neutrality		
Lack of bias	0.07**	0.11**
Honesty	0.23**	0.17***
Quality of decisions	0.17***	0.08
Trust in the authority	0.30***	0.27***
Ethicality (respect for rights; politeness)	0.21***	0.21***
R-squared	69%***	76%***

Entries are beta weights for an equation in which all terms are entered simultaneously. Beta weights reflect the relative influence of each factor distinct from the influence of other factors in the equation. R-squared is the amount of variance in the dependent variable explained by all the factors considered together.
*p < .05, **p < .01, ***p < .001.

SOURCE: "A Relational Model of Authority in Groups," by T. R. Tyler and E. A. Lind, 1992, in M. Zanna (Ed.), *Advances in Experimental Social Psychology, 25,* 115–191. Copyright 1992 Academic Press Inc. Adapted with permission.

personal situations—all very familiar situations for the respondents. Thus, both people's past experiences and the nature of their knowledge about the experiences of others may influence the criteria they consider when judging the fairness of a procedure.

Although there are clear variations in the importance of different criteria of procedural justice, there are also common features. A recent study examining the importance of outcomes and procedural concerns across both hierarchical and nonhierarchical settings demonstrates that relational concerns (e.g., neutrality, trustworthiness, status recognition) are important across all types of social settings (Sondak & Sheppard, 1995; see Table 4.5).

Trade-Offs

Unlike the trade-offs found within the distributive justice literature, Tyler (1988) finds very little evidence of trade-offs among criteria of procedural justice. Procedures rated high on one dimension were also generally rated high on others. However, there are trade-offs between fairness and nonfairness criteria. In particular, representation (providing participants a voice)

TABLE 4.5   Antecedents of Satisfaction Under Different Types of Authority

| | Authority Type | | | | |
Antecedent	Communal Sharing	Authority Ranking	Equality Matching	Market Pricing	Points
Outcome favorability	0.07	0.04	0.10	0.14	0.25
Control over outcomes	0.27	−0.03	−0.13	0.03	−0.01
Voice in decisions	−0.09	−0.07	0.24*	0.05	0.16
Neutrality, trust, status recognition	0.59***	0.60***	0.72***	0.69***	0.57***
R-squared	44%	41%	51%	60%	62%

Entries are beta weights for an equation with all terms entered simultaneously. Controls were made for sex and nationality of subjects and for judgments about aftermarket and politics (see Sondak and Sheppard, 1995).
*p < .05, ***p < .001.

and efficiency clash. Procedures that provide more opportunities for process control are more time consuming. Consequently, allocators of resources often resist providing "fair" procedures. Judges, for example, typically have very little time to handle cases and resist expanding litigants' opportunities to tell their side of the story.

Other studies also have suggested that greater procedural justice may have costs. MacCoun and Tyler (1988) find, for example, that twelve-person, unanimous-verdict juries are viewed as more representative and thorough in their deliberations but more costly than smaller juries, or ones that do not have to reach unanimous verdicts, or choosing to have no jury. Therefore, people are more likely to prefer such juries for serious cases and less likely to prefer them for more trivial cases. People's evaluations of the desirability of these procedures show a trade-off between decision quality and cost (see Figure 4.1). In Figure 4.1, the numbers are beta weights reflecting the size of different influences on the desirability of a particular jury. Similarly, Kerr (1978) demonstrates that people use a higher threshold of guilt when the penalties for rule breaking are more severe, and Erber (1990) demonstrates that procedural preferences shift toward more elaborate adversarial procedures when the penalties for rule breaking are more severe.

Micro Versus Macro Procedural Justice

Brickman and his colleagues (1981) discuss macrojustice in terms of distributive issues, but macrojustice is also a procedural justice concern. Just as people evaluate the overall distribution of outcomes within a society, they also con-

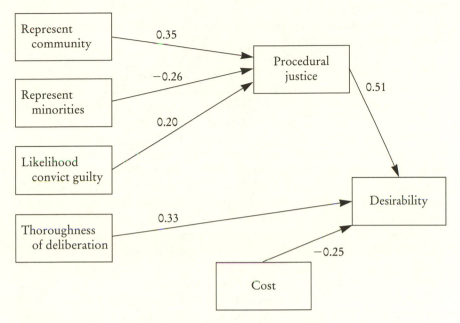

FIGURE 4.1   Model of jury procedural preferences. SOURCE: "The Basis of
Citizen's Preferences for Different Forms of Criminal Jury," by R. J. MacCoun and
T. R. Tyler, 1988, *Law and Human Behavior, 12*, 333–352. Copyright 1988 Plenum
Publishing Corp. Adapted with permission.

sider the overall form of social procedures. Many procedures, ranging from
jury trials to the use of lotteries to impose social burdens, can be evaluated
from a societal perspective. In fact, the macro level may be a natural level for
considering many procedural issues. For example, people consider whether
the jury is a fair procedure for determining guilt and innocence, whether elections are a fair procedure for determining leadership, and whether there
should be limits on campaign spending. In each case, the procedural issues are
considered independently of individual problems, disputes, or interests.

Several studies of macrojustice attend to issues of procedural justice
(Azzi, 1992, 1993a, 1993b; Azzi & Jost, 1992). They consider the particular
issue of subgroup balance, a concern identified by Brickman et al. (1981).
The subgroup principle recognizes that the balance of control in how
resources are allocated between majorities and minorities is a macro-level
justice concern. Azzi (1993a) explores this issue in the context of political
representation, using two possible principles of macrojustice. One is proportionality—one person, one vote in decisionmaking. Another is group

equality—one group, one vote in decisionmaking. He finds that minority group members judge group equality to be fairer, whereas majority group members judge proportionality to be fairer.

An example of a political system that uses both of these principles is the U.S. government. The Senate is based upon group equality, with each state receiving two senators irrespective of its population. The House of Representatives is based on proportionality, with seats allocated by population. Hence, the ideas Azzi (1993a) outlines have long been represented in American government. More recently, they have emerged with the increasing importance of ethnic identification in the form of suggestions that ethnic or cultural groups ought to receive political representation. Such arguments are not mere abstractions. There have been suggestions that voting schemes in congressional elections should be altered to increase the likelihood of electing minority representatives (Guinier, 1994).

One way for the majority and minority groups to resolve their conflict between using group equality versus proportionality would be to reach some form of consensus about a common principle of macrojustice. Azzi (1993a) suggests that the groups he studied compromised instead between the two principles through a procedure in which each had mutual control. Under mutual control, all groups have veto power over the actions of the overall group—as is true of individuals in a unanimous jury. Thus, each group can apply its own justice standards. Such a solution, although viewed as mutually fair, may make it difficult to arrive at social decisions.

Again, the solution that the subjects in Azzi's (1993a) study regarded as fair—mutual control—mirrors the solution enacted in forming the American government. For bills to become laws, they must be passed by both the Senate and the House of Representatives. That is, they must be acceptable to groups operating under both principles—group equality and proportionality.

Justice and Subgroup Identification

Azzi's (1993a, 1993b) approach to macrojustice assumes that people want control over outcomes. In other words, Azzi extends the micropsychology of Thibaut and Walker's (1975) instrumental view of justice to the macro level. In so doing, he does not consider the possibility that groups can develop a superordinate identity with the larger group that would compete with or supersede their loyalty to their own subgroups (see Chapter 10).

Justice and Self-Interest

The work of Azzi (1992, 1993a, 1993b) is also interesting because of its suggestions about the degree to which people are able to step behind the veil of ignorance—that is, to make judgments about an ideal society without knowing their own positions within that society (Rawls, 1971). In studies that ask people to indicate how rewards should be allocated across all of society, the concern is with whether there are general principles of justice divorced from one's personal situation. For example, are there general rules that might be endorsed by everyone in society, irrespective of their race, social class, education, and so forth? Consider the case of poverty. Would everyone—the poor, the middle class, and the wealthy—agree that no person should go hungry in our society? Would everyone agree that everyone is entitled to a car, to a house, to free medical care, to a satisfying job, and so on? Or, consider opinions about slavery. If we ask people whether slavery is just, their responses may be influenced by whether they know that they will be slaves. This influence is removed if people make their judgments behind the veil of ignorance (i.e., without knowing whether they will be slaves).

The question studied by justice researchers is whether people's judgments about what is fair are affected by their knowledge about their own positions in society. For example, are one's judgments about what the poor are entitled to have shaped by whether one is poor or wealthy? Ideally, people's responses would be independent of their knowledge of how those rules affect them. One hopes that people could put aside personal concerns and make idealized justice judgments. For example, Thibaut and Walker (1975) argue that people choose procedures for resolving disputes that they think are fair in abstract terms, such as favoring the disadvantaged party. They do not simply choose the procedure that will maximize the likelihood that they will win their particular cases.

In contrast, Azzi's (1992) research on procedural justice suggests that self-interest and group interest do influence fairness judgments. In other words, Azzi argues that people do not make judgments of fairness independently of their knowledge of their own positions in society. Members of minority factions are more likely to favor equal representation or veto power, whereas members of majority factions are more likely to favor proportional representation (Azzi, 1992).

Consistent with Azzi's (1992, 1993a, 1993b) work, empirical research on macrojudgments about distributive justice suggests that the situation in which people find themselves shapes both their perceptions of the fairest shape of aggregate distributions of income (Hermkens & Kreveld, 1992) and their reactions to such distributions when they see them (Taylor, Watson & Wong-Reiger, 1985).

In contrast to these studies, research by both Thibaut and Walker (1975) and Frohlich and Oppenheimer (1990) suggests that people's fairness judgments are not influenced primarily by their assessments of their own self-interest. Currently, there is no clear answer to the question of whether people's justice judgments are or are not affected by their ethnic group memberships, social position, or identification with different ethnic or economic classes or groups. Many studies that we have noted indicate at least some influence of self-interest on judgments of fairness. However, other studies indicate equally clearly that people are able to distinguish principles of justice from principles of self-interest and often base their evaluations and behaviors on justice principles that are clearly distinct from their own or their groups' interests. Thus, the relationship of self-interest and justice judgments is a question that needs further study.

It is also important to recognize that there are several questions about the relationship of self-interest and justice that might be asked. Tyler (1996) distinguishes two issues: defining fairness (a meaning model) and using fairness judgments in making evaluations of decisionmaking authorities (a weighting model). Using an experimental design, he shows that when people know the outcome of a procedure before judging its fairness, they still make procedural fairness judgments based upon procedural elements, not the outcome. For example, they still judge a procedure with voice to be fairer. Further, they put an equal weight on such pure procedural elements even if they know that the procedure led to an unfavorable outcome. This suggests that people can separate their assessment of the procedure's fairness from their knowledge of the procedure's impact on them. However, Tyler finds that people put less weight on whether the procedure is fair when evaluating the decisionmaking authority if they know the outcome of the procedure prior to hearing about its procedural qualities.

A similar finding occurs in Greenberg (1987a). Greenberg presented subjects with the opportunity to act following a specified experience of distributive and/or procedural fairness. Subjects leaving his experiment saw a sign asking subjects with complaints to call the human subjects committee. Greenberg counted the number of subjects who took this telephone number. He found that subjects acted only when they received unfairly low outcomes via an unfair procedure. But what about when an unfair procedure produced fair outcomes or produced unfairly high outcomes for the subject? Greenberg found that people took no action in response to unfairness. However, they still judged the procedures to be unfair. In other words, people recognized unfairness but did not use this unfairness information to shape their social behavior. Again, two issues need to be distinguished: how people evaluate justice and the role that justice plays in shaping their attitudes and behaviors.

Societal Implications

The procedural justice effect is important because it suggests a way to avoid the potential harm that resolving disputes can do to social relationships within a group or society. Poorly resolved disputes can threaten enduring relationships. Using procedures regarded by all parties as fair facilitates the maintenance of positive relations among group members and preserves the fabric of society, even in the face of the conflict of interest that exists in any group whose members want different things.

In any legal conflict, there is considerable skepticism about the decisions of legal authorities by at least some parties, and it is difficult for those authorities to make decisions that will be accepted by everyone, especially the loser. Consider the case of the murder trial of O. J. Simpson. How can a contentious issue such as O. J. Simpson's guilt or innocence be determined in a procedure that will be accepted by all sides to the dispute?

The problem posed by the O. J. Simpson case is especially important due to current racial divisions in the United States. We have already discussed the idea of fraternal deprivation. If people believe that a defendant has not received a fair trial because of his or her race, they are more likely to take action against the courts or society. Further, minorities often accept conspiracy theory explanations in which the police or other government agencies are seen as acting against minorities (Crocker, Broadnax, Luhtanen, & Blaine, 1995). In the case of O. J. Simpson, for example, Blacks were much more likely to believe that he was innocent and possibly framed by the police, whereas Whites typically thought that he was guilty and found conspiracy explanations difficult to accept (in this particular case). Hence, any verdict was inevitably going to seem unfair to some segment of society. In this respect, the O. J. Simpson case was a more highly visible example of a typical problem faced by courts—settling difficult and contentious disputes in which both parties cannot be given what they want or feel they deserve.

In this context, what is needed is a procedure that can create a solution acceptable to all the parties to the dispute. If procedures can do that, then they are crucial to enabling society to solve its problems. In the case of O. J. Simpson, there is some evidence to suggest that the trial procedure was at least somewhat effective in creating feelings of procedural fairness. Prior to the trial, 62 percent of Whites thought O. J. Simpson was guilty (Mydans, 1994); after the verdict, 64 percent still thought he was guilty, even though the jury judged him to be innocent (Terry, 1995). Interestingly, although the trial resulted in an outcome that many thought was wrong, the procedure itself was viewed as fair by 74 percent of Whites after the verdict (Terry, 1995). Thus, although the trial resulted in a verdict that many Whites thought was wrong, the procedure was robust enough to be nonetheless viewed as fair.

There is also evidence that this acceptance may not have been total. There have been calls for modifying the jury system, for example, by using nonunanimous verdicts. This suggests that viewing the trial also led some to question the fairness of the adversary jury trial system. This raises the more general question of how many seemingly unfair outcomes a procedure needs to deliver before people begin to question the procedure itself. Studies suggest that procedures are fairly robust and can deliver at least several seemingly unfair or negative outcomes before people begin to question their fairness (Lind & Tyler, 1988).

The other aspect of the procedural justice model involves the reactions of those who were more skeptical of the case against O. J. Simpson. In the O. J. Simpson case, only 38 percent of Blacks viewed him as guilty prior to the trial (Mydans, 1994), and 12 percent thought him guilty after the trial (Terry, 1995). Further, only 45 percent rated the trial as fair after he had been acquitted (a favorable outcome). It is unclear what effect a guilty verdict would have had. It would appear that there was no general feeling of procedural fairness among Blacks to cushion the discontent that could have been caused by a negative decision. Hence, discontent might have followed.

Consider a similar situation—the recent Los Angeles riots. When Rodney King was initially beaten by police officers, there was no riot. However, when the trial of the police officers involved in that beating was moved to the largely White-populated Simi Valley, an unfair trial procedure was created in the eyes of many minority respondents. When that unfair procedure produced an unfair outcome (acquittal of the police officers), riots occurred. Absent a fair procedure, a favorable outcome is needed to produce acceptance. Given widespread feelings among Blacks that the O. J. Simpson trial was unfair, a guilty verdict might have led to similar collective unrest.

Why is procedural justice so central to the evaluation of authorities? The reason for the preeminence of procedural-justice concerns in judgments of the legitimacy of authority is discussed by Thibaut and Walker (1978). In many social situations, it is not at all clear what decision or action is correct in an objective sense. Indeed, it could be argued that most groups' decisions concern questions for which there is no way of knowing what course of action is right or will work out best. In a trial, for example, jurors typically lack any completely clear evidence of guilt or innocence. They can never be certain whether their verdict is actually just in an objective sense.

Thibaut and Walker (1978) argue that what is critical to good decision-making in outcome-ambiguous situations is adherence to norms of fairness, and fairness is most evident when procedures that are accepted as just are used to generate the decision. In other words, absent objective indicators of the correctness of a decision, the best guarantee of a high-quality decision is the use of good—i.e., fair—procedures. Evaluations of the fairness of procedures serve as a heuristic that allows people to quickly evaluate the correctness of actions without really weighing all the benefits and costs associated with the action (Lind et al., 1993).

In social settings, cost-benefit calculations are complex, and a simpler solution is to assume that fair outcomes result from fair procedures. Consider a typical organizational situation—a comparison of outcomes among faculty. When a typical faculty member compares him- or herself with others, he or she considers their teaching load, their salary, their faculty rank, their committee assignments, their student-advising load, their office size, the amount of their laboratory space, their level of funding from their university, and many other issues. Addressing the fairly straightforward question, are you doing as well as others? turns out to be quite complex. Consequently, people focus on an easier question: Does the department chairperson allocate benefits fairly?

Another example of the use of cognitive heuristics involves Langer's (1992) work on mindlessness. This research indicates that people are likely to defer to an explanation, even if it is cognitively meaningless (e.g., "I need to use the copier machine because I need to use the copier machine."). It may be that people develop rules for central and peripheral processing (the elaboration-likelihood model, Petty & Cacioppo, 1986) in which many issues are reacted to without thought. Only some events trigger the type of cognitive effort that would invalidate the enactment of accustomed forms of interaction. One such event may be an experience of injustice. Thus, people may be slow to recognize the violation of forms reflecting justice norms in social interaction but quick to take offense when they do recognize such violations.

There are many situations in which outcome ambiguity is unavoidable. In the popular television series *Perry Mason*, the crime was always solved, the criminal always identified. In reality, however, most cases are not so clear. It will never be known, for example, whether O. J. Simpson is truly guilty, and this is true for almost all defendants. Hence, the correct outcome is usually unclear.

Similarly, in the case of citizen complaints against the police, there is usually no additional evidence beyond the victim's statement. In only 17 percent of such cases is there any other witness, and in only 7 percent is there any independent probative evidence. It is typically difficult to determine the accuracy of the victim's statement and victims seldom prevail. In cases of rape, a similar ambiguity prevails, with most cases involving conflicting statements about what occurred. In situations in which the truth is ambiguous and justified complaints may not be sustained, it is especially important that those involved in the legal system feel that the procedures used were fair.

The key idea here is that of the fairness heuristic—that is, that people evaluate their social experiences by evaluating the procedures they experience (Lind et al., 1993). Of course, a major theme of the literature on cognitive heuristics is that they lead people to make poor decisions. For example, the availability heuristic leads to major failures in correctly estimating risks. People overestimate the risk posed by striking vivid events, such as dying in an airplane accident, whereas they underestimate the risk posed by mundane everyday events such as dying by falling in one's bathtub. The fairness heuristic may also lead to errors.

Tyler and McGraw (1986) suggest that the occurrence of procedural justice effects provides an explanation for a traditionally puzzling problem in political science: why the poor do not revolt. In American society, as in most societies, those without wealth outnumber those with wealth. In a democracy, the large group of poorer citizens could use their political power to vote for massive income redistribution, yet they do not. A number of political psychologists have attempted to explain this absence of political mobilization by exploring the norms of fair outcome distribution held by the disadvantaged (i.e., distributive justice; see Hochschild, 1981; Lane, 1962). Tyler and McGraw suggest that the answer may be that the poor focus on procedural justice. In the United States, the procedures for allocating resources involve, at least in theory, a free and open contest in which those with intelligence and ability can rise to the top through their personal efforts. Since this contest-mobility system (Parkin, 1971) is viewed as a fair procedure, people accept its outcome.

5

RETRIBUTIVE JUSTICE

In our previous discussions, we focused on relative deprivation and distributive injustice—both outcome concerns. Those concerns were then supplemented with concerns over procedural justice—the fairness of the processes through which outcomes are determined. In this chapter, we want to consider the final form of justice—retributive justice. Retributive justice concerns arise when rules are broken and a group or individual must decide whether someone should be punished for rule breaking, what type of punishment is appropriate, and how severe that punishment should be.

The concerns with the fairness of procedures that were outlined in the previous chapter develop in the context of efforts to manage interpersonal or social conflicts (Thibaut & Walker, 1975). Groups, organizations, and societies respond to conflicts by creating authorities and institutions to make decisions about the allocation of scarce or disputed resources (Messick, Wilke, Brewer, Kramer, Zemke, & Lui, 1983; Tyler & Degoey, 1995). These authorities and institutions base decisions upon social norms that regulate behavior and provide a basis of shared understandings and expectations that allow social life to occur. Social norms indicate appropriate principles for exchange and for interpersonal conduct. They indicate the appropriate balance of rights and obligations in various settings. The ability of authorities and institutions to compel compliant behavior in instances of potential conflict is directly linked to perceptions of legitimacy (Tyler, 1990). One important source of legitimacy is the correspondence between institutional directives and social norms (Robinson & Darley, 1995). In cases of dispute, the meaning of those norms is interpreted and applied by legitimate authorities who make decisions that specify the appropriate interpretation of norms and rules. The existence of these norms, rules, and decisions and interpretations of legitimate authorities leads to a new justice concern: retributive justice.

Once specified, rules and norms can be broken, and the decisions of legitimate authorities can be disobeyed. In fact, studies of managerial, legal, and political authorities suggest that rules are often disobeyed and that the decisions of authorities are also often ignored (Tyler & Lind, 1992). Hence, the question of how to respond to rule breaking is central to the viability of organized groups.

Retributive justice research examines when people feel that some sanctioning reaction is needed in response to rule breaking, what types of sanctioning reactions they consider to be appropriate, and what are their considerations of how severe those sanctions should be. Underlying these questions is a concern with why and when people feel that rule breaking should be punished, that is, the psychology of retribution. The labels "psychology of retribution" or "retributive justice" suggest that the focus of this area of research is on retribution (commonly understood to mean "bringing suffering to bear on a wrongdoer"). This conception describes one of many facets of responses to wrongdoing. Accordingly, the psychology of retributive justice encompasses a wide variety of responses, ranging from the strictly punitive to efforts to reform offenders or restore the social breach created by an offense. Evidence suggests that responses to wrongdoing are employed to achieve a variety of goals (Warr, Meier, & Erickson, 1983). Although the psychology of retributive justice is currently less developed than that of distributive and procedural justice, there are signs that retributive justice represents an important frontier for future justice research.

What Is Retribution?

It is widely observed that people react against rule breakers. But is there something special about such reactions that involves some new form of justice concerns? It has already been noted that equity theory suggests that victims feel the need to try to restore equity after they have been victimized, for example, through compensation of material loses. Does retributive justice involve something more than such equity concerns?

Equity concerns are contained within discussions of retributive justice (Austin, Walster, & Utne, 1976; Brickmann, 1977). However, the nature of retributive concerns is much broader. People often feel that the restoration of equity is inadequate as a response to rule breaking. They feel that in addition to restoring equity, those who have broken rules should be punished in some additional way. For example, when someone hits a person, that person not only hits back but hits back harder. This additional response cannot be viewed in the context of equity theory since it again creates a situation of inequity (with the victim becoming a harm doer). It can be better viewed as an additional punishment for rule breaking.

The distinction between equity concerns and retributive concerns is perhaps best seen in research suggesting that people who intentionally break rules but do not cause a negative outcome are punished more severely than those who unintentionally cause a negative outcome (Horai, 1977). From an equity theory perspective, punishment should be a function of the amount of harm caused. This would predict a pattern of findings opposing those that Horai (1977) found. The suitability of compensation as a way of restoring equity in these types of situations is not the same, either. To accidentally hurt someone and try to restore justice by compensation is reasonable, whereas deliberately hurting someone and trying to "buy them off" is morally offensive and likely to be rejected.

In cases such as murder, rape, or bank robbery, people simply reject the idea that restoring equity is a just response to rule breaking. They regard offering to give the money back to be an inappropriate response to being arrested for bank robbery. This response may be linked to the instrumental judgment that such an equity-based response will encourage further rule breaking because the likelihood of apprehension is often low. Alternatively, the response may reflect the view that some crimes have a particularly symbolic (e.g., moral) significance for which material compensation is inadequate. In other words, some crimes (e.g., murder, rape, and so on) are morally wrong, and justice cannot be restored by material compensation. However, there is evidence to suggest that in such cases a form of moral compensation (e.g., expressions of remorse) partially restores justice (Felson & Ribner, 1981; Schwartz, Kane, Joseph, & Tedeschi, 1978). In fact, Ohbuchi, Kameda, and Agarie (1989) observe that such moral compensation has the effect of attenuating the aggressiveness of responses to wrongdoers.

Even with some crimes that could potentially be rectified through compensation, people reject compensation when they feel that the crime involves elements of immoral behavior. For example, research indicates that burglary victims are more upset and have greater difficulty coping with theft of personal pictures or jewelry than with the theft of televisions or other items of purely monetary value (B. B. Brown & Harris, 1989). In such cases, compensation is more difficult since the loss has a symbolic, emotional element. Similarly, displaying contempt for others by vandalizing their homes is considered an especially heinous crime, far worse than simply stealing property (B. B. Brown & Harris, 1989).

A particularly striking case of property crime that transcends material damage is seen in vandalism perpetrated by racist individuals or groups. A recent case in California involved the home of an African American family. Upon returning to their home, they found swastikas painted on every interior wall of the home and on a prominently placed portrait of Martin Luther King, Jr. Members of the ethnically diverse community in which the vandalism took place were deeply disturbed by the symbolic implications of the crime (Lee, 1995). These more troubling crimes not only lead to economic losses but also inflict symbolic harm. They threaten people's faith in their own safety by showing that others lack a commitment to following social rules that dictate respect for everyone's dignity and emotional well-being. In fact, recent changes in penal codes have incorporated additional penalties for crimes that have this added symbolic component (e.g., hate crimes).

The incompatibility of compensation and morality is illustrated by the asymmetry that people manifest in their reactions to rule breaking and rule following. Although rule following is a socially desirable behavior, people think the idea of compensating people for rule following does not make sense. Instead, virtue is considered its own reward. People who follow the law, for example, do not expect to be paid for their behavior. Similarly, people who break the law have committed a moral wrong and cannot completely restore justice simply by offering material compensation. It is important to note, however, that compensation of some form may be an important element of restoring justice in cases of wrongdoing (see Shultz & Darley, 1991).

America as a Retributive Society

Retributive justice is important because social responses to rule breaking are central to public views about society and social authority. The importance that people attach to issues of retribution is dramatically illustrated by the widespread evidence of public concern over the belief that our criminal justice system provides inadequate punishment of rule breakers. This includes general support for the view that more people should be punished for crimes (too many guilty go free), that court sentences are too lenient, and that society needs to use severe punishments such as the death penalty. Not only is such support widespread within the American public, but it has steadily increased in recent years (Ellsworth & Gross, 1994).

Whatever the reason for its increase, the steady growth in public punitiveness since the 1960s is striking. Consider public responses to questions about the leniency or harshness of the courts that are shown in Figure 5.1. The responses indicate (1) high levels of support for harsher punishments for those convicted of crimes and (2) rising levels of support for harsher punishments for criminals. To put these trends in perspective, consider support for the death penalty. Support for the death penalty is particularly interesting because it has been measured in public opinion polls for a very long time. The results of those polls, shown in Figure 5.2, reinforce the suggestion that punitiveness is both high and increasing.

Growth in public concerns about retribution is especially striking because it has occurred during a period in history in which there has been increasing social liberalism (Stinchcombe, Adams, Heimer, Scheppele, Smith, & Taylor, 1980). During this same period, Americans have become more tolerant of a wide variety of social behaviors, including premarital sex, homosexuality, abortion, and the expression of nontraditional ideas by homosexuals, Communists, and others. For example, people are more willing to say that the

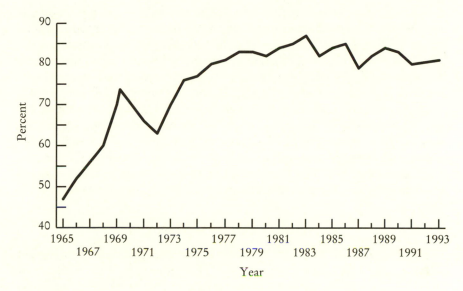

FIGURE 5.1 Percentage of the U.S. public saying the courts are too lenient on criminals. SOURCE: *Sourcebook of Criminal Justice Statistics.* Washington, DC: U.S. Department of Justice, Bureau of Justice Statistics.

FIGURE 5.2 Percent of adult U.S. citizens favoring the death penalty. SOURCE: The National Opinion Research Center, 1155 East 60th Street, Chicago, IL, 60637. Adapted with permission.

members of such groups should be allowed to teach or speak in public. It may be that this social liberalism is unrelated to punitiveness since, unlike crimes such as murder or rape, social liberalism involves victimless crimes. However, increasing social liberalism may actually encourage punitiveness because people may feel that it is increasingly important to show that there are some limits by strongly enforcing the few remaining social rules.

Of course, it is not necessary to look to criminal law and severe crimes to see how strongly people feel about rule violations. When someone cuts another person off in traffic or pushes into a movie line, a strong and immediate emotional response is created. In fact, it is the intensity of people's emotional responses to even relatively minor rule breaking that suggests the strength of the justice motive in the area of retributive justice (Hogan & Emler, 1981).

Why Are People Punitive?

The strong support for punishing rule breakers suggests that punishment fills some important need within society. The question is, What is that need and what has encouraged the rising concern over rule breaking? One model links punitiveness to instrumental concerns such as a fear of becoming crime victims. For example, high-profile crimes—such as the kidnapping of Polly Klaas, a child who was taken from her home in rural California and murdered by a stranger with prior criminal convictions—are widely credited with encouraging a public climate that supports harsher punishments of criminals. Similarly, Willie Horton—a criminal who was paroled and who subsequently committed new violent crimes—was a prominent image used in the 1988 national election to defeat Michael Dukakis in his bid for the presidency (Anderson, 1995). Of central importance are the elements of a crime that heighten public anger and punitiveness. Five elements have been noted: "[The crime] is violent, involving homicide, rape or a bloody assault; the victim is white and middle class; the victim is innocent; the victim is chosen at random; and the criminal has a record, suggesting that the crime might never have happened had the criminal-justice system worked right" (Anderson, 1995, p. 36). These factors suggest that many people believe that they are likely to be victims of random violence because previous punishments were not severe enough.

Another psychological model links the need to punish rule breakers to the need for cohesiveness and identification with groups, arguing that groups punish rule breakers to defend group identity and values (Boeckmann, 1993). From this perspective, the increasing need to punish rule breakers has been linked to feelings that social norms are unclear and diffuse (Stinchcombe et al, 1980). This interpretation also corresponds to the previously mentioned association between changing social values and increasing punitiveness on the part of American citizens.

One effort to disentangle these various motives is found in studies of the antecedents of support for the death penalty. Tyler and Weber (1983) explored attitudes toward the death penalty in a sample of citizens in the Midwest. They found that instrumental concerns had a small influence on support for the death penalty. However, the primary source of support was social values such as authoritarianism. This suggests that people's moral orientation toward rules dominates their response to rule breaking. The mediation of moral evaluations in retributive justice is consistent with the general model of responding to injustice described in Chapter 1. Interestingly, this moral orientation has been found to develop early in life, during childhood socialization. Therefore, basic moral orientation may determine responses to policy questions related to rules that develop during adult life.

One interpretation of these and similar findings is that deviant behavior offends people's values independently of any physical or monetary threat it may pose (Feather, 1996). Deviance symbolizes an erosion of values that is offensive and threatening to the normative system that people in groups rely upon. These symbolic implications of wrongdoing, then, are an important contribution to retributive-justice judgments.

These arguments are similar to the relational conceptualization of fairness judgments discussed in the procedural-justice literature (Lind & Tyler, 1988; Tyler, 1994a; Tyler & Lind, 1992). A relational conception of justice concerns links justice evaluations and behavior to concerns about the implications of behavior for the social bonds that exist between people in groups. The nature of relations between group members also contributes to the definition and character of the group. Behaviors that enhance feelings of recognition, strengthen social bonds, and contribute to a positive definition of the group are seen as fair from a relational perspective.

Recent research suggests that issues of group membership have an important influence on retributive justice (Boeckmann, 1993; Boeckmann & Tyler, 1996; Kerr, Hymes, Anderson, & Weathers, 1995). This may be due to violations of the normative expectations held for group members or it may be tied to social identity and self-esteem issues (Marques, 1990). Further, relational concerns may be manifested as concerns with the maintenance of the social group (Boeckmann, 1996a). This includes both concerns for the character of particular ongoing relationships between members of the group or society and concerns for the norms that underlie all relationships in society (Boeckmann & Tyler, 1996).

Tyler and Boeckmann (in press) explore the antecedents of support for punitive public policies. They consider two issues: (1) why people supported or opposed the recent California "three strikes" initiative that mandates life in prison for anyone convicted of three felonies and (2) why people favor or oppose general public policies designed to be punitive toward rule breakers.

The first factor considered in looking at these two issues is concern about crime. The results suggest that concern about crime influences support for both the initiative and general punitiveness. However, it is concern about crime as a social problem, not personal fear of crime, that influences support for the initiative. Both types of crime-related concerns influence general punitiveness.

The second factor—people's judgments about social conditions—is a stronger influence on support for the initiative and for general punitiveness. In particular, people are strongly influenced by their assessments of the situation within the family. The depth of concern over the lack of value socialization of teenagers and the development of gangs (the decline of the family) strongly predicts support for the initiative and for general punitiveness.

A final factor—social values—also is linked to support for the initiative and for general punitiveness. These values include authoritarianism and dogmatism. Those who are more authoritarian and/or dogmatic more strongly endorse both specific and general punitive actions toward rule breakers.

When the strength of these three types of antecedents to punitiveness is compared, two are seen to be primary sources of punitiveness. The first is assessments of social conditions, particularly the condition of the family. The second is social values. Crime-related issues play a lesser role. This is interesting because media presentations about public feelings often suggest that it is fear of violent crime that is driving public moods. Instead, it is concern about declining moral values that seems key.

Tyler and Boeckmann's (in press) study also explores the willingness of people to abandon procedural protections for criminal defendants. An interesting intersection of retributive and procedural justice occurs in the area of civil rights for criminals. Traditionally, American society has placed great weight on protecting the rights of individuals. For example, the exclusionary rule does not allow confessions into courts if they were coerced, irrespective of whether they are true. Further, the rule of a unanimous jury verdict makes the threshold of conviction high in criminal cases. Our society has believed that it is better to let ten guilty people go free than to convict one innocent person.

However, during times of concern about social conflict, there have always been arguments that some or all of these protections of the individual should be weakened or abandoned. For example, there have been proposals to (1) allow the police to hold suspects in jail as long as the police feel they need to, (2) allow confessions obtained illegally to be admitted in trials if they are true, (3) allow the police to wiretap citizens without warrants, and (4) require people to carry national identification cards that the police have a right to inspect. In addition, there have been calls for changing the jury system to have nonunanimous verdicts and in some cases, for simply abandoning juries. These suggestions flow from retributive concerns and conflict with traditional conceptions of procedural justice. The most radical form of such pressures occurs with a lynch mob, in which retribution takes place following, at best, minimal efforts to deal with issues of guilt or innocence.

The same tension between personal rights and social concerns is found in the area of tolerance for diverse political and social perspectives. In theory, our society is a democracy in which people are entitled to speak and teach about their political and social views, whatever they may be. In reality, there has been throughout American history a struggle over the degree to which people are entitled to express unpopular opinions and live unusual lifestyles. This struggle has involved a wide variety of unpopular groups, including Communists, homosexuals, and members of hate groups (McClosky & Brill, 1983; Sullivan, Piereson, & Marcus, 1982). Research suggests that the willingness to tolerate dissidents develops both from concerns about social values and from feelings about the dangers posed by those groups.

Tyler and Boeckmann's (in press) study exploring the antecedents of the willingness to abandon procedural protections suggests conclusions similar to those already outlined in the case of punitiveness. However, instrumental issues matter more in deciding whether to abandon procedural protections. Both instrumental concerns and concerns about cohesiveness are important influences on the willingness to abandon procedural protections.

Retribution in the Future:
Will the Future Become the Past?

Some have argued that punishment is an expression of frustration and concern over complex social problems in society. Increasingly, it is argued that people feel their leaders lack both solid policies and the capacity to solve social and political problems. People are frustrated by the slow pace of bureaucratic justice; criminals are not tried for their crimes until years after they have occurred; and it is not uncommon for criminals to be on death row for decades before being executed. Feeling abandoned by the formal legal system, people are left to manage their own psychological fears and uncertainties. One way is to express those feelings in reactions to rule breaking in particular and to adopt feelings of cynicism and disrespect for law and legal authorities in general:

> For centuries, expressive justice was the norm. In Europe and the American colonies, the role of government before the 18th century wasn't to control crime so much as to ventilate the community's outrage and exact revenge. The means were torture and execution—criminals were whipped, branded, scalded, mutilated, hanged, stoned, pressed and burned at the stake, and in public. The whole community participated in the rituals of retribution.

The new United States of America, the founding fathers believed, should do better; they wrote a ban on "cruel and unusual punishments" into the Eighth Amendment. The penitentiary, an American invention, developed after the Revolution. Instead of being flogged or hanged, convicts would work, pray and read the Bible in hopes penitence would bring salvation.

Not until the 1980's did corrections officials abandon their professed belief that programs and prisons could rehabilitate criminals. The public also appeared willing to sacrifice crime control to punishments that mainly express anger.

The most striking example is the death penalty, which fell into disuse in the 1960's, even before the Supreme Court ruled against existing provisions for carrying it out. In the 70's states began revising laws to satisfy the Court, and by the 1980's, the public, by huge majorities, demanded the return of capital punishment. (Anderson, 1995, pp. 36–37)

The key question, as yet unanswered, is the future direction of American policy toward rule breakers. America is already noteworthy for having a higher proportion of its adult citizens in prison than any other industrialized nation. Recent trends suggest an acceleration of this trend; the punitive "three strikes" initiative (i.e., three felonies lead to life in prison) passed in California, and similar rules have been supported in other states and enacted into federal law.

Ironically, the growth of prisons and the need to fund them have created a social dynamic that feeds upon itself. Research suggests that one of the primary antecedents of support for harsher punishments is being poorly educated (Tyler & Boeckmann, in press). When the public votes to spend more to build prisons and lock up criminals, the funds for such proposals typically come from a small pool of government money marked for discretionary spending. Such funds typically include spending for education. Hence, as states divert money away from education to the development and maintenance of an extensive prison system, they are facilitating the creation of a poorly educated society. Such a society, in turn, is more likely to support harsh punishments. Lower levels of education are also likely to lead to less tolerance of divergent social perspectives (Sullivan et al., 1982).

What about the future? Currently, American views about how to handle rule breaking seem to be very much in flux. As previously stated, compared with other industrialized nations, our society already incarcerates a larger proportion of its citizens, and it has harsher penalties for a variety of crimes. Nonetheless, there is widespread public dissatisfaction with the way our legal system handles rule breaking.

Further, there is support for even harsher punishments. For example, an American teenager was recently caned (i.e., beaten with a stick) for vandalizing cars in Singapore. Caning is a physically disfiguring punishment that can leave permanent scars. As such, it has been regarded as an unduly cruel punishment that is not used in the United States. However, although the

American government protested the punishment, public opinion polls suggested that large segments of the American public supported it. How far does this support for physical punishment extend? Will we actually move toward becoming the type of society that uses the punishments of the eighteenth century—punishments that directly inflict physical pain (e.g., whipping, caning) and are physically disfiguring (e.g., branding)? At this time, the future of American reactions to rule breaking is unclear.

Retribution as a Basic Human Motivation

Of all the justice motives, the feeling that rule breakers should be punished is "older, more universal, and socially more significant" than any other justice feeling (Hogan & Emler, 1981, p. 131). Both victims and others within social groups are upset and angry when social rules are violated, and they are motivated to take actions in response. Research indicates that both victims and observers are motivated to assign blame for wrongdoing and to try to sanction offenders for their behavior (Alicke, 1992; K. G. Shaver, 1970; Walster, 1966).

This primitive character is reflected in the widely noted emotional character of retributive feelings (Hogan & Emler, 1981; D. T. Miller & Vidmar, 1981; Vidmar & Miller, 1980). In fact, this primitive, emotional character has been contrasted to the more cognitive conceptualizations of distributive and procedural justice. Hogan and Emler (1981) suggest that retributive feelings, being highly emotional, have been viewed by psychologists as important in children and in primitive cultures but as less influential in the reactions of civilized adults.

Retributive Justice in Organized Groups

It has been argued that the retributive-justice motive arises in conjunction with organized groups or societies (Hogan & Emler, 1981; D. T. Miller & Vidmar, 1981; Vidmar & Miller, 1980). These arguments suggest that concerns about retribution involve issues of social order and are regulatory in nature. Everyone must restrain himself or herself in organized groups, following rules that delay or deny gratification. To justify such restraint, people monitor the environment to see whether virtue is rewarded and whether malefactors are punished (Hogan & Emler, 1981). In other words, people do not feel that others should get more than their share by violating social rules. If others can break rules with impunity, then everyone is tempted to do the same. Thus, moralities "provide the enabling conditions of social life; in the absence of a moral order, normal life is impossible" (Hogan and Emler, 1981, p. 138).

Hogan and Emler's (1981) argument has been stated more broadly by Campbell (1975, 1980), who argues for a social-evolutionary perspective on the development of social institutions. He suggests that the control of individual motivations can be socially adaptive. That control occurs through the development of and socialization of individuals who learn to use moral norms in governing their behavior. These moral rules coordinate and direct human interaction to everyone's mutual benefit.

An example of the development of rules is the previously mentioned study of Thibaut and Faucheux (1965). Messick and colleagues (1983) also show that people elect leaders to resolve problems of social coordination. In both studies, people responded to problems in interacting with others by trying to structure their interactions through the creation of rules and/or authorities.

One important implication of this social analysis of the evolution of rules is that rules will develop in situations in which social order is threatened by the free operation of individual motivations. As Thibaut and Faucheux (1965) argue, it is unlikely that rules will be developed "in the absence of temptations to violate them" (p. 101). In other words, one argument is that at least in part, rules emerge as they are needed to preserve mutually beneficial relationships that might otherwise fall apart. Thus, each party to an interaction must have some power over the other in order for rules to develop. No one unilaterally creates rules; he or she must feel that there is a need. Barrett-Howard and Tyler (1986) support this argument by showing that concerns about procedural justice are greatest in situations involving desirable but potentially unstable relationships—for example, friends who are working together. Hogan and Emler's (1981) argument extends the same logic to reactions to rule breaking. They suggest that people are likely to be most upset about rule breaking when an important relationship is threatened.

The Need for Punishing Rule Breakers

As has been noted, compensation can sometimes be a response to restoring justice following rule breaking. Brickman (1977) argues that more attention should be paid to compensation. Using a sports analogy, he argues that the advantage of compensation is that it allows the players to continue playing the game. The disadvantage, however, is that it legitimizes rule breaking. In basketball, for example, people do not consider it morally wrong to commit fouls. No moral stigma is attached to such an action—merely a calculation of probable gains and losses (e.g., "If I foul him he will miss his shot, but will he make his free throws?"). Such an amoral approach to crimes such as rape or murder is difficult to imagine.

Even Brickman (1977) suggests that there are instances of rule violations in sports and in life in which equity restoration is an inappropriate response. Rule breaking of this sort violates the basic assumptions of fair play without which the game could not continue. Cheating is a basic form of this unfair play. When infractions of this sort are observed, the player is often removed temporarily or permanently from play by a recognized authority. Similarly, rules of interpersonal conduct must be observed. For example, hitting or spitting on a referee is not acceptable. In society, a similar distinction is seen. Crimes that demonstrate a disregard for human life or liberty are violations of rules without which society could not function. Unsurprisingly, these violations evoke punitive responses rather than equity restoration.

Recent research suggests that the public accepts Brickman's (1977) argument that equity-based punishments are sometimes a reasonable means of restoring justice without permanently removing the "players" from society. For example, Umbreit's (1989) research finds that people are most strongly interested in the restoration of the social breach caused by the offense. This typically includes desires to communicate with the offender, to allow the negotiation of restitution, and to have apologies. These findings are consistent with much anecdotal evidence suggesting that people are as concerned with sincere apologies and acknowledgment from offenders as they are with punishing offenders. Such actions restore the balance of justice without punishing the offender.

One interpretation of Umbreit's (1989) results is that other research is in error when it suggests that Americans are increasingly punitive. However, it is important to note that Umbreit's results do not indicate that the public is less concerned with sanctioning rule breaking. Umbreit interprets his findings as suggesting that fairness or justice for the victims of crime includes the kinds of material and moral compensation discussed earlier. However, others have suggested that it is possible to have alternative sanctions without being "soft" on crime (cf. Petersilia & Deschenes, 1994; Robinson & Darley, 1996). In other words, people can both seek compensation and support punishment. What is unclear is how broadly people would accept substituting compensation for punishment.

Psychologists also argue that the precondition for the operation of society is that people expect rules to be enforced and violators to be punished (Hogan & Emler, 1981; D. T. Miller and Vidmar, 1981; Vidmar and Miller, 1980; Walster et al., 1978). People believe that is it important to respond actively to rule breaking through acts of vengeance or retribution. These acts may be carried out both personally and by friends and families of victims, but often they may be carried out by only vaguely self-interested people such as neighbors. As previously noted, acts of retribution tend to exceed the magnitude of the original act, so a spiral of violence can be created in which each act of retaliation leads to an even more violent response.

In order to forestall acts of personal vengeance and spiraling violence, society has created social institutions such as the police and courts to respond to rule breaking. These agencies represent the collective interest of society in enforcing social rules. These institutions have several important functions. First, they provide social authorities who define what is a just response to rule breaking. Hence, they predefine in general terms the appropriate level of punishment so that offended parties can feel that justice has been done. Second, these agencies are responsible for pursuing the attainment of justice. Authorities take on these roles to preclude the cycles of private retaliation that occur in the absence of state authority.

An example of a code of rules of personal vengeance and the variety of responses to harm is found in the Chechen area of the former Soviet Union, as illustrated in the following excerpt from a *Christian Science Monitor* article:

> Chechens have killed Russians, their enemies for centuries, without a second thought. But they do not kill other Chechens without carefully weighing the consequences specified in the ancient unwritten code called *adat* that acts as Caucasians' ethical framework, based on folk traditions.
>
> *Adat* is older than Islam, the predominant religion in the region, and a good deal more widely respected than the Russian penal code, which has never sunk very deeply into many Chechens' minds.
>
> Until the early years of this century, *adat* was interpreted in such a way as to ensure blood feuds that continued until whole clans had wiped each other out, in a spiral of violence fed by each revenge killing. (Ford, 1995, p. 13)

We have argued that retributive justice is a social mechanism that supports norms that are conducive to social harmony. It is obvious that historically, *adat* was not serving this function. Although formal authorities can prevent escalating violence, informal means of achieving this objective can also play a role. Change in the interpretation of the normative code of *adat* has resulted in a form that is more socially constructive:

> Not long ago, for example, in the course of an argument between two residents of a village near here, one man stabbed and wounded another. In quick revenge, a relative of the victim stabbed the original aggressor, intending to wound him too. Tragically, however, he killed him.
>
> Now that relative—even though his family was the first to be offended—has a price on his head. The dead man's sons would be within their rights, according to *adat*, to slay their father's killer.
>
> In fact, village elders are working on a more peaceful settlement of the dispute, given that the death was a mistake. In many cases nowadays, Chechens prefer to sort out their differences without resorting to the ultimate sanction. (Ford, 1995, p. 13)

The response to this instance of violence stresses several important points. First, it is evident that there is an effort to respond to violence in a manner that does not escalate negative social consequences. Second, intention is critical to the response. Specifically, there is an assessment of moral responsibility that moderates subsequent responses (see Figure. 1.1). Detailed discussion of the role of responsibility judgments in retributive justice is offered later in this chapter. Third, Chechens' responses appear focused on the ultimate goal of social harmony:

> Elders, still men of influence in rural areas of the Caucasus, and lawyers, who even here are seeking to wield more influence, are called on increasingly to arbitrate disputes and suggest peaceful resolutions.
>
> Sometimes not even their aid is needed: A victim's family may display what is known in the Chechen language as *rhilk*—extreme and unusual nobility—and actually forgive a wrongdoer.
>
> Churdayev, for example, visiting his native village of Shalaji, nestled in the foothills of the Caucasus Mountains during a break in the war, recalled how an uncle of his accidentally ran over and killed a neighbor.
>
> The victim's family "knew it was an accident, and they knew my uncle has three kids, so they showed their nobility and forgave him," Churdayev explains. "We went to the funeral with a cow, a sack of sugar, and some money, and offered them with respect. They accepted the cow and the sugar, but they refused the money. Their *rhilk* was higher than ours," he says. (Ford, 1995, p. 13)

This instance illustrates that responses to harm are not always purely punitive. Sincere gestures of conciliation and restitution on the part of perpetrators can serve as a partial means of redress and can lead to nonpunitive responses. The example also illustrates that formal authorities are not always necessary to avoid escalating conflict. It is apparent that both formal and informal mechanisms tend to serve this goal. The following example suggests there may be a compensatory relationship between the two forms of social control:

> And as modern ways make inroads into traditional lives, some Chechens are even ready to hand over their personal responsibility for exacting justice to the state. But only if the state satisfactorily shoulders that responsibility, as the following story illustrates.
>
> About ten years ago in Gehi chu, a small village North of Shalaji, a drinking bout one evening erupted into an argument, and in a drunken rage, one man stabbed another.
>
> He was arrested, charged, tried, and eventually sentenced to a long jail term, and the sons of the man he had killed decided that this punishment sufficed—that they would not take their revenge by killing one of the murderer's sons, as *adat* allowed them to do.
>
> But only a few years later, when General Dudayev seized power in Chechnya, he declared a general amnesty that emptied the republic's prisons, and the murderer went free.

"When the victims' sons saw that, they went back on their decision" Churdayev recounts. "He hadn't served his punishment, so they said they would take their revenge."

As for the murderer, he might as well still be in jail. He was certainly safer there before his release, and from that day to this, he has not dared step foot outside his home.

"The sons showed great *rhilk* when they didn't take revenge before," Churdayev explains. "They can't be expected to be so noble a second time." (Ford, 1995, p. 13)

Interestingly, recent research on public views about law in the United States suggests that the public has increasingly lost faith in legal authorities' ability to enforce rules. The consequence is greater public support, in the form of lenient jury verdicts, for those citizens who take the law into their own hands through self-defense or retaliation (Robinson & Darley, 1995). Like the Chechens, Americans are more willing to accept people taking justice into their own hands when they do not feel that the state is satisfactorily dealing with rule breakers.

In the situations examined by Robinson and Darley (1995) the citizens who acted were innocent victims of others—for example, people whose homes had been invaded. There was no suggestion that they had placed themselves in danger by their own rule-breaking behavior. The public might feel very differently about people who are themselves breaking a rule when they act in self-defense. For example, if a drug dealer kills a rival in a territorial dispute, the dealer may have felt provoked to take violent action, but a jury might not be sympathetic to the dealer's concerns (see Landy & Aronson, 1969).

Rule Typologies

Researchers note that rule breaking does not merely deprive victims of material goods or cause them physical harm. Being the victim of rule breaking also demeans the victim's standing within his or her group. One important function of punishment is to reassert the status of the victims and, more broadly, of the group to which they belong (Heider, 1958). In other words, there are symbolic harms that develop from rule breaking, and a goal of society is to reestablish appropriate status relationships among group members.

The nature of the response to rule violation is a function of the type of rule that has been broken (Boeckmann, 1996). People use information about the type of violation and the outcome of the violation to decide whether and how to respond. People who evaluate a negative outcome are likely to ask, What rule has been violated, or what has been damaged? Violations that lead to material harms are evaluated less severely than violations that lead to psychological or social harms (Alicke, 1990; Pontell, Granite, Keenan, & Geis, 1985; Rossi, Waite, Bose, & Berk, 1974). Not only is the intensity of the motive for retribution linked to the nature of the social rules broken, but also the nature of the rules influences decisions about how to react. For example, retribution is a more appropriate response to the violation of some types of rules. This is consistent with arguments made by Foa and his colleagues (Donnenwerth & Foa, 1974; Foa, Turner, & Foa, 1972). Their data suggest that people are sensitive to the nature of the violated rules and feel justice is best restored by responding in kind.

The rules that regulate the activities of members of social groups can be classified into four categories: rules that regulate personal-material resource transactions, rules that regulate personal-status resource transactions, rules that regulate the use of collective-material resources, and rules that support fundamental collective values (see Figure 5.3). The intensity and character of retributive responses depend on how the violation might be categorized in this model. It is acknowledged that offenses are often multifaceted, containing many characteristics and evoking many connotations. The proposed offense typology categorizes offenses along the most salient dimensions of an offense.

Violations of rules governing personal-material resource transactions can be seen in departures from equity, breaking contracts, violating the property of others, or failing to reciprocate. A large body of research discusses the efforts people make in response to violations of equity (Walster et al., 1978). Other examples of exchange-type violations include equity-based punishments in sports (Brickman, 1977) and tort law that specifies punishment in the form of restoring the wronged party's material status. In these instances, the goal of retributive justice is to restore the material balance between involved parties. Restitution or compensation of those who have suffered some material or financial loss at the hands of another is likely to be expected both by the affected party and by observers.

A second category of rules are those rules that support the social order by specifying how equal- and unequal-status people are to behave toward each other. Such norms can specify appropriate principles of distributive justice (high-status people get more) or of procedural justice (everyone is entitled to equally polite treatment from the police). Violations of this type of rule involve injury to status positions and often evoke strong motives for a retributive response. Such injuries may occur through insults or inappropriate behaviors that threaten status relationships (i.e., actions that are "rude" or "demeaning"). For example, Bies and Tripp (1996) find that employees who have been the subject of managers' insults express a sense of injustice and feel that some response is necessary to restore justice. Bies and Tripp note that many of the responses to such status injury are focused on restoring status levels through either securing a public apology or lowering the status of the perpetrator by bad-mouthing him or her.

		Who is the victim?	
		Personal/Individual	Society/Collective
What is lost?	Material resources	Robbing a person of money or damaging private property.	Embezzling government funds or damaging collective property.
	Symbolic or status resources	Insulting someone, slander, or libel.	Defiling national symbols (e.g., burning the American flag) or violating collective values (e.g., endangering children).

FIGURE 5.3   The nature of the rule-breaking offense

Breaches of status rules concern social-psychological resources that are difficult to specify or quantify. As such, equity-based responses are not as easily generated, and status-based adjustments are expected. The goal of retributive justice in this instance is to restore the former status quo (Heider, 1958; D. T. Miller & Vidmar, 1981). To achieve this, a demand for an apology is made. If no apology is forthcoming, retaliation or vengeance is likely (Ohbuchi et al., 1989), and insult is traded for insult (Hogan & Emler, 1981). These responses are directed at the involved parties and others in the social group and serve to restore social standing to the victim.

Rules that regulate the use of collective-material resources form the third category. Collective-material resources can take many forms, including material goods—such as public funds, improved public property, and natural resources—and more general public goods—such as a safe environment, clean air, and so forth. People react to rule breaking that poses a threat to collective resources. For example, Heider (1958) notes that juries sometimes give more severe sentences to rule breakers when they believe that there is a crime wave in their community. Those increased sentences are linked to the desire to protect the community resource of safety instead of to a model of individual deserving.

Responses to threats to collective-material resources are also found in other areas. For example, people are outraged when public funds are embezzled or when public property is vandalized, even in unimproved collective resources such as parks and natural resources. This concern is seen in environmental regulation aimed at preventing the spoilage of collective resources (Heberlein, 1972). The literature on social dilemmas (Dawes, 1980) suggests that these concerns about protecting collective resources develop from the persistent difficulty that organized groups have in effectively managing collective resources. Recent studies suggest that attitudes toward environmental laws are better predicted by concern for society than by self-interest concerns (Montada & Kals, 1995) and that justice considerations are important for the effective implementation of these solutions (DiMento, 1989; Tyler & Dawes, 1993; Tyler & Degoey, 1995). The character of responses to violations of this type of rule is suggested in recent research indicating that people are concerned with restitution and amelioration in response to environmental degradation (Baron, Gowda, & Kunreuther, 1993).

Rules that support the basic cultural and social values of a society form the fourth category. Examples of such basic values might include the sanctity of human life, the rights of individuals to not be physically violated, and the rights of children to a stable and nurturing environment. Violation of these types of norms or moral values may involve victims but can also include victimless crimes. Such crimes have a social meaning that extends beyond the preferences and desires of individual citizens. For example, people are not allowed to pay for sex or to buy a baby or a kidney, whether or not the parties to these transactions consent. Such behaviors violate social values and create injustice despite the equitable balance between interacting parties. Similarly, the police cannot torture prisoners to extract information, whether or not that information is valid.

The goal of retributive justice in these types of instances is to restore the validity of the violated norms or values and to ensure that they are not violated further (D. T. Miller & Vidmar, 1981). These goals require that the symbolism of punishment be communicated to society at large as well as to the offender. Responses to violations of these types of rules have a moral base.

This last category of responses to rule violation is frequently the subject of public-opinion surveys. Research indicates that people are often concerned with punishment of violations of this category of rules for symbolic reasons (Tyler & Weber, 1983; Vidmar, 1974) and are very angry at transgressors who break this type of rule (Alicke, 1990). In contrast to equity-based punishments, retributive responses may exceed the extent of suffering caused by violation. However, if the offender is sufficiently remorseful and contrite, the punishment may be more lenient (Felson & Ribner, 1981; Pepitone, 1975; Schwartz et al., 1978).

Research on justice generally has not examined how the response to rule breaking is linked to the nature of the broken rules. Consider, for example, the general finding that people see punishing the offender as more important than compensating the victim (Hogan & Emler, 1981). This may be more or less true for different types of rules. The typology suggested here indicates that punishment is a more important goal for status and value offenses, whereas compensation may be central to responses to material deprivations. Similarly, ensuring that perpetrators receive "just deserts" may be a more important punishment principle than deterring future infractions with some types of rules but not others (Vidmar, 1974).

Boeckmann (1996a) identifies two important consequences of the type of rule that is broken. First, the type of rule broken affects the severity of responses to rule breaking. People tend to react more severely when the rules broken have collective consequences and/or when symbolic resources have been violated. Hence, people react more strongly to violations of collective symbols or values such as burning the American flag than they do to violations with a more individual and material consequence such as a wallet theft. Second, the nature of offense consequences affects the type of goals that people emphasize in responding to wrongdoing. When people are asked to respond to violations that have primarily material consequences, they emphasize restitution (material restoration) to a greater extent than apologies. In contrast, when people evaluate offense with primarily symbolic consequences, they emphasize apologies (symbolic restoration) to a greater extent than restitution (Boeckmann, 1996b).

Retributive Justice Criteria

It is important to distinguish the abundant evidence that people care about justice issues in the context of rule breaking from concerns about the criteria used to evaluate justice or injustice in this context. There is widespread agreement that people strongly favor some type of reaction to rule breaking. However, there is disagreement about the criteria that people use to decide what constitutes rule-breaking behavior and whether or how severely to sanction. The majority of research and theory development in the psychology of retribution focuses on how people assign moral responsibility or blame to others for violations that lead to socially undesirable outcomes. This focus answers the question: On what basis do people evaluate whether people should be punished for rule breaking? This question is distinct from those that follow the decision that someone should be punished: What form should the punishment take? and How severe should the punishment be?

These latter questions are concerned with establishing the form of sanctioning that will restore justice in the wake of recognizing rule breaking.

The process of criteria evaluation illuminates the basic principles of retributive justice. Behavioral responses to rule violation are intended to encourage people to uphold rules that facilitate social living and to avoid significant future harms. These responses flow from moral judgments of responsibility and blameworthiness. Specifically, people making these types of judgments and responses search for features of behavior that communicate information about the perpetrator's actions vis-à-vis the rules as they evaluate the seriousness of the consequences of violation behavior.

Moral Reasoning

Much of the research on the attribution of responsibility and blame is based on Heider's (1958) pioneering discussion of responsibility. Heider distinguishes between causing an event to occur and being held morally responsible for that event. He argues that sanctioning behavior (e.g., punishment) flows from moral responsibility, not causality. Heider outlines five possible connections between causing an event and being held responsible for it. *Global association* links actors to events to which they are connected in any way. *Extended commission* holds people responsible for the consequences of events for which their behavior was necessary to cause the consequence irrespective of whether those consequences could have been foreseen or were intended. *Careless commission* holds people responsible for foreseeable events. *Purposive commission* holds people responsible for the things they intend to do. *Justified commission* holds people responsible for things they intend to do but also takes into account environmental forces that influence intentions. These five levels are presented in Figure 5.4.

According to Heider (1958), judgments based solely on intention represent purposive commission (level 4). In this case, people are held responsible for those things they intend to do. This stage represents the most direct extension of attribution logic from causality to moral reasoning since intention is the best guide to what people want to do. Thus, it tells us the most about their attitudes and values.

As predicted by Heider, one of the most important offender criteria in assessments of moral responsibility is intent. Intention is reliably associated with assessment of blame (D. T. Miller & Vidmar, 1981; Shultz, Schleifer, & Altman, 1981; Shultz & Wright, 1985) and to the severity of punishment responses (Darley & Huff, 1990; Horai & Bartek, 1978; Horan & Kaplan, 1983; Schwartz et al., 1978). The violator's character and behavior prior to and after the violation provide evidence about intent and are used in deciding whether responsibility should be assigned and whether a retributive-justice response is appropriate (Landy & Aronson, 1969; D. T. Miller & Vidmar, 1981;

Reasoning Level			*Nature of responsibility*
Most advanced	Level 5	Justified commission	Only responsible for intended actions when environmental pressures are considered.
	Level 4	Purposive commission	Responsible for intended actions.
	Level 3	Careless commission	Responsible for foreseeable actions.
	Level 2	Extended commission	Responsible for the effect of one's actions (whether or not foreseen or intended).
Most primitive	Level 1	Global association	Responsible for actions one is associated with in any way.

FIGURE 5.4   The association between causing an event and being morally responsible for that event.

Schwartz et al., 1978). For example, Schwartz and his colleagues (1978) find that if an offender expresses pleasure after committing an offense, observers attribute greater intention to the actor and assign more severe punishment.

Perceived freedom of action is also related to assessments of intention. Both lay judgment and legal codes demonstrate sensitivity to the general principle that a person must be able to freely and rationally choose the correct path of action to be held morally accountable for a failure to do so. When an actor is incapacitated in some manner for reasons beyond his or her control, responsibility is generally attenuated (Alicke, 1990; Fincham & Roberts, 1985; Robinson & Darley, 1995).

Actors can also be incapacitated for social reasons. For example, Kelman and Hamilton (1989) explore the ability of legitimate authorities to authorize subordinates to abandon their justice concerns and just follow orders. Their study of observers' reactions to crimes of obedience suggests that there is considerable variability in the extent to which observers consider the authoritative or coercive directives of superiors to be an acceptable excuse for crimes of obedience. There appears to be much more consensus that people should be able to avoid driving while drunk than that they should have the moral integrity or courage to disobey an unjust order from a superior.

The idea of incapacitation is central to judgments on the most advanced level of reasoning, justified commission (level 5). On this level, people take into account situational factors that might influence people's freedom to choose how to behave. The classic example is hostages or prisoners of war who act literally with a gun to their heads when they read a statement denouncing the crimes of their country. People take such environmental pressures into account. Of course, such discounting occurs within the framework of the fundamental attribution error—the tendency of people to give too little attention to environmental causes. Hence, people are generally unlikely to sufficiently discount such pressures, even when they do recognize their existence.

The law recognizes that causality can be mitigated by excusing conditions, so a person who causes an act to occur may not be held morally responsible for that action. The question is, What mitigating conditions are accepted? The classic mitigating circumstance is insanity. A person is causally responsible for an event but not morally responsible because his or her insanity made it difficult for the person to distinguish right from wrong. In recent American history, public opinion has pressured to have laws changed in order to make it more difficult to claim insanity as a defense (Silver, Cirincione, & Steadman, 1994).

Although insanity may have become a more difficult defense, other excusing conditions are flourishing in American law. Recent research suggests that Americans, at least under some conditions, take a wide variety of excusing conditions into account when assigning liability for wrongdoing (Robinson & Darley, 1995). One emerging condition is a history of battering: Battered wives or children kill their abusers and then argue that the history of battering made it impossible for them to realistically evaluate the threat to themselves and/or to tell right from wrong. Such defenses have become more accepted by law and more successful (Monahan & Walker, 1994). The defenses have also been used in cases in which the person injured someone other than the abuser. In situations of post-traumatic stress disorder, people kill innocent victims and then argue that their prior stress led to a more general inability to control their impulses. Recent defenses have also invoked more general excusing conditions, such as growing up in a poor environment ("rotten social background;" see Delgado, 1985), watching too much violent television, or coming from a culture with different values (Monahan & Walker, 1994).

Heider (1958) also argues for several levels of connection between causality and responsibility that do not simply involve intention. For example, careless commission involves actions that are not intended but might have been foreseen. Here, people typically apply the reasonable-person standard, holding people responsible for actions they might "reasonably" have foreseen. For example, behavior resulting from voluntary intoxication (e.g., drinking too much at a party) either enhances punishment responses (Alicke, 1990; Robinson & Darley, 1995) or provides no attenuation of punishment (C. Taylor and Kleinke, 1992). These effects occur because people expect a reasonable and responsible person to avoid becoming intoxicated prior to engaging in behaviors that require sound judgment (e.g., driving).

Research on the attribution of blame suggests that features of the situation are used in evaluating the event. If an accident is foreseeable and if there are means of taking precautions, people are expected to avoid harming others. Observers have the expectation that if possible, people should anticipate the consequences of their actions or inaction and respond appropriately or be held morally accountable—especially when consequences are or could be severe.

Abundant evidence suggests that people are motivated to attribute blame to people whose behavior leads to accidents (i.e., unintended events) with negative consequences (Burger, 1981; K. G. Shaver, 1985; Walster, 1966). Assessment of blame for accidents leads to punishment responses as described in Heider's (1958) "extended commission" and "careless commission" levels. One criterion that is particularly important in these contexts is outcome severity. Generally, the motivation to blame and punish bears a positive linear relationship to outcome severity. For example, C. Taylor and Kleinke (1992) observe that attributions of blame and punishment for drunk-driving accidents vary as a function of outcome severity, despite the fact that all drunk drivers intentionally break the same rule. Karlovac and Darley (1988) find that people who fail to avoid a foreseeable and serious accident are seen as more morally blameworthy than those who cause less serious accidents. Punishment responses for the former type of accident typically go beyond simple compensation for damages (Karlovac and Darley, 1988).

In judgments based on extended commission, people are held responsible for the severity of the outcomes they produce. So a more serious outcome leads to greater punishment, irrespective of people's intentions or whether they could foresee the outcomes. In Walster's (1966) classic study of unintentional harm, a person who sets his brake incorrectly and thus allows his/her car to roll down a hill receives a more severe punishment if it hits a child than if it hits a tree. Similarly, in the case of intended harm, a person who shoots and misses is treated more leniently than someone who shoots and hits, although both have the same intention. In other words, the severity of outcomes matters (Robinson & Darley, 1995), and people are punished more severely for being accurate shots.

Finally, the lowest level of association between causality and responsibility is global association, in which the person has no individual-level responsibility for the action. For example, one might be held responsible for the actions of people whom one oversees. Kelman and Hamilton (1989) refer to such responsibility as role responsibility. Similarly, one might be held responsible for the actions of others in one's family, as the earlier example of the Chechens illustrates. Or in a war, people in a village might be executed for the actions of partisans in the surrounding area without any indication that they personally approved of or participated in actions against the government. Similarly, the Israeli government dynamites the homes of the families of terrorists without seeking evidence that the families knew about or aided the terrorism being punished.

Theoretical Models of Criteria Utilization

Heider's (1958) analysis of responsibility contributes to most recent presentations of models of blame attribution (Shultz & Darley, 1991; Shultz et al., 1981; K. G. Shaver, 1985). These models also draw inspiration from moral philosophy and law. Their primary focus is on specifying how people combine information to arrive at the judgment that a retributive response is appropriate.

K. G. Shaver's (1985) conceptual model of blame attribution specifies the sequential causal relationship between a number of variables that intervene between simple causation of an act and moral accountability for that act. In this model, all acts with negative consequences are subject to an attributional analysis that begins with assessing the number of possible causes for the event. Multiple causes can lead to a diffusion of responsibility either to other actors or to mitigating factors in the situation and may lead to judgments of negligence on the part of the perpetrator. Identifying a single cause leads to an attributional analysis that includes whether the actor could have foreseen the negative consequences of his or her act; the existence of that possibility may also lead to attributions of negligence. Alternatively, a single actor may be seen as acting with intent. If this assessment is made, a decision as to whether the person freely chose to engage in the behavior follows. If an actor is seen as having been coerced, the person will be seen as responsible but not blameworthy.

When an actor is judged to have voluntarily acted to intentionally bring about a negative consequence, the assessment of blame is engaged. At this point, an observer assesses whether the actor had the capacity to appreciate the moral status of his or her action. If the person is judged to have the capacity to understand that his or her action was morally wrong (mens rea), an evaluation of accounts is made. If a person's account (justification or excuse) is accepted, then the person may be seen as responsible but not blameworthy. If the account is not accepted, the person is seen as blameworthy or morally accountable for his or her actions. Although the assignment of blame generally makes an actor the target of some retributive response, K. G. Shaver (1985) does not discuss sanctions at length.

The Shultz et al. (1981) model also considers the interrelationship between the same factors mentioned previously and subsequent punishment responses. Consistent with the K. G. Shaver (1985) model, the Shultz et al. information-processing model specifies that moral judgments proceed in a fixed sequence, with each judgment presupposing the previous one. To empirically evaluate the model, Shultz and colleagues presented subjects with scenarios that varied factors shaping judgments of causality (necessity and sufficiency) and responsibility (intervening causes, foreseeability, and voluntariness). Subjects then responded to the target person's behavior by making ratings of causality, responsibility, and appropriate severity of punishment. When the target person's actions were seen as necessary to produce the negative outcome (e.g., the event would not have occurred without their actions), the person was seen as more the cause of the outcome, more culpable for the outcome, and deserving of more severe punishment. Although some have argued that sufficiency information (e.g., whether the actions were enough to produce the event without action from others) is important from a legal perspective, the impact of sufficiency information in these empirical studies was relatively small.

An analysis of factors thought to affect responsibility judgments (intervening causes, foreseeability, and voluntariness) reveals that voluntariness or intention of an offender's actions has the greatest impact on judgments of causality, responsibility, and punishment. The more voluntary the behavior that leads to the negative outcome, the more certain the judgments of causality and moral responsibility and the more severe the recommended punishment. Intervening causation and foreseeability do not affect causation and severity ratings. However, the actor's foreknowledge of the consequences of the actions leads subjects to assign greater responsibility.

Shultz and colleagues (1981) use cause, responsibility, and punishment data to conduct a path analysis to test their sequential-judgment model. The results (already noted in Chapter 1) indicate a strong relationship between judgments of causation and responsibility and between judgments of responsibility and punishment. Consistent with the sequential-model predictions, there is no direct path from causation to punishment. As predicted by Heider, (1958) reactions to rule breaking flow through a justice-based interpretation of responsibility for those events and are not direct.

Although the conceptual analysis provided by K. G. Shaver (1985) and the empirical tests of the Shultz et al. (1981) model are important contributions to understanding behavior related to retributive justice, it is also important to note the limitations of these models. Both the Shaver analysis and the Shultz et al. studies generally emphasize the evaluation of behaviors that lead to accidental harms. They do not thoroughly consider behaviors that intentionally violate social rules; that are intended to harm others physically, socially, and psychologically; or that are violations that offend social or cultural values. Given the centrality of intent to most retributive justice theories, it is striking that most studies in this area focus on accidents. The judgment processes used to explain and respond to accidents may be quite different than those used with deliberate norm violations. The models discussed tell us about the former type of violation but may not generalize to the latter. Research on reactions to victims of deliberate harm suggests that judgments of the perpetrator's intention are central (Mikula, 1993).

In addition, emotion is not considered in these models of the evaluation and response to norm violation and harm doing. There is widespread anecdotal and empirical evidence that people are enraged by the misdeeds of others and anguished when wrongdoers are not punished to their satisfaction. This is the case even when the offender's behavior has no direct bearing on the interests of the evaluator. Evidence suggests that such emotion can influence both attributional processes (Alicke, 1990; Clore, Schwarz, & Conway, 1994) and behavioral responses (Schmidt & Weiner, 1988). For example, people in a positive mood prefer equality-based justice, but people in a negative mood prefer equity-based justice (Sinclair & Mark, 1991).

Another limitation of these information-processing models is that the motives and goals of the observers are not considered. The models tell us how people use and combine information but do not discuss why they combine the information in the fashion that they do or what their goals may be in applying a sanction.

Although the models outlined suggest that punishment is the key dependent variable, some studies suggest that a broader model of responsibility is possible. Shultz and Wright (1985), for example, distinguish between the factors that are antecedent to being held responsible both for harming and for benefiting another. These factors are not the same, with intention being more central to issues of harm. People do not, for example, receive credit for accidentally benefiting another, but they can be punished for accidentally harming another.

Apologies

Why is intent a critical factor in people's reactions to wrongdoing? D. T. Miller and Vidmar (1981) argue that intentional wrongdoing is seen as diagnostic of contempt for group rules and therefore threatening to social order. Thus, intentional acts evoke more certain and intense punishment. However, offender behavior that indicates some level of respect or acknowledgment of the principles of the broken rule, such as remorse, is less threatening. This acknowledgment satisfies to some extent the goals of retributive justice. For example, sincere expressions of remorse or contrition attenuate punishment reactions (Felson & Ribner, 1981; Kleinke, Wallis, & Stalder, 1992; D. T. Miller & Vidmar, 1981; Pepitone, 1975; Rumsey, 1976; Schwartz et al., 1978). This effect may be considered both from the perspective of society and from the perspective of the parties directly involved in the violation.

From an equity and self-presentational perspective, remorse serves as a means of restoring equity to the injured party. Remorse is seen as a form of apology that serves as a positive input that helps restore equity to the victim and offender's relationship (Darby & Schlenker, 1989). Apology also attenuates the retributive counteraggression of victims (Ohbuchi et al., 1989). However, calculated and insincere expressions of remorse can enhance punishment responses (Pepitone, 1975).

Remorse may also be interpreted as an indicator of regret and suffering on the part of the offender. An equity theory perspective predicts that such suffering will attenuate punishment responses (Austin et al., 1976). Austin and colleagues (1976) review experimental and anecdotal evidence suggesting that consideration of an offender's suffering is related to punishment decisions. The amount of restitution paid by the offender to his or her victim is also proposed to attenuate punishment reactions (Brickman, 1977; Darley & Shultz, 1990). Shultz and Darley's (1991) model explicitly incorporates suffering and restitution as moderating influences on the final punishment assignment.

Ohbuchi et al.'s (1989) analysis of the functions of apologies suggests apology and remorse expressions also have meaning for the broader social context. These expressions communicate information about the offender's present and future orientation toward status relations and group rules (cf. Heider, 1958). D. T. Miller and Vidmar (1981) argue that such expressions mitigate responses precisely because they acknowledge the validity of the rule that was broken.

Micro and Macro Retributive Justice

Just as people can evaluate the fairness of the overall procedures and distributions in society, they can also evaluate the overall fairness of retributive systems. People may judge the treatment of offenders by the criminal justice system to be too lenient or indicate that the appropriate punishment for murder is too severe. For example, people are asked whether they think the death penalty is an appropriate punishment for murder. Their responses indicate general views about punishment, rather than reactions to a particular criminal. In fact, people's responses to macro and micro judgments about punishment differ greatly (see Ellsworth, 1978).

Studies suggest that there is an inconsistency between these general attitudes and judgments of particular offenders and court cases (Cumberland & Zamble, 1992; Zamble & Kalm, 1990). When asked to make global evaluations of the criminal justice system and the treatment of criminals, people evaluate the current system to be too lenient, suggesting that they want more severe punishment. But when asked to make sentencing decisions after reading scenarios that contain specific information describing the crime and the offender, their decisions are remarkably close to the sentencing decisions made by judges and other participants in the criminal justice system (Zamble & Kalm, 1990). Ellsworth (1978) similarly shows that people support the death penalty for particular crimes on the macro level but are much less willing to vote to give the death penalty to a particular person who commits the same crimes.

This tension between macro- and micro-level judgments mirrors the earlier tension found between macro- and micro-level distributive justice judgments. In that setting, people rejected the macro-level income distributions resulting from the micro-level operation of equity principles. Here, people reject their macro-level punitiveness judgments when making judgments on the micro level. For example, in the abstract, 66 percent support the death penalty for killing a policeman, but in concrete cases, only 15 percent support it (Ellsworth, 1978).

Why are there differences between macro- and micro-level support for punishment? Doob and Roberts (1984) propose a cognitive explanation—that the nature of the information underlying public opinion affects leniency judgments. To test this idea, subjects were presented with information in one of two ways: media treatment and extended description. Subjects who evaluated information about the offenders' treatment that is presented in media fashion (brief, dramatic, and occasionally biased) supported severe punishment. In contrast, subjects who evaluated information presented in a more comprehensive and objective fashion (such as presentations by legal professionals) indicated they believed that the courts were treating offenders appropriately and, in some cases, too harshly. Hence, abstract justice judgments may be based on different information than are more personalized judgments.

Another possibility is that there are differences in the motivational bases for macro and micro judgments. It may be that people have different goals in retributive justice judgments when considering the macro or micro perspectives. When considering a particular case, an observer may attend to the justice needs of the victim and offender. This focus leads to the consideration of mitigating factors attributing blame and assigning punishment. People may, for example, respond to intention and remorse. These factors influence victims' judgments about whether the status quo has been restored. Observers may also feel compassion for the victim, or the offender, or both. In contrast, when observers consider the incidence of crime and the treatment of criminals in general, they are likely to attend to the concerns of society as a whole. This focus may lead to an emphasis on behavioral control and a desire for more severe punishment to achieve general deterrence. It also may lead to a focus on the symbolic or expressive role of punishment. When considering the problem of criminal deviance from a societal perspective, people may wish to punish severely in order to symbolically reassert the status of the violated rules.

Part 3

Behavioral Reactions to Justice and Injustice

In addition to affecting people's thinking, justice judgments often shape people's behavior in social settings. In fact, many of the most important behaviors that people exhibit in groups have been linked to their judgments about fairness. These include both positive behaviors—such as rule following and expending extra effort for the group—and negative behaviors—such as sabotage and aggression toward others. On a collective level, the behaviors include riots and civil disorder. Our goal here is to examine the nature of possible behavioral responses to injustice and the circumstances under which they occur.

6

Psychological Versus Behavioral Reactions to Injustice

One of the central insights demonstrated by justice research is that people actively interpret their own experiences. This activity is illustrated by two types of responses that can occur in reaction to harm doing: (1) the restoration of actual justice and (2) the restoration of psychological justice by distorting the situation.

The most extensive development of the idea of the psychological restoration of justice occurs within the literature on distributive injustice, particularly in the literature on equity theory. As discussed in Chapter 3, equity theory posits that people prefer fair allocations even when they are contrary to their self-interest. Yet one of the major contributions of the equity literature to the general field of social justice is the demonstration of the occurrence of psychological justifications for advantage. This phenomenon has been more broadly acknowledged within the distributive justice literature through the recognition that the economically and socially advantaged and disadvantaged tend to make psychological adjustments to their situations instead of changing their behavior. Although our discussion will emphasize the distributive justice literature, we will note several examples of similar ideas in the literature on procedural and retributive justice.

Distributive Justice

According to equity theory, the recognition of injustice produces an uncomfortable and distressing emotional state (Adams, 1965; Austin & Walster, 1980). When participants are treated unfairly in an experimental setting, they actually show signs of physiological distress (Markovsky, 1988; see Chapter 3). Therefore, people are motivated to restore justice. The question is how they decide to do so—(1) by changing their interpretation of events or (2) by changing their behavior. Psychological reaction to injustice is addressed in this chapter, and behavioral reaction is addressed in Chapter 7.

These two kinds of reactions can be illustrated by considering how employees might restore justice. For example, when workers are confronted with unfair overpayment, they can restore actual equity by working harder to justify their higher pay. Studies have shown that workers will change the amount or quality of their work to restore equity (Adams, 1965; Adams & Rosenbaum, 1962). The studies demonstrated, for instance, that workers who are told that they are overpaid work harder if they are paid on an hourly basis and do better work if they are paid for each piece of work they complete. In the study of displaced office workers described in Chapter 3 (Greenberg, 1988), workers initially responded to perceived injustice by varying their actual work performance.

Interestingly, workers change their work patterns even when the rate or quality of their work is private (Arrowood, 1961). That is, no one will know how hard they have worked or how much they have produced. Hence, their behavior is unlikely to be a response to the desire to behave in a socially desirable manner. Instead, they seem genuinely motivated to respond to the existence of unfairness.

Workers also can restore equity psychologically by deciding that their work is more difficult or important. This justifies their higher pay. For example, Gergen, Morse, and Bode (1974) showed that overpaid workers justified their higher pay by deciding that their work was more worthwhile. Gergen had subjects perform the difficult task of trying to discern voices out of a background of white noise. He found that subjects who were told that they were being overpaid for this work rated the difficulty of doing the task to be greater.

Either of the two mechanisms outlined—behavioral and psychological—will restore the perceived balance between what people get and what they deserve. Thus, a crucial beginning to an analysis of behavioral reactions to injustice is an understanding of when people respond to injustice behaviorally and when they respond psychologically.

Studies examining what workers do over time show that those who are unfairly overpaid first restore equity by changing their actual behavior (increasing their effort). However, over time, they increasingly restore equity psychologically (Lawler, 1968). Consequently their work effort drops back to its original level. Greenberg's (1988) study of displaced workers measured workers' reactions to injustice over time. Although people initially responded to perceptions of injustice by adjusting their actual work performance, over time the work performance of all the groups Greenberg studied converged at their original level. In other words, by the third week of Greenberg's longitudinal study, workers in the overcompensated, undercompensated, and fairly compensated groups all performed at the same level. These findings suggest that after some time has passed, workers may turn to restoring equity using a strategy emphasizing psychological approaches. This shift from restoring actual equity to restoring psychological equity reflects the benefits that advantaged workers find in using the latter approach. A psychological solution allows workers to justify their higher wages without extra effort, whereas a behavioral solution requires additional work production. Why the disadvantaged also show this pattern is less clear.

Underlying Psychological Motives

Up until this point, the discussion of people's justice judgments has implicitly assumed that these judgments reflect people's efforts to make sense of their social experience following rational processes. This assumption suggests that people want to know the truth about the world and knowing the truth, want to behave justly. This rational or truth-seeking image of the person is central to many cognitive models (see S. T. Fiske & Taylor, 1991). These models suggest that although people may use a variety of heuristics or shortcuts in processing information, people are motivated by the desire to develop an accurate view of the world.

Social psychologists also recognize that people can be motivated to distort their judgments about their experiences to enhance their attainment of other social objectives—such as bolstering their feelings of competence or security—or to keep resources and opportunities for themselves. This alternative image emphasizes that people can be rationalizers who seek to justify their situation.

A classic example of the rationalizing person is found in research on cognitive dissonance. In a typical study of cognitive dissonance, people are enticed to perform an act counter to their normal attitudes through subtle social pressure. Since people typically underestimate the influence of situational pressures on their own behavior (the fundamental attribution error), they are left without a compelling explanation for having done so. In this situation, subjects are in a similar situation to the unfairly advantaged: They can either acknowledge having done something that is contrary to their self-image, or they can try to rationalize their behavior. Cognitive dissonance studies find that at least to some degree, people rationalize their behavior. They do so by changing their attitudes to make them more consistent with their behavior.

The conflict between these two objectives of behaving rationally and preserving self-image is found in the conflicting motives of the previously discussed overpaid workers. On the one hand, workers would like to see the world as it is, recognizing their true market value. However, this objective knowledge would tell them that they are overpaid for their work, creating inequity distress. On the other hand, workers would like to keep the advantages that they have received through overpayment, and keeping them requires psychological justification.

Psychologists have recognized the strength of this second motivation in instrumental models based upon people's desire to maximize their gains in interactions with others. They have also shown that people generally see themselves as more capable and competent than they really are (S. E. Taylor & Brown, 1988). These exaggerated judgments facilitate psychological justification by providing rationales for keeping overpayments.

In contrast to these more specific individual motives for distorting unjust situations, Lerner (1981) proposes that people have a general desire for justice. The just world hypothesis states that people have a need to believe in a just world in which everyone gets what he/she deserves and therefore deserves what he/she gets (Lerner, 1981). For example, when people are powerless to alter an unfairly disadvantaged person's fate, they reject and devalue the person, especially if they think they will continue to see the person suffer (Lerner & Simmons, 1965). Victim derogation—seeing victims as lazy, stupid, naive, inferior, or morally defective—is a typical means of justifying harm and disadvantage (e.g., "People are poor because they do not want to work"; "She would not have been raped if she had worn a respectable dress"). In addition, people can also minimize the extent of the victim's suffering and/or deny their own responsibility for the victim's plight (e.g., "If the homeless were really unhappy with their situation, they could move into shelters, so they must like living as they do"). The phenomenon of victim derogation and blame is seen in the most extreme form in times of war.

Although most just world research has focused on the reactions to the suffering or deprivation of others, it is equally plausible that victims of injustice might use self-derogation to make sense of their personal situations (Jost & Banaji, 1994; Mark & Folger, 1984). In an experimental study, those who believed strongly in a just world were more likely to view their personal failure to win a desirable prize as fair than were those who did not believe so strongly (Hafer & Olson, 1989). Other research provides evidence that people use their personal outcomes as an anchor for evaluating their performance, even when the relationship between performance and outcome is tenuous or arbitrary (Steil, 1983). For example, school children arbitrarily assigned to a disadvantageous position made significantly less effort in and showed less comprehension of the experimental task than those who were arbitrarily assigned to an advantageous position, even though their objective performances were the same (Steil, 1983). The hypothesized need for personal control suggests that the assumption of personal responsibility for failure by the disadvantaged reflects attempts at psychological control (Bulman & Wortman, 1977).

Psychological justifications for particular outcomes, therefore, occur within a general framework of people's efforts to view themselves in ways that make sense of their situations and make the situations as palatable as possible (Baumeister, 1982). As already noted, these general tendencies have interfered with the ability of equity judgments to create satisfaction with pay and promotion decisions in organizational settings. In those cases, these same justifying or rationalizing tendencies facilitate the development of psychological justifications for unfair advantages.

Three Perspectives

In considering the distinction between the restoration of actual and psychological equity, it is important to distinguish between three perspectives: (1) the perspective of the unfairly advantaged (the harm doers), (2) the perspective of the unfairly disadvantaged (the victims), and (3) the perspective of society. As with the previously discussed workers, there are two possible types of responses that each group might have to justice violations: behavioral and psychological (see Walster, Walster, & Berscheid, 1978).

Harm doers (the unfairly advantaged). Consider the situation of harm doers—people who have gotten too much either by actions they have taken (i.e., harming others) or through chance, accident, or the benefit of unequal social conditions (e.g., being born at the right time). Those people might restore equity by compensating victims or by in some way injuring or depriving themselves. If people are receiving or have received too much, they can restore fairness if they work harder, lower their rewards, or redistribute resources to others. These actions will restore actual equity at the cost of self-interest.

However, they might restore equity psychologically by justifying their advantage (for example, by viewing the victims as deserving their fate). They might reevaluate the situation and decide that their work is of greater value (i.e., that they deserve more) or that others' contributions are of lesser value (i.e., that they deserve less). These cognitive changes justify their unfair level of rewards, restoring psychological justice without costs to self-interest. Such justifications avoid the need for compensation or restitution (Lerner, 1981; Mikula, 1986). For these reasons, it has been suggested that the advantaged are more likely to engage in psychological strategies to reduce feelings of inequity (D. H. Taylor & Moghaddam, 1994).

A second motive for distorting unfair advantages is to protect a positive self-image. It may be difficult to reconcile unjust actions with perceptions of oneself or one's society as being moral and fair (Deutsch & Steil, 1988). Often, when people use their power to take resources or to behave in ways that hurt others, those actions are accompanied by cognitive justifications of harm. For example, those who commit acts of cruelty or injury during wars justify their actions by viewing their victims as deserving their fate (Darley, 1992). This process of cognitive distortion makes acts of injustice and inhumanity seem more acceptable to those who commit them.

On a societal level, those who are advantaged may try to justify their advantages by distorting norms of distributive justice. Relative power and position shape people's distributive orientations (Kabinoff, 1991) and their reactions to distributive inequities (K. S. Cook & Hegtvedt, 1986; Steil, 1983). For example, those with more resources and power prefer equity-based distributions, whereas those with fewer resources prefer principles of equality and need (Kabinoff, 1991). Similarly, those who benefit from distributive inequities are more likely to view the distribution (and the procedures that produced that distribution) as fairer than those who do not benefit (Azzi, 1992; Cook & Hegtvedt, 1986). The advantaged may add insult to injury by justifying their material advantages by enhancing their evaluations of their own virtues and/or derogating the characteristics of those receiving lesser outcomes.

An example of an ideology that justifies advantages is the American belief in free markets. Americans strongly endorse the idea that what determines how far one gets in society is how hard one works (Kleugel & Smith, 1986). This ideology suggests that people are responsible for their own fate. Moreover, there is little reason for government to intervene in markets since markets are fair. Thus, the wealthy regard themselves as intelligent and hard working because they have succeeded in a free contest, and they see little reason to be sympathetic toward those who are less well-off.

Although the advantaged may be inclined toward psychological distortion, studies make clear that the advantaged do not always simply justify their advantage, evaluating whatever is in their interest as fair. If they did so, this would render justice an epiphenomenal construct that contributes nothing unique to the understanding of social behavior. In fact, one of the most impressive findings of equity-inspired research is the demonstration that both the feelings and the actual behaviors of the advantaged are shaped by justice concerns.

Consider the work of Montada and Schneider (1989), who examine reactions to the poor and homeless in Germany. They found that moral outrage and existential guilt led people to be more willing to support spending money for the disadvantaged. Moral outrage reflected a general judgment that it was wrong for there to be poor or homeless people. Existential guilt reflected feelings that the respondent was unfairly advantaged relative to these disadvantaged groups. Finally, sympathy reflected an emotional attachment to the poor or disadvantaged. The findings suggest that both moral outrage and existential guilt had strong effects on the willingness to support spending money for the disadvantaged. Affective sympathy had little influence. Overall, justice-based judgments had a strong influence on behavioral intentions.

Similarly, consider the case of economic markets. The belief that there are unfair disadvantages that influence the outcomes of individuals in economic markets is significantly related to support for redistributive policies (H. J. Smith & Tyler, 1996; Tougas & Veilleux, 1988) and redistributive behavior (Berscheid & Walster, 1967). Such policies and behaviors seek to restore equity when the advantaged believe that their advantages are undeserved, even if they have to relinquish some of those advantages.

For example, H. J. Smith and Tyler (1996) found that respondents who regarded markets as unfair were more willing to support policies for redistributing resources. As shown in Figure 6.1, the more that people viewed the market outcomes for the disadvantaged to be unfair, the more they supported redistributive policies. Similarly, the more unfair people viewed the market procedures to be, the more they supported redistributive policies. In fact, the greatest support for redistributive policies came from people who thought both market outcomes and procedures were unfair.

Victims (the unfairly disadvantaged). Victims also can respond to injustice either by changing behavior or by making psychological adjustments. One type of actual response is retaliation. This behavior makes clear that the victim regards the harm doer's behavior as unjust. It also helps to restore equity because the harm flowing from retaliation balances out the harm doer's gain. For reasons of self-interest, their preference should be for restoring actual equity via individual compensation or retaliation (Walster, 1978) or via collective political and social actions such as ballot initiatives, riots, and strikes (D. M. Taylor & Moghaddam, 1994).

One interesting argument made within the equity literature is that the disadvantaged may gain by challenging injustice, even if they do not gain the lost resources or opportunities. By challenging the injustice, the disadvantaged can avoid being victimized twice: once by the initial injustice and a second time by the justifying distortion that they deserved their unfair fate (e.g., secondary victimization). If harm doers are challenged by the victims of injustice and deal successfully with that challenge, the harm doers will not subsequently feel the need to derogate the victims. Elsewhere, Hogan and Emler (1981) argue that seeking redress is also important for saving face in front of the larger social audience. A victim's failure to seek redress from the perpetrator may result in low status and communicates to others that the victim is weak, inviting further injustice (Hogan & Emler, 1981).

However, the unfairly disadvantaged often do not act in the face of injustice (Major, 1994; Martin, 1986a; S. C. Wright, Taylor & Moghaddam, 1990b). Research suggests that the disadvantaged are in a difficult position. On the one hand, they have a strong motive to acknowledge injustice and seek compensation for current and past harms. On the other hand, such acknowledgment brings the disadvantaged into confrontation with the advantaged, who control jobs, wealth, and agencies of social control (e.g., the police). Those who seek to restore actual justice must contend with the

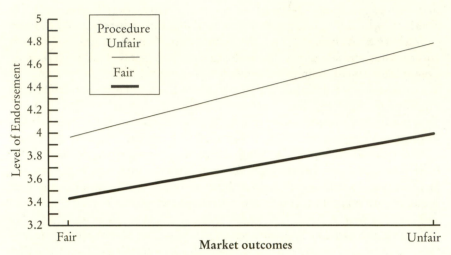

Higher scores indicate greater policy endorsement.

FIGURE 6.1   Willingness to support social policies

objective realities of powerlessness. The disadvantaged, then, have a strong motive to deny injustice or disadvantage. Unfortunately, such denial is psychologically damaging; people turn to drugs, alcohol, or acts of self-destruction in frustration. Denial also prevents potentially constructive social change.

However, lack of action found among the disadvantaged also can simply represent powerlessness. People may judge that injustice is occurring and may feel angry, but they may not act for fear of losing their jobs, being shot in the street by the police, or other reasons.

Contrary to this image, social scientists have noted widespread evidence that differences in objective conditions do not lead to subjective experiences of injustice. Typically, the disadvantaged do not translate personal experiences with objective inequality into feelings of outrage and resentment (Martin, 1986a). In other words, widespread differences in the actual nature and quality of people's lives do not translate into feelings of anger. Like Sherlock Holmes's famous question: Why didn't the dog bark?, social scientists ask Why do the disadvantaged not feel that injustice has occurred and express more outrage and discontent? A central question emerging from social science research is why the large objective differences found in the quality of people's lives are not more strongly reflected in differences in their views about justice and society. There is something about people's interpretation of their experiences that dampens potential feelings of injustice and anger.

One explanation for the finding that the unfairly disadvantaged do not feel that injustice exists is that the comparison processes through which experience is interpreted may lead to the acceptance of objective disadvantages (see Chapter 2). Major (1994) argues that natural patterns of social comparison prevent the awareness of objective disadvantage. She suggests that people compare themselves with others who are proximal and similar to themselves—others who most likely share the same disadvantages. Further, they compare themselves with themselves at other points in time, so their previous disadvantages become the standard of comparison. These comparison tendencies blunt the development of feelings of injustice.

In addition, the interpretation of experience occurs through a filter of beliefs about legitimacy. If people view a negative event or negative comparison as the product of a legitimate situation, it is unlikely that they will develop feelings of injustice (Folger, 1987; Tedeschi & Nesler, 1994). Tyler (1990) demonstrates that prior views about the legitimacy of legal authorities influence evaluations of the procedural justice, but not the distributive justice, of personal experiences with those authorities.

Also, Tyler et al. (1989) find that prior evaluations of the legitimacy of legal authorities influence evaluations of the procedural justice, but not the distributive justice, of case disposition procedures (e.g., trials, plea bargaining) among people charged with felonies. Takenishi and Takenishi (1992) similarly find that prior commitment to government authorities influences the fairness criteria used to judge government actions.

There is also a tendency for people to legitimize the status quo, seeing "what is" as "what ought to be" regardless of the fairness of their objective position (Hochschild, 1981; Kluegel & Smith, 1986; Major, 1994). As has been noted, one striking example of this occurs in the case of attributions of causality and responsibility for success and failure.

Studies of economic achievement in the United States show that people take personal responsibility for their own success and/or failure in life (Kluegel & Smith, 1986). In other words, people assume that the distribution of resources generally reflects people's relative worth (Della Fave, 1980). Furthermore, people who view themselves and others as personally responsible for their successes or failures are more likely to assume that societal inequities are legitimate (Martin, 1986b). This research shows that people view justice in individual terms, focusing on personal characteristics (e.g., one's personal identity) and issues of personal relative deprivation in contrast to focusing on shared group membership characteristics (e.g., one's social identity) and issues of group relative deprivation. Interestingly, this pattern of results reflects an individualistic, meritocratic ideology. Furthermore, disadvantaged people's uncritical acceptance of equity and meritocratic explanations of economic success serves neither the person nor the disadvantaged group; however, it does serve to justify the status quo (Jost & Banaji, 1994; Tyler & McGraw, 1985).

To be able to question an ideology such as the legitimacy of economic institutions, people need to have some type of alternative ideology that is at least as powerful (Kelman & Hamilton, 1989). For example, people historically have been willing to question the government when they had religious authority on their side. Further, when people have an alternative ideology, they are more likely to interpret their experiences as an injustice. For example, gays accepted police harassment for the "crime" of homosexual behavior for many years without organized protest. However, a number of social changes, including the climate of protest against the Vietnam War and the awakening of feelings of injustice through the Civil Rights movement, led to an increasing awareness of injustice. This greater awareness led to crystallizing events such as the 1969 Stonewall Inn riots that helped to launch the gay liberation movement (Duberman, 1994). On this occasion, police harassment was defined as unfair, creating a new interpretation of events.

People often endure unpleasant events without thinking of those events as unfair and of themselves as victims. For example, Luker (1984) describes how women underwent illegal and secret abortions in the United States without feeling they were being unjustly treated. After the women's liberation movement changed social consciousness and abortion became legal, many women reinterpreted their earlier experiences and decided that they had been unfairly treated. At the time, however, they regarded their experiences as simply part of life.

Consider the case of the legitimacy of the police and courts. In a random-sample survey of 1,575 citizens in Chicago Tyler (1990) found that race and social status had no effect on judgments of the legitimacy of legal authorities. To illustrate, we will examine one aspect of legitimacy—feelings of obligation to obey the law (see Table 6.1). Dividing respondents in Tyler's sample by ethnicity or by income produced similar results. There was little variation in perceptions of legitimacy due to either ethnicity or income.

In contrast, consider the 652 of those respondents who had reported recent personal experiences with legal authorities. Those respondents who were non-White and/or poor reported more negative experiences with the police and courts (see Table 6.2). How can the discrepancy between differences in treatment and lack of differences in judgments about legitimacy be explained? If the disadvantaged are actually having more negative experiences with legal authorities, why do they not feel that those authorities are less legitimate?

In contrast to more structural explanations, there is a motivational explanation for why the disadvantaged fail to see their disadvantage as an instance of injustice. Crosby (1984) argues that the disadvantaged are motivated to deny that they are the personal victims of injustice. She infers denial from the finding that disadvantaged people, particularly working women, recognize

TABLE 6.1 Legitimacy of Authority

| | Percentage Agreeing | | | |
| | Ethnicity | | Income | |
	White	Non-White	Low	High
People should obey the law even if it goes against what they think is right.	80	84	83	81
I always try and follow the law even if I think it is wrong.	81	83	82	82
Disobeying the law is seldom justified.	80	79	80	78
It is difficult to break the law and keep one's self-respect.	65	73	85	84
If a person is doing something and a police officer tells them to stop, they should stop even if they feel that what they are doing is legal.	84	85	85	84
Average	78	81	81	78

SOURCE: *Why People Obey the Law,* by T. R. Tyler, 1990, New Haven, CT: Yale University Press. Copyright 1990 Yale University Press. Adapted with permission.

wage injustice on a collective level but do not report personal injustice, even though the objective data show evidence for both individual and collective discrimination. This pattern has been widely replicated in studies of other disadvantaged groups (D. M. Taylor, Wright & Porter, 1994).

The denial of injustice can reflect several different motives. Acknowledging disadvantage means accepting one's victimized position. This is potentially damaging to one's self-esteem and sense of control over the world (Bulman & Wortman, 1977; Mikula, 1993). According to the just-world hypothesis (Lerner, 1981), people get what they deserve in life and consequently deserve what they get. Hence, victims of discrimination may feel that accepting victim status suggests a flaw in their own character, or at least that others will view them as being flawed. Furthermore, the recognition of injustice often requires victims to identify a particular perpetrator or to act in some way to correct the injustice (Crosby & Gonzalez-Intal, 1984; Montada, 1991). In many situations, these actions may prove costly (e.g., losing one's job, the expense of litigation).

The psychological denial of personal injustice is illustrated by comparisons between people's assessments of their personal experience of injustice and assessments of the injustice their respective group experiences. When evaluations of personal and collective injustice are compared, members of disadvan-

TABLE 6.2   Experience with Legal Authorities

	Percentage Agreeing			
	Ethnicity		Income	
	White	*Non-White*	*Low*	*High*
Outcomes				
When you compare the outcome of your call to the outcome people generally receive when they call the police with similar problems, did you receive the same outcome as others or a better or worse outcome? (percentage worse)	8	10	10	8
Do you think that you received a worse outcome than others because of your race, sex, age, nationality, or some other characteristic of you as a person? (percentage yes)	33	76	64	41
Was the outcome of your call to the police what you thought it would be when you called them, or was it better or worse than you expected? (percentage worse)	23	28	27	24
Procedures				
Were the police polite to you? (percentage yes)	72	69	67	74
Did they show concern for your rights? (percentage yes)	67	58	58	68
Did the police do anything improper? (percentage yes)	14	28	27	15
Did the methods used by the police favor one person? (percentage yes)	28	41	33	33

SOURCE: *Why People Obey the Law,* by T. R. Tyler, 1990, New Haven, CT: Yale University Press. Copyright 1990 Yale University Press. Adapted with permission.

taged groups are less likely to deny collective disadvantages than personal disadvantages (Crosby, 1982; Crosby, Pufall, Snyder, O'Connell, & Whalen, 1989; D. M. Taylor, Wright, Moghaddam, & Lalonde, 1990; Taylor et al., 1994). Most explanations for the discrepancy between personal and group evaluations share an emphasis on the benefits of denying personal disadvantages or injustices. However, more recent research suggests the researchers' emphasis on the denial of personal injustice by the disadvantaged is misplaced. Taylor et al. (1994) argue that the focus on the denial of personal injustice hinges on the assumption that people are motivated to deny *any* personal discrimination because as long as people recognize some personal discrimination, the psychological benefits of denial are lost. Once some personal injustice is acknowledged, a perpetrator must be identified, some action must be undertaken, and the threat of stigma is possible. However, empirical research suggests that people minimize rather than deny personal injustice (D. M. Taylor et al., 1990; D. M. Taylor et al., 1994). Therefore, it is worthwhile to consider the possibility that members of disadvantaged groups might exaggerate the amount of collective injustice (D. M. Taylor et al., 1994).

Taylor et al. (1994) directly compare models based on the idea of an individual need for denial (that suggest people will be unable to acknowledge personal deprivation)—to group exaggeration models—(that argue that the discrepancies outlined develop from the tendency to exaggerate the collective disadvantage of their group). They find that although both models receive some support, most of their evidence supports the group exaggeration model. There are two reasons why people might be motivated to exaggerate or emphasize the amount of collective injustice. First, collective injustice can provide an external attribution for personal failure or make personal success even more impressive (Crocker & Major, 1989). Second, it can help establish collective claims for obtaining valued resources (Bourhis & Hill, 1982; Patchen, 1958; D. M. Taylor et al., 1990; van Knippenberg & van Oers, 1984).

However, it is important to recognize that not all disadvantaged group members deny or minimize the injustice of their personal situation relative to the situation for their group (Vanneman & Pettigrew, 1972). In fact, a small minority of women in Crosby's (1982) original study reported both that they personally and that women in general suffered injustice. Furthermore, African Americans who reported both that African Americans in general were mistreated by the police and that they personally had been mistreated were most likely to support radical political protest (Dibble, 1981). An adequate explanation for the tendency of the unfairly disadvantaged to minimize personal injustice or exaggerate collective injustice must be able to explain why some people do not report a discrepancy.

Society.   There is a potential conflict between individuals and the social group concerning how to respond to injustice. For example, harm doers prefer to justify their actions rather than compensate their victims. By justifying their actions, they can serve both justice and self-interest motives at the same time—keeping what they have stolen but feeling good about themselves. However, allowing harm doers to restore equity psychologically can encourage retaliation by victims, create social dissension through derogation and stereotyping of victims and their social groups, and over time, disrupt the social fabric of society.

Equity theory suggests that the unjustly advantaged are in conflict both with society with their victims. The violation of a fair exchange threatens the future viability of fair exchanges for all the members of the larger group. Therefore, equity theorists argue that society values the restoration of actual equity. If those who commit harm restore equity through psychological means, that benefits them personally in the short term but creates heightened social tension in the long term. Over time, society is undermined. Thus, social institutions and authorities such as the courts are responsible for pressuring harm doers to make actual restitution. One way in which they do so is to undermine psychological justifications for harm doing.

Basic justice concerns also argue for limiting the ability to psychologically justify harm. In such a situation, the victim suffers twice. First, they lose objective resources. Then, they are derogated and left bitter and maligned. This is not only socially dysfunctional but also contrary to the goal of social justice. It leaves the original victim injured by material or physical harm, demeaned socially, and angry and alienated from both the harm doer and others in society.

To facilitate the actual restoration of equity, societal institutions and authorities such as judges mandate the restoration of equity when injustice has occurred. If, for example, your employer refuses to pay you for your work, you can sue your employer and go to court to collect the money. You have a mechanism for restoring actual equity. The existence of mechanisms for correcting errors has already been noted to be one element in the fairness of procedures (i.e., in the Leventhal 1980 model). The courts are such a correction mechanism, as is the ability to appeal to a union, to higher management, to relatives, or to others who might intervene on one's behalf.

An important reason for societies to have collective agencies for dealing with injustice is to lessen negative and antisocial actions such as appeals to friends or family for revenge. By managing the restoration of justice, the state can minimize miscarriages of justice. In gang wars, for example, the spiraling cycle of revenge and counterrevenge often also leads to innocent deaths of bystanders shot down on the street.

In addition to the need to minimize private efforts at revenge, society has an interest in facilitating the creation of social conditions that allow people to trust one another. Much of social life is linked to trusting others. If people cannot trust, then social exchange is crippled (Tyler & Kramer, 1996). Hence, society wants to encourage people to follow social rules and not to victimize others.

Of course, in other situations the perpetrator may be seen as a representative of the larger social group, and the victim may be seen as a deviant. For example, police officers are empowered by society to control people who may be violating social rules, and the officers exercise considerable discretion in situations that are often ambiguous and confusing. Because this is the officers' function, society makes it very difficult for victims to successfully sue and collect damages from them. In such cases, the norms of the larger society may prevent the restoration of actual equity and may encourage the restoration of psychological equity. When a low-status or morally decrepit person is victimized, the event may be seen as justified (Pepitone, 1975), or the offense may not be evaluated as being so severe (Landy & Aronson, 1969).

In dealing with legal and political authorities, people often make demands for rights and/or restitution based on moral claims. Social authorities are typically reluctant to grant such claims, recognizing that using the authorities and institutions of society to redistribute societal resources opens the door for further claims of injustice. Thus, both individuals and groups often engage in lengthy struggles before their claims to redress are acknowledged. This was exemplified by the struggle for school desegregation that culminated in the 1954 *Brown v. Board of Education* decision. A similar struggle has occurred over monetary compensation for Japanese Americans and their families who were interned in relocation camps during World War II (Nagata, 1993). Although the harms occurred during the 1940s, debates about compensation continued into the 1980s. Similarly, compensation for women forced into prostitution during World War II by the Japanese and even the issue of a Japanese apology for the war are still being debated.

Finally, rationalizing or denying injustice can enable the larger society to keep or protect valuable resources. For example, there has been little pressure from the U.S. government to return major portions of the frontier to the original Native American inhabitants, even though the injustice of the treatment of Native Americans throughout this nation's history is widely acknowledged.

When Will People Acknowledge Injustice?

Whether people prefer to restore equity psychologically or behaviorally may depend upon (1) practical concerns such as the likelihood of success and/or retaliation and (2) the ambiguity of the situation (e.g., the ease with which reality can be distorted).

One factor that influences whether the unfairly advantaged offer actual compensation is the amount involved in such compensation. People are more likely to compensate victims if the amount involved is small. This accords with simple self-interest: More sacrifice creates greater pressure to justify harm.

The actual amount of compensation can also shape the reactions of the unfairly disadvantaged. If a person has real power disadvantages in actual situations of injustice, gaining the restoration of justice can be costly or impossible. For example, Mikula's (1986) interviews with victims of injustice found that confrontations with higher-power individuals seldom resulted in the redistribution of resources. Such conclusions are not confined to everyday injustices. A recent survey of women's responses to sexual harassment suggests that women who report acts of harassment often experience negative consequences, including loss of promotion opportunities, loss of jobs, and various psychological problems (Koss et al., 1994). It is not surprising, therefore, that the same study found that most women ignored and did not report incidents of sexual harassment.

In situations with serious personal consequences, estimates of the likelihood of success are likely to be central to decisions about how to respond to injustice. If the likelihood of compensation or successful retaliation is low and the costs are high, the disadvantaged will be more likely to psychologically distort the situation. Similarly, resource mobilization models of collective action propose that people's willingness to protest collectively is a direct reflection of their estimates of success or efficacy (Klandermans, 1993; Martin, Brickman, & Murray, 1984).

Second, the establishment of a clear amount facilitates compensation. Presenting the harm doer with the exact dollar amount needed to redress injustice facilitates compensation because it provides the harm doer with clear and concrete evidence of the possibility of resolving the injustice. Hence, clarifying an ambiguous situation to indicate that there is both an injustice and a set of actions that could correct that injustice makes the actual restoration of justice more likely (K. S. Cook & Hegtvedt, 1986; Deci, Reis, Johnston & Smith, 1977; Taylor & Moghaddam, 1994).

Studies indicate that an amount clearly adequate to compensate for the wrongful act is more likely to be given than an amount that is not clearly adequate (Berscheid & Walster, 1967). In their study, Berscheid and Walster (1967) gave churchgoers the opportunity to cheat at a work task by giving inaccurate performance information and receive trading stamps dishonestly. They explored the circumstances under which people would give those unjustly obtained trading stamps back. One circumstance that facilitated the return of the stamps was the establishment of an exact amount of compensation for the original theft. Whether people would give back their stamps was not linked to the amount they had to give up; they would give up more if they knew that it was adequate compensation. In other words, although harm doers generally disliked compensating greater amounts, they were more willing to do so if they felt that the amounts involved were the exact amounts needed to restore fairness and compensate for the harm caused.

It is not difficult to see why people would like to compensate an exact amount. If people partially compensate, they are acknowledging wrongdoing but not restoring equity. Hence, they are opening themselves up to psychological pain and guilt and to further demands for restitution. If, though, they acknowledge wrongdoing but immediately restore equity through complete compensation, they have no reason to continue feeling bad.

The principle that requesting a smaller amount facilitates actual compensation argues that victims should not exaggerate their suffering if they want compensation. Instead, they should ask for an amount that can feasibly be given to them. Of course, this idea works better in a laboratory setting, where suffering is minimal. What amount of money compensates for years of slavery (African Americans); for the massacre of one's ancestors (Native Americans) or friends and relatives (the Armenians in Turkey); for being removed from one's home and losing land, possessions, and economic opportunities (Japanese Americans during World War II); or for being forced into prostitution (Korean "comfort women")?

Two questions are central here: Can money compensate for harms? If so, how is the amount to be determined? For example, women who were forced into prostitution by Japan during World War II were offered $20,000 each in compensation. How can it be determined whether this is an appropriate amount? Further, does compensation actually respond to the need for some social response created by the original harm? Would the victims react more favorably to an apology?

Another factor that encourages compensation is the lack of a clear justification for the original harm. When people have disputes, both sides typically think themselves to be in the right. Both sides justify their positions, seeing themselves as more just and justified than the other party. Such a situation makes distortions about the other person and the other's position easy to develop and maintain. Further, one typical response to conflict is to cut off communication with the other party, making it less likely that discussion or other interaction will lead to a recognition of distortions.

The courts facilitate compensation by giving clear moral pronouncements about right and wrong. The judge tells the parties which party is right or wrong in the eyes of the law, giving an authoritative pronouncement of who is correct in terms of society's rules. These authoritative pronouncements make it more difficult for the harm doer to avoid moral responsibility for harms. In the face of a clear moral statement from an accepted authority such as a judge, people are less likely to try to justify their wrongdoing.

In general, the distortions underlying justifications are difficult to create and maintain since they involve distortions of reality. People are more likely to be able to sustain them when they involve minor distortions of reality. Further, if people have information from respected others—for example, information indicating that their position is wrong—they have a harder time sustaining it.

In addition, it is hard to sustain distortions when people have everyday contact with the person involved. In other words, as much as harm doers might wish to justify their harm, forces in the social world may limit their ability to do so. It is difficult to maintain distorted views of reality, especially in the face of personal experience. Therefore, it is not surprising that residential, work, and educational segregation helps maintain social stereotypes. If the members of different ethnic and racial groups do not interact, it is much easier for people to maintain negative (and often inaccurate) stereotypes of the members of other groups. When people interact, those stereotypes can clash with direct personal experience and are more difficult to maintain. The unfairly advantaged also are less likely to distort unfair situations cognitively when they expect future contact with the victim and/or see themselves as similar to or sharing a close relationship with the victim (Mikula, 1994; Walster et al., 1978).

Procedural Justice

Although distributive justice has been the focus of most research, writing on procedural justice in organizational and legal contexts also suggests the possibility that the advantaged may manipulate perceptions of procedural fairness to justify unjustice actions. Greenberg (1990b), for example, argues that management uses fair procedures as an impression-control strategy. By presenting the appearance of fairness, managers are able to perpetrate distributive injustice. Employees who are taken in by this performance do not perceive that they are victims despite the distributive inequities that they bear.

Similarly, Haney (1991) argues that powerful authorities use fair procedures to their advantage. By giving the impression of due process and consideration, bodies such as the Supreme Court are able to perpetuate the status quo. By providing the appearance of fair procedures, authorities can avoid the significant challenges that may result from perceptions of injustice.

Retributive Justice

Finally, psychological distortion or justification of harm is seen in the domain of retributive justice as well. In particular, perpetrators of rape are seen to shift responsibility for the rape to the victim (Burt, 1983; Herbert & Dunkel-Schetter, 1992). Through processes of derogating the rape victim's character and behavior, the injustice perpetrated upon the victim is justified. By shifting the blame in this manner, the rapist expects that the behavior will be justified and that punishment will be considerably reduced. More surprisingly, derogation of rape victims is seen from the perspective of society as well. When a rape is described in an ambiguous fashion, men and women attribute some blame to the rape victim. Both the belief in a just world (Lerner, 1980) and the concept of defensive attribution (K. G. Shaver, 1970) have been identified as motivating victim derogation (Bell, Kuriloff, & Lottes, 1994; Whatley & Riggio, 1993).

7

BEHAVIORAL REACTIONS
TO INJUSTICE

A General Model of Responses to Grievances

The previous chapter outlined some of the pressures encouraging people to distort situations cognitively in ways that justify the status quo. However, it is clear that not all members of advantaged groups deny inequities between their situations and the situations of the disadvantaged (Montada & Schneider, 1989), nor do all members of disadvantaged groups appear to deny or minimize personal discrimination or injustice (e.g., Crosby, 1982; D. M. Taylor et al., 1994). The recognition of injustice and the resulting feelings of anger or guilt should motivate people to behave in a variety of ways (Crosby, 1976; Mark & Folger, 1984).

Research generally has addressed two issues. The first is understanding the various types of behavior in which people can engage. The second is understanding what judgments about the situation (e.g., feasibility of change, costs, and benefits) lead people to engage in one form of behavior as opposed to another.

Possible Behaviors

An overall look at the types of behavioral responses to deprivation and discrimination proposed by researchers suggests two dimensions that distinguish the various forms of people's reactions to injustice (Crosby, 1976; Ellemers, 1993; Kawakami & Dion, 1992; Lalonde & Cameron, 1994; Mark & Folger, 1985; S. C. Wright, Taylor, & Moghaddam, 1990b). The types of possible behavior are shown in Figure 7.1.

The first and most heavily researched distinction is between individual and collective behaviors—between reactions designed to improve or rectify one's personal situation and reactions designed to improve or rectify the situation for one's larger reference group. This distinction focuses on the motive underlying behavior. The distinction between individual and collective

Who is the object of injustice?		
	Individual	Collective
Nonnormative (destructive, negative)	• Stress symptoms (alcoholism) • Personal vengeance	• Riots • Separatist movements
Normative (constructive, positive)	• Self improvement	• Social change (political lobbying, class action suits)

Perspective of society is the row label spanning both Nonnormative and Normative rows.

FIGURE 7.1   Behavioral reactions to injustice

behavior is not based on the number of people who participate; rather, it is based on people's intentions. For example, people can riot for individual reasons (e.g., "Now is my chance to get the color TV that I deserve") or for collective reasons (e.g., "Now is our chance to protest how the 'system' treats our group").

The second distinction is between normative behaviors—reactions that conform to the standards of the larger social system and negative, or nonnormative, behaviors—reactions that are outside the confines of existing social rules (Kawakami & Dion, 1992).

Of course, it is only from a societal perspective that constructive, normative behaviors are considered positive and nonnormative behaviors are viewed as negative. Negative behaviors such as riots can be viewed as positive by those seeking social change, and constructive normative behaviors can be viewed as negative. From a radical perspective, people need to see the way in which their everyday problems are a product of the social system. They need to be encouraged to think and act collectively. For example, if people decide that they are responsible for their own plight and decide to go back to school, they are unlikely to join a group seeking social change.

Consider the case of people with grievances against merchants within their own neighborhoods. When those cases are taken to court, they are typically settled through mediation or other informal dispute resolution mechanisms. These mechanisms can be very satisfying to the individual with a grievance since they may receive compensation for at least some of what they had previously lost. However, mediation is very dissatisfying to community activists because the piecemeal settlement of individual complaints allows dishonest merchants to continue deceptive and exploitive practices. Activists would prefer that there were no informal mechanisms for dispute resolution. In that case, community anger might build to a point at which collective actions would lead to legal or structural changes that would end the deceptive practices. Individuals must act collectively in order to achieve such systemwide changes. Collective action is unlikely to occur if the worst victims are provided with individually satisfactory methods of resolving their grievances. The key question is whether it is good to resist solving problems for individuals so as to build up pressure for collective action. Answers to this question depend upon a political analysis of society, and such an analysis is beyond the scope of psychological theories.

Individual-Level Responses to Injustice

A number of studies have examined individual-level responses to injustice. The first possible individual response is for people not to react even though they recognize the situation to be unfair. People may simply accept the current situation (Mikula, 1986). In descriptions of dissatisfying close relationships or economic exchanges, acceptance of the situation is often described as loyalty or resignation (Hirschman, 1970; Mikula, 1986; Rusbult, 1987). Similarly, studies of disputing behavior suggest that the most common response to a grievance against another person or organization is to do nothing (Felstiner, Abel, & Sarat, 1980–1981).

Accepting injustice is not without costs. For example, feelings of personal relative deprivation are associated with greater psychological depression and reports of symptoms indicating physical stress (Abrams, 1990; Hafer & Olson, 1993; Keith & Schafer, 1985; Parker & Kleiner, 1966; Walker & Mann, 1987). More dramatically, people may direct their frustration toward themselves by suicide, drug use, or alcoholism.

Finally, previous acceptance of injustices or of inadequate compensation for injustices can mean that when a triggering event occurs, reactions are stronger and more aggressive than what otherwise might be expected (Tedeschi & Nesler, 1994). The intense emotion of spontaneous acts of violence such as riots or vigilante actions reflects both the accumulation of frustrations over time and some recent example of injustice that releases those emotions. One negative consequence of such emotional release is that both innocent bystanders and harm doers may be subjected to extreme violence and even killed, when under calmer circumstances, their actions would not have merited such consequences.

One immediate individual-level reaction to possible injustice is to seek verification or social support from other people (Koss et al., 1994). Ambiguous situations or a lack of information often makes it difficult to determine whether a negative event is actually an unfair event. Therefore, people often turn to their peers to verify or support their interpretation of the situation. For example, in one study, employees often ruminated about an unfair event or insult from a supervisor long after the event had occurred (Bies & Tripp, 1996). More importantly, this rumination was often social: Employees discussed their opinions and descriptions of the event with others (Bies & Tripp, 1996). This tendency to seek social support or verification has rarely been considered in empirical investigations of reactions to injustice, but it might prove to be the most frequent response to unfair events.

The opportunity for discussion may also stimulate action in response to perceived injustice. For example, Gamson (1982) presented people with an illegitimate request from an authority. His concern was with the circumstances under which people would reject this unjust demand. His study found that people were much more likely to do so if they had an opportunity to talk to other people also subjected to the demand. If people could talk with each other, they were likely to develop an injustice framework within which they collectively viewed the demand as unreasonable. This framework, in turn, led to greater willingness to confront the authority and to refuse the behavior that was being requested.

A second active personal response to injustice is to seek to restore fairness from the person perceived to be responsible. For example, victims may ask the harm doers to compensate them. One relatively unexplored area of research is victims' reactions to compensation once it is offered (deCarufel, 1986). In one study, initially unfairly paid subjects later received fair pay plus some compensation for their earlier underpayment. They reported as much dissatisfaction as did unfairly paid subjects who continued to receive unfair pay, suggesting that the partial compensation that was offered served to legitimate the injustice. However, it did not adequately compensate for it because the original amount taken had not been returned (deCarufel & Schopler, 1979). Interestingly, these results mirror the trading-stamp study (Berscheid & Walster, 1967) described in the previous chapter. In that study, the unfairly advantaged were willing to compensate the victims only if they believed the compensation adequately covered the victims' losses.

Interestingly, if the harm doer was forced by social authorities to make the partial compensation, people receiving that compensation were more satisfied than when they received similar partial compensation voluntarily from the harm doer (deCarufel & Schopler, 1979). This suggests that harm doers offering partial compensation are viewed as trying to get away with something. They may be trying to end their feelings of guilt without restoring actual equity. However, the efforts of social authorities are appreciated when they at least partially restore justice. Social authorities can publicly label the behavior involved to be wrong, shaming the other party in the eyes of the community.

Other personal-level responses are nonnormative and violate social rules. For example, most people agree that bombing the building of one's former employer or other acts of vengeance designed to harm the wrongdoer violate shared norms. When employees feel unfairly treated, they are much more likely to steal from their employers (Greenberg, 1990a, 1993), sabotage them (Hafer & Olson, 1993), or bad-mouth and publicly embarrass them (Bies & Tripp, 1996). In close relationships, people may use the "silent treatment" or ostracism as a method of punishment (Somer & Williams, 1994). When they do so, they are violating the norm that people in relationships discuss their problems and grievances with each other. By making clear that one is offended and angry but refusing to explain why, a person is violating the normative framework of relationships.

Instead of restoring justice by direct retaliation against a specific harm doer, the offended party may make a retaliatory gesture toward a more general audience. People can engage in individual acts of violence toward others. For example, a person may bring a gun to work and kill coworkers, or a person may kill people on the street, at a school, or in a train or bus. These cases are frequently associated with perceptions that management or society has treated the violent worker unfairly.

Interestingly, in such cases the effort to identify and find the actual harm doer often seems minimal, so the harm doer often escapes punishment and others are victimized. Perhaps the specific harm doer is only important as a representative of a larger organization or group, and seemingly unfocused attempts perhaps reflect the interchangeability of group members (R. J. Brown & Turner, 1981). For oppressed minorities, killing any member of the disliked majority group has similar psychological meaning. For example, "On December 6, 1989, at the Université de Montreal, Canada, a man entered a classroom of engineering students waving a semiautomatic rifle. He forced the male students from the room, and to the women he yelled, 'You are feminists. I hate feminists.' He killed fourteen women, injured more, then turned the rifle on himself. His suicide note made apparent his intentions to send 'the feminists, who have always ruined my life, to their Maker'" (M. D. Foster & Matheson, 1995, p. 1167). From the perspective of the gunman, all of the women in the room represented the feminists that he hated, so it was irrelevant who he killed.

In addition to committing acts of revenge or violence, people may join revolts, rebellions, or riots that are aimed at changing the nature of the social system that produced the harm. Of course, joining such actions is heavily dependent on their availability (since they are collective acts that occur at particular times and geographical locations). If collective actions are available, the individual may choose to join them for many reasons. If not, people may rebel against relationships with others or with society by rejecting social rules and becoming a beatnik, a hippie, or a member of some other socially deviant group (see Stenner & Marshall, 1995). Such actions may be a rejection of society or of particular relationships and expectations (for example, the expectations of one's parents).

A final reaction to personal injustice is to leave the unjust relationship or group (Hirschman, 1970; Mikula, 1986; Rusbult, 1987; D. M. Taylor & Moghaddam, 1994). In a six-week field study, clerks hired at one pay scale returned the second day to learn that a new pay structure would be used instead. Under the new pay scale, clerks who were equitably paid or overpaid continued to participate, but 27 percent of the clerks who were underpaid under the new pay scale quit the study (Valenzi & Andrews, 1971). Other research suggests that employees often avoid or withhold help and support for other employees or supervisors who treat them unfairly (Bies & Tripp, 1996).

Neglect of particular close relationships is a more passive form of psychological exit that occurs when people are unable to leave the relationships (Rusbult, 1987). When people are not motivated to try to solve the problems in their relationships but lack alternatives, they may begin to work late at the office, join civic or religious groups that keep them away from home, begin a job that requires traveling, or even take a job in another location and commute back on (infrequent) occasions. In all of these cases, the individual maintains the connection but does not invest psychological energy in the relationship and its problems.

Possible Responses to Rule Breaking

There are also a variety of ways in which people might respond on the individual level when rules are broken. On the simplest level, for example, people can cooperate with the police to resolve crimes. In fact, "over three-fourths of all arrests occur as a result of reports initiated by bystanders or victims" (Shotland & Goodstein, 1984, p. 9). Observers can also intervene indirectly or directly into ongoing crimes, stopping those crimes and holding criminals for the police. The most extreme actions involve punishing criminals—that is, vengeance. If people are unsatisfied with formal retribution or punishment or doubt the ability of formal institutions to punish offenders adequately, they might respond individually with acts of personal vengeance (Robinson & Darley, 1995).

When do individual observers act? First, when the situation is morally clear. If people know who is to blame and are clear about the circumstances of the crime, action is more likely. People are more likely to act when the situation involves the violation of collective rules (see Figure 7.2). For example, when people see a couple having an argument at the mall, they often feel very reluctant to intervene, even if they think the behavior they see (for example, a husband hitting his wife) is wrong, because they feel family matters are outside the collective. However, people will actively intervene to stop a person stealing the purse of an old woman or trying to kidnap a child on the playground. In such situations, collective rules are clearly being violated, and observers feel responsible for stepping forward (Huggins, 1991; Shotland & Goldstein, 1984).

Further, people are more likely to act when they feel competent to intervene. Individuals are much more likely to act as individuals if they believe they can personally influence the situation (Martin et al., 1984). For example, ex-police officers or those with a military background are more likely to know how to deal with violence and, therefore, more likely to intervene.

What happens when people without experience intervene? Consider the problems that occur when citizens buy handguns and keep them in their homes. Two consequences are that (1) they injure themselves or family members or (2) they are disarmed by criminals who steal their guns. Without experience in identifying and dealing effectively with situations of violence, typical citizens do not know how to act prudently. So they may, for example, shoot a family member, mistaking him or her for a burglar. This suggests that there is a practical aspect to people's behavior: Although people may recognize an injustice, they will only take action if they feel they are capable of addressing the injustice (e.g., apprehending the criminal).

Group-Level Responses to Injustice

When a person breaks a rule by, for example, murdering someone, society as a group is offended. Even those who are not victims or did not even know the victim of a crime want to see justice restored. The goal is to protect the status quo, the rules and values that make social living possible, by meting out retribution and symbolically reasserting the broken rule (D. T. Miller & Vidmar, 1981). Collective responses to rule breaking can occur formally (e.g., via a legal system) or informally (e.g., insults, refusing to associate with a person, and so on.). In most societies that have central governing bodies, severe sanctions are administered through a legal and penal system.

It is likely that for more serious moral offenses, collective sanctions are achieved both formally and informally. For example, communities often isolate or discriminate against released or paroled offenders who have served formal sentences, and lawyers refuse to deal with other lawyers who violate informal norms (H. L. Ross, 1980). After O. J. Simpson was acquitted of

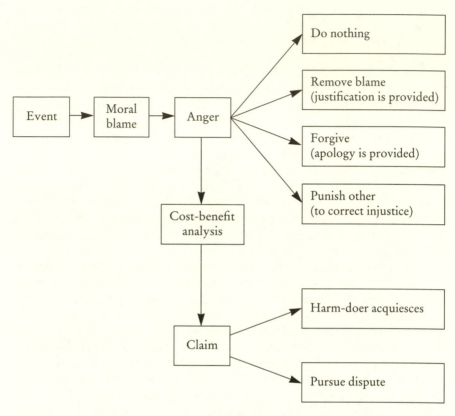

FIGURE 7.2   Process model of social responses to undesirable events

murder, he was encouraged not to visit his country club by his former social group. Similarly, child molesters and rapists trying to return to their communities after serving their formal sentences often find that they are ostracized and publicly labeled as deviants by their communities.

Collective Behaviors Following Rule Breaking

People also respond collectively to rule breaking (Shotland, 1976). Society wants to see the individual punished and to see justice restored. For example, in the case of rule breaking, victims' rights groups often form in response to what the members perceive as punishment that is too lenient. Alternatively, lynch mobs or vigilante groups may pursue retribution outside of the formal system of punishment. Such actions are motivated by the desire to defend group rules and rectify injustice (Toch, 1993). Because vigilante actions are undertaken by groups, the ability to overwhelm the individual rule breaker usually exists. Hence, group members are less concerned with their individual competence to control the offender since they can overwhelm the person with numbers.

People also act when they feel that the groups of which they are a member are treated unjustly by other groups or the larger society. When confronted with collective mistreatment, disadvantaged group members may seek to restore justice in two ways. On the one hand, they may pursue collective change in ways that are acceptable within the larger system (e.g., voting as a bloc, political lobbying, or labor negotiations). They may even turn to third parties to intervene (e.g., class-action suits or referring decisions to the International Court of Justice).

Disadvantaged group members may also pursue change in ways that directly challenge the current system (e.g., riots, rebellion, terrorism). In this case, the collective reaction to injustice is not considered normative by the larger society's standards. A final reaction of subordinate groups to the perceived unjust treatment by an authority representing the larger group (i.e., a superordinate authority) is to exit or disengage from the larger society (Azzi, 1993a; Taylor & Moghaddam, 1994). Separatist movements and civil wars reflect a collective desire to exit or disengage from the larger society.

Naming, Blaming, and Claiming

Which features of the situation determine when people engage in one form of behavior rather than another? A sequence defining how people respond behaviorally to grievances and feelings of injustice is proposed by Tedeshi and Nesler (1994). It draws heavily on the seminal work of Felstiner et al. (1980–1981). Tedeshi and Nesler delineate the sequence as follows: recognizing an injury, establishing blame, feeling anger, and pursuing a grievance (see Figure 7.2). Imagine reading a report written by your boss in which many of your ideas are included but your authorship is not acknowledged. According to this model, before you will confront your boss, you first must recognize that your ideas were included without acknowledgment, you must then blame your boss for the omission, and then you feel angry about it.

Central to the issue of pursuing grievances is the motivation underlying decisions about whether or not to take action. Tedeshi and Nesler (1993), like Felstiner et al. (1980–1981), suggest that people make instrumental decisions about the probable gains and losses of pursing further actions. In the previous example, if you are angry that your boss failed to acknowledge your contribution, you might be reluctant to confront him or her because he or she might fire you, prevent you from gaining a promotion or pay raise, or refuse to write a recommendation letter.

Although people consider such issues, pragmatism is not a complete explanation of people's behavior. Typically, almost all forms of litigation are not cost-effective (Feeley, 1979). Thus, some other form of motivation must also underlie efforts to hold others accountable for unacceptable actions. Consider the case of the pretrial mediation sessions studied by Lind, Ambrose, de Vera Park, and Kulik (1990). In this study, businesses had to decide between accepting a mediator's recommendations or going on to a trial. In fact, going to trial typically is not a cost-effective decision because trial outcomes seldom exceed mediation outcomes. What determined whether people pursued their grievances was their judgments about the fairness of the mediation hearings. In other words, people made a justice-based judgment, not a judgment based on economic efficiency.

One reason that people's behavioral responses to injustice might deviate from rational assessments of cost and benefit is that injustice contains an element of emotion (S. C. Wright et al., 1990a). When people describe their emotional reactions to injustice, they do not describe cost-benefit analyses but instead describe emotional reactions: They are "inflamed and enraged," or "mad, angry, and bitter" (Bies & Tripp, 1996, p. 254). S. C. Wright and his colleagues demonstrate that emotional feelings of frustration and resentment have an important influence on whether or not people take actions. Interestingly, emotion is most important in determining whether actions will occur, not what form actions will take. The type of action is more responsive to cognitive judgments. Wright et al. conclude that "these feelings are clearly inconsistent with [cost-benefit analyses]" (p. 244), since emotions have a strong effect on whether people behave in reaction to injustice.

Similarly, Bies and Tyler (1993) examine the antecedents of people's willingness to sue their employers. In a sample of employees, they found that the primary antecedent of willingness to sue was an assessment of the fairness of company procedures. Although Bies and Tyler assessed the expected costs and benefits of litigation, those were not the major factors shaping the intention to sue. If people felt that the procedures by which they had, for example, been discharged were fair, they did not sue their employers.

These findings suggest that pursuing grievances reflects a response to judgments about those with whom one has a grievance. If those parties are viewed as immoral or unjust, people pursue claims. These effects are distinct from judgments about the likelihood of winning or losing the case. In other words, people are not simply instrumental in their decisions about whether to pursue grievances as individuals.

The decision to pursue a grievance has an important element of perceived injustice or lack of morality on the part of the other party. Merry and Silbey (1984) argue that the rational choice view of disputing behavior, a view that emphasizes the rational pursuit of instrumental goals, does not explain people's actual behavior in disputes. Instead, people are engaged in conflicts over moral values and principles and want to obtain justice. It is the lack of a suitable response to principled complaints that leads people to pursue their complaints with third parties such as mediators or court officials. It is not surprising, then, that people's reactions to their experiences in small-claims courts are heavily linked to their judgments about the fairness of those experiences (Adler et al., 1983).

Consider why people would ever be willing to reject informal legal settlements (i.e., plea bargaining or pretrial settlement offers), since "Litigation is a negative-sum proposition for the litigants—the longer the process continues, the lower their aggregate wealth" (Loewenstein, Issacharoff, Camerer, & Babcock, 1993, p. 135). The authors suggest that one reason is that "people are influenced powerfully by considerations of fairness [such that] judgments of fairness will exert a significant influence on pretrial negotiations. [In fact], disputants seemed more concerned with achieving what they considered to be a fair settlement of the case than maximizing their own expected value" (p. 139). Rather than "seeking to maximize their own payoffs," litigants were "seeking simply to obtain what they deem fair" (p. 159).

This suggestion is similar to the previously noted discussion of the antecedents of riots and other collective actions. Such collective actions are often spontaneous and driven by a sense of shared social grievance. They occur even when their likelihood of success is minimal (Klandermans, 1989; N. E. Muller, 1980). As N. E. Muller's analysis of the antecedents of aggressive political behavior suggests, "[the finding] clearly indicates that utilitarian justification is by no means the only—or even the major—determinant of participation in aggressive political behavior. There are just too many people with quite high aggressive behavior scores who see little utilitarian justification for such action" (Muller, 1979, p. 79). But what might drive them to participate, despite the feeling of low utilitarian justification? Muller identifies several moral or justice-based factors that are important, including the belief that one's outcomes are unfairly low (just deserts frustration) and normative justifications for aggression (belief in the low legitimacy of government and having a political ideology that suggests violence is acceptable) (Muller, 1979, p. 79).

Walster et al. (1978) suggest that people move in sequence when they react to perceived injustices. They first try to gain compensation; if this fails, they try retribution. Why engage in retribution? Remember that in our earlier discussion we noted that harm doers derogate their victims to justify harm. The argument for retribution is that like compensation, it restores the balance between the parties. Consequently, the harm doer, knowing that equity has been restored, does not need to derogate the victim. However, preventing this second wave of harm (i.e., derogation) is obviously less desirable from the victim's point of view than is restoring actual justice through compensation.

People's reactions may reflect whether they perceive the offense to be material or symbolic in nature (Boeckmann, 1996a). When the offense is perceived to be material, compensation is sought, but if the offense is perceived to be symbolic, retribution is pursued. For example, in contract law, failure to meet the terms of a contract is not a large moral wrong. People must simply pay the injured party under the terms of the contract—that is, what that party probably would have received if the contract had been carried out or what it will cost to replace the defaulting party. In other words, restoring fairness is a simple matter of establishing the appropriate amount for compensation.

However, a symbolic offense such as spitting on the flag or insulting someone's mother is unlikely to be settled by simple compensation. Instead, some type of social response such as an apology is needed. An apology is important because it communicates respect for the rules that have been violated or for the people who have been maligned. In fact, trying to respond to having insulted someone by offering the person money would be viewed as a further insult. The harm doers need to acknowledge their guilt for violating a symbolic rule—in addition to potentially compensating the victim. For example, the Japanese prime minister recently acknowledged fault in the matter of using Korean women as forced prostitutes during World War II. Initially, compensation for the victims was provided. However, this was seen as an inadequate response and an apology was demanded. Such an apology was resisted and debated in the Japanese parliament—even though the parliament had authorized compensation—because it recognized that by apologizing, the Japanese were acknowledging that they had broken moral rules in their original behavior. Interestingly, offering to pay compensation was not regarded as acknowledging having committed a moral wrong, at least to the same degree as apologizing would have been.

When Will People Act Collectively?

Most empirical research has examined the more specific question, When will people react to injustice collectively rather than individually? A variety of research investigations suggest that disadvantageous intergroup comparisons and associated feelings of group relative deprivation promote support or participation in collective behavior (Dube & Guimond, 1986; Hafer & Olson, 1993; Dion, 1986; Olson and Hafer, 1994; Tougas & Veilleux, 1988; I. Walker & Mann, 1987). According to this research, individuals can act as representatives for the entire group; they feel deprived and respond on behalf of the entire group. The manner in which they think about their experience determines how they respond to it behaviorally.

Imagine a female word processor who learns that her male colleague earns two dollars more an hour. On the one hand, she may focus on herself as an individual. In this case, she might decide that she is not all that good or that she does not work that hard, so she does not deserve to receive that extra two dollars herself. On the other hand, she may focus on herself as a *female* word processor. In this case, she may notice not only that she does not earn the same as her male colleague but also that most of the female word processors in her company earn less than their male colleagues. In this latter case, she might decide that there is something wrong with the system and ask her boss for a raise. She might also move toward collective action, trying to organize other female employees to engage in a strike.

These ideas point to the importance of how people frame problems or issues. The idea of framing develops out of the research of Kahneman (1992) that demonstrates that the same experience can have different psychological impacts depending on how it is framed. For example, people are more willing to take risks with gains; therefore, framing a problem as a possible gain leads people to take greater risks than does framing it as a loss. This is true even when the same objective risks are involved. In this case, framing also occurs, but the dimension of framing is individual versus group. For example, if one feels that an injustice occurred because of one's individual characteristics (e.g., being rude, poorly dressed, or unqualified), one reacts differently than if one believes that it was because of one's group characteristics (e.g., being non-White, female, or old). Hence, the core question is how people interpret their experiences.

Thinking of oneself as a unique individual or as a group member (see Chapter 2) can influence people's evaluations of outcomes in unfair situations. For example, in an experimental study (H. J. Smith & Spears, 1996), participants were unfairly deprived of a cash bonus. Participants who were primed to think of themselves as members of a disadvantaged group were much more likely to acknowledge wanting the money than were participants who were primed to think of themselves as unique individuals. In other words, framing the situation in group terms made rationalizing one's fate much less likely. Before people can react to injustice, they must acknowledge it. This research suggests that how people frame their experience is a key influence.

Retributive justice responses also show a sensitivity to whether harm is framed in individual or group terms. If harm is understood as having an impact on the collective, it is punished more severely than if the harm is focused on an individual. This is observed to be the case for both monetary damages (Boeckmann, 1996a) and symbolic harms (Boeckmann & Liew, 1996). Similarly, the individual-versus-collective distinction is seen in punishment for cases of sexual assault (S. C. Wright, Ropp, Jenson, Blucher, & Darrow, 1996). When rape is portrayed as one individual victimizing another, it is punished less severely than when it is portrayed as a hate crime perpetrated against women in general (S. C. Wright et al., 1996).

Distributive and Procedural Injustice

Relative deprivation research often assumes that the key judgment for feelings of group deprivation is the judgment of distributive injustice between groups. However, judgments about differences in the procedural issue of how members of different groups are treated are more strongly related to group resentment and support for collective action than to judgments about outcomes (Dion, 1992). For example, ethnic conflicts generally focus on the degree of ethnic group political participation and representation, recognition of the group's distinct culture, or the elimination of discriminatory institutions and practices—all procedural rather than distributive concerns (Azzi, 1993a, 1993b, 1994). In fact, whether people acknowledge distributive inequities may depend on their perceptions of how those inequities are produced. For example, defendants who believe that judges are neutral and nonbiased evaluate their verdicts to be fairer regardless of whether they are judged innocent or guilty (Tyler, 1990). In other words, procedural justice (or injustice) can act as a heuristic for determining whether the outcomes one (or one's group) receives are fair (Lind, Huo, & Tyler, 1994).

Other research suggests that collective action is motivated by a combination of procedural and distributive injustice. People are most likely to challenge a situation collectively if they believe that the procedures used are unfair and if they have personally suffered because of the injustice (Dibble, 1981). For example, in a study of work tasks, students were most likely to complain to a third-party authority (a campus ethics committee) when they were treated unfairly and received unfavorable outcomes (Greenberg, 1987a). In another study, Greenberg (1993) demonstrated that people were more likely to steal organizational resources if they perceived their outcomes as unfairly low and the procedures used to produce those outcomes as unfair. The potent combination of unfair (collective) treatment and unfair personal outcomes is reminiscent of earlier descriptions of double deprivation (Folger, 1987; Runciman, 1966; Vanneman and Pettigrew, 1972). The study of work tasks also showed that students were more likely to take action when the procedural injustice they experienced reflected institutional policy than when it reflected the actions of a single person (Greenberg, 1987a).

Interestingly, fair procedures appear to mitigate dissatisfaction with unfavorable or unfair outcomes, but it is less clear that they increase satisfaction when outcomes are favorable (see Brockner & Weisenfeld, 1996, for a review). The typical pattern found in studies of procedural justice suggests that people are less upset and angry after receiving a negative or unfair outcome if that outcome is generated by a fair procedure. However, people seem equally satisfied after receiving a fair outcome via a fair or an

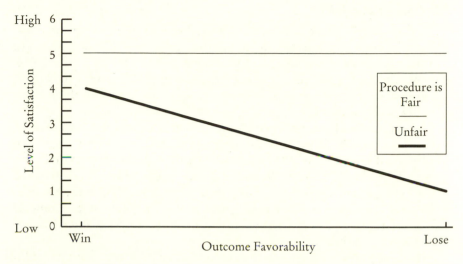

FIGURE 7.3   The influence of outcome and procedure on satisfaction

unfair procedure, even though they recognize the unfairness of the procedure (see Figure 7.3). Thus, outcome favorability and procedural justice
do not impact cumulatively on satisfaction. The key situation is one of
unfair outcomes. If those outcomes are delivered via a fair process, satisfaction is higher.

Intervening Cognitions Between Perceptions of Injustice and Collective Behavior

Although feelings of anger and frustration might prime or motivate people
for particular behaviors, they might not necessarily produce direct engagement in collective action (Ellemers, 1993; Petta & Walker, 1992; S. C. Wright
et al., 1990b). Just as a variety of cognitions determine whether people will
recognize injustice, a second set of cognitions helps determine how people
will react to injustice once they recognize it (Crosby, 1976). Researchers
have explored the influence of three types of factors on the choice to support or participate in collective behavior: (1) people's optimism or pessimism that the situation might change (T. D. Cook, Crosby & Hennigan,
1977; Folger, 1986, 1987), (2) people's beliefs about the relevant intergroup
situation (Ellemers, 1993; Tajfel, 1982), and (3) the pragmatic costs and benefits of collective behavior (Martin, 1986b).

Is Change Possible?

The first set of factors that can promote a collective reaction to group injustice is people's beliefs about the possibility of change. The possibility of future change has been identified by Folger (1986, 1987), Crosby (1976, 1984), Ellemers (1993), and Martin (1981) as a precondition for feelings of deprivation. However, these authors do not agree about how to think about the possibility of future change and what its implications are.

Several authors focus on when people will feel resentful. T. D. Cook et al. (1977) distinguish between future and past expectations. They argue that resentment is most likely to occur when past expectations are high but future feasibility (i.e., the likelihood of change in the future) is low (see also Gurr, 1970). Similarly, Folger (1987) argues that although past expectations can serve as referent outcomes (i.e., outcomes with which people compare their own outcomes), feelings of resentment are unlikely unless future change is not probable.

Other authors focus on whether people will act. Without any hope for change, participation in collective action appears unlikely (Kelly & Kelly, 1994; Lalonde & Cameron, 1994). If the situation is impossible to change, why should people risk reacting to it? More recently, authors have suggested that beliefs about one's (or one's group's) ability to accomplish change shape one's reactions. In fact, several authors have proposed the concept of feelings of collective efficacy (i.e., the belief that as a group, people can accomplish change) as an important determinant of collective behavior (Azzi, 1992; Dion, 1986; Klandermans, 1989). More specifically, Azzi (1992) suggests three types of efficacy beliefs that are important in determining whether people will participate in collective action: (1) individual efficacy (e.g., "I can make a difference"), (2) collective efficacy (e.g., "The group can make a difference"), and (3) participatory efficacy (e.g., "Successful collective action requires my participation"). Participation in collective action is most likely to occur if people believe that their group will be effective only if they participate.

Together, this research suggests that the relationship between future feasibility and participation in collective behavior is likely to be curvilinear, with the most collective behavior occurring at intermediate levels of feasibility. If people believe that a rotten situation will improve without any action, feeling resentful is unlikely; and active reactions to the bad situation perhaps are even more unlikely (Crosby, 1976; Folger, 1987). But if people believe that they or their group cannot make a difference, it is equally unlikely that they will react collectively to perceived injustices (Hogg & Abrams, 1988; Martin, 1986b; Tajfel, 1982).

Martin (1982) distinguishes between two types of deprivation. The first—optimistic group relative deprivation—reflects unexpected violations and should be related to constructive attempts to change the system. This perspective holds that justice has occurred in the past, and justice will occur again in the future. In this context, fairness is normative and procedures exist for correcting deviations from fairness (Leventhal, 1980). As a consequence, people work within the system to right injustice. For example, when people find corruption in city government, they often organize a reform party and seek to put someone new in office. They assume that such constructive actions will be allowed to succeed if they can build sufficient public support. The second type—pessimistic group relative deprivation—reflects expected violations and should be related to violence against the system. In this context, injustice is normative. People expect violations of fairness, and they have no reason to believe that appeals within the system to right injustice will be addressed. Consequently, people must address injustice by creating a new social structure. For example, if people live in an authoritarian society, they expect elections to be rigged, so they will try to destroy the government rather than work with it to create reform. In other words, this perspective holds that there has been no justice in the past, and no justice is to be expected in the future.

Beliefs About the Intergroup Situation

In contrast to the focus by relative deprivation researchers on people's general feelings of optimism or pessimism, social-identity researchers have focused on a second set of variables that might influence whether people will act collectively or individually—their beliefs about the relevant intergroup situation (Ellemers, 1993; Hogg & Abrams, 1988; Tajfel, 1982). According to social-identity theory, there are three important variables that influence beliefs about the intergroup situation. One important variable is whether deprived or disadvantaged group members believe the boundaries between groups are *permeable*. A permeable boundary is one that people can pass through. In the classic Horatio Alger story, Horatio was a poor boy who began working in a company and eventually became a company boss. He passed through the boundary between workers and managers. (How? He married the boss's daughter!)

If people believe the boundaries of groups are permeable, they may try to pass through or assimilate into a higher-status group (D. M. Taylor & McKirnan, 1984; S. C. Wright et al., 1990a). In fact, most people will continue to prefer individual over collective strategies of action even if they believe the collective situation is unjust (S. C. Wright et al., 1990a). However, if group members believe the boundaries between groups are impermeable (i.e., closed) and that passing through is impossible, they are more likely to focus on collective strategies. For example, many workers in early twentieth-century America did not believe that they could work hard and become owners and bosses. So they focused their energy on organizing collective workers' unions that made demands for changes in their social and economic status.

Permeability is directly examined by S. C. Wright et al. (1990b), who explore the antecedents of doing nothing, acting individually, and acting collectively. They find that as predicted by social-identity theory, people respond to open group boundaries with individual efforts—that is, by trying to pass into the higher-status group. They respond to closed group boundaries by collective efforts to improve the status of the group (see Figure 7.4).

Interestingly, this research illustrates that as long as a few token members of disadvantaged groups are able to assimilate into a higher-status group (thereby demonstrating permeability), people respond to injustice individually. Looking at Figure 7.4, one sees very little difference between a 2 percent and a 30 percent quota in collective nonnormative behavior. Only a closed system significantly increases such behavior. Hence, systems benefit from allowing a few of the members of disadvantaged groups to pass upward (S. C. Wright et al., 1990b).

This discussion makes clear that whether people can move from group to group is a crucial determinant of social dynamics within society. Some societies, including the American society, base group distinctions on achieved characteristics such as education that allow all people to potentially pass from group to group. In contrast, societies based upon ascribed characteristics, such as ethnicity or race, create some groups that have more difficulty being mobile. In India, for example, people were traditionally born into a caste that defined their status in life, and little mobility was possible.

In America, immigrants whose physical appearances were indistinguishable from "mainstream" European Americans historically assimilated more easily than African Americans, whose physical differences from European Americans were readily identifiable. Similarly, today those immigrants from Russia who are physically indistinguishable from European-Americans assimilate more easily than those, for example, from Asia who are physically distinct. Indeed, one could argue that during World War II, it was much more feasible to identify and place Japanese Americans in concentration camps than to take the same actions against Italian Americans and German Americans who could not be physically distinguished from other European Americans. As this shows, Japanese Americans had greater difficulty passing as Americans.

However, it is important not to overstate the role of physical characteristics in creating social distinctions. Categories are socially constructed and can be based upon many types of physical (e.g., appearance, speech, and so forth) or psychological characteristics (i.e., attitudes and values). People are capable of making clear and important social distinctions where minor physical characteristics exist. For example, people in Northern Ireland make

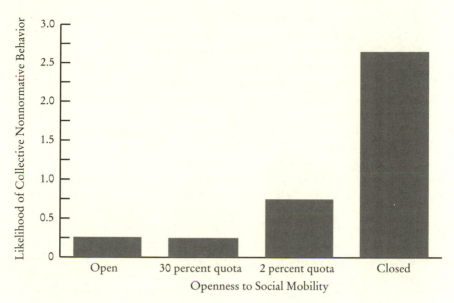

FIGURE 7.4   Group openness and the likelihood of collective nonnormative behavior. SOURCE: "Responding to Membership in a Disadvantaged Group: From Acceptance to Collective Protest," by S. C. Wright, D. M. Taylor, and F. M. Moghaddam, 1990, *Journal of Personality and Social Psychology, 58,* 994–1003. Copyright 1990 American Psychological Association. Adapted with permission.

a distinction between being Protestant and being Catholic, even though this difference is not directly related to obvious physical differences (Stringer & Lavery, 1987). Nonetheless, this distinction has been the basis for creating a social hierarchy, rewarding in-group members, punishing the members of out-groups, and even fighting wars.

Our previous discussion of procedural justice pointed out the possibility of voice effects—that is, the effects of having influence over decisions. People were found to feel more fairly treated if they were given the opportunity to speak, even when their arguments did not influence the decisions made. Similarly, S. C. Wright et al. (1990b) find that people are more satisfied with partially open systems, even when those systems provide very little opportunity for true mobility. In both cases, the structural features of the procedure (i.e., voice or openness) lead to satisfaction, even when those features have very little effect on the outcomes obtained by the disadvantaged.

These findings suggest that people may focus on the appearance of justice, as reflected by procedural features, and not on the attainment of justice, as reflected in favorable opportunities or outcomes. Social critics have referred to this tendency as the creation of false consciousness—a belief that justice is being obtained when in fact it is not. Critics of social institutions such as the courts suggest that the symbols of justice associated with the courts—for example, the statues depicting justice found in many courts—are intended to convey the image of procedural fairness on a structural level. This image in turn encourages people to feel that their concerns are being addressed and their needs are being met by the courts.

On a societal level, similar arguments have been made about the U.S. Supreme Court. Scheingold's 1974 book *The Politics of Rights* argues that disadvantaged groups use appeals to the Court as a way of claiming rights, rights that can then entitle them to increased social resources. Scheingold suggests that the Court seldom grants such rights but provides opportunities for expressing and articulating grievances. In a comment on this symbolic feature of the courts, Haney (1991) uses the provocative title "Let Them Eat Due Process" to suggest that the courts provide symbolic but not real (i.e., distributive) justice. In other words, the courts create the impression that boundaries are more permeable than they actually are. This analysis assumes that increased resources, not respect, is what people really want (or at least ought to want) from society (see Chapter 8).

A second key variable identified by social-identity theorists is whether people believe the relationships between different groups are stable or unstable (e.g., whether the group's position as a whole can change or switch with another group's position). Deprived or disadvantaged group members who view the relationship as unstable are more likely to compete directly and collectively with the higher-status group (Ellemers, 1993; Hogg & Abrams, 1988; Major, 1994).

For example, consider the long-term rivalry between the University of California at Berkeley and Stanford University. In addition to physical proximity, this rivalry is fueled by the fact that the strengths of each university are approximately in balance, leading each to feel that it can be the higher-status group. In fact, in some years Berkeley academic departments are ranked higher than Stanford departments in national comparisons, and in other years the opposite occurs.

The Berkeley-Stanford rivalry also illustrates the social construction of status in the way each university presents itself in comparison to the other. For example, Berkeley recently used national status ratings to argue that it is the highest status university in America. To do so, it emphasized that thirty-five of thirty-six Berkeley departments were rated in the top ten in their field (including the Classics, German Literature, and Music Departments). In contrast, Stanford outranked Berkeley in many (but not all) key departments such as the Departments of Neurosciences, Computer Sciences, Economics, and Psychology. The point is not which of these two excellent universities is actually "more" excellent. It is that groups try to frame status comparisons in ways that emphasize their own merits. The point is that this rivalry is encouraged by the feeling in both groups that the status hierarchy is unstable and either group could move ahead.

In contrast, in situations in which change seems unlikely, people are less invested in issues of status. The caste system of Hindu society in India is an example of a status hierarchy that traditionally was very stable. Since status was based upon ascribed characteristics, there was little people could do to change their status. Interestingly, in recent years, the caste system has become more open to change. For example, McKibben (1996) notes that the caste system in the Kerala region was traditionally associated with status differences and promoted economic injustices. This unjust system remained unchallenged for much of the region's history until a reformer created the impression that the system could be challenged. The reformer's efforts were focused upon questioning the moral legitimacy of the caste system. Subsequently, the caste system was reformed, resulting in greater social and economic justice in Kerala (McKibben, 1996).

The focus on the caste system's moral legitimacy illustrates the third key variable: whether people believe the relationships between groups are legitimate or illegitimate. Feelings of group deprivation assume prior assessments of entitlement at the group level, just as feelings of personal deprivation assume prior assessments of entitlement at the personal level (Crosby, 1976; Major, 1994). One important antecedent to feelings of group deprivation is beliefs about the legitimacy of the intergroup situation (Ellemers, 1993; Major, 1994; Tajfel, 1982). If status relations between groups are perceived to be legitimate, high-status and low-status groups will not be considered comparable, and objective inequalities will be considered irrelevant (Ellemers, 1993; Major, 1994). In contrast, the belief that intergroup status relations are illegitimate should promote social comparisons between groups. Furthermore, the belief that the position for the entire group is illegitimate (as opposed to one's personal inclusion in the group) promotes increased identification with the group. This makes it more likely that people will experience feelings of group rather than individual relative deprivation (Ellemers, 1993). Finally, if intergroup relations are perceived to be illegitimate, people may be more likely to consider alternative arrangements. Similarly, if people can imagine alternative arrangements, they will be more likely to view the current situation as illegitimate. For example, in South Africa, people accepted segregation for many years. However, when change became possible, the traditional system was increasingly viewed as illegitimate.

It is the combination of these three variables that forms people's beliefs and reactions to a particular intergroup situation. For example, disadvantaged group members will prefer to compete with an advantaged group directly through political lobbying, terrorism, revolution, war, or civil rights activity if they perceive the relationships between the groups to be illegitimate and unstable and the boundaries between groups to be impermeable (Hogg & Abrams, 1988).

Costs and Benefits of Action

The third set of factors that might influence whether people react collectively or individually is assessments of personal costs and benefits. For example, research indicates that people show a greater willingness to engage in collective behavior when there are more mobilization resources present, independent of their feelings of resentment (Martin, 1986b). This research suggests that collective behavior may be determined both by the potential costs of the behavior and by psychological comparisons (Klandermans, 1989; Martin, 1986b, Van Knippenberg, 1989). In other words, people begin with the least costly strategy. For example, the acceptance of an unfair situation or the attempt to pass (i.e., change group membership) rather than to challenge the status quo directly may not reflect differences in feelings of group-oriented deprivation. Rather, it may reflect differences in the anticipated costs and benefits of different behaviors.

An example of a cost-benefit analysis for close relationships is provided by Rusbult (1987). Rusbult uses the investment model to examine the antecedents of exit (leaving a situation), voice (trying to change the situation), loyalty (waiting for improvement), and neglect (ignoring problems). She argues that two judgments are central to people's behavioral decisions: how much they have invested in the situation and the quality of their alternatives. Greater investment encourages voice; lower investment, exit. Higher quality alternatives encourage exit and inhibit loyalty. In each case, the nature of people's behavioral response to injustice is believed to be linked to assessments of outcome gain and loss.

One limitation of many analyses of costs and benefits is that they neglect the psychological consequences for different behavioral choices. For example, passing or assimilating to another group is not without its psychological costs to the person involved. Disadvantaged group members are often faced with a choice between being a low-status member of a high-status group and being a high-status member of a low-status group (Tyler, Degoey & Smith, 1996). Passing upward to a higher status group improves a person's group status, often at a cost to one's personal status within the group. In fact, one's personal position in a group is more closely related to feelings of self-worth than the group's position in the larger society, suggesting one reason why moving from a low-status to higher-status group is not always attractive (Tyler, Degoey, & Smith, 1996). In other words, the self-esteem of disadvantaged individuals often suffers when those individuals move into higher-status groups.

In addition, fellow members of disadvantaged groups or categories can hold people accountable to the group, thereby making assimilation to other groups difficult. For example, workers typically keep their job applications to other organizations secret from their coworkers, fearing negative reactions. Similarly, in recent years, young research-oriented faculty have sometimes taken jobs in less prestigious schools, hoping to move up. These young faculty members do research in the hope that they will secure positions in higher-status research-oriented schools. But they often encounter both subtle and overt social pressures from the colleagues at their current school to not be disloyal by publishing more than the norm. Consequently, the young faculty members often minimize discussing their research and writing activities with their current colleagues, but they emphasize the activities when applying for other (higher status) jobs.

Disadvantaged groups can also discourage assimilation by providing social support and emotional resources for dealing with potential difficulties and threats from outside the group (Abrams, 1990; Hyman & Singer, 1968). By building social bonds with talented group members, the group can discourage them from trying to leave the group.

A second difficulty with the current emphasis on the costs and benefits of participation in collective action is that it provides a better explanation of who does *not* participate than who does (Klandermans, 1993). Klandermans notes that people often participate in collective action in spite of formidable obstacles (e.g., group meetings are outlawed) and huge potential costs (e.g., physical danger). Empirical research also shows that people often participate in social movements even when the chance of success is slight (Klandermans, 1993). For example, both participants and nonparticipants in the Dutch Peace Demonstrations in the early 1980s believed that they could not control the nuclear arms race. However, participants in the demonstrations were significantly more likely to have friends and relatives who also demonstrated, and they valued the general goal of nuclear weapons reduction more highly than did nonparticipants (Klandermans and Oegema, 1987). This research suggests that having interpersonal connections and ideological commitments are as important to determining participation in collective action as making an analysis of potential costs and benefits. Furthermore, an emphasis on costs and benefits does not recognize that people vary in the strength of their feelings. On the contrary, those with greater feelings of injustice will be motivated to overcome higher barriers to participation, to seek resources that are not easily available, and to be more receptive to ideological alternatives to the status quo.

Rule Breaking Versus Rule Following

Clearly, both individual and collective nonnormative responses to injustice create significant social problems for the larger society. If individual workers, for example, engage in sabotage or slacking off on the job, they hurt their company. Similarly, collective disorders such as riots threaten public safety and often cause widespread death and destruction.

One means of avoiding these problems is by fostering the conditions that lead to normative, as opposed to nonnormative, responses on the part of individuals or groups. Normative responses include voluntary decision acceptance, voluntary compliance with rules, and voluntary efforts to help the group. The study of legitimacy addresses these issues. Concern about the legitimacy of authority leads to a recognition that the study of the occurrence of rule breaking behavior (the dominant focus of the previous research) needs to be supplemented with research focused on the antecedents of rule acceptance and rule following. Such a shift further leads to increased attention to procedural issues. This is because studies suggest that people who experience procedural justice when they deal with authorities are more likely to view those authorities as legitimate, to accept their decisions, and to obey social rules (Earley & Lind, 1987; Friedland, Thibaut, & Walker, 1973; Lind, Kanfer, & Earley, 1990; Lind, Kulik, Ambrose, & Park, 1993; MacCoun et al., 1988; McEwen & Maiman, 1984; Pruitt, Pierce, McGillicuddy, Welton, & Castrianno, 1993; Rasinski, 1987; Rasinski & Tyler, 1987; Thibaut, Friedland, & Walker, 1974; Tyler, 1990, 1994a; Tyler & Lind, 1992).

More generally, procedural justice is found to promote a positive climate within organizations. For example, it encourages commitment to the organization, and it encourages the willingness to accept third-party decisions (Greenberg, 1987a; Lind, 1990; Lind et al., 1993; MacCoun et al., 1988), accept arbitration awards (Lind, 1990), follow group rules (Friedland et al., 1973; Greenberg, 1994; Thibaut et al., 1974), and engage in organizational citizenship behaviors such as volunteering to work on behalf of the group (Moorman, 1991; Moorman, Neihoff, & Organ, 1993; Niehoff & Moorman, 1993; Organ & Moorman, 1993).

Procedural justice also diminishes certain other aspects of behavior. Research has shown, for example, that perceptions of procedural justice mitigate the intention to leave the organization (Dailey & Kirk, 1992; Konovsky & Cropanzano, 1991; Schaubroeck, May, & Brown, 1994), the intention to sue in court (Bies & Tyler, 1993), and the willingness to support strikes and sit-ins (Leung, Chiu, & Au, 1993). In other words, procedural justice encourages people not to take actions that hurt their group or organization.

To authorities in organized groups, legitimacy is the primary focus of concern when considering the ability of authorities to function effectively. Morality, although important, can work either in favor of or against the actions of authorities. People might support authorities because they think their actions are moral, or they might oppose them because they think their actions are not moral. Legitimacy—the feeling of obligation to follow the decisions of group authorities and group rules—works to the benefit of group authorities. What causes legitimacy? Tyler (1990) examined this issue by considering the subset of his larger group of respondents who had recent personal experiences with police officers or judges. He found that the primary factor shaping the impact of experience on legitimacy was a judgment about the fairness of the decisionmaking procedure. This linkage of procedural justice to legitimacy and, through legitimacy, to rule following behavior has been widely confirmed.

Tyler (1990) examined the antecedents of rule following behavior in a random sample of 1,575 citizens in Chicago. He found that both feelings about the morality of rule following and judgments about the legitimacy of legal authorities affected people's everyday rule following behavior. That is, those who felt that it was morally wrong to break rules and those who felt an obligation to obey legal authorities were more likely to voluntarily follow the law. His first conclusion was that rule following behavior is strongly influenced by moral and legitimacy-based judgments. Those judgments were as or more important than evaluations of the likelihood of being caught and punished for rule breaking. This finding is consistent with other research suggesting that fear of punishment has, at best, a minor influence on rule following behavior.

MacCoun (1993) estimates that in the area of drug use, variations in the perceived severity or certainty of punishment explain approximately 5 percent of the variance in drug use. Hence, rule following behavior is primarily responsive to moral concerns and judgments about legitimacy. In discussions of the acceptance of decisions and rules made by national authorities, procedural justice similarly is widely hypothesized to be an antecedent of legitimacy and acceptance for political and legal authorities (Easton, 1965, 1975; Kelman, 1969). Theoretical discussions of authority distinguish between support for the policies and decisions of incumbent authorities and support for the procedures and institutions of government. This latter, diffuse form of support is viewed as the key to the willingness to accept decisions and rules. This diffuse-support hypothesis is supported empirically in studies of both national legal authorities such as the Supreme Court (Murphy & Tanenhaus, 1969; Tyler & Mitchell, 1994) and national political authorities such as Congress (Tyler, 1994b; Tyler, Rasinski, & McGraw, 1985).

These arguments suggest that procedures can act as a cushion of support, allowing authorities to deliver unpopular decisions without losing support in the eyes of the public. To an important extent, people are satisfied irrespective of their decision because of the fairness of the procedure. However, if the procedure is viewed as unfair, dissatisfaction is linked to the favorability of the outcome.

In our earlier discussion of distributive justice (Chapter 3), we noted Deutsch's (1975, p. 147) "crude hypothesis of social relations." Deutsch argues that the principles used to define distributive justice both arise from and define the nature of social relationships. Similarly, procedural justice both arises from and defines legitimacy. If people think that the procedures of government are fair, they regard government as more legitimate. Conversely, if they regard government as legitimate, they regard the procedures of government as fairer.

Part 4

Why Do People Care About Justice?

The first two parts of this book were concerned with establishing the important role of justice in shaping people's psychological and behavioral reactions to their social experiences. But it is not enough to know that justice matters. It is also important to ask why justice matters. We will now turn to an examination of psychological theories that explore people's motivations for caring about issues of justice.

Two basic bodies of theory have defined people's relationships to groups: resource based theories and identity based theories. Resource-based theories suggest that people interact with others because they value the resources they gain. Identity based theories suggest that people interact with others because they use their experiences with others to help them define their own identities and to assess their self-worth. Each of these basic psychological theories has led to the development of a psychological perspective on the justice motive. This section outlines each perspective and then looks at research that compares them.

8

THE NATURE OF
THE JUSTICE MOTIVE

Theories of Justice

Resource Based Theories

A core question within social psychology is why people or groups engage in social interactions with others. One psychological model that has been proposed to address this general question emphasizes the desire to more effectively obtain personally desired resources. Although it is possible for each individual or group to create all of the resources needed to live without interacting with others, there are clear advantages to specialization in the production of food and other life essentials. Robinson Crusoe may have been able to live alone on a desert island, but the quality of his life clearly would have been better if he had been able to cooperate with others with whom he could exchange resources.

Everyone, including those who have tried to move furniture alone, recognizes that there are benefits to being able to exchange help and resources with others. Indeed, specialization *requires* the ability to exchange resources with others. Devoting one's life to becoming excellent in some skill, whether it is brain surgery or plumbing, requires being able to rely upon others for resources. One cannot, for example, grow one's own food and build one's own shelter while spending twelve-hour days learning brain surgery. Hence, exchange with others introduces the advantages—but also the problems—of social interaction between people and groups.

The argument that people are instrumental in their orientation and enter into social interactions to gain resources for themselves and their group is central to two theories within social psychology. On the group level, this theoretical model is called realistic group conflict theory; on the individual level, it is called social exchange theory.

Realistic group conflict theory is an instrumental theory of intergroup behavior. It assumes that people are self-interested and try to maximize their own rewards in their dealings with others. This motivation is further reflected in the groups to which people belong. Consequently, the nature of interactions among groups is determined primarily by the nature of the interdependence between groups. If groups are in competition, conflict will result. If their interests are compatible, they will cooperate.

An example of realistic group conflict is provided by a study by Sherif and colleagues (Sherif, Harvey, White, Hood, & Sherif, 1961). In that study, a group of eleven-year-old children were recruited to participate in a summer camp. Initially, all of the children were part of one group. However, in the second stage of the experiment, two groups were created—the "rattlers" and the "eagles." These two groups were then put into competition. The researchers found that this competition produced in-group friendships and hostility toward the other group. That hostility led to conflict. In the third stage, both groups were required to work together to achieve mutually beneficial goals. For example, the two groups had to pool their money to rent a film both groups wanted to see. The joint cooperation lessened hostility.

In each stage, the climate within each group and between groups was shaped by the objective nature of the interdependence between the groups. When the groups were competing for resources, hostility arose; when they were cooperating, friendship arose. Thus, group conflict was predicted by the objective (i.e., realistic) relationship between the groups (see R. Levine & Campbell, 1972). An example of the application of this approach is the jigsaw classroom (Aronson, Stephan, Sikes, Blaney, & Snapp, 1978). In such a classroom, members of different groups have information or skills crucial to the success of the group project. Only if members of different groups work together can the project go well.

A second instrumental theory is social-exchange theory. The common theme linking realistic group conflict theory and social-exchange theory is the assumption that people or groups enter into interactions with the motive of gaining resources and that this motive governs (1) their behaviors within interactions, (2) their choices about whether to stay or leave, and (3) their feelings. In social-exchange theory, individuals are the focus of analysis. However, the assumptions about those individuals are similar to those outlined about groups. Thibaut and Kelley (1959) argue, for example, that (1) one's satisfaction is determined by one's level of obtained resources relative to a comparison level and (2) one's behavior reflects one's judgment of the most profitable actions in which to engage. This judgment results from comparing one's current behavior and its expected gains and loses to the expected gains and losses of alternative behaviors in which one might be engaged.

There are many variations of basic instrumental models, depending on the degree to which they emphasize concerns over short-term self-interest. In the context of ongoing relations with others, an instrumentally motivated person might take a long-term view, thinking that membership in a group or relationship, although initially costly, will be beneficial in the long run. People often engage in costly and difficult courses of action—such as going to law school or medical school—because they anticipate that in the long run, these actions will be personally beneficial. The manner in which judgments can be transformed to incorporate long-term concerns is outlined by Kelley and Thibaut (1978).

The dominant psychological models of the justice motive begin with the assumption that people are basically motivated by self-interest when they interact with others (Walster et al., 1978; Thibaut & Walker, 1975). The social-exchange model of justice begins with the assumption that people want to regularize their interactions with others. To do so in social interactions, people collectively develop mutually accepted systems for allocating resources, systems with rules that are codified in terms of fairness. People expect others to follow these rules and expect to follow the same rules themselves (Walster et al., 1978).

Hence, justice concerns arise out of the motivation to gain long-term benefits from social interactions. People follow justice rules as long as it is in their interest to do so. Similarly, they enforce those rules because it is in their own interest to do so. Although people are concerned about issues of justice, that concern supports their efforts to maximize their own gains in interactions by preserving mutually beneficial exchange relationships (Thibaut & Walker, 1975).

Like Walster et al. (1978), Thibaut and Walker (1975) make instrumental issues central to their model of justice. In Thibaut and Walker's studies, judgments are made about control. They argue that in all social interactions, people want to maximize their control over outcomes so as to best satisfy their own self-interest. Normally, people want to have direct control over their outcomes in exchanges with others. This occurs in market situations in which people are free to accept or reject buying a good at the price indicated by the seller. People are free to simply walk away.

However, in conflicts, people are often in situations in which they need to reach some type of settlement. Typically, conflicts occur in the context of ongoing interactions, so people either do not wish to or are not free to simply walk away from the relationship. For example, when businesses cannot meet the terms of a contract, they must somehow accommodate those with whom they have an agreement. Similarly, neighbors, coworkers, and family members must interact in the future and need to find some way to cooperate.

In such situations, people often turn to third parties to help them resolve a dispute. Such third parties can be informal authorities such as a parent, community leader, or mutual friend. They can also be judges, mediators, therapists, or members of the clergy. Whoever they are, such third parties take some of the powers away from the disputants and use it to try to resolve the dispute. In situations such as mediation—in which they have little power—third parties give advice. In situations such as a court proceeding or arbitration—in which they have more power—they can control what the solution will be.

When people give up outcome control, they seek to maximize their remaining control through control over the process of presenting evidence. Hence, people like the adversary system and view it as fair precisely because it gives them high levels of control over evidence presentation (through their lawyers) in the context of low levels of control over the outcome. The adversary system is effective at resolving disputes because third parties have the power to make binding decisions and, perhaps more important, because people feel that they have been given an opportunity to influence those decisions. According to Thibaut and Walker (1975), people do not simply see this system as leading to favorable decisions; they also regard it as fair. This sense of fairness develops from the feeling that it is a fair procedure and that it leads to fair outcomes (for cases of conflict of interest, see Thibaut & Walker, 1978).

The instrumental models of justice outlined have an interesting irony. In previous chapters, we have detailed the widespread and important impact of justice on people's thoughts and behaviors. We might be inclined to move from that demonstration to the view that people are intrinsically moral or concerned about justice. Yet, the models outlined make no such claim. Instead, they view people as basically self-interested. Their concerns about justice develop out of such self-interested concerns. In other words, justice is good business!

According to instrumental models, people should not care about justice unless it is in their self-interest. That is, people should not care about justice in anonymous situations in which their responses cannot be publicly determined. However, we have already noted that people do care about justice in anonymous situations, suggesting that people have some basic commitment to justice. Yet, there may still be situations in which instrumental concerns are important.

Identity Based Theories

In contrast to instrumental models, an identity perspective suggests that people are motivated by their desire for positive regard from important others. This perspective reflects the sociological tradition of symbolic-interaction and role-theory research that assumes that people construct their sense of self based on how they feel others view them (see the idea of reflected appraisals, Mead, 1934, and the "looking glass self," Cooley, 1902). Social identity theory (Tajfel & Turner, 1986) follows this basic premise, but it more specifically suggests that an important part of people's self-concept is based on membership in important groups and social categories—their social identity. Those group identifications, combined with unique individual characteristics, merge to form people's self-concepts. Social identity theorists argue that people are interested in creating positive social identities that lead them to feel self-respect and self-esteem. As part of this effort, people prefer to identify themselves with positively valued groups.

This approach is fundamentally different from an instrumental approach because it suggests that people interact with others out of a desire to gain identity-relevant information. The social identity perspective emphasizes people's desire to belong to positively valued groups. The pride that people feel in memberships in those groups positively enhances their feelings of self-worth and their self-esteem. This enhancement occurs both intrinsically and through favorable comparisons with out-groups (Tyler, Huo, & Smith, 1995). Thus, people are motivated to join groups with favorable evaluations. Once in those groups, they are motivated both to feel good about those group memberships and to enhance their self-worth by comparing themselves with less favorable groups. Both membership in positive groups and group distinctiveness (being better than other groups) enhance self-esteem.

Although social identity theory emphasizes the importance of belonging to positively evaluated groups (i.e., from their position as a member of different groups), other identity models suggest that people also derive identity-relevant information from their positions within groups. The respect that people feel they have within their group (e.g., their reputation within their community) also contributes to people's feelings of self-esteem and self-worth (Tyler et al., 1996). Like social identity, this model argues that people interact with others because of a desire to feel good about themselves.

An example of the basic argument of social identity theory is provided by the minimal group experiments of Tajfel and Turner (1979). In these studies, students were arbitrarily divided into groups that were not in competition over resources, and membership in a given group did not reflect any real or important distinction between the people involved in other groups. For example, in one experiment, students were divided into groups based upon their ability to estimate the number of dots on a screen (overestimaters versus underestimaters); in another experiment, a different group was divided based on the flip of a coin. Participants were told to award points for accomplishing certain tasks to members of their group and members of the other group. Their choices were completely anonymous, and their choices would not influence whether they would gain points for themselves or not. Interestingly, people exhibited in-group favoritism, giving more points to persons in their group and evaluating their own group more positively than the other group. Tajfel and Turner argue that this finding reflects people's ability to identify with groups defined by even the most trivial criteria and their consequent desire to belong to the best group.

Social-identity theory has been applied to the justice arena in the group value model of procedural justice (Lind & Tyler, 1988). Based on social identity models of the person, the group-value model argues that people use evidence that they are receiving distributive, procedural, and retributive justice as an indicator of the quality of their social relationship to the group and its authorities (Lind & Tyler, 1988; Tyler & Lind, 1992). If people receive unfairly low outcomes, are subjected to rude or insensitive treatment, or fail to have wrongs against them avenged, these experiences communicate information indicating marginal social status. Conversely, if people receive fair outcomes from others, are listened to, and have wrongs against them corrected by society—through retribution, compensation, or other mechanisms—they feel respected and valued by their group.

A variety of terms have been used to discuss the general class of models that we will call identity-based models. These models all focus on social relationships as a cause of people's judgments and behaviors. Further, they all consider how people's connections to others are linked to their efforts to use their social relationships to form their identities. These identities shape conceptions of self and judgments of self-esteem and self-worth. The group value model of justice argues that people define justice by focusing on the social meaning of others' actions. In other words, people use the justice of their experiences with others to understand their status. The relational model of authority extends this argument by suggesting that the relational indices of interpersonal respect, trustworthiness and neutral treatment, which are key antecedents of procedural justice, also communicate social information. That is, the way that people are treated by group authorities tells them about their status within the group. Further, social identity theory suggests that people more generally draw self-identity from group memberships, and that these identities shape their sense of self and their behavior toward others within their group and toward outsiders.

Identity-based models also make the broader point that group rules, norms, and values define the group. Hence, those group rules, norms, and values define the people within groups because they are using group information to construct their social identities. The actions of group authorities are symbolic and reflect the manner in which the group defines itself. This symbolic, or moral, function of rules recognizes that rules and authorities are representatives of the group and reflect group values. When we talk about the symbolic function of rules, we are talking about the manner in which those rules reflect the underlying social values about right and wrong held by members of society. Such values, which are internalized by group members as part of the socialization process, define the group and its rules, authorities, and institutions. They also define the social identities of group members.

The group value model of justice recognizes two ways in which the procedures people experience are important. First, as noted previously, people receive information about their status from their treatment by groups. Second, people receive information about the status of the group itself. For example, most groups pay considerable attention to treating group members publicly with respect and dignity and showing respect for their rights. In a trial, the rights of defendants are publicly acknowledged. These public actions demonstrate to group members that their group is highly desirable and that membership within it is valuable. In other words, they reinforce the judgment that the group itself is a high status group.

A key difference between the group value model and social exchange models of justice is the assumption that people do not evaluate their social relationships solely in terms of the number of resources they receive from others. People use their outcomes and treatment by authorities as a source of information about their position within their group. Knowing that one is a valuable and worthy member of the group has positive implications for self-esteem and feelings of self-worth (Vermunt, van den Bos & Lind, 1993; Tyler, Degoey & Smith, 1996). According to the group-value model, justice is connected to people's feelings about their group membership, social status, self-worth, and self-concepts (Lind & Tyler, 1988; Tyler & Lind, 1992).

The centrality of relational concerns—neutrality, trustworthiness, and status recognition—to procedural justice explains the important role of procedural justice in shaping judgments about authorities and institutions. Authorities and institutions embody the cultural and social values of the group. Their actions speak for the group. Political theorists (Lane, 1988; Rawls, 1971) recognize that self-respect is affected by assessments about how one is treated by authorities. In fact, such assessments are especially strongly affected by treatment by political, legal, and managerial authorities.

One's position in the group is not only an issue of self-esteem and self-worth. Group members with more advantageous positions also believe that the authorities involved will treat them fairly, so they will not be disadvantaged by group membership. In other words, people care about the quality of their outcomes over time. In this regard, social-exchange and identity models of the justice motive are similar. Both argue that people have a concern about their long-term outcomes in social interactions. The key distinction lies in the broader focus of identity models on intergroup and intragroup social status and the quality of the connections individuals have with the social group.

The group-value model refers to the motivations underlying people's concerns about justice. Tyler and Lind (1992) also extend this model to discuss the antecedents of support for social authorities and rules. This model is referred to as the relational model of authority. It develops from the finding, already outlined, that procedural justice is a key antecedent of judgments about authorities and rules (Tyler, 1990).

Possible Other Models

A group value model is one alternative to the instrumental or social exchange model. However, it is important to recognize the possibility that other, as yet undeveloped, models exist. People may care about noninstrumental issues besides social identity and group status. Other possibilities include social and sociostructural responsibilities. J. G. Miller and Bersoff (1992) argue that in some contexts, justice concerns arise from obligations to be responsive to the wants and needs of members of one's social group. Similarly, Kelman and Hamilton (1989) argue that accepting particular social or organizational roles (e.g., manager) carries with it a set of obligations. These obligations may include distributive concerns such as meeting the needs of subordinates, procedural concerns such as treating subordinates with neutrality, and retributive concerns such as accepting responsibility for the misdeeds of subordinates.

Other models could be based on the types of emotional relationships people have with others. For example, studies of children's willingness to help their aging parents find that liking is an important mediator of willingness to help (Pratt, Schmall, & Wright, 1987).

In addition, recent discussions in evolutionary psychology have suggested that justice motivations are "hardwired" (R. Wright, 1994). The evolutionary argument is that conflicts between the motivation to engage in self-interested behavior and the need for cooperation faced by human ancestors in interdependence relationships have selected for those who display a sense of justice. This innate sense is said to be the biological check that makes reciprocal altruism an effective strategy for social groups. In other words, groups that are able to cooperate have an advantage over solitary actors, so those groups have prevailed. To cooperate, groups have needed to have a sense of justice and injustice—that is, a sense of how to appropriately give and take in cooperation situations.

Evidence from Research

Comparing Psychological Models by Examining How People Define the Fairness of Procedures

One approach to comparing the instrumental and the group value models is to examine the antecedents of justice judgments. Considerable research of this type has occurred in the area of procedural justice during the last twenty years. This work has been inspired by the research of Thibaut and Walker (1975), research grounded in their control model.

The control model of Thibaut and Walker (1975) has been widely studied in the context of people's evaluations of their experiences with third parties. The findings of the research support the Thibaut and Walker model in that people judge procedures to be fairer when those procedures give them control over outcomes (Lind & Tyler, 1988). However, findings of studies of control do not simply follow the instrumental model suggested by Thibaut and Walker. That model links the value of process control to its influence on decision control, arguing that people care about process control because it gives them influence over outcomes.

Contrary to the instrumental predictions of control theory, studies suggest that process control is often more important than decision control (Lind et al., 1983; Tyler, 1987; Tyler, Rasinski & Spodick, 1985). Further, studies suggest that people value process control even when it does not influence decision control (Lind, Kanfer, & Earley, 1990; Musante, Gilbert, & Thibaut, 1983; Tyler, Rasinski, & Spodick, 1985). The most compelling demonstration is the experiment by Lind, Kanfer, and Earley (1990). The findings, shown in Table 8.1, indicate that people value voice even after the decision has been made. In fact, the only precondition for the occurrence of the process control effect seems to be that people feel their views are being considered by the decisionmaker (Tyler, Rasinski & Spodick, 1985).

Control studies typically find that both decision control and process control have independent influences on procedural justice (Shapiro & Brett, 1993; Tyler, 1987; Tyler, Rasinski, & Spodick, 1985)—that is, process control effects are partially, but not completely, explainable in terms of indirect decision control. To at least some extent, process control effects are noninstrumental in character. Such effects have been labeled value-expressive. Studies make clear that at least to some degree, people regard procedures as fairer simply because they are allowed voice or process control in

TABLE 8.1   Procedural Justice and Timing of Input

Dependent Measures	Experimental Condition		
	No Input	*Postdecision Input*	*Predecision Input*
Procedural justice	2.43	3.15	3.70
Acceptance of goal	4.33	5.67	5.93

Higher scores indicate more justice and greater willingness to accept the goal.

SOURCE: From "Voice, Control, and Procedural Justice: Instrumental and Noninstrumental Concerns in Fairness Judgments," by A. E. Lind, R. Kanfer, and P. C. Earley, 1990, *Journal of Personality and Social Psychology, 59*. Copyright 1990 American Psychological Association. Adapted with permission.

"Sorry, no water. We're just a support group."

FIGURE 8.1   SOURCE: Drawing by Cheney. Copyright © 1993 *The New Yorker* Magazine, Inc. Reprinted with permission.

those procedures, irrespective of whether that process control is linked to influence over outcomes. For example, Lind, Kanfer, and Earley (1990) allowed people to present evidence in one of two ways: (1) before a decision that affected them and (2) after the decision had already been made. These two conditions were compared with a situation in which people had no input into the decision. The results indicate that although the magnitude of the process control effect diminished, it did not disappear in the post-decision input condition. In other words, a good process can lead to satisfaction in the absence of influencing the likelihood of obtaining desired outcomes.

The implications of the research outlined above are hinted at in Figure 8.1. People can accept social support instead of actual influence or control over desired resources. In the experiments outlined, people who present evidence to authorities receive positive social feedback. In the post-decision input condition, that social feedback substitutes for actual influence over the decisions made. Like the people in the support group depicted in the cartoon, social rewards are substituting for obtaining a desired resource—control over outcomes.

Other findings also suggest that an instrumental perspective on justice is inadequate to account for procedural-justice findings. Mikula et al. (1990)

coded everyday instances of injustice and found that "a considerable proportion of the injustices which are reported do not concern distributive or procedural issues in the narrow sense but refer to the manner in which people are treated in interpersonal interactions and encounters"(p. 133).

Several efforts have been made to directly test a relational conception of justice. One type of test involves examining the role of relational indicators in shaping procedural justice judgments. Tyler (1988, 1989, 1990, 1994a; Tyler & Lind, 1992) examines the influence of relational criteria (e.g., the trustworthiness of decisionmakers) on procedural justice in studies of citizen experiences with police officers and judges and employee experiences with managers. In both settings, each relational aspect of experience independently influences procedural justice judgments, and the combined relational criteria are more central to such definitions of procedural justice than are instrumental evaluations of outcome favorability and/or control. The findings suggest that people are concerned about their long-term social relationships with the group and group authorities.

People are affected by three relational issues. One is their evaluation of the neutrality of decisionmaking procedures—the degree to which they are unbiased, honest, and make decisions based on evidence. People value being on a level playing field in which the rules do not systematically favor one party over another. Such favoritism could reflect giving one side unfair advantages, making decisions based upon personal relationships with one party to the dispute, or basing decisions on the decisionmaker's whims or prejudices.

A second relational issue involves the assessment of the trustworthiness of others in the relationship, particularly authorities (Lind & Lissak, 1985; Pruitt et al., 1993; Tyler, 1988, 1990). People place great weight on their inferences about the motives and intentions of the authorities with whom they deal. In fact, such judgments are typically the primary antecedent of procedural justice judgments.

The centrality of trust to reactions to authorities explains two paradoxical findings in procedural justice studies. First, when people encounter treatment that is apparently unfair (e.g., bias, poor quality decisionmaking, and so on), they sometimes do not interpret that behavior as unfair (Tyler, 1990). This finding is explained by including motive attributions in the analysis. If people believe that authorities have "their heart in the right place," they focus less strongly on their actual behavior in making fairness judgments. Conversely, people do not rate procedures that appear to be fair as actually being fair if they feel that those creating or implementing those procedures are not motivated to act fairly. For example, as has already been noted, people do not value having the structural opportunity to speak unless they think what they say is being considered by the decisionmaker.

The importance of having evidence that one's arguments are considered by the decisionmaker explains the widespread finding that decisions are more acceptable if they are excused, justified, or otherwise explained (Bies, 1987; Bies & Shapiro, 1988; Bies, Shapiro, & Cummings, 1988; Brockner, DeWitt, Grover, & Reed, 1990; Schaubroeck et al., 1994; Shapiro, 1993). Greenberg (1990b) extends this finding to a more general argument that justice findings suggest the basis for an impression management strategy by authorities.

Finally, the third relational dimension—status recognition—reflects the degree to which people's social status and standing in the community is respected through (1) the dignity of a procedure, (2) the respect and politeness of their treatment, and (3) the respect shown for their rights (Bies & Moag, 1986; MacCoun et al., 1988; Tyler, 1988, 1990). When people are treated politely and with dignity, their feelings of positive standing within the group or relationship are enhanced, with positive implications for feelings of self-esteem. Conversely, undignified, disrespectful, or impolite treatment carries the implication that a person is not a full member of the group. Segregated schools, for example, not only caused material harm to African Americans but also communicated an important, negative message about their status within American society. It is for this reason that separate is inherently unequal because it denotes the inferiority of one social group, a problem that cannot be rectified by equalizing spending across schools.

The three relational issues outlined are not the same in conceptual terms. Neutrality in behavior and in procedures reflects something that an authority or an institution does. Features of neutrality are often built into the framework of procedures. For example, trial procedures create a level playing field by giving both parties the opportunity to have an attorney and by giving those attorneys equal opportunities to present arguments and question witnesses. Status recognition is also reflected in the behavior of authorities, and politeness and treatment with dignity are strongly linked to how particular authorities implement procedures. Finally, motive inferences about trustworthiness are made by people based on behaviors they experience. The importance of motive inferences supports Heider's suggestion (1958) that people in general believe that understanding the motives underlying volitional behavior provides the most effective basis for predicting future behavior. It may also be true that the motives of others in an interaction provide the most direct evidence of social standing.

Comparing Psychological Models of Justice by Examining What Procedural Justice Influences

Thibaut and Walker's (1975) original research emphasized outcome satisfaction. This reflects a control model focus. And studies have widely supported the suggestion that procedural justice shapes not only outcome satisfaction but also the willingness to voluntarily accept decisions (see Lind & Tyler, 1988). However, procedural justice has also been found to have a much broader impact. It also influences willingness to comply with group rules (Tyler, 1990), willingness to remain in the group (Brockner et al., 1992; Tansky, 1993), and willingness to help the group (Tyler & Degoey, 1995).

Perhaps the most striking support for the relational perspective comes from studies demonstrating that procedural justice influences self-esteem (Koper et al., 1993; H. J. Smith & Tyler, 1996; Tyler et al., 1996) and self-efficacy (Gilliland, 1994). In an experimental study (Koper et al., 1993), the research assistant either graded only the student's first three answers on an academic skills test and offered no explanation for this decision—the unfair treatment experimental condition—or graded the entire test extremely carefully—the fair treatment experimental condition. When the academic skills test was presented to subjects as very diagnostic of their academic skills, how they were treated by the research assistant significantly influenced their self-esteem. Those who were treated fairly had significantly higher self-esteem than those who were treated unfairly.

According to a relational perspective, authorities act as group representatives. Their behavior and the procedures they use communicate information about the group's general opinions (Hogg & Abrams, 1988; Tyler & Lind, 1992). Fair treatment indicates that the person is a valuable group member, whereas unfair treatment indicates marginality and even exclusion. The knowledge that one is valued and worthy should increase self-esteem, whereas the knowledge of marginality should decrease it. Thus, justice is important and self-relevant because it has relational value, not just instrumental value.

Of course, we do not want to overstate the case. Outcomes also influence people's status in their group. This is clear to anyone who has ever compared his or her salary to that of coworkers, and it is a central argument of relative deprivation theory and distributive justice models of justice. Hence, an interesting question is how long could people continue to receive unfavorable outcomes via fair procedures before they would start to raise questions about those procedures and the authorities using them? Little research exists to address this question.

However, research suggests that procedures are fairly robust against negative outcomes (Lind & Tyler, 1988). Both laboratory experiments and field studies suggest that people maintain their faith in procedures after receiving several unfair or unfavorable outcomes. An important topic for future research is identifying the limits of the cushion of support provided by procedures.

Comparing Psychological Models by Examining When Procedural Justice Matters

The research already outlined compares the instrumental and relational models by looking at both the criteria people consider when judging procedures and the impact that procedural evaluations have. Another approach to comparing the models involves looking at when people care about procedural justice and/or when they consider the issues outlined by group-value theory—voice, treatment with respect and dignity, judgments about the trustworthiness of the motives of authorities, and neutrality of decision-making procedures (i.e., relational concerns; Tyler & Lind, 1992).

Outcome importance.   Some have suggested that people will stop caring about procedures when the stakes are high enough. However, research does not find this to be true. In fact, people care more about procedures as the stakes rise (Lind & Tyler, 1988). It is difficult to explain from an instrumental perspective why people still care about procedural justice even when the outcomes involved are very important. For example, Lind et al. (1993) examine the role of procedural judgments in decisions to accept mediation awards in civil suits. The amounts of money at issue in their study ranged up to $800,000. The findings indicate that the primary judgments shaping decisions about whether to accept mediation decisions are assessments of the procedural qualities of the mediation session, not its outcome. A similar test in the criminal justice arena suggests that people faced with substantial deprivations in liberty (up to twenty years in prison) also evaluate their experience with the law—in this case the felony disposition process—primarily in procedural terms (Casper, Tyler, & Fisher, 1988; Tyler, Casper & Fisher, 1989).

Nature of the social relationship.   The relational model also predicts that the importance of relational issues will vary depending on the nature of the social relationships involved. Tyler and Degoey (1996) examine this possibility by exploring one of the strongest relationships found—the connection between trust in the motives of authorities and the willingness to voluntarily accept third-party decisions. Their analysis is based upon a sample of employees in Chicago who discussed their relationships with their supervisors and their work organizations.

Tyler and Degoey (1996) first examine whether the existence of a past or expected future relationship influences the role of trust in shaping the willingness to accept decisions. The results of regression analysis suggest that the existence of a relationship increases the importance of trust. When employees think of their work supervisor as their friend, they care more about whether they are trustworthy. Further, employees care more about trust if they share the organization's values and/or draw their personal identity from their work. However, variations in instrumental issues such as the degree to which employees feel that their jobs are secure does not influence the importance of trust.

Comparing Procedural and Distributive Justice

Although these findings strongly support the suggestion that procedural justice judgments are relational in character, it is important not to assume that all justice judgments have a similar psychological character. Tyler (1994a), for example, directly compares the antecedents of judgments about procedural and distributive justice in legal and managerial settings. In his study, distributive justice was more strongly influenced by instrumental judgments than was procedural justice (although relational judgments continued to have a direct effect on both types of justice). These findings are shown in Figure 8.2. They suggest that the psychological motives underlying distributive and procedural justice are not the same. Therefore, it is important to consider the psychological characteristics of each form of justice separately.

The connection between the relational issues outlined, judgments about justice, and views about authority is further illustrated by Tyler's (1995) study that examines the effect of judgments about authorities on views about their legitimacy. The study used six data sets that included a wide variety of authorities, including parents, judges, managers, and so forth (the total number of subjects was 2,298). The results are shown in Figure 8.3. They indicate that procedural justice judgments are primarily relational in character. Further, legitimacy is primarily responsive to procedural justice concerns.

Distributive Justice Research

In contrast to the literature on procedural justice, instrumental perspectives dominate the distributive justice literature (Tyler, 1994a). For example, the merit principle of equity theory assumes that justice is the consequence of an analysis of relevant contributions and rewards. The utilitarian nature of assumed distributive justice motivations is also illustrated by the types of research conducted. One set of studies shows that people are more concerned with distributive justice in allocating pay when their behavior will be public, but they are less concerned when they believe their behavior will be private. This suggests that people act fairly at least in part out of fear of the social consequences of self-interested behavior. People are also found to prefer principles of distributive equity that favor their personal situation. For example, older workers favor pay systems based on seniority, whereas younger workers prefer pay systems based on productivity (Karsh & Cole, 1968). As noted previously, several recent studies (Tyler, 1994a) support the suggestion that instrumental motivations are more central to judgments about distributive justice.

However, not all evidence supports an instrumental orientation on distributive justice. Sometimes people are found to act in ways contrary to their self-interest in order to achieve distributive justice goals (Montada, 1991; H. J. Smith & Tyler, 1996), a finding difficult to explain from a self-interest or instrumental perspective. Further, relationships influence people's interpretation of fairness in ways that are not related to instrumental costs and benefits.

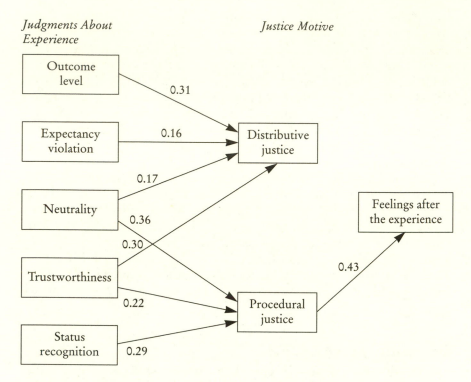

Judgments About Experience

Justice Motive

FIGURE 8.2   The psychology of the justice motive in a managerial setting.
SOURCE: "Psychological Models of the Justice Motive: Antecedents of Distributive and Procedural Justice," by T. R. Tyler, 1994, *Journal of Personality and Social Psychology, 67,* 850–863. Copyright 1994 American Psychological Association. Adapted with permission.

Also, as shown in Figure 8.2, there are significant direct paths between relational concerns and distributive justice judgments.

Even in the economic marketplace, an arena in which people might not expect to receive justice or give it to others (e.g., "let the buyer beware"), research on people's distributive justice judgments suggests that people are concerned with relational forms of justice (Kahneman, Knetsch, & Thaler, 1986). For example, people believe that employers have an obligation to their existing employees but not to future employees (Kahneman et al., 1986). Landlords have an obligation to current tenants but not to future tenants. Further, people have an obligation to maintain ongoing levels of exchange in existing relationships even when shortages develop. For instance, a store should not exploit shortages to charge its regular customers

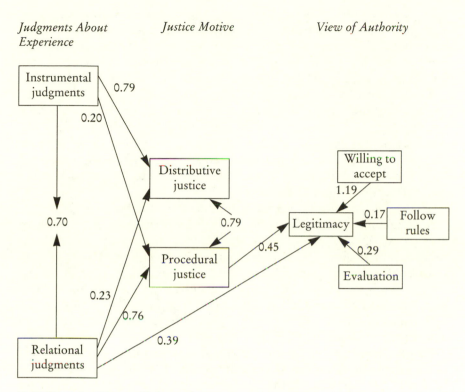

FIGURE 8.3   The psychology of legitimacy

more, nor should a team raise prices for play-off tickets and exploit loyal fans. Again, these obligations are to ongoing relationships. One can fairly solicit bids from strangers in one's own house, unlike a play-off ticket that should not be auctioned off but sold in some way that respects the entitlement of ongoing fans. Notice that the potential costs and benefits of the transactions remain the same regardless of whether a relationship exists.

People feel there is a psychological contract that develops in ongoing social relationships that specifies justice norms and entitlement (Rousseau & Anton, 1993; Rousseau & Aquino, 1988; Rousseau & Parks, 1993). Rousseau (1995) suggests that people develop a sense of an "implied" contract—that is, workers feel that the organization with whom they are dealing has obligations because of a social relationship even if the obligations are not specifically stated in any employment contracts. Anton (1990) finds that such perceived entitlements can include the expectation of honest information regarding work performance, meaningful work (challenging, creative), treatment with respect and dignity, opportunities for participation, and a safe work environment. Anton further demonstrates that respecting perceived entitlements is not just a nice thing to do. Employees are less satisfied, less trusting, and more likely to quit if their perceived entitlements are not recognized by their work organizations.

The influence of social relationships on distributive justice is also suggested by research (described in Chapter 3) showing that the use of equity, equality, and need as principles of allocation is linked to the nature of the social relationship among the parties to an allocation. For example, people are more likely to distribute resources equally if they are friends with the other person involved, whereas equity is more likely to be used as a principle of allocation among strangers.

The finding that group membership influences distributive justice judgments suggests another piece of evidence for a relational perspective (see Hogg & Abrams, 1988; Messick & Mackie, 1989; Tajfel & Turner, 1986, for reviews). For example, in minimal group studies (Tajfel, 1982), subjects are categorized arbitrarily into different groups (through estimation of dots or the flip of a coin) and are then asked to allocate points among anonymous members of their group and members of the other group (see Table 8.2). The total number of points each member is given often is translated into a small amount of actual money.

An instrumental model might predict that subjects would prefer an allocation strategy that maximizes the number of points for the in-group member (strategy 1). It is possible that they might expect other in-group members to give them the most points (Rabbie, Schot, & Visser, 1989). Alternately, subjects might prefer an allocation strategy that maximizes the total number of points (strategy 2, giving the subjects more money). A third alternative is to allocate rewards equally to the two people (strategy 3). Instead, the results from these studies suggest that subjects prefer the fourth strategy outlined in Table 8.2. In that strategy, subjects maximize the difference between the number of points given to the in-group member and the out-group member. Subjects prefer this strategy even if it means that the in-group member will actually get fewer points (compare strategies 1 and 4; see Hogg & Abrams, 1988; Messick & Mackie, 1989; Tajfel & Turner, 1986, for reviews and a discussion of this method).

Social identity theorists argue that subjects prefer this fourth strategy for allocating points to in-group and out-group members because they want to positively differentiate their in-group from the out-group. They want to show that their in-group is better than the out-group. This desire to belong to a positively valued group, or to have a positive social identity, reflects a relational motive. Giving in-group and out-group members different amounts of points is the only way they can do this in the minimal group experimental situation. Notice that this choice does not instrumentally benefit the subjects.

TABLE 8.2   Group Membership and Allocation Strategies

Point Allocation	Possible Strategies			
	Maximize In-Group Profit (Strategy 1)	Maximize Joint Profit (Strategy 2)	Maximize Equality (Strategy 3)	Maximize Difference Between Groups (Strategy 4)
In-group member	10	9	7	6
Out-group member	6	8	7	1
Difference between the two	4	1	0	5
Total for two	16	17	14	7

Other research shows that the advantaged are more willing to support the redistribution of their advantages to the disadvantaged if they value or identify with a larger shared superordinate category ("U.S. citizen"). H. J. Smith and Tyler (1996) establish that people are more willing to defer to laws passed by Congress that give resources to the disadvantaged if they trust Congress. This is the relational effect that has been described earlier. In this case, it is reflected in a significant influence of relational evaluations of Congress on policy endorsement. In addition, Smith and Tyler show that this tendency is stronger when people identify with the United States (a superordinate category to which both the advantaged and the disadvantaged belong).

This research suggests that advantaged group members who value the larger superordinate category ("United States") are interested in the fair treatment of both disadvantaged and advantaged group members for two reasons. The treatment of any category member communicates information about individual group members' value to the group and it further, communicates information about the group's norms or the group's values (Lind & Tyler, 1988; Tyler & Lind, 1990). This analysis implies that the discovery that an important group behaves unjustly should be particularly upsetting for those who identify most closely with the group, even if they continue to benefit instrumentally from their membership. For example, in one study, survivors of layoffs were more upset with unfair organization policies when they were more identified with the organization before the layoff began (Brockner et al., 1992).

The importance of relational issues also appears to be recognized by leaders. An analysis of revolutionary leaders' speeches shows that leaders direct attention away from procedural justice and toward distributive inequities. Further, leaders seeking to motivate their followers to fight for change focus not only on differences in material resources and well-being but also on differences in emotional well-being and ideological resources (such as moral righteousness; Martin, Scully, & Levitt, 1990).

Retributive Justice Research

An instrumental understanding of retributive justice is linked to seeking punishment out of a desire to control the future behavior of the rule breaker and other potential rule breakers (D. T. Miller & Vidmar, 1981). People value rule following and seek to punish rule breakers both to prevent them from breaking rules and to serve as an example to others. The instrumental view predicts punishment will be the direct consequence of a perceived threat to self-interest, particularly when punishment is perceived to be effective in reducing that threat. Thus, instrumentalists reason that taking criminals out of society through incapacitation reduces threats to self-interest because those criminals are no longer able to attack members of the general public. Incapacitation both gets criminals off the street and scares others who might consider committing a crime, creating deterrence effects.

In contrast to the behavioral control model, theoretical statements on retributive justice (Hogan & Emler, 1981; D. T. Miller & Vidmar, 1981) suggest support for an identity based, group value model of justice. Rule breaking is viewed as a threat to the status of victims and to the status of social rules (Hogan & Emler, 1981; Miller & Vidmar, 1981). An offense "has symbolic consequences for the individual" and the social group because rule breaking is "an affront to [the victim's] values and status" (D. T. Miller & Vidmar, 1981, p. 155; cf. Heider, 1958). In addition to physical and material harm, victims suffer the psychosocial harm of humiliation and degradation. Restoring the victim's status requires punishing the rule breaker.

Rule breaking also threatens the status of group rules and underlying values of the group. From this perspective, wrong doing harms the social fabric of the group and its members (Kerr et al., 1995; Marques, 1990). Hogan and Emler (1981) call such breaches failures of the moral values that are the "enabling conditions for social life" (p.138). Healing these breaches has important implications for the maintenance of group norms, cohesiveness, and quality of social relations in the group (D. T. Miller & Vidmar, 1981). This perspective stresses the importance of punishment as a symbol to restore the structure of society and the positive social characteristics of the group. Deviance within a group has implications for the status of the group. It has been argued that punishment may be motivated in part by an effort to avoid having a few bad apples tarnish the overall reputation of the group and the social identity of group members (Boeckmann, 1993; Felson & Tedeschi, 1995; Kerr et al., 1995; Marques, 1990; D. T. Miller & Vidmar,

1981). Marques (1990) refers to the process of devaluing undesirable in-group members as the "black sheep effect."

Kerr and colleagues (1995) reasoned that these processes may be mani-fested in judgments of guilt and the severity of recommended sentences. They used a simulated jury paradigm to assess the extent to which the black sheep effect may be manifested in these judgments. In their studies, they independently varied the ethnic and religious affiliations of the defendant and the jury participants. Consistent with the black sheep hypothesis, defendants with affiliations similar to the jury were seen as more guilty than defendants with different affiliations. However, a significant interaction between similarity of affiliation and strength of evidence was observed. When evidence was ambiguous, similar defendants were judged leniently, whereas when evidence was strong, similar defendants were judged harshly relative to defendants who were different (Kerr et al., 1995).

Boeckmann and Tyler (1996) argue that the symbolic perspective outlined corresponds to the relational ideas contained within the group value model and the relational model. This occurs because retributive justice judgments are linked to similar concerns about the group. Specifically, responding to wrongdoing is seen to be linked to the values that define the group, the eval-uation of the group and the implications this has for social identity, and the nature and quality of social bonds within the group. Like the symbolic per-spective, they see the key issue in responding to deviance as being the impli-cations these actions have for the identity of the group and social relation-ships within the group.

Tyler and Boeckmann (1996) test this idea in their study of public support for punitive policies regarding rule breakers. They compared two models. One links punitiveness to instrumental issues of dangerousness and fear. The other links punitiveness to relational judgments regarding issues of cohesiveness—the view that society's moral values and social bonds are deteriorating. A comparison of the two models, shown in Figure 8.4, sup-ports the predictions of the relational model. Cohesiveness influenced both support for the three strikes initiative and general punitiveness.

The Strength of Instrumental and Relational Motives

Several different areas of research support an instrumental or behavioral-control model of retribution. Behavior-control models suggest that people should express support for making an example of an offender to deter simi-lar crimes by others. Empirical research supports the suggestion that people are motivated by the desire to deter future crimes. For example, Vidmar (1974) found that 63 percent of those he interviewed gave behavior control as their primary reason for supporting the death penalty, but only 37 per-cent gave deservedness.

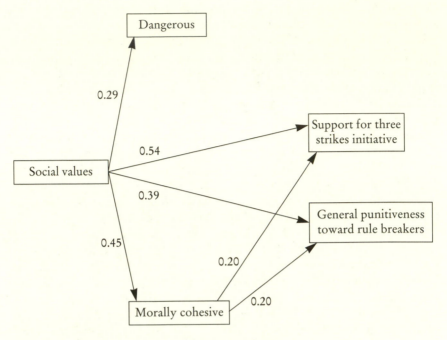

FIGURE 8.4   The antecedents of public punitiveness

In other research, respondents were given information indicating that deterrence (in this case the death penalty) does not lower crime. This information should have negated the instrumental reason for supporting punishment, leading to lower punitiveness (Ellsworth, 1978; Ellsworth & Ross, 1983; Sarat & Vidmar, 1976). These studies provide intermediate levels of support for an instrumental model; some respondents reported less support, but others did not.

The deservedness model that links punishment to the degree of disrespect for social rules is supported by research on public attitudes about rule breaking. First, punitiveness is typically strongly related to social and political values. A number of studies, for example, link authoritarianism (Narby, Cutler, & Moran, 1993; Tyler & Weber, 1983), conservatism (Tyler & Weber, 1983), and the belief in a just world (Lerner, 1980) to punitiveness.

The instrumental and relational perspectives on rule breaking can be directly compared by examining the strength of each motivation in reactions to rule breaking. As we have noted, the study by Tyler and Boeckmann (1996) directly compares the two and finds that relational motives are more important antecedents of support for the "three strikes" initiative and of general punitiveness.

When Rule Breaking Matters

The behavior-control model hypothesizes that rule breaking should be especially troubling under some circumstances. For example, people should be especially punitive toward criminals who they think are likely to commit future crimes since punishment is intended to deter future crime (specific deterrence).

A behavioral control model also suggests that people should be more troubled when rule breaking is personally threatening. In other words, those potentially affected by a crime should be more punitive than those less affected. For example, women should be especially likely to punish rapists. Further, people should be more punitive when they feel that crime rates are too high.

Although studies of punitiveness provide some support for an instrumental perspective on punishment, that support is not strong. Studies do not find that fear of personal harm through victimization (fear of crime), judgments that rule breaking is widespread (evaluations of the crime rate), or having been a victim of rule breaking behavior is a strong predictor of punitiveness.

A moral or relationally based model of punishment assumes that people will be more punitive when they feel that rule breaking shows a lack of moral character (e.g., a disrespect for social rules). For example, it has already been noted that defendants are more harshly punished when they seem to feel no remorse after they have broken rules (Felson & Ribner, 1981; Rumsey, 1976).

The relational perspective is supported by evidence that retributive motives are more strongly aroused when people break social rules that are more central to maintaining the social and moral order (Pepitone, 1975). In addition, those who feel closely connected to the group punish in-group perpetrators more severely than out-group perpetrators (Boeckmann, 1993). Boeckmann (1993) finds that people are more troubled when the person who breaks a rule is a group member. Why? It has already been noted that people are more relational when dealing with others inside their group. Hence, it is more of an affront and a betrayal of group values when a person within the group violates group rules or injures others (materially or symbolically). As Grossman (1995) suggests, "deviant behavior by members of our own group is perceived as more disturbing and produces stronger retaliation than that of others with whom we are less involved" (p. 25). Consequently, civil wars are usually the most bloody, prolonged, and unrestrained in their violence. Similarly, domestic violence is often strikingly brutal.

Boeckmann and Tyler (1996) extend this analysis in a study of support for punitiveness toward rule breakers. They find that people care more about relational issues (i.e., treating the person with dignity and respect) if they believe the person committing crimes is an in-group member. Further, they are more concerned with extending procedural rights to that individual.

It may also be more difficult for people to believe that members of their group would break rules. For example, when Caesar asked in dismay, "And you also, Brutus?" as he was being assassinated with the complicity of his close friend, he was reflecting the shock that most people feel when they realize that a person with whom they identify and share social bonds has broken social rules. One response to such information is to deny that group members would be capable of rule breaking. In the aftermath of the Kobe earthquake in Japan, the members of that tightly knit society were shocked to learn that there had been looting in the ruins. The response was to decide that "These looters weren't Japanese. They were foreigners" (Kristof, 1995). Similarly, disbelief often accompanies the revelation that a community member has sexually abused children, run a pornography ring, or committed a violent act toward their family or coworkers. People want to believe that a mistake, a misidentification, has been made since they want to believe that no member of their group could be guilty of such counternormative actions (Marques, 1990).

Policy Implications

The distinction between instrumental and moral reactions to rule following is not simply an academic one. There is a fundamental tension between these two perspectives on reactions to rule violation that is highlighted by current debates about criminal justice policy. With its forward looking perspective, the instrumental model focuses on those conditions that lead to future rule following. In contrast, punitiveness is directed at punishment for past crimes.

The utilitarian focus of the instrumental model suggests focusing on the conditions that will lessen rule breaking in the future. Two punishment goals are important: deterrence and incapacitation. Deterrence is achieved through making punishment sufficiently aversive that behavior is not repeated by either the criminal or by others. Unfortunately, psychological research suggests that punishment is not particularly effective in altering long-term behavior unless there can be effective behavioral control in future situations. Incapacitation is achieved through removing the criminal from society and to a lesser extent, through electronic monitoring of the offender's whereabouts. Through these means, the offender is prevented from creating any further harm. Support for this type of approach is seen in endorsement of programs to warehouse criminals in institutions for their remaining lives and in substantially monitoring and restricting the movements of offenders who are released (i.e., sex offenders).

A punishment goal that serves both behavioral-control and moral or relational perspectives is rehabilitation. Rehabilitation appears to be a particularly important strategy to pursue given the ineffectiveness of deterrence and the considerable expense of incapacitation. Rehabilitation is achieved by encouraging offenders to internalize group values (a relational concern) in an effort to reduced future deviations from them (a behavioral-control concern). Ironically, however, the conditions that enhance internalization involve (1) developing values of individual responsibility through freely making value choices, (2) taking responsibility for choices and obligations in situations without supervision, and (3) developing occupational skills that make following the rules a viable career option. When efforts have been made to create programs that provide such a rehabilitative environment in criminal justice settings (e.g., work release programs or training and education programs in prisons) there has been public opposition. This opposition is based on the belief that people who commit crimes should be punished by living in an aversive environment—that they deserve to suffer because they have broken social rules.

This conflict is also linked to differences of opinion about whether people can be changed. In the past, the rehabilitation ideal dominated corrections policy. More recently, people have become much more pessimistic about the possibilities of character change. This has led to declining support for rehabilitative programs. The differences in opinion about whether offenders can be encouraged to internalize group norms and values may also be linked to the perceived relational climate of society. Putnam (1995) argues that there is a decline in the number and strength of social connections in American society. Concomitant with this change is a decline in trust extended to the average person in society. People are less certain that others are committed to the same basic values. These observations suggest that people are increasingly viewing others in society as untrustworthy strangers.

As previously outlined, Boeckmann and Tyler (1995b) find that the perception of criminals as strangers is linked to heightened attention to instrumental concerns when dealing with rule breakers. In contrast, the perception of criminals as insiders is linked to attention to relational and moral concerns in dealing with rule breakers. It is hardly surprising, then, that a good number of Americans are losing faith in rehabilitation and are focusing instead on threatening potential deviants and incapacitating identified criminals. For example, the public increasingly supports programs to warehouse criminals for their remaining lives.

The incomparability of instrumental and moral reactions to rule breaking also arises on the macro level during times of social change. Following a revolution or other changes in power, new leaders must decide whether to integrate past officials into their new society or to have investigations and trials in an effort to punish former officials for their past crimes. Although new leaders often follow the path of ignoring or pardoning past crimes, there are strong pressures from the families of victims and the members of injured groups to uncover the truth about past crimes and bring the guilty to justice.

The Relationship of Procedural and Retributive Justice

A group value model suggests insights for understanding the connection between procedural and retributive justice. Normally, procedural and retributive justice work in conjunction. Procedures for dealing with rule breaking function to reinforce social structure and group identity. Through procedures, commitment to the group is developed and emphasized. For example, those accused of crimes must show deference to social authorities (e.g., rising when the judge enters the courtroom) to indicate respect for social rules. In fact, the failure to respect social procedures (contempt for the court) is a separate, additional crime for which a defendant can be punished. Hence, the procedures of a trial, in which responsibility for rule breaking is determined, and the punishment meted out reinforce the symbolic structure of society and the symbols of justice (such as a blindfolded woman holding a scale) often found in court buildings. Procedures complement punishment, and both reassert the status of the victim and of social rules. The punishing of wrongdoers reasserts social status. Procedures also reinforce commitment to society because they allow the rights of the individual to be demonstrated.

By according rights and due process of law to those accused of crimes, society also reasserts that the status of people within the group is protected. Interestingly, although Boeckmann (1993) finds that in-group members are more severely punished for violating rules, he also finds that in-group members are accorded more procedural protections while their guilt is being determined.

However, rule breaking can also provoke a conflict between procedural and retributive justice. People may react to heinous or shocking crimes like the sexual abuse of children by denying that the offender shares the values of the group. For example, discussions of mass murderers or child molesters often emphasize that such people were loners and never fit into society. In other words, they were never group members who held the values of the group. Such distancing is important because the actions of misfits or outcasts are less threatening to group values.

Further, misfits may be more subject to spontaneous community actions such as lynching, being railroaded through a cursory investigation and trial, or other efforts to violently reassert the group's rules and status (Huggins, 1991). The California police express increasing concern about extralegal violence, citing the following example as illustrative: A teenage male was suspected of molesting two young girls. His accusers sought him out to address the injustice. When they found him in his home, they held a gun to his head while several female residents of his community beat him savagely (*San Francisco Chronicle*, 1995, May 10).

Part 5

When Does Justice Matter?

In Chapter 8, two possible motives for why people care about justice were discussed. We showed that people pay more attention to justice relevant information when they share a social bond with others, but an instrumental outcome orientation dominates interactions among people who do not share important social ties. This section explores in detail the external conditions under which the importance or meaning of justice may change in social interactions. This contextual view is contrasted with a universalistic view that suggests that a concern with justice is a basic human characteristic found in all social situations.

9

SOCIAL STRUCTURAL INFLUENCES

An important question raised in this chapter is the extent to which justice is a basic human motive. If the concern for justice is an inherent human characteristic, then it should be found in its varying forms—"fairness," "equity," and "just desert"—in whatever context justice is studied. In contrast, to the degree that justice concerns become more or less important across different situations, the idea of a universal justice motive becomes difficult to uphold. However, even if the evidence suggests that a general concern for justice exists, we need to ask whether (1) the way people think about and define justice changes from situation to situation or (2) different people in different settings show varying attention to justice. Both the issues of relative importance and meaning of justice across situations are addressed in this chapter.

Justice as a Basic Motive

One model of the psychology of the person suggests that a concern for justice is an inherent human characteristic. Lerner (1980, 1981, 1982) argues that people are intrinsically motivated to behave fairly. He suggests that people have a basic desire to behave fairly and to believe that justice exists in the world (i.e., the belief-in-a-just-world phenomenon). If justice concerns arise from basic human motivations, we would expect to find common justice concerns across people, social groups, and societies.

One type of support for Lerner's universalistic argument is evidence that people engage in cognitive distortions to maintain the belief that the world is a just place in which people get what they deserve (see Chapter 6). If people see someone else suffer, for example, they distort their judgments to draw the conclusion that the victim deserved to suffer, even if given evidence that the suffering is actually randomly determined. In other words, people can and do engage in psychological distortions to maintain the deeply held belief that the world is an orderly system in which both bad and good outcomes are justly deserved.

Similarly, even when people have power over others and can do to them whatever they desire (as in wars), they typically engage in considerable cognitive effort to justify their actions and make them seem moral and good (Kelman & Hamilton, 1989). People find it difficult to hurt others and have to resort to dehumanizing their victims before they can impose injustice and harm on them. This suggests that people are motivated to distort "objective reality" not only to justify the actions and situations of others but to justify their own actions.

In addition to evidence that people feel the need to justify events to maintain their belief in a just world, the idea of a basic justice motive is also supported by the finding that people care about justice in their everyday social interactions. Earlier chapters in this book have documented the widespread influence of justice concerns on people's thoughts, feelings, and behaviors across a broad range of situations. Our analysis of the literature on distributive, procedural, and retributive justice suggests that justice of each type is important to how people feel about themselves, how they respond to social situations, and how they interact with others.

Further, there is wide consensus about the criteria for making justice judgments within particular settings in American society (Lane, 1986). This consensus has two aspects. First, within a particular situation, people who differ in their demographic characteristics—age, education, sex, race, and so forth—seem to have similar views about how justice should be defined (Tyler, 1988; Tyler, 1994b). Public opinion polls also show that the public agrees about what constitutes a punishable crime (J. L. Miller, Rossi & Simpson, 1986) and about the appropriate level of sanctioning for specific crimes. Judgments of the seriousness of different types of crimes appear to be relatively stable across different samples (Pontell et al., 1985) and over time (Coombs, 1967).

People also agree that different justice principles apply in different situations. People have templates that identify situational characteristics that activate particular justice principles. For example, within American society there is a broad consensus that equity applies to business and work settings; equality applies to legal and political settings; and need, to the family (Deutsch, 1975, 1985).

The Scope of Justice

Notwithstanding the evidence outlined for a basic justice motive, Deutsch (1985) argues that there is a scope or limited range to the application of justice principles. He argues, "Unless one shares Albert Schweitzer's reverence for all living creatures, one would not feel it to be unjust if one killed an annoying mosquito or caught a fish to eat for dinner" (Deutsch, 1985, p 36). He further argues that justice principles are not applied to interactions with "heathens, inferior races, heretics, and perverts"—those who are perceived to be outside one's moral community.

In a similar vein, Cohen (1991) suggests that our understanding of how people think about and react to justice issues in social life will be incomplete without a careful consideration of "how we draw the boundaries of the 'moral community' within which all matters of justice are confronted" (p. 247). He argues the idea of distributive justice assumes membership in a moral community and that distributive principles are applied only to those who fall within the relevant community. It follows that membership within moral communities entitles individuals to a fair distribution of both material resources (e.g., money) and symbolic resources (political rights), and exclusion from membership leads to a denial of such desired resources.

The idea of a scope of justice or moral community is formalized in the concept of moral exclusion (Opotow, 1990). Opotow defines moral exclusion as the process whereby "individuals or groups are perceived to be outside the boundary in which moral values, rules, and considerations of fairness apply" (p. 1). She further suggests that those who are excluded are perceived as "nonentities," "expendable," or "undeserving," and harming them becomes viewed as "acceptable," "appropriate," and "just." In addition to providing a formal, working definition of exclusion, Opotow is also responsible for bringing this important concept to the attention of justice researchers and hence making it the focus of recent theoretical developments and empirical efforts in social justice research. In an effort to contribute to the development of moral exclusion as a line of justice research, our goal in this chapter is to explore what is currently known about the boundary conditions or "scope" of justice effects.

Psychological research on the phenomenon of moral exclusion covers a remarkably broad range of issues and spans a wide range of social contexts. Opotow (1990; 1994) and Plous (1993) demonstrate how nonhuman species often are excluded from justice considerations. Nagata (1990) describes the conditions under which Japanese Americans were excluded from legal protection in the United States during World War II. Cook (1990) discusses the historical exclusion of African Americans from equality in the distribution of social resources. Fine (1990) describes how public schools engage in systematic exclusion of disadvantaged students. Kelman and Hamilton (1989) outline how human rights are denied in times of war. And Huo (1995) shows that people exclude members of disliked social and political groups from access to resources, procedural rights, and fair treatment. These examples are provided as an illustration of the breadth of the issues covered in research on moral exclusion, and the list is by no means exhaustive. As Opotow noted, moral exclusion is a general phenomenon that takes on various forms and can be useful in understanding a range of social issues (Opotow, 1990).

Although the concept of moral exclusion has only recently been formally introduced to the psychology literature, related issues such as political tolerance have long been an important concern in the social sciences. For example, political scientists have for many years struggled with the problem posed by a majority of citizens who want to exclude unpopular minority groups from full engagement in the democratic process (e.g., Sullivan, Piereson & Marcus, 1982). What are people's motivations for denying others the right to speak in public or to teach children? A more careful examination of the psychological antecedents of moral exclusion will both help us to better understand people's conceptions of justice and be of relevance in addressing important societal problems such as exclusion from full participation in a democratic society.

Two Views of the Scope of Justice

Limits to the scope of justice can be explained in two ways. An instrumental view suggests that the scope of justice is determined by issues of self- or group interest. For example, people exclude others who are competitors for valuable resources. In contrast, a relational perspective suggests that the scope of justice is determined by normative and social concerns. For example, people exclude others because those who are excluded are not like them, do not behave as they do, and do not share their cultural and social values.

The study by Nagata (1990, 1993) is particularly illustrative of the contrast between the instrumental and relational explanations of scope of justice effects. Nagata asks the question: Why were Japanese Americans interned during World War II, whereas German Americans and Italian Americans were not interned? Since all were descendants of people from countries with which the United States was then at war, why were the Japanese Americans treated differently? In particular, why were American citizens of Japanese descent suddenly placed outside the moral community and denied basic legal rights—such as hearings to establish that they had or were likely to commit some treasonous actions—before being placed in prison camps? (For a discussion of the political forces operating at this time in history see Smith, 1995.)

Nagata's analysis suggests that the internment of Japanese Americans can be explained via instrumental factors and relational factors. Two instrumental concerns were hypothesized to underlie support for the internment. Some feared that Japanese Americans would remain loyal to the Emperor of Japan and engage in acts of sabotage to undermine the U.S. interest in the war. A second instrumental concern involved economic considerations. There were reports at the time that farmers in California were feeling threatened by the success of Japanese American farmers in a competitive agricultural market.

Alternatively, support for the internment could have stemmed from more relational motives. Many people felt that people of Japanese ancestry living in the United States should be punished for the attack on Pearl Harbor. This explanation suggests that support for the internment was, in part, a reaction to harm done to the group and the desire to punish those perceived to be responsible. Another relational factor is that at the time of World War II, Japanese Americans were perceived by many to be "different" from other Americans. These perceptions were reinforced by racial stereotypes that portrayed Japanese Americans' values as distinct from "mainstream American values." This latter explanation may best account for why Japanese Americans were treated differently than Italian Americans and German Americans were treated. In sum, according to a relational perspective, threats to cultural views and/or societal goals form the psychological basis of people's willingness to exclude others from normal justice considerations.

In addition to supporting policies such as the internment of Japanese Americans, instrumental and relational motives also underlie a range of exclusionary attitudes and behaviors. Consistent with an instrumental perspective, exclusionary periods in history have been linked to economic downturns. Staub (1989) notes that one of the preconditions of the extermination of Jews in World War II was the prolonged economic depression Germans had experienced between the two world wars. Similarly, the growing anti-immigration sentiment in the United States today is suggested to be partly the result of economic recession and the resulting unemployment of American citizens. Current political rhetoric suggests that illegal immigrants pose an economic threat to American workers because they are willing to work for lower pay.

Opotow (1995) examines the psychological antecedents of exclusion from the scope of justice within the context of environmental debates. She found that in deciding whether or not to include an endangered species (e.g., the bombardier beetle) within their scope of justice, people in her study were influenced by the utility of the beetles to humans and by the degree of conflict of interest between the beetles and humans.

Interestingly, feelings of similarity to the beetle did not influence people's decisions to exclude the beetle from their scope of justice. Opotow's findings support an instrumental perspective on exclusion. An important contribution of Opotow's study is that it is one of the first to systematically examine the various antecedents of moral exclusion. Rather than rely on historical anecdotes, she employs an experimental paradigm to tease out the independent effects of perceived similarity, utility, and threat on the desire to exclude a nonhuman species from the scope of justice.

A relational perspective suggests that issues of social identification and, particularly, threats to social identities motivate exclusion. In line with this argument, people react more strongly to injustice to others if they include those others within groups that are important to them (Brockner, 1990). In one study, Brockner and his colleagues investigated layoff survivors' commitment to the organization. Survivors who had close personal or professional relationship with coworkers (members of the moral community) who were unfairly laid off were significantly less committed to the organization. When those with whom we identify are treated unfairly, our sense of identity is threatened and we react negatively. Similarly, people evaluate in-group members who violate important group norms more negatively than out-group members (Boeckmann, 1993; Marques, 1990). The black sheep in one's group is excluded because they threaten the group's sense of positive social identity.

It is possible that both instrumental and relational motivations simultaneously influence exclusion. Both motivations can be important at the same time. For example, gay activists who objected to the Ku Klux Klan holding a public demonstration against homosexuals cited both relational and instrumental reasons for their objections. First, they objected to the demonstration because of the Klan's violation of basic social norms (e.g., bigotry and disregard for humanity; Gibson, 1987), a relational concern. Furthermore, the activists cited fears that Klan members would turn violent, a well justified but more instrumental motivation.

Exclusion is a multidimensional phenomenon. In addition to studying the general phenomenon of exclusion from the scope of justice, it is important to examine how people think about specific forms of exclusion. Huo (1995) systematically examined the multidimensional nature of exclusion in a study that asked college students to evaluate political and social groups that they liked and political and social groups that they disliked. The results show that people are less willing to give resources, rights, and fair treatment to disliked groups than to liked groups. This pattern of findings suggests that the disliked groups were excluded from people's scope of justice (see Figure 9.1).

More importantly, Huo looked at how people's judgments varied depending on the type of exclusion considered. The most specific and concrete form of exclusion examined was that of withholding access to shared community resources. A second form of exclusion is the denial of equal right to political participation and legal protection that has been of interest to political scientists who study political tolerance (e.g., Sullivan, Piereson, & Marcus, 1979). The exclusion of certain people from speaking in public or voting in elections represents this form of exclusion. Finally, a third form of exclusion involves demeaning, biased treatment toward the excluded group. The reference to adult male Blacks as "boys" or the North Vietnamese soldiers as "gooks" are examples of this dehumanizing form of exclusion.

As shown in Figure 9.1, the results indicate that people are most willing to deny members of disliked groups resources and least willing to deny them

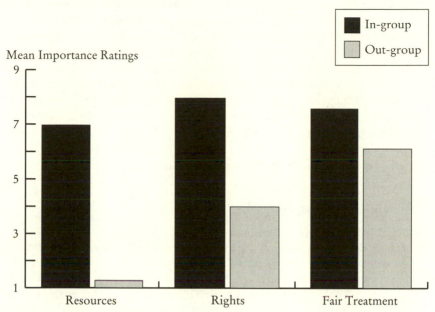

Mean Importance Ratings

High scores indicate importance

FIGURE 9.1 The importance of extending justice to in-groups and out-groups

dignified, fair treatment; the denial of procedural rights falls in between. The findings suggest that the most serious form of exclusion is the denial of respectful and dignified treatment. Even political groups whose views we abhor are felt to be entitled to fair and dignified treatment. The implication is that exclusion from fair treatment is reserved for those few select individuals or groups whom we find to be most morally repugnant and who fall furthermost from the center of our moral community.

The line of reasoning outlined is consistent with Staub's description of the phenomenon of escalating harm in historical cases of extreme harm such as the Holocaust. During the Nazi regime in Germany, Jews were at first denied relatively minor entitlements compared to the eventual atrocities many suffered later in the war. As the war escalated and the Jews became more dehumanized in the eyes of the Nazi soldiers, they were subjected to more extreme forms of harm that culminated in torture and mass extermination. It appears that negative social conditions can push individuals or groups of individuals farther away from the core of the moral community. The consequence of being pushed out of the moral community is increased vulnerability to more severe forms of harm.

In a recent experimental study, Huo (1996) directly tests the operation of instrumental and relational mechanisms in determining attitudes toward each of the three types of exclusion she identified in the earlier study—denial of resources, rights, and fair treatment. Two findings are notable. First, the study replicated the pattern of findings from her earlier correlational study by showing that people are least willing to deny counternormative groups fair treatment and most willing to deny to them access to community resources. Second and more interestingly, the findings suggest that relational motives (i.e., disagreements about social norms) have a more powerful influence on exclusion than instrumental motives (i.e., gaining material resources) on all three forms of exclusion.

Shrinking and Expanding the Scope of Justice

As we noted earlier, the boundary and composition of moral communities are socially constructed and hence subject to change. For example, negative social conditions can dramatically shrink the scope of justice. This observation was made many years ago by the social psychologist Gordon Allport, who noted that when times have changed for the worse, group boundaries tighten and the "stranger is suspect and excluded" (Allport, 1979, p. 35). More recently, Staub (1989) came to a similar conclusion after studying four cases of mass genocide and extreme harm doing, including the Nazi Holocaust, the killing of Armenians in Turkey in the early part of the twentieth century, the Cambodian autogenocide, and the disappearances of leftist rebels in Argentina in the 1970s. He argues that difficult life conditions such as economic hardships, political conflicts, war, violence, and rapid changes in culture and society threaten people's sense of self, security, and physical well-being. This leads to a breakdown of social bonds between people and the exclusion of marginal subgroups from the larger group's scope of justice or moral community. The excluded group is then vulnerable to a variety of harms, ranging from social derogation to genocide.

Given the above analysis, an interesting and important question to ask is how can the moral community be expanded to include those who have been wrongfully excluded? If we consider the two views of scope of justice effects discussed earlier, then the moral community can be increased in at least one of two ways: (1) making more resources available and hence decreasing economic competition (an instrumental approach) or (2) increasing identification with a shared group membership or similarity to others (a relational approach).

The problem with an instrumental approach is that objective conditions impose a natural limit on the extent to which more resources can be made readily available. A relational approach, in contrast, should not be hindered by the lack of availability of desired resources and would instead involve efforts to heighten the psychological connection among people (see Tyler & Lind, 1990, for a discussion). Related research has demonstrated that a sense of shared common group membership has positive consequences for intergroup relations. For example, high school students in a multiethnic high school who checked both an ethnic group membership and "American" when asked to identify themselves were significantly less likely to derogate members of other ethnic groups than were those students who only checked their ethnic group (Gaertner et al., 1994). Similarly, Plous (1993) shows that people's concern for animals is strongly related to their perceptions of how similar the animals are to humans. The more similar people viewed an animal to be to humans, the more willing they were to protect them from harm and the more disturbed they were by watching a videotape of the animal being abused.

Batson (1990) suggests that people find it easier to empathize with similar others and that people are more disturbed by and more willing to help reduce the distress of those with whom they most identify. Batson's work implies that people can use this perspective as a mechanism by which they can view excluded others to be deserving of considerations of justice. Ironically, when people feel particularly empathetic toward a single individual, they find it difficult to apply more general justice principles such as equity (Batson, Klein, Highberger, & Shaw, 1993). For example, when students heard about the plight of one particular needy child, they endorsed helping this child first even though other equally and more deserving children were ahead in the queue. Although empathy may lead one to include a particular individual within the moral community, the inclusion may come at the cost of others.

Active and Passive Exclusion

An important distinction that needs to be made in the moral exclusion literature is the difference between actively excluding others and passively not including others (Deutsch, 1995; Opotow, 1990). For example, the Nazis who persecuted Jews and the Americans who interned Japanese Americans in concentration camps were actively pursuing a policy of exclusion. However, people are sometimes excluded passively by others who do not feel threatened by them or have no desire for retribution. For example, the American Declaration of Independence states that it is "self-evident" that "all Men are created equal." However, that definition by omission passively excludes women, Native Americans, African Americans, and other social minorities.

Each form of exclusion—active and passive—has important consequences for those who are excluded as well as for those who are perpetrators of exclusion. For the excluded, a policy of active exclusion and persecution is likely to result in greater and more immediate harm than a policy of passive exclusion. For the perpetrators, participating in active exclusion may lead to higher levels of psychological stress than passive exclusion, as they try to reconcile the desire to view themselves as good, moral people with their destructive actions (Lerner, 1981).

The degree of psychological stress suffered by ordinary, morally upright people who are ordered to harm others is described in an account of the experiences of the members of a German police battalion (Browning, 1992). When these average, middle-class men were commanded to kill entire communities of Jews during the German invasion of Poland in 1943, they experienced deep psychological conflicts. Alcohol was served during the slaughter to calm their nerves and to ease the deep revulsion they felt at the horrific task that they were engaged in. After the killings, the police officers felt depressed, angry, embittered, and shaken. In the case of Nazi doctors who had the task of selecting people for extermination, they coped with the extreme stress of the duties assigned to them by psychologically splitting their life outside of the extermination camps from their professional role within the camps (Lifton, 1986). This process of "doubling" allowed them to bring extreme harm onto others and still see themselves as good, decent people.

A more common way for people to reconcile their image of themselves as moral beings with the destructive consequences of their actions is to create a social reality in which they can perceive those who are excluded as deserving of their fate. For example, the victims can be perceived to be a threat to the larger community or to deserve punishment for their deviant behaviors. In fact, there is a long social history of scapegoating victims of social and political injustice. Whether the victims are African Americans in the South or Jews in Nazi Germany, actions that exploit, harm, or otherwise injure the members of stigmatized groups are typically preceded by justifications that deny the humanity of the members of those groups. Such dehumanizing efforts are often seen in propaganda against enemies in war. Enemies are portrayed as subhuman and amoral, characteristics that justify harming them.

Why is stereotyping and dehumanization necessary? People find it very difficult to take advantage of or to do harm to others. The most extreme case is doing violence to others. In a recent book on killing, for example, Grossman (1995) argues that even soldiers in war have difficulty killing other people. Based upon studies conducted by the army, Grossman suggests that during past wars most soldiers have been unwilling to fire their weapons at the enemy. For example, during World War II, only 15 percent to 20 percent of soldiers in battles actively fired at the enemy. Instead, most soldiers were not trying to kill the enemy. Most of them appear to have not even wanted to fire in the enemy's general direction (p. 22). He argues, "The simple fact is that when faced with a living, breathing opponent instead of a target, a significant majority of the soldiers revert to a posturing mode in which they fire over their enemy's heads" (p. 11). They do so because "the average and healthy individual . . . has such an inner and usually unrealized resistance toward killing a fellow man that he will not of his own volition take life if it is possible to turn away from that responsibility" (p. 29).

Interestingly, those in combat who do not actually have contact with their victims—artillery personnel, the crews of bombers, sailors on battleships—do not experience the aversion to killing that has been outlined. This is because physical distance and the mechanistic, repetitive nature of their work make it easy for them to avoid acknowledging that they are killing other human beings. This finding accords with Milgram's (1965) finding that physical separation enhanced the willingness of people to harm others (Milgram, 1965). In Milgram's experiment, subjects were asked to administer an electric shock to "learners." The subjects were least willing to harm the learner if they had to physically hold the victim's hand on the shock plate. They were most willing to do harm if the victim was in a different room.

How can killing be facilitated? Kelman and Hamilton (1989) identify three specific psychological forces that promote the willingness to engage in actions inconsistent with one's own moral code and sense of justice or injustice. The first is dehumanization—the stripping of human status from victims. As has been noted, it is easier not to apply moral values if the victims are not seen as fully human. Psychological distance is created by portraying victims as different. That is, as Grossman says,

> to get men to think of the potential enemies they will have to face as inferior forms of life [with films] biased to present the enemy as less than human: The stupidity of local customs is ridiculed, local personalities are presented as evil demigods. . . . It is so much easier to kill someone if they look distinctly different from you. If your propaganda machine can convince your soldiers that their opponents are not really human but are "inferior forms of life," then their natural resistance to killing their own species will be reduced. Often the enemies' humanity is denied by referring to them as "Gooks" "Krauts" or "Nips". In Vietnam this process was assisted by the "body count" mentality, in which we referred to and thought of the enemy as numbers. One Vietnam vet told me that this permitted him to think that killing the NVA and VC was like "stepping on ants" (Grossman, 1995, p. 161).

The second force is routinization. Embedding actions in routines diminishes the likelihood that moral considerations will arise. In other words, once people are involved in a course of action, they think differently about that course of action than they do when initially considering whether to become involved. In particular, issues of justice or injustice are less likely to arise. People no longer ask whether the policy itself makes sense; they instead consider how to implement it. For example, in the many discussion held by American presidents about Vietnam after the United States became involved, the primary focus was on implementing that decision, not questioning its wisdom or morality (Halberstam, 1972).

The power of routinization is recognized in the literature on entrapment in escalating commitments (Brockner & Rubin, 1985; Pruitt & Rubin, 1986). It has been found that organizations that have embarked on a course of action such as the war in Vietnam become focused upon the tactics of success and typically do not reconsider the wisdom of the actions. Hence, the organizations are vulnerable to putting increasing resources into the task, resources far greater than those that were envisioned in the original decision to commit to the action. In other words, groups become entrapped in their course of action, letting go of their original rational decisions and becoming emotionally invested in success. What groups need are clear limits to how much they are willing to commit to a course of action—that is, points at which the wisdom of the original action is reconsidered. In bargaining, a bottom line serves as such a limit. Prior to bargaining, a person writes down the price that they will not move beyond. If, in the emotion of negotiation, one is moved to offer more, the principle of not moving beyond the bottom line prevents that action. Similarly, organizations need clear points at which the wisdom of their actions will be reconsidered.

Like organizations, people need clear points at which they will reconsider the wisdom of suspending their personal consideration of the morality of their actions in favor of obedience to a legitimate authority. For example, when soldiers in Vietnam were ordered to kill women and children, they might have reconsidered their obligation to obey orders, just as corporate executives told to lie to government regulators or suppress internal documents might reconsider whether their actions are appropriate. In fact, some do so, as is evidenced by the existence of whistle-blowers, people who go to government or legal authorities with information about corporate wrongdoing. For example, in 1970 Frank Serpico, a New York City police officer, provided *The New York Times* with a detailed description of police corruption. His efforts, in part, led to the establishment of the Knapp Commission on police corruption. However, before the Challenger disaster (in which the space shuttle was launched and exploded), engineers were aware of the technical flaws in the O-rings that made such a disaster likely; yet they did not stop the launch (Vaughan, 1996).

The third force is authorization. In hierarchies, the orders of superiors override standard moral considerations. In other words, people put aside their own moral or justice-based standards and rely on their superiors to make moral decisions. They focus on obeying orders and do not feel morally responsible for their actions. For example, Arendt's (1964) portrayal of Adolf Eichmann, the German officer responsible for transporting Jews to their death during World War II, suggests that Eichmann was less a moral monster than a bureaucrat who was primarily focused on following the orders of his superiors.

People are more willing to defer to authorities when they feel that the orders they receive are both socially and morally legitimate and hence ought to be obeyed. Contrast the feeling of moral righteousness that made participating in World War II and the Korean War seem to flow from a seemingly undisputed just cause with the feelings of moral ambiguity that troubled those Americans who fought in Vietnam.

Future Research on Moral Exclusion

The active-passive continuum of moral exclusion raises several interesting questions for future research. One question concerns the manner in which moral communities evolve. Are people initially included unless rules for exclusion are derived, or are people initially excluded unless rules for inclusion can be found?

Another important issue for future research is further investigation into the factors and the interactions of factors that shape the boundaries of people's moral communities. Although such boundaries may change over time and across situations, what seems clear is that they exist in one form or another. For example, people who would today regard it as immoral to exclude women from equal political participation would not feel that moral issues are raised at all in killing a cow or a carrot. However, with the rise of the animal liberation movement, it is possible that one day boundaries could shift to include cows (and in the very distant future, even carrots) within one's moral community. Future research needs to systematically examine the factors that lead to the creation, maintenance, and evolution of moral communities.

Further, it is important to distinguish between excluding people who are already in a moral community (pushing out insiders) and excluding those who were never a part of the community (keeping outsiders out). First, consider the exclusion of those who are already members of a community. What was especially disturbing about the Japanese American internment was that many of those interned were U.S. citizens who were excluded because they were perceived to be different and socially marginal. Similarly, though many factors contributed to the Holocaust, including a long history of anti-Semitism, German Jews were shocked by their treatment because they were German citizens who were making important contributions to society. One of the troubling aspects of these two situations is that racism seems to have played a significant part in pushing out people who were members of an organized community.

The situation is quite different when a group is deciding which outsiders to allow into the group. For example, consider recent efforts by Americans to reform immigration policies. These discussion seem to involve more instrumental considerations. The general public favors restricting the number of immigrants allowed into the country because of its concerns about the negative economic impact a large influx of new residents would have on American society. Similarly, existing immigration policy favors immigrants who can bring financial investments or business ventures into the United States.

It may be that people are much more instrumental when dealing with outsiders seeking to enter their group than when considering how to react to people who are already in the group. Excluding members of the community based on instrumental motivations may be perceived to be immoral and hence difficult to justify. In contrast, preventing strangers from joining the community on the same basis seems to be more acceptable. Once ties have been made, however tenuous, moral obligations develop and may take precedence over instrumental considerations in importance. At this point, these predictions are mere speculations, and their evolution into full research hypotheses would have to rely on future theoretical developments and additional empirical research.

Last, discussions of the scope of justice focus on those circumstances under which people exclude others from their scope of justice concerns. However, there is also a less studied issue of when people include themselves in a moral community. People of varying centrality to their community (i.e., differing in their subjective feelings of inclusion) have been found to differ in their reliance on justice concerns (Tyler & Lind, 1990). Tyler and Lind argue that people of intermediate centrality to the group are the most concerned about procedural justice and related relational issues because they are particularly concerned about their status within their group. People with high status (who feel secure about their social position) and those with low status (who recognize their marginal position) focus relatively more on instrumental concerns. In the future, it would be interesting to examine how people's standing in moral communities impact their willingness to exclude or include others from the same community.

Social Context Effects

The argument that there is a scope of justice can be stated more generally as the suggestion that justice concerns are shaped by the social context. For example, Leventhal (1980) argues that people are not always concerned with justice issues. He suggests that justice rules are often routine or invariant aspects of interactions and fade into the background. Only under some circumstances are justice concerns activated. For example, justice may be a clear concern when new institutions and organizations are created but are not as important in the day-to-day life of an institution.

There are two views about how the nature of justice concerns changes as relationships become institutionalized. One view is that people focus less strongly on justice issues in the context of ongoing relationships, focusing instead on other issues such as good outcomes. This is similar to the suggestion made earlier (Lind & Tyler, 1990) that people who are securely attached to others in their group do not focus on procedural justice but focus on other concerns. A different argument is that people in organized groups simply expect that they will receive justice. In other words, they appear not to be focused on justice issues, but they will rapidly become concerned about justice if they do not receive it. This argument flows from the idea of a fairness heuristic (Lind, Kulik, Ambrose, & de Vera Park, 1993); when a relationship is going well, fair treatment is expected and people do not pay close attention to whether they are being treated fairly.

The social context may shape justice in two ways. It may determine the relative importance of justice, or it may shape the criteria used to define justice. Current research suggests that justice issues remain important across a variety of situations but that the criteria and meaning of justice vary. Several types of contextual influences have been examined, including the influence of scarcity and structural and role influences.

Scarcity and Abundance

One set of contextual factors involves the scarcity or abundance of social resources or opportunities. A popular theme in movies and literature is a group of people who find themselves stranded on a desert island or in a life raft, trapped in a prison camp during war, or in some other way placed in a situation of scarcity and conflict with others. The question is, How will people respond to this situation? Will they become self-centered and selfish, or will they continue to care about others and about principles of fairness and justice?

Some argue that justice concerns are a curvilinear function of resource availability, with justice being most important in intermediate situations. Hogan and Emler (1981), for example, suggest that justice concerns are minor in times of abundance and primarily arise when there are conflicts of interest over the allocation of moderate levels of resources. Under this situation, scarcity conflicts will arise and people will be concerned with justice and with the implications injustice may have for immediate and long-term outcomes. As the severity of resource scarcity increases, justice becomes limited again and will only apply to those with whom one has significant exchange or social relationships. Finally, self-interest may be the terminal form of justice when scarcity imposes threats on the basic necessities of life (Booth, 1983; de Carufel, 1981).

This argument extends the general argument of Thibaut and Faucheux (1965) that rules are likely to arise in profitable but unstable social relations. That is, rules arise in intermediate situations in which people can still cooperate to their mutual benefit but in which there is the possibility that cooperation will collapse (see Barrett-Howard & Tyler, 1986, for evidence supporting this proposition).

Evidence suggests that justice concerns remain important when resources are scarce, but the justice rules people use to define fairness and the extent to which those rules are applied vary. For example, need and efficiency are viewed as more appropriate distributive-justice principles than equity when the particular resource is scarce (Greenberg, 1981). According to the contingency model of distributive justice (Skitka & Tetlock, 1992), scarcity promotes cognitive effort on the part of the allocator in evaluating claims for the desired resource. Under conditions of low scarcity, only the personally responsible claimants with low priority (low need and unlikely to use resources efficiently) are denied resources. Under conditions of high scarcity, only claimants with high priority (high need and likely to use resources with efficiency) are given resources.

Other research suggests that scarcity may affect the scope of justice concerns in addition to affecting the principles of justice used. Sociological theories of responses to scarcity based on field observation (Booth, 1983) suggest that distributive justice norms may have an increasingly restricted range of applicability in times of scarcity. Towson, Lerner, and de Carufel (1981) demonstrate a shift to in-group favoritism from equitable allocations in response to high competition in a laboratory setting. Elster (1993) similarly argues that scarcity prompts people to limit the scope of justice to members of the same social or ethnic group in the distribution of scarce and valuable resources. Examples of this phenomenon include efforts to introduce legislation that would bar foreign nationals from utilizing organ pools in the United States and the preference expressed by African American kidney donors that their kidneys not be provided to Caucasian patients.

Studies also suggest that how people respond to scarcity depends on their political and social ideology. Whether resources are scarce or plentiful, political conservatives tend to focus on an assessment of personal responsibility and withhold resources from claimants who are personally responsible for their plight (Skitka & Tetlock, 1993). The basis of their reactions is not affected by level of scarcity. In contrast, political liberals' allocation behavior appears more responsive to the extent of resource scarcity. Under conditions of abundance, liberals tend to allocate resources to all claimants. However, under conditions of scarcity, egalitarian values are not practical, and painful discriminations must be made. In this event, the behavior of liberals begins to resemble that of conservatives, and claimants who are personally responsible for their problems (for example, people who need a new kidney because their own failed due to excessive drinking) are denied resources.

Some research has suggested that the experience of allocating under conditions of scarcity may have enduring effects (M. Ross & Ellard, 1986). Skitka (1996) finds that liberals who have allocated resources under conditions of scarcity are less likely to allocate resources to all claimants when scarcity constraints are relaxed. It is reasoned that to reduce the painful and socially awkward trade-offs associated with making allocation decisions under scarcity, liberals accentuate the deservedness of the chosen and the undeservedness of the rejected. These justifications then outlive the period of scarcity and affect future allocation decisions.

In addition to influencing distributive justice, scarcity may have an effect on retributive justice. For example, Sales's (1973) analysis of archival data finds that punitiveness toward violators of in-group rules increases when society faces economic threats. This is indexed at the collective level by a relative increase in expenditures for police, law and order themes in political speeches, and attitudes in favor of the death penalty during times of economic recession.

The influence of scarcity on the choice of justice principles can be understood as the product of either relational concerns or of instrumental concerns. An instrumental analysis suggests that under conditions of diminished resources, justice principles would be chosen in ways that serve self-interest. If a person is more likely to benefit from justice rules that emphasize the efficient distribution of resources, he or she will support that principle. If a person is more likely to benefit from rules that emphasize a distribution of resources based on need, he or she will support that principle (Greenberg, 1981). Similarly, increased scarcity should mean that people will limit their scope of justice to those with whom they have a productive exchange relationship (Deutsch, 1985).

In contrast, a relational analysis emphasizes values and social influences on justice considerations during times of scarcity rather than direct costs and benefits. One type of evidence that supports a relational analysis is that when resources are scarce, societies and individuals think about justice in macro terms. One macro concern is efficiency—what is good for the overall society. For example, historically in the Inuit society, the elderly voluntarily wander off to die in the snow when they can no longer contribute to the group, and in wartime, doctors conduct triage to determine who will receive medical treatment. During times of scarcity, individuals focus on what is good for the group rather than on what is good for themselves or for other individuals. Greenberg (1981) provides evidence that under conditions of scarcity, overall efficiency becomes a central justice principle.

The issue of scarcity provides an excellent arena within which to compare the instrumental and relational models of the justice motive. If the instrumental model of the justice motive is correct, then people should increasingly abandon their justice concerns for self-interested behavior as resources become scarce. In extreme situations, people should simply care about themselves, their families, and perhaps their immediate social group. These feelings should be especially strong when people are losing accustomed resources, since prospect theory indicates that losses loom larger than gains in subjective calculations (Kahneman, 1979). But from an instrumental perspective, abundance should be a time when there is an absence of resource conflicts (Hogan & Emler, 1981).

In contrast, the relational model suggests that people should be concerned about status and identity issues under conditions of scarcity. However, it is interesting to note that scarcity does not always lead to status or identity problems. Consider the military police officers studied in the original research on relative deprivation (Stouffer et al., 1949). Those officers faced a scarcity of promotion opportunities with apparent equanimity. In contrast, the pilots faced an abundance of promotion opportunities with unhappiness and dissatisfaction. A relational perspective suggests that the changes in status—and consequent identity—that occur during times of abundance may be more troubling than the resource problems encountered during times of scarcity.

The argument that times of abundance may be difficult for individuals and societies to deal with is supported by both Brickman and Campbell (1971) and Greenberg (1981). They argue that people rapidly increase their expectations as resources increase; consequently, it becomes difficult to create the psychological feeling of abundance. Instead, resources increasingly take on a symbolic role, reflecting relational issues of status and self-worth. Thus, high levels of objective abundance do not necessarily lead to positive feelings. As an illustration, anecdotal evidence from the news media suggests that although East Germans' objective standard of living has increased dramatically since the German reunification, their level of satisfaction has not (personal communication, Bierbrauer, 1996, March 15). Although there is very little research comparing the instrumental and relational models under conditions of scarcity, it appears to be a promising arena for future studies.

Role and Structural Effects

Another set of contextual factors that influences considerations of justice is role or structural differences. Leventhal (1980) suggests that the degree to which justice concerns are activated depends in part on the nature of the social structure. For example, justice concerns are more salient in pluralistic systems that lack a single set of values and are less central in monolithic systems. This suggests that the increasing diversity of societies such as the United States may lead to greater attention to issues of justice or injustice. Similarly, justice issues are more prominent when organizations are being created and rules are being developed (Azzi & Jost, 1992). Hence, justice issues should matter when relationships or organizations are being formed or are dissolving.

We have already noted that justice concerns may change as social interactions become institutionalized. Recent descriptions of the role of justice in close relationships (Lerner & Mikula, 1994) support a similar argument— that justice issues may be less central in ongoing relationships but may become salient when a relationship is disintegrating. When relationships are going well, justice concerns fade into the background. None of the parties to the relationship are actively considering whether they are being fairly or unfairly treated. In contrast, when relationships start to deteriorate, people become more concerned with the injustice of their situation (Attridge & Berscheid, 1994; Brehm, 1992).

Not all researchers, though, agree that justice concerns are absent in satisfying close relationships (Lerner & Mikula, 1994). For example, justice may be defined differently in satisfying relationships (e.g., need rather than equity) than in deteriorating relationships (e.g., equity rather than need). This argument is consistent with the previously outlined literature on the influence of the nature of relationships on the distributive justice principles used within them (Deutsch, 1975, 1985).

In hierarchically oriented relationships, justice concerns may also recede into the background. Subordinates often defer their moral obligations and evaluations to their supervisors and leaders, acting as agents for the collective will rather than as autonomous individuals (Milgram, 1974). Kelman and Hamilton (1989) provide numerous examples of people's willingness to suspend consideration of their moral principles to support the actions of legitimate authorities. As Darley (1992) comments, "organizations are required to produce evil actions" (p. 204) since they provide the social forces that encourage individuals to abandon their personal moral considerations. Similarly, Kelman and Hamilton suggest that under certain conditions, people authorize legitimate others to make moral judgments for them.

In order for people to defer to authorities, they must believe that those authorities are legitimate (Tyler, 1990). Interestingly, legitimacy is strongly linked to judgments about the justice of authorities' actions. However, as we have noted, the key antecedent of legitimacy is procedural justice, not distributive justice (Tyler, 1990). Hence, people defer to authorities when they think those authorities engage in fair decisionmaking procedures. They do not rely on the fairness of the outcome of the decisions. Again, it may not be that justice concerns have disappeared; instead, the criterion for determining justice may have changed from a general moral evaluation to more specific evaluations of procedural fairness.

An interesting example of the power of procedural justice to promote legitimacy is provided in a recent study of public support for the United States Supreme Court (Tyler & Mitchell, 1994). The study explored the public's views about abortion among a random sample of the American population. It found that many of those who were interviewed felt that abortion was immoral. However, these views were found to have little impact on the legitimacy of the Court that makes policy decisions about the legal status of abortions. Instead, people judged the legitimacy of the Court by evaluating the fairness of Court decisionmaking procedures. If the decisionmaking procedures were judged to be fair, people felt that the court was legitimate and should be empowered to make abortion policies, irrespective of whether they agreed with those policies. People felt that following fair procedures authorized the Court to exercise power. This finding provides evidence that evaluations of Court decisionmaking procedures had a stronger influence on people's willingness to defer to the Court than did personal moral values and beliefs.

Role Effects

Another structural factor that determines the extent and degree to which justice concerns are activated is the social role in which people engage. A first and perhaps obvious role difference is between victim and victimizer. Mikula (1994) finds evidence that victims in close relationships perceive unfair events as more serious, more undeserved, and more unjust, and they attribute more responsibility and blame to the victimizers than do the victimizers themselves. Interestingly, the less satisfied partners are with their relationship, the greater the divergence in their explanations for unjust events.

Not only do perceptions of unjust events diverge between victims and victimizers, but also their understandings of retributive behavior differ. For example, when romantic partners use the silent treatment as punishment, they assume the violator knows that he or she has committed an offense and is unwilling to apologize. In contrast, as the targets of such treatment, they report having no idea that their actions have offended their partner. More importantly, when people are the target of the silent treatment, they report feeling extremely angry and aggressive, but when they use the silent treatment themselves, they minimize the target's emotional reactions and focus instead on its effectiveness (Somer & Williams, 1994). In other words, these divergent perspectives reflect an egocentric bias in which one's behavior, or one's reaction to another's behavior, is seen as more reasonable and good than the other's reaction and behavior (e.g., deRidder & Tripathi, 1992; Mummendey & Otten, 1993).

A second important role difference is between allocators and recipients of resources. Those who are allocators must consider issues of macrojustice, examining the various trade-offs involved in enacting fair procedures and finding fair solutions (Elster, 1992; Leventhal, 1980; Skitka & Tetlock, 1992). Allocators must make proactive social justice judgments (Greenberg, 1987b), whereas recipients make reactive judgments. Further, the trade-offs important to allocators are very different from the trade-offs important to the recipients (Elster, 1993).

Certainly, the issues important to allocators and recipients are different. For example, allocators may be particularly interested in how their decisions will be received and how those decisions will affect social relationships. In contrast, recipients are more interested in how they are affected by decisions and the implications of those decisions for their self-concept and their standing within important social groups. The influence of role on views about justice is demonstrated in studies of work supervisors and police officers (Lissak & Sheppard, 1983; Sheppard & Lewicki, 1987). These studies find that allocators place a greater emphasis on instrumental issues than on relational issues vis-à-vis subordinates and citizens. This accords with Hogan, Curphy, and Hogan's (1994) suggestion that subordinates' evaluations of authorities are more strongly affected by relational issues than are authorities' evaluations of subordinates.

The influence of role and structural effects on social justice concerns can also be understood from either an instrumental or a relational perspective. An instrumental perspective suggests that it is in the interest of those who may have caused an injustice to minimize their responsibility for the unjust event; however, it is in the interest of those who feel they are victims to emphasize the seriousness and injustice of the same event. For example, recipients, according to an instrumental perspective, will endorse as fair any distribution that benefits them.

However, because allocators and recipients often have opposing interests, there are natural limits to the plausibility of a self-interest argument. Although allocators are motivated to be efficient, this efficiency is tempered by feelings of accountability to recipients because they know that recipients will react to the allocations they receive (Skitka & Tetlock, 1993). In the arena of retributive justice, similar dynamics may be at work. For example, it is in the interest of those who punish to emphasize the effectiveness and reasonableness of the punishment, and it is in the interest of those who are the targets to emphasize how the punishment is undeserved and unfair.

An instrumental perspective suggests that roles and social structure can be understood as a series of instrumentally beneficial exchange relationships. In contrast, a relational perspective suggests that roles and social structure can be understood as a web of social relationships and moral responsibilities. A relational understanding of role and structural differences can explain why some couples' explanations of unfair events converge and other couples' explanations do not. After all, it is not in the perpetrator's self-interest to acknowledge his or her role in creating an injustice. Therefore, it is difficult to account for this variability from a purely instrumental perspective. A relational perspective suggests that other goals (e.g., mutual responsiveness; Clark & Mills, 1993) might be important in some relationships and not in others, independent of any instrumental costs and benefits.

Allocator and recipient differences may reflect differences in social responsibilities. For example, allocators' structural role in the group makes authorities responsible for considering the moral implications of their actions (Kelman & Hamilton, 1989), whereas subordinates react based on their feelings of obligation to authorities and to the group. To date, studies have not yet provided a clear differentiation of the motives underlying role effects on social justice judgments.

10

CULTURE

In Chapter 9, we examined variations in the importance and meaning of justice that occur in different social conditions. For example, we explored how the scarcity or abundance of resources changes social allocation rules. We also considered how the nature of the social structure influences the importance and meaning of justice. This focus on the nature of the social structure leads to a more general discussion of a rapidly growing area of social justice research—the study of cultural differences in the importance and meaning of justice. In this chapter, we examine research on people's views about justice in differing cultural contexts.

In general, cross-cultural research in psychology is concerned with establishing the characteristics of people that are basic and universal and the characteristics of people that are influenced by the cultural context. Moving beyond the traditional assumption of universalism in psychology, researchers and theorists have acknowledged the important role that culture plays in shaping human interactions. Evidence of the extent of culture's impact on the field of social psychology can be found in recent efforts to develop culturally valid theories of the self (Markus & Kitayama, 1992) and of social relations (Fiske, 1992). In keeping with this general trend, justice researchers have also begun to try to understand how cultural context shapes people's views about what is right and wrong and what is fair or unfair.

Research on people's views about justice has slowly moved away from assuming that findings of a study conducted in one culture represent basic human processes to questioning and testing the cross-cultural validity of existing theories and research programs. For example, in the 1970s, equity theory was the dominant paradigm used to understand people's sense of justice, and equity was assumed to be a basic principle that guides social interactions in all societies (Berkowitz & Walster, 1976). Since then, the study of justice has become far more complicated, and researchers have examined the influence of a wide variety of factors on views about justice. Past reviews of the justice literature have evaluated the impact of gender and individual differences (Major & Deaux, 1982) as well as national culture (Leung, 1988). These reviews suggest that "culture" in a broad sense, plays at least some role in shaping people's views about justice and should be considered seriously.

There are several factors that fuel the growing interest in the influence of culture on people's views about justice. One of the main motivating factors is the desire to respond to critics who propose that some of the most basic theories of justice are culture bound and of limited generalizability (Gergen, Morse, & Gergen, 1982; Hayden & Anderson, 1979; Hogan & Elmer, 1978; Pepitone, 1976; Sampson, 1976).

A second reason for focusing on cultural influences is more functional in nature. In a world in which mass migrations, international business ventures, and global politics are becoming commonplace, cross-cultural interactions are more likely to occur than ever before. Cultural differences in perceptions of morality and fairness can lead to open conflict and disrupt important relationships. Hence, it is important to understand whether there are any observable differences in people's views about justice across cultural contexts and how such differences would impact cross-cultural interactions.

A third motivating factor is that cross-cultural research can lead to the development of concepts that are not likely to be discovered through research conducted within a single culture (Leung, 1989; Sugawara & Huo, 1994). To the degree that there are cultural differences, the study of each unique culture will contribute new elements to an overall understanding of the parameters of individual relationships.

In writing this chapter, we have made two major assumptions. Our first assumption is that there are both universal and culture specific aspects to the way people think about and react to justice issues. Our second assumption is that it is useful to distinguish the possible influence of culture at two levels—the individual and the group. Hence, we will begin our discussion of cross-cultural research on justice by examining the extent to which individual- and group-level responses to issues of justice are influenced by the cultural context (see Figure 10.1). At the individual level, the question is whether the cultural context influences the individual's views about justice. For example, do individuals who live in a collectively oriented society define justice differently than individuals who live in an individualistic society? In contrast, at the group level the question is whether the cultural context shapes the way a collective (e.g., a group of individuals) deals with justice concerns. For example, a community that has to deal with scarcity may develop different rules for allocating resources than a community that exists under conditions of abundance.

A Universal Perspective

The idea of universal justice standards suggests that there may be basic human characteristics. Such characteristics may be genetic or biological, as

Level of analysis	Nature of justice concern	
	Universal	Culture specific
Individual	Common human needs and concerns	Effects of cultural rules on individual's sense of justice
Group	Common societal problems	Effects of the environment on the development of cultural values

FIGURE 10.1   Bases of observed cultural similarities and differences

suggested by sociobiology (Wright, 1994), or they may reflect the basic structure of the human mind (Fiske, 1992). When considering a universalistic argument at the level of the collective, we acknowledge that societies or groups are not people and do not have similar unfolding characteristics. However, it is possible to make a similar distinction between universal and culture-specific social characteristics. That distinction is linked to the nature of the problems with which societies must cope. Societies that face a similar set of core problems are likely to adopt similar justice rules to cope with these problems, leading to a universality in justice rules.

The Individual

At the level of the individual, a universalistic argument assumes that humans have a basic set of needs and concerns, irrespective of the cultural context within which they live. It follows that individuals who are members of different cultures should share some similar views about justice and should respond to problems of resource allocation, conflict resolution, and retribution in a like fashion. Lind and Earley (1992) refer to these views as intrinsic to the person. Such views are identified by their invariant occurrence across different cultures.

Support for such a universalistic argument can be found in theories of cognitive development like that of Piaget. He suggests that personal cognitive development reflects the unfolding over time of internal stages of reasoning and should occur universally across cultures. This view of development has been extended by Piaget (1948) and Kohlberg (1969) to the development of conceptions of justice and morality. Within the justice literature, a similar argument for universal human motives is found in the work of Lerner, who argues for an underlying justice motive (1981).

An example of an intrinsic conception about justice is the "voice effect" documented in the procedural justice literature. Lind and Earley (1992) suggest that people's desire for the opportunity to express their views rises out of a basic human need for positive regard within important reference groups. For an individual, to be given the opportunity for "voice" is to have some indication that he or she is respected by other group members. Because a concern about having "voice" is linked to a motive intrinsic to the individual, such a concern is likely to be expressed by all people across different cultural contexts.

An illustration of research that seeks to test the intrinsic justice motive argument for the "voice effect" is a study by Lind, Erickson, Friedland, and Dickenberger (1978). The study examined people's preferences for adversarial versus nonadversarial dispute resolution mechanisms across nations with different formal legal systems. It distinguished two possible explanations for the original finding that Americans prefer the adversarial method and view it as fairer than the nonadversarial (i.e., inquisitorial) method. One explanation for the effect is that it reflects an inherent preference for a particular method of dispute resolution. An adversarial system is preferred because it provides the opportunity for "voice" not provided by the inquisitorial system. If the argument is valid that people seek out opportunities for "voice" in order to fulfill a basic need for respect, then individuals from a variety of cultures should agree that the adversarial system is more fair and prefer it over the inquisitorial system.

An alternative explanation for the American preference for the adversary system is socialization—that is, since Americans are socialized into a legal system that defines the adversarial method as just and right, it is not particularly surprising that they prefer this method of resolving disputes.

In testing procedural preferences across four different nations (United States, England, France, and Germany) with two different formal legal systems, Lind et al. provide evidence to suggest that even in countries with an inquisitorial legal system (France and Germany), individuals indicated a preference for the adversarial system and perceived it to be more fair. The preference for an adversarial legal system in societies that do not have it suggests that people view a procedure that provides an opportunity for voice as inherently fairer than one that does not. This provides support for the argument that there is a basic psychological model of procedural justice.

The Group

At the level of the collective, a universalistic argument assumes that there is a set of core problems that must be dealt with by any social group. Examples of some basic social problems that occur across different societies include "turn taking" (social coordination), creating hierarchies, allocating resources, and punishing rule breakers. There may be basic social characteristics that develop across all societies as a result of common efforts to solve these core social problems. Such common social characteristics may in turn lead societies to develop similar justice rules. Presumably, justice rules arise because they have some functional value to societies seeking to deal with the problems of maintaining social order, maintaining cohesiveness, and enhancing productivity (Campbell, 1975).

Consider the example of social coordination. Individuals may avoid dealing with turn taking by always working alone. If, however, they collaborate with others, they are forced to confront issues of allocating rewards and burdens, and they must articulate principles to guide those efforts. Such principles are a reflection of a common social problem and may lead to the development of comparable justice rules.

A Culture Specific Perspective

In contrast to the universalistic argument, a culture specific perspective suggests that human motives and behaviors are shaped in large part by the cultural context. The assumption is that cultural norms and values color and shape individuals' views about the relevance and meaning of justice in social interactions. For example, cultural differences may lead to differing definitions of such basic concepts as morality and just deserts. At the level of the collective, the environment within which a group exists shapes the kind of justice rules the groups adopts. Just as societies facing similar problems develop similar justice rules, societies facing different problems develop different justice rules to cope with the unique problems posed by their environments.

The Individual

The culture specific perspective is reflected in the term "extrinsic standards" (Lind & Earley, 1992). In contrast to intrinsic, universal standards, Lind and Earley define extrinsic standards of justice as those that do not reflect the operation of basic human motives. Extrinsic standards are linked to the properties of social systems and reflect the values of specific groups. In the case of extrinsic standards, there is no expectation that people will display similar concerns about justice across societies. On the contrary, people's views about and reactions to justice should vary depending upon the norms and values of the particular cultural context in which they were socialized.

Support for the culture specific perspective can be found in the widely held view that individuals from traditional cultures prefer to resolve their disputes through informal, conciliatory procedures, not through formal, adversarial procedures (Nader & Todd, 1978). In a direct comparison of two distinct cultures, Leung (1987; Leung & Lind, 1986) demonstrated that students in Hong Kong prefer nonadversarial procedures more than do American students. The findings suggest that the observed difference can be attributed to differing perceptions of the procedures by Hong Kong and American students. Although students in both countries considered criteria such as how fair the procedure is and how likely it is that the procedure will reduce animosity to be equally important, they had different beliefs about the extent to which the procedures would lead to these desired outcomes. For example, Chinese subjects are more likely to think that an adversarial trial would damage social harmony. Through their social experiences within different cultures, these students have developed different beliefs about the characteristics of dispute resolution procedures and its associated outcomes. These studies provide evidence that culture can affect the individual and his/her views about justice relevant matters.

The Group

At the level of the collective, the unique problems encountered by societies can lead to the development of culture bound conceptions of justice. Earlier, we suggested that societies share some common problems, and efforts to resolve these basic problems can lead to the development of similar justice rules. In addition to facing some common problems, societies may also face differing problems that develop from their distinctive geographies, the nature of their economic resources and their economies, and the histories of the people who live within those societies. These culture specific social characteristics give rise to unique justice conceptions within cultures.

Earlier, we noted that equity theory has been put forward as a universal model of justice. However, cross-cultural research shows that equity is not the universal distributive rule it was thought to be (Berman, Murphy-Berman, & Singh, 1985; Murphy-Berman et al., 1984). For example, research shows that people in India have a preference for need over equity as a general distributive rule. This difference is explained as a reaction to different environmental conditions. In India, where the level of desired resources is scarce, greater cultural value is placed on people's needs; hence need becomes a more culturally acceptable criterion for the distribution of valued resources than equity. In other words, the level of scarcity in India led the society to develop a culture-specific conception of need as a basis for resource allocation. However, in a society of relative resource abundance, individual effort is considered to be a more appropriate distribution criterion.

Empirical Issues

Relative to monocultural research, theoretically and empirically valid cross-cultural research is a difficult endeavor with many added complications. Consequently, it is important to consider certain problems that may arise in the process of conducting cross-cultural research on people's views about justice. Here we consider a few of the empirical issues raised in cross-cultural research.

Interpreting Evidence

First and most importantly, we need to consider the kind of research evidence that constitutes support for either a universalistic or culture specific view of justice. Inevitably, evidence from cross-cultural studies consists of findings of cultural similarity or findings of cultural difference. If there are commonalties, this suggests one of two possibilities: (1) that people have similar core justice concerns and/or (2) that societies must solve similar social problems and develop similar justice conceptions in their efforts to deal with those problems. Either way, similarity across cultures suggests clear support for a universalistic perspective to the extent that the phenomenon can be replicated across a range of different cultures.

In contrast, it is less clear how findings of difference should be interpreted. One possibility is that differences occur because people lack intrinsic conceptions of justice. It is also possible, however, that people have intrinsic conceptions of justice but that such basic human motives are overridden by the pressures of cultural socialization (Tyler & McGraw, 1986). In the latter case, we would expect to find indirect evidence of intrinsic standards, such as feelings of confusion or discomfort with socially imposed standards of fairness. Although people might publicly, and perhaps even privately, accept socially imposed standards, they should be like the disadvantaged who have psychologically adjusted to their position. Although this group appears on the surface to have denied their feelings of injustice, there are indirect indications of unhappiness (e.g., drug use, alcoholism, and so forth).

As our previous discussion of justice makes clear, the question of cultural effects is not a simple question of whether culture influences general justice concerns. There are a series of ways in which culture might potentially affect the psychology of justice. First, culture might influence the importance of distributive, procedural, and/or retributive justice. For example, some researchers suggest that the members of certain cultures lack a conception of justice—or more accurately, a western conception of justice (Kidder & Muller, 1991).

Second, culture might influence the meaning of distributive, procedural, and/or retributive justice. People might agree that justice is important but define it differently.

Finally, culture might influence the impact of situational factors on the importance and meaning of justice. In the last chapter, we noted that the psychology of justice is responsive to social factors, and such factors may differ across cultures. For example, cultures may differ in the degree to which they are hierarchical or in the degree to which people participate in governance, and these differences may shape the psychology of justice within those cultures.

Defining Culture

It is important to note that an examination of the relationship between culture and justice concerns is not exclusively about comparisons between nations (the United States versus Japan, England versus Sweden, and so on). It can also concern differences within nations. In fact, the nation-state is a fairly recent historical phenomenon (Azzi, in press). Traditionally, a people's culture has been linked to religious and/or social groupings that often were forcibly eradicated or suppressed in the creation of nation-states. For example, people may draw more of their cultural identity from being Christian, Buddhist, or Muslim than they do from being English or American. If so, it is these cultural boundaries that are of concern in the study of culture and the psychology of justice. The issue of cultural diversity within nations and how it affects interpretations and reactions to justice is a pressing social concern in many societies around the world today. We will address that question at the conclusion of this chapter.

Evidence from Empirical Research

In this section, we provide a brief review of the existing research literature on the influence of culture on conceptions of distributive, procedural, and retributive justice. First, we review evidence in support of the universalism position, and then we review evidence in support of the cultural particularism position.

Universalism

Research suggests that justice is a widespread, if not a universal, concern across culture groups (James, 1993). Justice seems to matter to people in widely varying cultures. This does not mean that cultural effects on the importance of justice are not found—they are. But the dominant finding is that concerns about justice are similar across cultures.

The importance placed on justice across different cultures is illustrated by cross-cultural research on procedural justice. Research evidence suggests that procedural justice is the most important predictor of preferences for dispute resolution strategies among different ethnic groups within the United States (Lind, Huo, & Tyler, 1994) and among people from different Western nations (LaTour, Houlden, Walker, & Thibaut, 1976). In addition, a study in Japan, a non-Western culture, showed that procedural justice is the most important criterion people consider when deciding how to resolve legal disputes (Sugawara & Huo, 1994). Such evidence suggests that concerns about procedural justice are at least widespread, if not universal.

Research on retributive justice also provides evidence for the universalism argument. Such studies demonstrate that the desire to punish rule breaking is prevalent across cultures (Hamilton & Saunders, 1992). In particular, cross-cultural research shows that there is considerable agreement among cultures about which offenses warrant punishment and how serious those offenses are (Evans & Scott, 1984).

Particularism

Although evidence suggests that justice is valued by people across different cultures, it appears that it is also shaped by cultural factors (Lind & Earley, 1992). Evidence for a more particularistic approach is presented by researchers who argue that the concern for fairness (as defined by a concern for individual rights and entitlement) is a particularly Western construction (Kidder & Muller, 1993; Miller & Bersoff, 1992). For example, Kidder and Muller (1993) report that the Japanese language does not include a word for fair. This observation might reflect either an absence of justice concerns or varying definitions of justice. Kidder and Muller argue that the lack of a specific word for fairness reflects the greater emphasis in Japanese society on what is respectful or polite than on what is just or right. Similarly, in the domain of moral judgments, it is suggested that different cultures have different definitions of what is moral and immoral (Haidt, Koller, & Dias, 1993). Furthermore, other research shows that the relationship between experiencing injustice and feeling anger varies across European societies (Babad & Wallbott, 1986; Wallbott & Scherer, 1986). This suggests that the degree to which justice affects people's thoughts and feelings, our central concern in Chapters 2, 3, 4, and 5, might not be constant across social groups.

Evidence suggests that cultural norms also shape views about retributive justice and the meaning of criminal offenses. Roberts (1992) notes that although there is considerable cross-cultural similarity in reactions to some types of crimes, reactions to other types of offenses vary across cultures. For example, French and North American respondents agree that the offense of rape is serious. In contrast, the French are much more concerned about the fraudulent labeling of wine than North Americans (a crime the French placed at the same level of seriousness as having sex with a minor). These findings suggest that the centrality of a norm to the maintenance of cultural identity may be one determinant of cultural variation in responding to justice.

Cultural context clearly shapes the relative importance placed on justice considerations. In a comparison between Indian and American subjects, Miller and Bersoff (1992) show cultural differences in the importance placed on behaving according to justice norms in the resolution of a social conflict. In that study, Indian and American participants are asked about the appropriate resolution for a conflict that requires making a choice between favoring justice considerations (e.g., individual rights, claims, and the prevention of harm) or favoring role-related interpersonal responsibilities. Subjects are asked, for example, to consider a situation in which they go on a trip but lose their money while away and cannot purchase a train ticket home. Their return is required so that they can attend a relative's wedding. Subjects are asked whether it is better to steal money to return for the wedding (meeting interpersonal obligations) or to follow justice principles and miss the wedding. Indian adults and children preferred solutions that favored interpersonal responsibilities, suggesting less concern about issues of justice (Miller & Bersoff, 1992). Americans, in contrast, preferred to miss the wedding.

Miller and Bersoff's analysis illustrates some of the difficulties of interpreting cross-cultural findings. First, it may not be that people in some cultures value justice less, but rather that they define it differently (i.e., the meaning of justice changes). The interpersonal responsibilities of importance to Indian subjects may also represent justice judgments. It may be that Indian subjects, for example, give preference to the principle of need, feeling that their family needs their presence at the wedding more than the victim needs the stolen money. If so, then it is the meaning of justice that changes, not its importance.

It is also possible that the level at which justice considerations are conceptualized is different across cultures. The group is suggested to be more important to the self-concept of Indian subjects (as members of a more collectivist culture) than it is for American subjects (as members of a more individualist culture). Microjustice principles of individual rights and responsibility may not represent the best level at which to capture collectivist justice concerns. Justice for collectivist cultures may be better defined at the group level (Azzi, 1994; Brickman, et al., 1981). Again, the key issue may be not whether justice matters, but how it is conceptualized.

The other question is whether situational variations in the importance and meaning of justice are similar across cultures. In the area of distributive justice, considerable evidence suggests that different rules are applied in different social domains. For example, within the United States, where most of the studies on the topic are conducted, research suggests that there is general consensus within American society about the distributive goals that are appropriate to different types of settings (Tyler, 1985). In particular, equity seems to most Americans to be fair in work settings but unfair in other situations. In law and government, however, people resist equity. Proposals to weigh votes by political knowledge, for example, are not viewed as fair. In political/governmental settings, people endorse the use of equality and needs as principles. For example, police protection should be equally distributed across neighborhoods, or more police should go to those areas in need. Those who pay more taxes should not receive more police protection or have more votes (even though both ideas are consistent with an equity model) because resources should be distributed equally in the political arena (Walzer, 1983). Hence, there is considerable consensus within situations but no general principles of justice that explain distributive justice judgments in all settings.

The finding that there is considerable consensus about which justice principles are to be applied in particular settings suggests that justice rules may be the result of childhood socialization and the adoption of important cultural values and norms. This would argue that in other cultures, the rules governing the appropriate principles for distributing resources in particular situations (work, family, law, and so on) might not be the same as those within the United States. For example, societies differ in the emphasis they place on providing benefits for the disadvantaged. They do not universally embrace the use of equity to distribute social and economic benefits.

Consider an example comparing the United States and France. During the fall of 1994, France experienced a series of strikes by government workers upset at proposed cuts in their work benefits. Workers argued that equality and fraternity are not mere slogans (in France). Instead, the support of the state for disadvantaged workers is a core social value, with the result that France is "a far more egalitarian society than most Western industrial countries" and provides benefits to workers and their families that allow the "children of the disadvantaged a fair chance to jump to middle-class status in one generation." A consequence of these policies is "a way of life that brought cohesion and social peace to France for decades" (*New York Times*, 1995, December 20). In contrast, the United States is characterized by wide disparities in income and wealth and a diminishing state-financed social net to protect the disadvantaged. Thurow (1995) predicted that these disparities are likely to lead to "individual disaffection" and "social disorganization." Further, he said, "if the democratic political process cannot reverse the trend to inequality, democracy will eventually be discredited. What we do know is that a large group of hostile voters who draw no benefits from the economic system and don't think the government cares is not a particularly promising recipe for economic or political success."

The Role of Cultural Dimensions

In empirical research, differences in the way people define justice have been typically linked to dimensions of national cultures first identified by Hofstede (1980) in his international survey of workers. The most heavily researched dimension arising out of that research contrasts collectivist cultures—in which group goals and needs take precedence over individual needs—with individualistic cultures—in which individual needs and goals take precedence over group needs and goals (James, 1993; Triandis, 1989).

Although a detailed discussion of individualism versus collectivism is beyond the scope of this book, it is important to explain the nature of the group to which collectivists are predicted to have loyalties. Collectivists are hypothesized to show a greater focus on groups by definition, but the types of groups they focus on are not necessarily countries or cultures. Collectivism may, for example, involve loyalty to one's family or clan rather than loyalty to the country. Hence, attaching greater importance to group goals does not translate into attaching greater attention to the larger society. In a collectivist culture, people are more likely to think of justice in terms of justice for groups such as their family or ethnic group rather than for themselves as individuals.

It has been widely suggested that collectivist cultures focus more strongly on the distributive principles of equality and need, whereas individualistic cultures focus on the principle of equity (Deutsch, 1975; Hasegawa, 1986; James, 1993; Triandis, 1972, 1989). This hypothesis is supported by numerous studies (Berman, Murphy-Burman, & Singh, 1985; Bond, Leung, & Wan, 1982; Leung & Bond, 1982, 1984; Kashima, Siegal, Tanaka, & Isaka, 1988; Mahler, Greenberg, & Hayashi, 1981; Marin, 1981; Meindl, Hunt, & Cheng, 1994; Mikula, 1974; Murphy-Berman, Berman, Singh, Pachauri, & Kumar, 1984; Siegal & Shwalb, 1985; Tornblom & Foa, 1983).

However, the greater use of equality to allocate outcomes in collectivist cultures depends upon who the recipient is. If the recipient is a member of an out-group, members of collectivist cultures make greater use of equity norms (Leung & Bond, 1984; Leung, 1988). This pattern of results supports other evidence of increased ethnocentrism and in-group bias in collectivist cultures. This evidence suggests that members of collectivist cultures are more sensitive to group memberships than are members of more individualistic cultures (Gundykunst, 1988; Triandis, 1989). This research also illustrates that even in collectivist cultures, there are situations in which people will prefer justice principles that serve productivity and competition, and in individualist cultures, there are situations in which people will prefer justice principles and procedures that enhance and maintain group harmony (James, 1993).

Two other dimensions of national culture have also been related to differences in people's preferences for distributive justice principles: power distance and femininity-masculinity. Power distance describes differences in people's beliefs about the naturalness and permeability of social hierarchies (Hofstede, 1980). The more egalitarian a society is, the less likely individual and group-based inequities will be tolerated (Scase, 1977; Stern & Keller, 1953). In more egalitarian societies, people are more likely to respond to social injustices with anger (Gundykunst & Ting-Toomey, 1988).

Other research suggests that more feminine cultures that focus on the nurturing aspects of social relationships will prefer justice principles that enhance harmony and cooperation; but more masculine cultures that are best described by an achievement orientation will prefer justice principles that lead to competition (James, 1993). For example, Swedish and Dutch subjects, members of feminine cultures, prefer equality as a distributive principle to a greater extent than American subjects, members of a masculine culture (Nauta, 1983; Tornblom & Foa, 1983).

In the domain of procedural justice research, evidence provides some support for the cultural particularism position. For example, it has been suggested that because members of collectivist cultures place relatively greater importance on the maintenance of social relationships, they prefer procedures that are likely to reduce conflict over procedures that are considered fair but likely to lead to greater animosity. However, evidence on this point has been inconsistent. Cross-cultural investigations of procedural preferences show that collectivists such as Chinese students in Hong Kong and Kurdish and Lebanese immigrants in Germany show a stronger preference for conciliatory procedures than do American students (Leung, 1987; Leung & Lind, 1986; Bierbauer, 1990). However, in a study comparing individuals from different ethnic groups within the United States, Lind, Huo, and Tyler (1994) found similar patterns of procedural preferences across all the groups.

There is evidence for both cross-cultural similarity and difference in how people define procedural justice. Studies in Japan (Sugawara & Huo, 1994), Europe (Thibaut & Walker, 1975), Hong Kong (Leung, 1987; Leung & Lind, 1986), and among different subgroups of American society find great similarity in the criteria people use to define procedural justice. However, more recent research suggests that differences in power distance influence both the meaning and importance of justice in shaping reactions to authorities (Tyler, Lind & Huo, 1994).

The distinction between collectivism and individualism has also been related to reactions to rule breaking. In collectivist societies, rule breaking is viewed as a failure of society to socialize and guide the person properly

(Hamilton & Sanders, 1988). Therefore, rehabilitation and reintegration into society is emphasized. In individualist societies, rule breaking is viewed as a personal failure for which society is not responsible. Therefore, punishment and separation from society is emphasized.

The distinction between collectivist and individualist cultures in views about punishment is linked to the nature of the social relations within a group, as predicted by the relational view of justice. For example, social groups in Japan are much more closely knit and homogeneous than comparable groups in the United States. Further, in collectivist societies, there is a greater sense of obligation and responsibility to others (Hagiwara, 1992; Hamilton & Hagiwara, 1992; Hamilton & Sanders, 1983; Kurosawa, 1992). Consequently, shaming a rule breaker is a much more effective punishment in Japan than it is in the United States (Braithwaite, 1989).

Cultures also differ in the goals they assign to punishment. For example, citizens in the United States are more interested in retribution, incapacitation, and general deterrence; but Japanese citizens emphasize rehabilitation and social labeling (Hamilton & Sanders, 1988, 1992). In Japan, the emphasis is on the need to bring the individual back into society through restitution, apology, or some other similar means. In the United States, people who break rules are isolated to punish them for their crimes. Interestingly, both societies equally favor punishment, but they differ in their beliefs about the goals of punishment.

Response to Environmental Conditions

Research on differences in cultural values assumes that cultural differences are the product of different values, norms, and beliefs. In contrast, the observed differences may be a direct response to environmental conditions. This point was illustrated by the description of the allocation preferences between Indian and American subjects presented earlier in the chapter (Murphy-Berman et al., 1984). That study showed that when resources are scarce, allocation based on need is seen as more just than when resources are plentiful. Similarly, when resources are scarce, people are less likely to view the world as just (Furnham, 1993). Finally, Meindl, Hunt, and Cheng (1994) explain the shift among Chinese managers from more egalitarian to more meritocratic principles of justice as a reflection of the shift from a more collectivist centralized economy to a more market-oriented one. Other researchers link differences in definitions of justice to different beliefs about the consequences of using different conflict resolution procedures rather than to differences in underlying values (Bond, Leung & Schwartz, 1992; Leung & Lind, 1986).

To test whether observed differences are the result of the values people hold or a direct instrumental response to environment conditions, it is necessary to control one factor and look at the impact of the other factor on justice beliefs. For example, Siegal and Schwalb (1984) examined Japan and Australia, two nations that were economically comparable but had very different cultural heritages. They found that the need norm is more important in Japan. By controlling on level of resources, the findings provide clearer evidence that the observed differences in allocation preferences can be attributed to differences in values, norms, and beliefs. Alternatively, an instrumental explanation can be supported if a study were to examine two nations that shared similar cultural values but had different economic conditions and found that justice judgments varied in the predicted direction.

Although the research outlined makes it clear that there are many problems involved in the interpretation of cross-cultural findings, it is clear that cross-cultural research is serving the important function of broadening knowledge about the diversity of human concerns. Justice research in non-Western settings has revealed new justice concerns that have not been investigated in earlier research on Western cultures. For example, Japanese participants expressed great concern for clarity in procedures, an aspect of justice that does not emerge in open-ended interviews with Americans and has not been investigated directly in studies of American subjects (Sugawara & Huo, 1994). A concern for clarity of procedures is a natural extension of the hierarchical nature of Japanese society. In such a situation, people are interested in understanding what the rules are so that they can be followed.

The Social Construction of Justice Beliefs

One difficulty with explanations of cultural differences based on values or general environmental conditions is that they do not take into account people's individual experiences. In addition, they do not suggest whether and how people might change their views across their lives. Darley and Shultz (1990) present a more individualized approach to socialization that emphasizes the interpersonal aspects of the socialization process. It focuses on both peer interactions and children's interactions with adults. Adults play a particularly central role in moral socialization; children construct their sense of justice through interactions with parents and teachers. This social constructionist model argues that principles of justice evolve as acceptable explanations for behavior. These explanations are learned through negotiation with adults.

Still, cultural scripts will limit the influence of personal experiences in the development of views about society (Tyler & McGraw, 1986). For example, the disadvantaged may have objective experiences that their basic feelings about justice say are unfair, but they may interpret those experiences as deserved and just because of cultural socialization. Slaves, for example, often believed that slavery was legitimate, just as the authors of the Declaration of

Independence could proclaim "all Men are created equal" without meaning to include slaves or women in the arena of basic human rights. Similarly, in a study of just-world beliefs in South Africa, Furnham (1985) found that even in an unjust culture, just-world beliefs were still strong. He argued that the dominant class supported the adoption of such beliefs despite the reality of injustice in order to preserve the existing social order.

The argument that children learn their moral codes through interaction with particular adults is supported by the finding that adult behavior when socializing children is linked to whether children develop moral codes. Blasi (1980) has suggested that growing up with a lack of moral values (i.e., being a sociopath) can be linked at least in part to inconsistent parenting behavior. If parents do not reward and punish children's behavior in a consistent way or explain why behavior is wrong, for example, children are not found to develop a clear sense of right and wrong. Further, if children do not develop emotional bonds with parents or engage in discussions of right and wrong, then there is no motivation on the child's part to internalize moral values. Hence, each individual's justice rules will reflect idiosyncratic elements developed through negotiations with particular authorities.

If people learn what is just through cultural socialization or through negotiation with particular adult authorities (education), this raises the question of how such justice rules arise on the societal level so they can be taught. How, for example, do parents determine which moral rules they should be seeking to enforce when dealing with their children. How do the parents know what is right? As we have noted, one possibility is that justice rules are developed because they help to deal with basic societal problems (Campbell, 1975).

Socialization, whether at a cultural level or via personal experiences with others, may interact with the unfolding of basic human needs and cognitive frameworks. In their treatment of moral development, Piaget and Kohlberg focus on the evolution of feelings about right and wrong as the sophistication of people's reasoning develops over time. The development of moral reasoning is attributed to both cognitive maturity and engagement in social experiences. Development involves changes in the way people think about justice. For example, Kohlberg argues that people move through three stages of development, each with a distinct way of viewing justice issues. In the *pre-conventional* stage, people think about justice in self-interested terms. In the *conventional* stage, they think about justice in terms of the obligation to obey social rules. Finally, in the *postconventional* stage, people derive justice rules from the principles or goals that they think ought to be achieved.

Multiculturalism, Diversity, and Social Justice

As has been noted, cross-cultural research is not only about the relationship among people within different countries. It is also about situations of multiculturalism (members of different cultures coexisting within a society). Multicultural situations can occur within the context of a single nation or in an organization or community within culturally diverse societies like the United States, Canada, and the former Soviet Union. They can also occur when people interact across national boundaries as they do in international trade.

Cultures do not necessarily correspond to national boundaries, as is evidenced by the cultural diversity of American society. American society has traditionally been a society of immigrants who brought with them both the objective characteristics of different cultural backgrounds—clothing, language, and so forth—and different cultural values, identifications, and views about boundaries in society. America's future is also predicted to be diverse. For example, it is projected that in the year 2020, there will be no majority ethnic group in California. Instead, 41 percent of the state's population will be European Americans; 41 percent Latino Americans; 12 percent Asian Americans; and 6 percent African Americans (Dockson, 1993). Hence, research on culture and justice in the United States can help us to understand the future of an increasingly diverse society.

Beyond a simple change in demographics, a change in the social dynamics of relationships among ethnic and cultural groups is occurring. Minority groups are increasingly rejecting the idea that they should assimilate into mainstream American culture and abandon their own cultural values. Instead, groups are seeking to retain and legitimize their own groups (Rose, 1993). This trend will lead to a "mosaic" society in which the cultural traditions of different groups are recognized by the larger society.

Although many people argue that there are benefits to such a mosaic society, two important problems are likely to arise. First, the more obvious problem is that differences in cultural values may lead to an escalation of both instrumental and normative conflicts. Government, organizational, and social authorities in multicultural societies must allocate resources and interpret normative systems. Scarce societal resources must be allocated, and different groups in society are likely to view each other as being in conflict over the outcomes of allocation procedures. Additionally, distinct cultures may have disagreements about what constitutes appropriate social norms (Bierbrauer, 1992). Authorities process such disagreements and must decide which normative system or compromise of systems is to be used by the multicultural society. In either form of conflict, the decisions of authorities must be accepted in order to maintain effective governance (Gibson, 1996). How distinct groups perceive each other and the authority are importantly related to how effectively authorities can govern and hence maintain the stability of a multicultural society.

Second, a related problem that may arise in diverse societies is that salient differences between cultural groups can readily form the basis of social categorization. Although such categorizations and resulting judgments of dissimilarity are not sufficient for moral exclusion and the subsequent denial of full justice considerations, they are often the precondition to moral exclusion (Opotow, 1990). The process of categorization thus sets the stage for injustices: Groups with superior economic and political power in society may marginalize or turn a blind eye to injustices endured by culturally distinct groups. For example, the undervaluation of legal immigrants' labor and the existence of hazardous working conditions may be tolerated so long as the immigrant group is effectively categorized as outsiders.

The perception of difference may be facilitated by a focus on cultural diversity that points to differences among groups of people. As we observed in Chapter 9, categorization along lines of perceived similarity can influence whether people will deny full justice considerations to dissimilar others (Huo, 1995). This denial could be instrumentally based, or it could reflect relational concerns (Chapter 8). One tradition within social psychology suggests that such exclusion is based upon the perception that different groups are in competition for a fixed pie of resources (Levine & Campbell, 1972). This perspective suggests that the specter of exclusion in a diverse society would disappear with sufficiently high levels of productivity. In contrast, the moral or symbolic perspective suggests that exclusion is based on a lack of identification and feelings of dissimilarity. From this point of view, people who are perceived to be different may be excluded from fair distributions of resources even under conditions of relative abundance (Huo, 1996).

Another source of evidence that suggests that conflict over resources is a limited explanation for exclusion is seen in research that focuses on retributive justice. This research suggests that criminals who are perceived as out-group members (not sharing the in-group's values) are denied procedural protections afforded to in-group members (Boeckmann & Tyler, 1996). This and similar findings suggest that issues of normative similarity are proximal to judgments about social justice. A related concern in diverse societies is the issue of conflicts over norms and reactions to the procedures used to resolve them.

Resolving Normative Conflicts

The meaning of nonnormative behavior becomes particularly troublesome in a culturally diverse society in which there may be wide disagreement about basic values and moral principles. This problem bears directly on the issue of retributive justice. For example, among the Hmong (a group of Asian immigrants in California), it is normative for an older man to select a young bride and take (i.e., kidnap) her. Following her capture, the man negotiates a marriage agreement (including financial arrangements) with the

young woman's parents. From the normative perspective of many Californians and state law, this practice is interpreted as kidnapping. And since the
brides are typically in their early teens, this practice is seen as violating laws
about sex with minors. Further, it can be viewed as parents selling their children. Prosecution and punishment for these practices have been interpreted
by some as intolerance of diversity, but others see it is simply the upholding
of basic social values. Another example is the practice of vaginal circumci-
sion—the mutilation of the external female genitals. Although this practice
is common among some cultures in Africa, it has been widely criticized as
mutilation and as child abuse.

In recent legal cases as diverse as eating one's dog and killing one's children, the courts have been willing to consider some arguments based upon
the customs and moral rules of the defendant's culture. Similarly, Robinson
and Darley's research suggests that jurors are likely to reduce liability for
offenders whose cultural background in some way prevented them from
fully appreciating the consequences of their actions within a new cultural
context (Robinson & Darley, 1995). Although both the courts and jurors
appear to be increasingly more accepting of cultural arguments, this conces-
sion to multiculturalism has been opposed by some (Dockson, 1993).

The question of critical importance is whether a mosaic society can function effectively. Many such societies—including the former Soviet Union, the
former Yugoslavia, and Canada—have experienced or are experiencing serious political problems. In fact, that may be the general character of societies
without a common core of social values and/or cultural or ethnic identifications. For example, Canada has had in place an official policy of multiculturalism for over twenty years. Yet, recently this policy has come under increasing
attack by people who feel that the recognition of different cultural norms
undermines Canadians' sense of national identity. As one Canadian puts it,
"Multiculturalism was supposed to coalesce into a new sense of Canadian
identity. Instead it has helped tear Canada's identity apart" (Clayton, 1995). In
a similar sentiment, Rawls writes, "How is it possible for there to exist over
time a just and stable society of free and equal citizens, who remain pro-
foundly divided by reasonable religious, philosophical, and moral doctrines?
History suggests that it rarely is" (1993, p. 4). Why might such societies have
problems? The reason is that there is no common core of social values indicating what is moral—no agreement about distributive and retributive justice.

What might function to hold such societies together without agreement
about what is right or wrong? Our previous discussion points to procedural
justice as a key antecedent of managerial and government effectiveness.
Hence, the key question is whether procedural justice works in multicultural or cross-cultural settings.

One possibility is that people from varying cultural backgrounds differ in
their preferences for procedures to resolve disputes. Research suggests that

preferences about how to resolve disputes are not dramatically different among the members of different ethnic groups (Lind, Huo & Tyler, 1994; see Figure 10.2). Consistent with Thibaut and Walker's control theory of procedural justice described in Chapter 4, most people prefer to use procedures that give them control over their own outcomes—persuasion and negotiation. Further, in choosing between the two procedures by going to a neutral third party for help, people preferred mediation to arbitration. What is most striking about the Lind et al. findings is the overall similarity of procedural preference patterns across four different ethnic groups. These results suggest that little accommodation is needed in terms of the procedural preferences of the members of different ethnic groups. Further, as noted in Chapter 4, the members of different ethnic groups seem to agree that procedural justice is the key criterion for evaluating the fairness of dispute resolution procedures.

In addition to general preferences, a related concern is whether ethnicity influences the basis of people's reactions to experiences with authorities. In other words, do the members of all ethnic or racial groups act in a way that suggests that procedural justice is the most important issue they consider when reacting to a third party's decision? Tyler (1994) examined people's evaluations of the fairness of congressional decisionmaking procedures; he found no differences in the criteria used to evaluate procedural fairness that could be linked to the demographic characteristics of the respondents. None of the demographic characteristics he tested—race, gender, education, income, age, or ideology—interacted with relational evaluations in predicting procedural justice judgments. Instead, the weight people placed on outcomes, voice, and relational factors (neutrality, trust, status recognition) do not vary across different demographic groups. A study by Tyler, Huo, and Lind (1995) compared the basis on which employees evaluated their supervisor's decisions. The results indicate that there is considerable consistency in the basis of people's responses—i.e., the members of all ethnic groups focused on procedural fairness. These findings suggest that a focus on the fairness of procedures is a phenomenon that exists in very different social and cultural groups.

People across different ethnic backgrounds agree on appropriate procedures for resolving conflicts. Furthermore, they consider similar issues when evaluating procedures. These findings provide important information for developing social procedures that are acceptable to people of varying cultural and ethnic backgrounds—i.e., approaches to decisionmaking that are "robust" across variations in the background of those who experience them, leading to solutions that are equally satisfactory to all involved. This evidence suggests that procedural justice holds a key to bridging across conflicts in normative belief systems.

One interpretation of disagreements between the normative standards used by different cultural groups (such as the Hmong) in society is that such

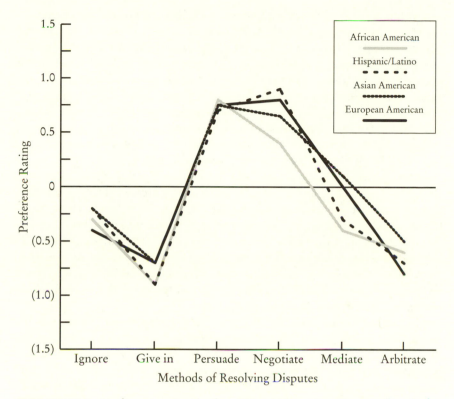

FIGURE 10.2   Preference ratings by four U.S. ethnic groups. SOURCE: ". . . And Justice for All: Ethnicity and Gender Preferences for Dispute Resolution Procedures," by A. E. Lind, Y. J. Huo, and T. R. Tyler, 1994, *Law and Human Behavior, 18,* 269–290. Copyright 1994 Plenum Publishing Corp. Reprinted with permission.

groups are in conflict with one another. Although normative systems may conflict, the essential aspects of procedural fairness from the relational perspective (Tyler & Lind, 1992) provide the opportunity for understanding and appreciating diversity. Specifically, opportunities for voice, respectful and dignified treatment, and neutrality (hypothesized to represent intrinsic characteristics of the person) all allow for the parties involved to understand and appreciate difference.

Legal scholars recognize the need for common normative systems for the effective governance of society. This desideratum necessarily may entail outcomes that will, on average, be unfavorable for some immigrant group or another. However, two important goals are served through procedurally fair dispute resolution. First, as argued in Chapter 4, people are likely to accept and voluntarily comply with unfavorable decisions delivered by fair procedures. Hence, authority legitimacy and social cohesion can be maintained. Second, but perhaps more important, authorities become knowledgeable about the differences that exist in a diverse society. This knowledge is increasingly incorporated into the interpretation and development of normative systems and laws (Dockson, 1993). These observations suggest that procedural justice is a key element to effective governance in a multicultural society. It provides the opportunity for people with different normative values to settle their differences peacefully and to engage in actions that would lead to mutual accommodation and compromise.

Overall, these findings suggest that multiculturalism is not as much of a threat to the effectiveness of authorities as is often feared. Instead, findings suggest considerable consensus about the meaning and importance of procedural justice concerns as well as similar procedural preferences. Interestingly, there are larger differences in views about distributive and retributive justice. However, those differences are not central to the effectiveness of authorities. If authorities follow fair decisionmaking procedures, people will defer to them even if their decisions are not in accord with people's assessments of distributive and retributive justice.

The discussion of procedural justice in a diverse society thus far has focused upon the perspective of authorities and society. In particular, the effectiveness of procedural justice in creating and sustaining perceptions of legitimacy and for compelling compliance are emphasized. It is important for issues of substantive justice to consider the perspective of different cultural groups. As currently stated, the benefits of procedural justice primarily accrue to the authority structure. A system that is procedurally fair but repeatedly gives unfavorable outcomes to one or another group fails in providing substantive justice. In order for substantive justice to be provided for all groups in society in the long run, normative systems need to avoid systematic discrimination. Moreover, they must be shaped by the input that people from different groups contribute during the procedures described above (cf. Lind, 1995).

Categorization and the Meaning of Fairness

Despite a notable lack of cultural differences in the interpretation of fair procedures, the promise of effective governance in a multicultural society is not necessarily secure. The social categorization processes that are likely to occur in situations of salient cultural differences have been demonstrated to affect justice judgments related to procedures and outcomes (Huo et al., 1995). These findings suggest that there may be limits to the "cushion of support" that authorities rely upon when managing conflicts that arise in a diverse society.

The group value model of procedural justice makes predictions about social categorization. It predicts that people will be more concerned about relational issues when interactions occur within group boundaries. In contrast, people may be more influenced by outcome issues when interactions occur across group boundaries. Hence, if people define their interactions as crossing group boundaries (as is likely to happen in a diverse society), this may influence how people interpret and respond to how those interactions occur.

This hypothesis is tested by Tyler, Lind, and Huo (1994) in the context of judgments about authorities (Figure 10.3). In their study, workers were interviewed about conflicts with their supervisors. In some cases, the supervisor was of the same ethnicity, but in other cases ethnicity differed. The issue was what determined the employee's feelings about the legitimacy of their supervisor.

Both studies suggest that interactions are more instrumental when they occur with people who are perceived to be outsiders (i.e., people who are of a different nationality or ethnicity). Hence, multiculturalism will create problems if it creates psychological boundaries between groups that must interact in society. Specifically, when people are involved in a dispute, they are likely to react to the situation in terms of outcome favorability in intergroup contexts. Given that many disputes are resolved with one or more parties receiving unfavorable outcomes, such an instrumental orientation is destabilizing for the authorities involved. These findings suggest that in intergroup contexts, one or more parties (and the groups that they represent) will depart from the interaction feeling dissatisfied and angry. This perception has been related to a number of problems for society (Tyler, 1990) such as people's unwillingness to accept and follow decisions made by authorities.

Our previous discussion of the cross-cultural generality of the group value model and the relational model of authority implied that procedural justice is an effective means of managing diversity. The present discussion casts a shadow upon the promise of procedural justice and the viability of multicultural societies. The research discussed here builds on our earlier discussion of the scope of justice. It suggests that one important determinant of the scope of justice is people's definitions of the boundaries of their groups. In other words, categorization shapes people's reactions to others. This finding supports a central tenet of social identity theory (Hogg & Abrams, 1988) that suggests that people have a need to see their group as better than other groups. A critical question for multicultural societies is whether there is a means of maintaining social justice while preserving cultural diversity. Recent research incorporating insights from social identity theory have begun to address this key question.

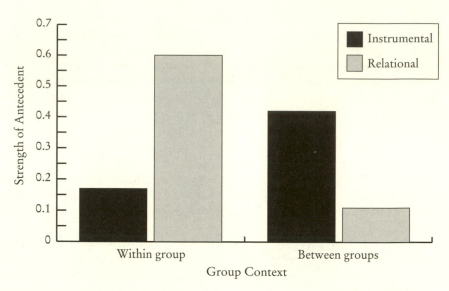

FIGURE 10.3 Antecedents of third-party legitimacy for disputes within and across group boundaries. SOURCE: Data from Tylor, Lind, and Huo (1995, unpublished).

The Promise of Superordinate Identity

Social identity theory proposes that there are multiple levels of identification (Hogg & Abrams, 1988). For example, a person may draw her sense of identity and esteem from being a surgeon, a doctor, a medical professional, an African American, a woman, or a U.S. citizen. Obviously these different social categorizations vary in terms of their inclusiveness. It is also possible for any one of them to serve as a means of comparison that creates a group of insiders and a group of outsiders. For example, the doctor category effectively makes interactions with nurses an interaction with an outsider.

The intersection of categorization and comparison processes suggests that the choice of categorization level affects the inclusiveness of who is considered an outsider. At one extreme is the category of "I" that leaves the entire world as outsiders; at the other extreme is the category of "world citizen" that excludes no one. Categories that are inclusive of subcategories are referred to as superordinate categories. For example, the superordinate social category of "American citizen" includes many social categories such as Asian American, African American, Scottish American, or Catholic American. It is important to note that social identification is a subjective process. It is quite possible that people can identify with groups with which they have no objective connection. For example, many Whites were involved in the Civil Rights movement of the South in the 1960s. The level at which one categorizes oneself has implications for the scope of justice, how it is defined, and how people react to the decisions of authorities.

Inhibiting Moral Exclusion

One consequence of sharing a common ("superordinate") category is that people will be less likely to perceive other members of the superordinate group as different. The perception of an overarching similarity between groups inhibits perceptions of difference that can lead to moral exclusion. The development of a superordinate category for members of a diverse society is therefore likely to avert social injustices.

Research focusing on the distribution of resources suggests that the development of a common identity between social groups is key to avoiding exploitation and the ineffective use of resources (Kramer & Brewer, 1984). This same line of research suggests that the nomination of an authority who has been identified by members of various groups sharing resources avoids problems of exploitation and facilitates socially efficient use of resources (Messick, Wilke, Brewer, Kramer, Zemke, & Lui, 1983).

The key suggestion flowing from categorization findings is that social groupings should be framed in ways that emphasize common categorizations. For example, instead of thinking of individuals as members of "labor" or "management," everyone should be thought of as a member of the same organization. Similarly, the degree to which we are all "Americans" should be emphasized rather than framing issues in terms of conflict between groups of varying ethnicity, gender, or class.

Identification

The previous discussion focused upon the categories that people use to frame their social world. However, simply placing yourself inside or outside a group is a limited way of thinking about the social world. It is also important how strongly people identify with the groups to which they feel they belong. Identification refers to the degree to which people feel close to others in their group or to group values, rules, or authorities. Identification is linked to the extent that people draw their social identity from a particular group.

The group value model predicts that the relational information communicated by procedures and relevant authorities will be more important the more the person values or identifies with the larger group (Huo, Smith, Tyler & Lind, 1995; Smith & Tyler, 1995; Tyler, Degoey & Smith, 1996). In other words, people will care more about their status within groups that are important to their social identity. Hence, they will pay more attention to and be more influenced by their treatment by others, treatment that communicates information about their status in the eyes of others. Conversely, when people are less identified with the group, instrumental information is more important.

One study that shows the identification effect is Tyler and Degoey (1995). That study examines the influence of identification with the community on the basis of people's evaluations of government authorities. The findings indicate that legitimacy judgments are primarily relational in character, as we have already noted in our discussion of legitimacy. Further, in this study, people make more relational and less instrumental evaluations if they identify strongly with the community. In other words, those people who identify more strongly with their community judge community authorities more in terms of whether they think the authorities are trying to be fair and less in terms of whether the authorities deliver favorable outcomes.

Similarly, Huo, Smith, Tyler, and Lind (1995) show that workers evaluate their managers' decisions more relationally if they identify with their work organization. As expected, employees generally evaluated their supervisors in relational terms, not instrumentally. In addition, there is an interaction between relational judgments and identification with the organization. Those who identified more strongly with the organization weight relational concerns more strongly. Conversely, those who identify more strongly with the organization weight instrumental concerns less strongly.

Of course, the existence of a relationship does not indicate directly that it is an identity motive that is important. To test this more directly, Tyler and Degoey (1996) examined the influence of sharing an organization's values and drawing one's personal identity from work. They found that both sharing the values of an organization and drawing one's identity from work increased the importance of relational issues in shaping willingness to accept the decisions of organizational authorities.

Studies that include attention to identification with the group the authority represents suggest that such identification changes the way group members conceptualize the meaning of justice. In particular, it leads to a de-emphasis on personal control over outcomes. Heightened identification with the group the authority represents leads to a greater ability to reach consensus, to less concern about personal or group gain, and/or to a greater willingness to defer to group authorities if those authorities are seen to be acting fairly.

The pattern shown suggests that there are strategies that group authorities can adopt to manage internal diversity. In situations in which there is identification with the group, they can utilize procedural justice approaches. As we have already noted, leaders benefit from being able to act in the long

term interest of the group, without having to worry about delivering immediate benefits to everyone. Hence, the ability to manage groups is enhanced
when there is identification with the group and its authorities.

An important and interesting question raised by Azzi (in press) is the natural form and level of identification. The nation-state, which has dominated
the last 100 years, may represent a form of social organization that does not
fit easily into people's thinking. It may be easier to identify with small
groups. Hence, it may be natural that the Soviet Union splintered into
smaller units when the pressure of competition with the United States
became less of an issue. The theory of optimal distinctiveness (Brewer, 1991)
supports the argument that overly diffuse groups may have difficulties in
maintaining themselves over time. The theory is based on the assumption
that people experience a fundamental tension between their need for vali-
dation and similarity to others and their need for uniqueness and individ-
uation. Hence, group maintenance depends on the group's ability to satisfy
its members' needs for both affiliation and distinctiveness. In this case,
groups that are too large and diffuse may not satisfy people's needs for affiliation. We would predict that as groups become larger and more diffuse, the
tendency to identify with subgroups should increase. An important arena
for future research is the natural or "optimal" level of psychological identification—the family, the kin group, the community, the state, the region, the
nation-state, and so on.

Subgroup Identification

Of course, the favorable findings on identification also suggest a possible
limit to relational approaches. What if the issue is not superordinate identification, but identification with an ethnic or religious subgroup within the
larger group? In that situation the converse social dynamic might be found,
with people who identify with their subgroup reacting to subgroup authorities relationally and to superordinate authorities in instrumental terms. To
examine this possibility, Huo, Smith, Tyler, and Lind (1995) adapted a
typology that Berry (1984) proposed for understanding how immigrants
adapt to a new culture. Identification with the superordinate group (e.g., the
nation-state, the work organization) and identification with a subgroup
(e.g., one's ethnic group membership) represent independent dimensions
that we can use to create four categories of respondents (see Figure 10.4).
Assimilators are those who have strong identification with the superordinate group but low identification with the subgroup. Biculturalists identify
strongly with both groups. Separatists have strong identification with their
subgroup but low identification with the superordinate group. Finally, the
alienated are those who do not identify strongly with either group.

Subgroup Identification	Superordinate Identification		
		High	Low
	High	Biculturalist	Separatist
	Low	Assimilated	Alienated

FIGURE 10.4   Superordinate and subgroup identification. SOURCE: "Cultural Re-
lations in Plural Societies: Alternatives to Segregation and Their Sociopsychological
Implications," by J. W. Berry, 1984, in *Groups in Contact*, N. Miller and M. Brewer
(Eds.), San Diego: Academic Press, Inc., 11–27. Copyright 1984 Academic Press,
Inc. Adapted with permission.

Huo, Smith, Tyler, and Lind (1996) interviewed employees in a public
sector work organization about their level of identification with the work
organization (the superordinate group) and with their ethnic group (the
subgroup). They examined the basis for accepting the decisions of authorities (work supervisors) among employees who were assimilators, biculturalists, and separatists. The alienated were not included in the analysis
because no theoretical predictions could be made because of their lack of
identification with either of the relevant groups. The results are shown in
Figure 10.5 They indicate that assimilated workers and bicultural workers
are very similar in the bases of their reactions to supervisors. Members of
both groups deferred to supervisors if they thought those supervisors were
neutral and trustworthy and if the supervisors demonstrated status recognition. In contrast, separatists reacted to the decisions of their supervisors in
instrumental terms—considering what they had won and lost.

A similar analysis can be performed on the data of Smith and Tyler (1996).
In this case, the issue is the degree to which European Americans identified
with "America" as opposed to "Whites." As before, those who identify most
strongly with America judge policies by whether authorities are acting fairly.
A similar pattern is found among those who identify with both American
and their own ethnic group ("Whites"). But, those who identify primarily
with their own ethnic group judge the policies of Congress by asking how
those policies help or hurt their group—an instrumental orientation.

We can extend this analysis to conflicts between political and religious
authorities. Kelman and Hamilton point out that historically such conflicts
are central to societies. Tyler, Smith, and Huo (1996) examine such conflicts
in an analysis of citizens interviewed about their views on abortion. In this

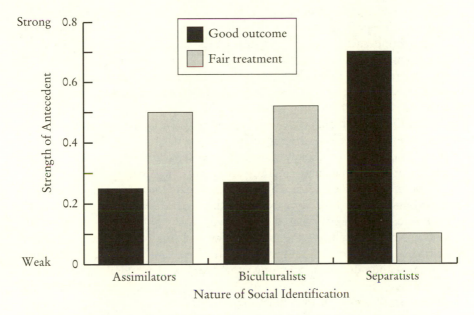

FIGURE 10.5 Antecedents of willingness of assimilators, biculturalists, and separatists to volun-tarily accept decisions. SOURCE: "Superordinate Identification, Subgroup Identifi-cation, and Justice Concerns: Is Separatism the Problem; Is Assimilation the Answer?" by Y. J. Huo, H. J. Smith, T. R. Tyler, and A. E. Lind, 1996, *Psycho-logical Science, 7*, 43. Copyright 1996 Cambridge University Press. Adopted with permission of Cambridge University Press.

analysis identification with government (the Supreme Court) is compared to identification with religious moral values for or against abortion. As before, the pattern of authority relations changes most dramatically among those citizens who are more identified with their moral values than with govern-ment. That group reacts to government not by judging the fairness of gov-ernment authorities, but by evaluating the degree to which they agree with the decisions made.

The key point of the analyses just presented is that as predicted by a group-value approach, subgroup identification can undermine the relational basis of deference to authorities. Hence, both the findings regarding super-ordinate identification and those regarding subgroup identification support the argument that identification shapes when relational indices of justice will define reactions to authorities.

A second point is that biculturalists and assimilators share a similar psy-chology. Hence, there is little reason to feel that people should be encour-

aged to assimilate to the mainstream and dissociate with important subgroups. The pattern shown indicates that the importance attributed to
"assimilation" may be misplaced, at least the idea that people need to abandon their subgroup identities. Biculturalists—those who identify with both
the superordinate and the subgroup—still based their evaluations of leaders
on procedural justice. Only separatists reacted to the superordinate group
authority in an instrumental way.

If, as these results suggest, identification with the group the authority represents encourages reliance on relational evaluations and affects the way
people define fairness, a key question to pose from the perspective of the
authority is, what facilitates identification with the superordinate group?

One mechanism through which superordinate identity can be promoted
is through socialization. For example, through education, children learn a
common history and a shared set of social and political values. Symbolic
exercises such as saluting the national flag and singing the national anthem
reinforce commitment to a group and its core values. Organizations also
recognize the value of encouraging superordinate group identification. They
encourage the adoption of shared norms among employees through the
development of unique organizational cultures.

An alternative mechanism through which superordinate identification can
be encouraged is to increase task interdependence or a feeling of sharing a
common fate. Research outlined earlier in the book suggests that cooperation
on group tasks will facilitate the adoption of a shared identity. For example,
Sherif et al. (1961) convincingly demonstrated that intergroup hostilities
greatly decreased after members of two groups worked together to achieve a
common goal. Similarly, research on the jigsaw classroom (Aronson et al.,
1978) showed that students who had to rely on each other in order to complete a class assignment developed more positive intergroup attitudes.

Identification can also be promoted by sharing a common enemy. In the
past, differences among various subgroups in the United States were minimized by having the common opponent of the Soviet Union. More recently,
having an external enemy in the form of Saddam Hussein served to unite
Americans during the 1991 Gulf War. In the Sherif et al. (1961) research mentioned previously, there was strong evidence that having a common enemy
altered intragroup dynamics. When the two groups of boys at the summer
camp engaged in competition against each other, the groups became more
cohesive. Moreover, when asked to indicate their best friend, 90 percent of
the boys chose someone in their own group even though their best friends
before the intergroup competition had been placed in the other group.

A fourth way to encourage superordinate identification is through the
administration of procedural justice. Although current research cannot adequately address the issue of causal relationship, it is likely that the relationship
between superordinate identification and procedural justice is bidirectional.

People who identify with the group the authority represents are more likely to focus on procedures and relational evaluations.

Conversely, people who are treated with dignity and respect by an authority may come to identify more strongly with the group that the authority represents. For those who are new to a nation, a community, or a work organization, treatment with dignity and respect may be extremely important in facilitating identification with the new group. For those minorities who have experienced a long history of discrimination, procedural justice may be a less effective strategy for encouraging loyalty to the superordinate group. Such people are likely to have developed a separatist identification and ideology in an effort to cope with their experiences with discrimination. For such individuals, trust in an illegitimate system may be difficult to engender through procedures and better facilitated through the granting of positive outcomes. However, the reliance on outcomes may foster a relationship based on instrumental concerns. As noted earlier, a focus on getting favorable outcomes poses serious problems for authorities and for the group they represent. An important line of future research is to examine the conditions under which the disenfranchised can develop trust in the social system.

The implication of these findings is that in order for governance to be effective, authorities need people to develop superordinate identifications. Such concerns are also apparent in the criminal justice system. Boeckmann and Tyler (1996) study the relationship between support for judicial authorities' discretion and identification with members of society. Of particular relevance in this context are the judgments made about members of society who break the law. Respondents in the Boeckmann and Tyler study indicated the extent to which they perceive deviants as sharing a common community identity with themselves. Respondents were divided into two groups: those believing that deviants are fundamentally different in their values (and are not really members of society) and those believing that deviants share a common superordinate identification with the respondent (and are members of society). When criminals were viewed as insiders, people were both more willing to give rule breakers procedural protections and more willing to defer to the decisions of group authorities (i.e., judges) about how to handle rule breakers.

The Tightrope of Multiculturalism and Social Justice

The discussion of the interaction between cultural differences, categorization, and social justice suggests that achieving social justice in a diverse society requires a delicate balancing act. Increasingly, cultural groups in American society are making demands for recognition and respect of their differences. These trends are in contrast to earlier assimilationist approaches to the integration of immigrants into American society. The appeal made by ethnic groups to respect and celebrate difference appears to many as a legitimate claim that is consistent with the American creed of tolerance first expressed by the founding fathers. One goal of these early Americans was to create a society that would tolerate diversity of religious cultures. They saw an intolerance of cultural diversity as injustice in the form of restricting liberties. Clearly then, intolerance of diversity is incompatible with social justice and the American credo.

However, research evidence and the lessons of history strongly suggest that is possible for a society to have too much diversity. Without a common identity of some kind, members of a society have difficulties coexisting. These problems can be manifested in the distribution of resources, reactions to norm violations, and responses to the decisions of authorities. The creation and perception of social injustice is clearly related to an emphasis on diversity at the expense of acknowledging common bonds between members of society.

The discussion of biculturalists suggests that a skillful balancing act between respecting differences and appreciating the core similarities among people in society is a means of preserving social justice in society. A rigid assimilation policy that suppresses basic human rights falls short of balancing the needs of society and social justice. An assimilationist approach contains two dangers. First, the imposition of a homogeneous set of values prevents the recognition and discussion of real cultural differences. Second, experimental research suggests that group members will resist situations that do not allow the expression of group differences (Brown & Wade, 1987). If groups are forced to perform similar roles, they express greater dislike for other groups with whom they must cooperate than if they are allowed to perform distinctive roles (Brown & Wade, 1987). Likewise, an extreme multicultural policy encourages separatist movements that may also fall short of social justice. A culturally and socially fractured society is fertile ground for xenophobic sentiments and moral exclusion. The focus on group interests of separatist movements and their lack of willingness to compromise render authorities ineffective in helping to resolve difficult social problems.

The majority of research reviewed here suggests that concerns for social justice are a robust, pan-cultural phenomenon. The problems that arise in a multicultural society do not stem from disagreements about the importance of social justice. Rather, the problems associated with cultural diversity arise from the use of cultural differences as a means of categorization and defining group boundaries. However, research indicates that identification need not be exclusively tied to categorical differences between cultural groups (Berry, 1984). The example of the biculturalist and the subjective nature of identification provide an optimistic picture of the realization of social justice in a diverse society.

REFERENCES

Abrams, D. (1990). Political identity: Relative deprivation, social identity and the case of Scottish nationalism. *Economic and Social Research Council* 16–19 Initiative—Occasional Papers.

Adams, J. S. (1965). Inequity in social exchange. In L. Berkowitz (Ed.), *Advances in Experimental Social Psychology* (Vol. 2, pp. 267–299). New York: Academic Press.

Adams, J. S., and Freedman, S. (1976). Equity theory revisited: Comments and annotated bibliography. In L. Berkowitz and E. Walster (Eds.), *Advances in Experimental Social Psychology* (Vol. 9, pp. 43–56). New York: Academic Press.

Adams, J. S., and Rosenbaum, W. B. (1962). The relationship of worker productivity to cognitive dissonance about wage inequities. *Journal of Applied Psychology, 46,* 161–164.

Adler, J. W., Hensler, D. R., and Nelson, C. E. (1983). *Simple justice: How litigants fare in the Pittsburgh Court Arbitration Program.* Santa Monica, CA: RAND.

Affleck, G., Tennen, H., Pfiffer, C., and Fifield, J. (1987). Appraisals of control and predictability in adapting to a chronic disease. *Journal of Personality and Social Psychology, 53, 2,* 273–279.

Alexander, S., and Ruderman, A. (1987). The role of procedural and distributive justice in organizational behavior. *Social Justice Research, 1,* 177–198.

Alicke, M. D. (1990). Incapacitating conditions and alteration of blame. *Journal of Social Behavior and Personality, 5,* 651–664.

Alicke, M. D. (1992). Culpable causation. *Journal of Personality and Social Psychology, 63,* 368–378.

Allport, G. W. (1979). *The nature of prejudice* (25th anniversary ed.). Reading, MA: Addison-Wesley.

Ambrose, M. L., Harland, L. K., and Kulik, C. T. (1991). Influences of social comparisons on perceptions of organizational fairness. *Journal of Applied Psychology, 76,* 239–246.

Anderson, D. C. (1995, January 15). Expressive justice is all the rage. *New York Times Magazine,* pp. 36, 37.

Anton, R. (1990). Emerging employee rights: Their existence and their effects on attitudes and behavior in the workplace. Unpublished doctoral dissertation, Northwestern University, Chicago.

Arendt, H. (1964). *Eichmann in Jerusalem.* New York: Viking.

Aronson, E., Stephan, C., Sikes, J., Blaney, N., and Snapp, M. (1978). *The jigsaw classroom.* Beverly Hills, CA: Sage.

Attridge, M., and Berscheid, E. (1994). Entitlement in romantic relationships in the United States: A social exchange perspective. In M. J. Lerner and G. Mikula

(Eds.), *Entitlement and the Affectional Bond: Justice in Close Relationships.* New York: Plenum.

Augoustinos, M., and Walker, I. (1995). *Social Cognition: An integrated introduction.* London: Sage.

Austin, W., McGinn, N. C., and Susmilch, C. (1980). Internal standards revisited: Effects of social comparisons and expectancies on judgments of fairness and satisfaction. *Journal of Experimental Social Psychology, 16,* 426–441.

Austin, W., and Tobiasen, J. M. (1985). Legal justice and the psychology of conflict resolution. In R. Folger (Ed.), *The sense of injustice.* New York: Plenum.

Austin, W., and Walster, E. (1980). Reactions to confirmations and disconfirmations of expectancies of equity and inequity. *Journal of Personality and Social Psychology, 30,* 208–216.

Austin, W., Walster, E., and Utne, M. (1976). Equity and the law: The effect of "suffering in the act" on liking and assigned punishment. In L. Berkowitz and E. Walster (Eds.), *Advances in Experimental Social Psychology* (Vol. 9, pp. 163–190). New York: Academic Press.

Azzi, A. (1992). Procedural justice and the allocation of power in intergroup relations: Studies in the United States and South Africa. *Personality and Social Psychology Bulletin, 18,* 736–747.

Azzi, A. (1993a). Group representation and procedural justice in multigroup decision-making bodies. *Social Justice Research, 6,* 195–217.

Azzi, A. (1993b). Implicit and category-based allocations of decision-making power in majority-minority relations. *Journal of Experimental Social Psychology, 29,* 203–228.

Azzi, A. (1994). From competitive interests, perceived injustice and identity needs to collective action: Psychological mechanisms in ethnic nationalism. In B. Kapferer (Ed.), *Nationalism, Ethnicity and Violence.* Oxford, UK: Oxford University Press.

Azzi, A., and Jost, J. (1992). Votes without power: Procedural justice as mutual control in majority-minority relations. Unpublished manuscript.

Babad, E. Y., and Wallbott, H. G. (1986). The effects of social factors on emotional reactions. In K. S. Scherer, H. G. Wallbott, and A. B. Summerfield (Eds.), *Experiencing emotion: A cross-cultural study* (pp. 154–172). Cambridge, UK: Cambridge University Press.

Baron, J., Gowda, R., and Kunreuther, H. (1993). Attitudes toward managing hazardous waste: What should be cleaned up and who should pay for it? *Risk Analysis, 13,* 183–192.

Barrett-Howard, E., and Tyler, T. R. (1986). Procedural justice as a criterion in allocation decisions. *Journal of Personality and Social Psychology, 50,* 296–304.

Batson, C. D. (1990). How social an animal? The human capacity for caring. *American Psychologist, 45,* 336–346.

Batson, C. D., Klein, T. R., Highberger, L., and Shaw, L. L. (1993). Immorality from empathy-induced altruism: When compassion and justice conflict. *Journal of Personality and Social Psychology, 68,* 1042–1054.

Baumeister, R. F. (1982). A self-presentational view of social phenomenon. *Psychological Bulletin, 91,* 3–26.

Bell, S. T., Kuriloff, P. J., and Lottes, I. (1994). Understanding attributions of blame in stranger rape and date rape situations: An examination of gender, race, identification, and students' social perceptions of rape victims. *Journal of Applied Social Psychology, 24,* 1719–1734.

Belleveau, M. A. (1995). Blind ambition?: The effects of social networks and institution on the compensation of elite coeducational and women's college graduates. Working paper, Duke University, Durham, NC.

Berger, J., Fisek, H., Norman, R. Z., and Wagner, D. G. (1983). The formation of reward expectations in status situations. In D. Messick and K. S. Cook (Eds.), *Equity theory: Psychological and sociological perspectives.* New York: Praeger.

Berkowitz, L., and Walster, E. (Eds.) (1976). Equity theory: Toward a general theory of social interaction. *Advances in experimental social psychology* (Vol. 9). New York: Academic Press.

Berman, J. J., Murphy-Berman, V., and Singh, P. (1985). Cross-cultural similarities and differences in perceptions of fairness. *Journal of Cross-Cultural Psychology, 16,* 55–67.

Bernstein, A. (1994, August 15). Inequality: How the gap between rich and poor hurts the economy. *Business Week,* pp. 77–83.

Berry, J. W. (1984). Cultural relations in plural societies: Alternatives to segregation and their sociopsychological implications. In N. Miller and M. Brewer (Eds.), *Groups in contact* (pp. 11–27). San Diego: Academic Press.

Berscheid, E. (1983). Emotion. In H. Kelley, E. Berscheid, A. Christensen, J. H. Harvey, T. L. Huston, G. Levinger, E. McClintock, L. A. Peplau, and D. R. Peterson (Eds.), *Close relationships.* New York: W. H. Freeman and Company.

Berscheid, E., and Walster, E. (1967). When does a harm-doer compensate a victim? *Journal of Personality and Social Psychology, 6,* 433–441.

Bierbrauer, G. (1990). Toward an understanding of legal culture: Variations in individualism and collectivism between Kurds, Lebanese, and Germans. *Law and Society Review, 28,* 243–264.

Bies, R. J. (1987). The predicament of injustice: The management of moral outrage. In L. L. Cummings and B. M. Staw (Eds.), *Research in organizational behavior* (Vol. 9, pp. 289–319). Greenwich, CT: JAI.

Bies, R. J., and Moag, J. S. (1986). Interactional justice: Communication criteria of fairness. In R. J. Lewicki, B. M. Sheppard, and M. H. Bazerman (Eds.), *Research on negotiations in organizations* (Vol. 1, pp. 43–55). Greenwich, CT: JAI.

Bies, R. J., and Shapiro, D. (1988). Voice and justification: Their influence on procedural fairness judgments. *Academy of Management Journal, 31,* 676–685.

Bies, R. J., Shapiro, D., and Cummings, L. L. (1988). Causal accounts and managing organizational conflict: Is it enough to say it's not my fault? *Communication Research, 15,* 381–399.

Bies, R. J., and Tripp, T. M. (1996). Beyond distrust: "getting even" and the need for revenge. In R. Kramer and T. R. Tyler (Eds.), *Trust in organizations.* Beverly Hills, CA: Sage.

Bies, R. J., and Tyler, T. R. (1993). The "litigation mentality" in organizations. *Organizational Science, 4,* 352–366.

Blasi, A. (1980). Bridging moral cognition and moral action. *Psychological Bulletin, 88,* 1–45.

Bluhm, L. H. (1975). Relative deprivation and level of living among Brazilian farmers. *Rural Sociology, 40,* 233–249.

Boeckmann, R. J. (1993). *Social identification effects on retributive and procedural justice judgments.* Unpublished master's thesis, University of California, Berkeley.

Boeckmann, R. J. (1996a). *An alternative conceptual framework for offense evaluation: Implications for a social maintenance model of retributive justice.* Unpublished doctoral dissertation, University of California.

Boeckmann, R. J. (1996b, August). *Punishment goals as a function of qualitative offense characteristics: Implications for the psychology of retributive justice.* Poster session presented at the annual meeting of the American Psychological Society, San Francisco, CA.

Boeckmann, R. J., and Liew, J. C. (1996, April) *Hate speech: ethnic minorities' punishment and response.* Poster session presented at the annual meeting of the Western Psychological Association, San Jose, CA.

Boeckmann, R. J., and Tyler, T. R. (1996) *Liabilities and assets of group membership: Social identification and categorization influences on retributive and procedural justice.* Unpublished manuscript, University of California, Berkeley.

Bond, M. H., Leung, K., and Schwartz, S. (1992). Explaining choices in procedural and distributive justice across cultures. *International Journal of Psychology, 27,* 211–225.

Bond, M. H., Leung, K., and Wan, K. C. (1982). How does cultural collectivism operate? The impact of tack maintenance contributions on reward distribution. *Journal of Cross-Cultural Psychology, 13,* 186–200.

Booth, A. (1983). Social responses to protracted scarcity. In S. Welch and R. Miewald (Eds.), *Scarce natural resources: The challenge to public policy makers.* Beverly Hills, CA: Sage.

Bourhis, R., and Hill, P. (1982). Intergroup perceptions in British higher education: A field study. In H. Tajfel (Ed.), *Social identification and intergroup relations.* New York: Cambridge University Press.

Braithwaite, J. (1989). *Crime, shame, and reintegration.* Cambridge, UK: Cambridge University Press.

Brehm, S. (1992). *Intimate relationships.* New York: McGraw-Hill.

Brewer, M. B., and Kramer, R. M. (1986). Choice behavior in social dilemmas: Effects of social identity, group size and decision framing. *Journal of Personality and Social Psychology, 50,* 543–549.

Brickman, P. (1977). Crime and punishment in sports and society. *Journal of Social Issues, 33* (1), 140–164.

Brickman, P., and Campbell, D. T. (1971). Hedonic relativism and planning the good society. In M. H. Appley (Ed.), *Adaptation-level theory.* New York: Academic Press.

Brickman, P., Coates, D., and Janoff-Bulman, R. (1978). Lottery winners and accident victims: Is happiness relative? *Journal of Personality and Social Psychology, 36,* 917–927.

Brickman, P., Folger, R., Goode, E. and Schul, Y. (1981). Microjustice and macrojustice. In M. J. Lerner and S. C. Lerner (Eds.), *The justice motive in social behavior.* New York: Plenum.

Brisbin, R. A., and Hunter, S. (1992). Perceptions of justice: Clientele evaluations of conflict adjustment by a utility regulatory agency. *Social Justice Research, 5,* 3–30.

Brockner, J. (1990). Scope of justice in the workplace: How survivors react to co-worker layoffs. *Journal of Social Issues, 46* (1), 95–106.

Brockner, J., DeWitt, R., Grover, S., and Reed, T. (1990). When it is especially important to explain why: Factors affecting the relationship between managers' explanations of a layoff and survivors' reactions to the layoff. *Journal of Experimental Social Psychology, 26,* 389–407.

Brockner, J., Tyler, T. R., and Cooper-Schneider, R. (1992). The influence of prior commitment to an institution on reactions to perceived unfairness: The higher they are, the harder they fall. *Administrative Science Quarterly, 37,* 241–261.

Brockner, J., and Weisenfeld, B. M. (1994). The interactive impact of procedural and outcome fairness on reactions to a decision: The effects of what you do depend on how you do it. *Psychological Bulletin, 120,* 189–208.

Brown v. Board of Education, 347 U.S. 483 (1954).

Brown, B. B., and Harris, P. B. (1989). Residential burglary victimization: Reactions to the invasion of a primary territory. *Journal of Environmental Psychology, 9,* 119–132.

Brown, R. J. (1978). Divided we fall: An analysis of relations between sections of a factory work-force. In H. Tajfel (Ed.), *Differentiation between social groups: Studies in the social psychology of intergroup relations.* London: Academic Press.

Brown, R. J., and Turner, J. C. (1981). Interpersonal and intergroup behavior. In J. C. Turner and H. Giles (Eds.), *Intergroup behavior.* Oxford, UK: Blackwell.

Brown, R. J., and Wade, G. S. (1987). Superordinate goals and intergroup behavior: The effects of role ambiguity and status on intergroup attitudes and task performance. *European Journal of Social Psychology, 17,* 131–142.

Browning, C. R. (1992). *Ordinary men: Reserve police battalion 101 and the final solution in Poland.* New York: HarperCollins Publishers, Inc.

Bulman, R. J., and Wortman, C. B. (1977). Attributions of blame and coping in the "real world": Severe accident victims react to their lot. *Journal of Personality and Social Psychology, 51,* 277–283.

Burger, J. M. (1981). Motivational biases in the attribution of responsibility: A meta-analysis of the defensive-attribution hypothesis. *Psychological Bulletin, 90,* 496–512.

Burt, M. R. (1983). Justifying personal violence: A comparison of rapists and the general public. *Victimology, 8* (3–4), 131–150.

Campbell, D. T. (1975). On the conflicts between biological and social evolution and between psychology and moral tradition. *American Psychologist, 30,* 1103–1126.

Campbell, D. T. (1980). Social morality norms as evidence of conflict between biological human nature and social system requirements. In G. S. Stent (Ed.), *Morality as a biological phenomenon.* Berkeley: University of California Press.

Caplan, N., and Paige, J. M. (1968). A study of ghetto rioters. *Scientific American, 219,* 15–21.

Casper, J. D., Tyler, T. R., and Fisher, B. (1988). Procedural justice in felony cases. *Law and Society Review, 22,* 483–507.

Citera, M., and Rentsch, J. R. (1993). Is there justice in organizational acquisitions? In R. Cropanzano (Ed.), *Justice in the workplace.* Hillsdale, NJ: Lawrence Erlbaum.

Clark, M. S. (1984). Record keeping in two types of relationships. *Journal of Personality and Social Psychology, 47*, 549–557.

Clark, M. S., and Chrisman, K. (1994). Resource allocation in intimate relationships. In A. L. Weber and J. H. Harvey (Eds.), *Perspectives on close relationships* (pp. 176–192). Boston: Allyn and Bacon, Inc.

Clark, M. S., and Mills, J. (1993). The difference between communal and exchange relationships: What it is and is not. *Personality and Social Psychology Bulletin, 19*, 684–691.

Clark, M. S., Mills, J. R., and Corcoran, D. M. (1989). Keeping track of needs and inputs of friends and strangers. *Personality and Social Psychology Bulletin, 15*, 533–542.

Clark, M. S., Mills, J., and Powell, M. C. (1986). Keeping track of needs in communal and exchange relationships. *Journal of Personality and Social Psychology, 51*, 333–338.

Clayton, M. (1995, April 25.) Canadians tire of multiculturalism. *Christian Science Monitor,* pp. 1, 7.

Clemmer, E. C. (1993). An investigation into the relationship of fairness and customer satisfaction with services. In R. Cropanzano (Ed.), *Justice in the workplace.* Hillsdale, NJ: Lawrence Erlbaum.

Clore, G. L., Schwarz, N., and Conway, M. (1994). Affective causes and consequences of social information processing. In R. S. Wyer, Jr. and T. K. Srull (Eds.), *Handbook of social cognition: Vol. 1: Basic processes* (pp. 323–417). Hillsdale, NJ: Lawrence Erlbaum.

Cohen, R. L. (1991). Membership, intergroup relations, and justice. In R. Vermunt and H. Steensma (Eds.), *Social justice in human relations: Vol. 1: Societal and psychological origins of justice* (pp. 239–258). New York: Plenum.

Conlon, D. E. (1993). Some tests of the self-interest and group-value models of procedural justice: Evidence from an organizational appeal procedure. *Academy of Management Journal, 36*, 1109–1124.

Cook, K. S., and Hegtvedt, K. A. (1986). Justice and power: An exchange analysis. In H. W. Bierhoff, R. L. Cohen, and J. Greenberg (Eds.), *Justice in social relations.* New York: Plenum.

Cook, S. W. (1990). Toward a psychology of improving justice: Research on extending the equality principle to victims of social injustice. *Journal of Social Issues, 46* (1), 147–162.

Cook, T. D., Crosby, F., and Hennigan, K. M. (1977). The construct validity of relative deprivation. In J. M. Suls and R. L. Miller (Eds.), *Social comparison processes.* Washington, DC: Hemisphere.

Cooley, C. H. (1902). *Human nature and the social order.* New York: Scribner's.

Coombs, C. H. (1967). Thurstone's measurement of social values revisited forty years later. *Journal of Personality and Social Psychology, 6*(1), 85–91.

Crocker, J., Broadnax, S., Luhtanen, R., and Blaine, B. (1995). *Belief in U.S. government conspiracies against Blacks: Powerlessness or group consciousness.* Unpublished manuscript, University of Michigan.

Crocker, J., and Major, B. (1989). Social stigma and self-esteem: The self protective properties of stigma. *Psychological Review, 96*, 608–630.

Crosby, F. (1976). A model of egoistical relative deprivation. *Psychological Review*, *83*, 85–113.

Crosby, F. (1982). *Relative deprivation and working women*. New York: Oxford University Press.

Crosby, F. (1984). Relative deprivation in organizational settings. *Research in Organizational Behavior*, *6*, 51–93.

Crosby, F., and Gonzalez-Intal, A. (1984). Relative deprivation and equity theories: Felt injustice and the undeserved benefits of others. In R. Folger (Ed.), *The sense of injustice: Social psychological perspectives*. New York: Plenum.

Crosby, F., Muehrer, P., and Loewenstein, G. (1986). Relative deprivation and explanation: Models and concepts. In J. M. Olson, C. P. Herman, and M. P. Zanna (Eds.), *Relative deprivation and social comparison: The Ontario symposium*. Hillsdale, NJ: Lawrence Erlbaum.

Crosby, F. J., Pufall, A., Snyder, R. C., O'Connell, M., and Whalen, P. (1989). The denial of personal disadvantage among you, me, and all the other ostriches. In M. Crawford and M. Gentry (Eds.), *Gender and thought: Psychological perspectives*. New York: Springer-Verlag.

Cumberland, J., and Zamble, E. (1992). General and specific measures of attitudes toward early release of criminal offenders. *Canadian Journal of Behavioral Science*, *24*, 442–455.

Dailey, R. C., and Kirk, D. J. (1992). Distributive and procedural justice as antecedents of job dissatisfaction and intention to turnover. *Human Relations, 45*, 305–317.

Darby, B. W., and Schlenker, B. R. (1989). Children's reactions to transgressions: Effects of the actor's apology, reputation and remorse. *British Journal of Social Psychology*, *28*, 353–364.

Darley, J. (1992). Social organization for the production of evil. *Psychological Inquiry*, *3*, 199–218.

Darley, J., and Huff, C. W. (1990). Heightened damage assessment as a result of the intentionality of the damage-causing act. *British Journal of Social Psychology*, *29*, 181–188.

Darley, J., and Shultz, T. (1990). Moral rules: Their content and acquisition. *Annual Review of Psychology*, *41*, 525–556.

Davidson, B. (1984). A test of the equity theory for marital adjustment. *Social Psychology Quarterly*, *47*, 36–42.

Davidson, B., Balswick, J., and Halverson, C. (1983). Affective self-disclosure and marital adjustment: A test of equity theory. *Journal of Marriage and the Family*, *45*, 93–102.

Davies, J. C. (1962). Toward a theory of revolution. *American Sociological Review*, *27*, 5–19.

Davis, J. H. (1980). Group decisions and procedural justice. In M. Fishbein (Ed.), *Progress in social psychology* (pp. 157–229). Hillsdale, NJ: Lawrence Erlbaum.

Dawes, R. M. (1980). Social dilemmas. *Annual Review of Psychology*, *31*, 169–193.

de Carufel, A. (1981). The allocation and acquisition of resources in times of scarcity. In M. J. Lerner and S. C. Lerner (Eds.), *The justice motive in social behavior*. New York: Plenum.

de Carufel, A. (1986). Pay secrecy, social comparisons and relative deprivation in organizations. In J. M. Olson, C. P. Herman, and M. P. Zanna (Eds.), *Relative deprivation and social comparison: The Ontario symposium*. Hillsdale, NJ: Lawrence Erlbaum.

de Carufel, A., and Schopler, J. (1979). Evaluation of outcome improvement resulting from threats and appeals. *Journal of Personality and Social Psychology, 37,* 662–673.

Deci, E. L., Reis, H. T., Johnston, E. J., and Smith, R. (1977). Toward reconciling equity theory and insufficient justification. *Personality and Social Psychology Bulletin, 3,* 224–227.

de Dreu, C. W., Lualhati, J. C., and McCusker, C. (1994). Effects of gain-loss frames on satisfaction with self-other outcome differences. *European Journal of Social Psychology, 34,* 497–510.

Delgado, R. (1985). "Rotten social background": Should the criminal law recognize a defense of severe environmental deprivation? *Law and Inequality, 3,* 9–90.

Della Fave, L. R. (1980). The meek shall not inherit the Earth: Self-evaluations and the legitimacy of stratification. *American Sociological Review, 45,* 955–971.

deRidder, R., and Tripathi, R. C. (1992). *Norm violation and intergroup relations.* Oxford, UK: Clarendon.

Deutsch, M. (1975). Equity, equality, and need: What determines which value will be used as the basis for distributive justice? *Journal of Social Issues, 31* (3), 137–149.

Deutsch, M. (1982). Interdependence and psychological orientation. In V. J. Delilega and J. Grzelak (Eds.), *Cooperation and helping behavior.* New York: Academic Press.

Deutsch, M. (1985). *Distributive justice.* New Haven: Yale University Press.

Deutsch, M. (1987). Experimental studies of the effects of different systems of distributive justice. In J. C. Masters and W. P. Smith (Eds.), *Social comparison, social justice, and relative deprivation*. Hillsdale, NJ: Lawrence Erlbaum.

Deutsch, M., and Steil, J. M. (1988). Awakening the sense of injustice. *Social Justice Research, 2,* 2–23.

Dibble, U. (1981). Socially shared deprivation and the approval of violence: Another look at the experience of American blacks during the 1960s. *Ethnicity, 8,* 149–169.

DiMento, J. F. (1989). Can Social Science Explain Organizational Noncompliance with Environmental Law? *Journal of Social Issues, 45* (1), 109–132.

Dion, K. L. (1986). Responses to perceived discrimination and relative deprivation. In J. M. Olson, C. P. Herman, and M. P. Zanna (Eds.), *Relative deprivation and social comparison: The Ontario symposium*. Hillsdale, NJ: Lawrence Erlbaum.

Dion, K. L. (1992, July). Relative deprivation, perceived discrimination and militancy. Paper presented at the International Congress of Psychology, Brussels, Belgium.

Dockson, R. R. (1993). *Justice in the balance 2020: Report of the Commission on the Future of the California Courts.* San Francisco: Supreme Court of California.

Dollard, J. L., Doob, N., Miller, N. E., Mowrer, O., and Sears, R. (1939). *Frustration and aggression.* New Haven: Yale University Press.

Donnenwerth, G. V., and Foa, U. G. (1974). Effect of resource class on retaliation to injustice in interpersonal exchange. *Journal of Personality and Social Psychology, 29,* 785–793.

Doob, A. N., and Roberts, J. V. (1984). Social psychology, social attitudes, and attitudes toward sentencing. *Canadian Journal of Behavioral Science, 16,* 269–280.

Dube, L., and Guimond, S. (1986). Relative deprivation and social protest: The personal group issue. In J. Olson, C. P. Herman, and M. Zanna (Eds.), *Relative deprivation and social comparison.* Hillsdale, NJ: Lawrence Erlbaum.

Duberman, M. (1994). *Stonewall.* New York: Penguin books.

Duster, T. (1995). A review of the bell curve. *Contemporary Sociology, 24,* 158–161.

Earley, P. C., and Lind, E. A. (1987). Procedural justice and participation in task selection: The role of control in mediating justice judgments. *Journal of Personality and Social Psychology, 52,* 1148–1160.

Easton, D. (1965). *A systems analysis of political life.* Chicago: University of Chicago Press.

Easton, D. (1975). A reassessment of the concept of political support. *British Journal of Political Science, 5,* 435–457.

Eisner, R., and Zimmerman, R. (1989). Individual entitlement to the financial benefits of a professional degree. *Journal of Law Reform, 22,* 333–364.

Ellemers, N. (1993). The Influence of Socio-structural Variables on Identity Management Strategies. In W. Stroebe and M. Hewstone (Eds.), *European Review of Social Psychology* (Vol. 4). London: John Wiley.

Ellsworth, P. (1978, November). Attitudes towards capital punishment: From application to theory. Paper presented at the Annual Meeting of the Society for Experimental Social Psychology, Stanford, CA.

Ellsworth, P., and Ross, L. (1983). Public opinion and capital punishment: A close examination of the views of abolitionists and retentionists. *Crime and Delinquency, 29,* 116–169.

Ellsworth, P., and Gross, S. R., (1994). Hardening of the attitudes: American's views on the death penalty. *Journal of Social Issues, 50* (2), 19–52.

Elster, J. (1992). *Local justice: How institutions allocate scarce goods and necessary burdens.* New York: Russell Sage.

Elster, J. (1993). Justice and the allocation of scarce resources. In B. A. Mellers and J. Baron (Eds.), *Psychological perspectives on justice.* Cambridge, UK: Cambridge University Press.

Emery, R. E., Mathews, S. G., and Kitzmann, K. M. (1994). Child custody mediation and litigation: Parents' satisfaction and functioning one year after settlement. *Journal of Consulting & Clinical Psychology, 62,* 124–129.

Erber, M. W. (1990). Context effects on procedural justice: Effects of interrelatedness, trust, and penalty on procedural preferences. *Social Justice Research, 4,* 337–353.

Evans, S. S., and Scott, J. E. (1984). The seriousness of crime cross-culturally. *Criminology, 22,* 39–59.

Feather, N. T. (1996). Reactions to penalties for an offense in relation to authoritarianism, values, perceived responsibility, perceived seriousness, and deservingness. *Jounal of Personality and Social Psychology, 71,* 571–587.

Feeley, M. (1979). *The process is punishment: handling cases in a lower criminal court.* New York: Russell Sage.

Feierabend, I. K., Feierabend, R. L., and Nesvold, B. A. (1969). Social and political violence: Cross-national perspectives. In H. D. Graham and T. R. Gurr (Eds.), *Violence in America.* New York: Spence.

Felson, R. B., and Ribner, S. A., (1981). An attributional approach to accounts and sanctions for criminal violence. *Social Psychology Quarterly, 44,* 137–142.

Felson, R. B., and Tedeschi, J. T., (1995) A social interactionist approach to violence: Cross cultural applications. In R. B. Ruback and N. A. Weiner (Eds.), *Interpersonal violent behaviors: Social and cultural aspects* (pp. 153–170). Springer, New York.

Felstiner, W.L.F., Abel, R. L., and Sarat, A. (1980–1981). The emergence and transformation of disputes: Naming, blaming, claiming. *Law and Society Review, 15,* 631–654.

Festinger, L. (1954). A theory of social comparison processes. *Human Relations, 7,* 117–140.

Feuille, P., and Delaney, J. T. (1992). The individual pursuit of organizational justice: Grievance procedures in nonunion workplaces. *Research in Personnel and Human Resources Management, 10,* 187–232.

Fincham, F. D., and Roberts, C. (1985). Intervening causation and the mitigation of responsibility for harm-doing. *Journal of Experimental Social Psychology, 21,* 178–194.

Fine, M. (1990). "The public" in public schools: The social construction/constriction of moral communities. *Journal of Social Issues, 46,* 107–119.

Finkel, S., and Rule, J. (1987). Relative deprivation and related psychological theories of civil violence: A critical review. *Research in Social Movements: Conflicts and Change, 9,* 47–69.

Fiske, A. P. (1991). *Structures of social life: The four elementary forms of human relations.* New York: Free Press.

Fiske, A. P. (1992). The four elementary forms of sociality: Framework for a Unified Theory of Social Relations. *Psychological Review, 99,* 689–723.

Fiske, S. T. (1995). Controlling other people: The impact of power on stereotyping. In N.R. Goldberger, J. Bennet Veroff, (Eds.), *The Culture and Psychology Reader,* New York: New York University Press.

Fiske, S. T., and Taylor, S. E. (1991). *Social cognition* (2nd ed.). New York: McGraw-Hill.

Foa, E. B., and Foa, U. G. (1976). Resource theory of social exchange. In J. W. Thibaut, J. T. Spence, and R. C. Carson (Eds.), *Contemporary topics in social psychology.* Morristown, NY: General Learning Press.

Foa, E. B., Turner, J. L., and Foa, U. G. (1972). Response generalization in aggression. *Human Relations, 25,* 337–350.

Foa, U. G., Converse, J., Jr., Tornblom, K. Y., and Foa, E. B. (Eds.) (1993). *Resource theory explorations and applications.* New York: Academic Press.

Folger, R. (1977). Distributive and procedural justice: Combined impact of "voice" and improvement on experienced inequity. *Journal of Personality and Social Psychology, 35,* 108–119.

Folger, R. (1986). A referent cognitions theory of relative deprivation. In J. Olson, C. P. Herman, and M. Zanna (Eds.), *Relative deprivation and social comparison: The Ontario symposium.* Hillsdale, NJ: Lawrence Erlbaum.

Folger, R. (1987). Reformulating the preconditions of resentments: A referent cognitions model. In J. Masters and W. Smith (Eds.), *Social comparison, social justice and relative deprivation.* Hillsdale, NJ: Lawrence Erlbaum.

Folger, R., and Greenberg, J. (1985). Procedural justice: An interpretive analysis of personnel systems. In K. Rowland and G. Ferris (Ed.), *Research in personnel and human resources management* (Vol. 3, pp. 141–183). Greenwich, CT: JAI.

Folger, R., and Konovsky, M. A. (1989). Effects of procedural and distributive justice on reactions to pay raise decisions. *Academy of Management Journal, 32*, 115–130.

Folger, R., Konovsky, M. A., and Cropanzano, R. (1992). A due process metaphor for performance appraisal. *Research in Organizational Behavior, 14*, 129–177.

Folger, R., Rosenfield, D., Rheame, K., and Martin, C. (1983). Relative deprivation and referent cognitions. *Journal of Experimental Psychology, 19*, 172–184.

Folger, R., Rosenfield, D., and Robinson, T. (1983). Relative deprivation and procedural justification. *Journal of Personality and Social Psychology, 45*, 268–273.

Ford, P. (1995, March 8). Chechens' eye-for-eye vendettas shape war. *Christian Science Monitor*, pp. 1, 13.

Foster, D. (1991a). Relative deprivation theory: Theoretical and empirical status. In D. Foster and J. Louw-Potgieter (Eds.), *Social psychology in South Africa* (pp. 245–270). Johannesburg, South Africa: Lexicon.

Foster, D. (1991b). Social influence III: Crowds and collective violence. In D. Foster and J. Louw-Potgieter (Eds.), *Social psychology in South Africa* (pp. 441–483). Johannesburg, South Africa: Lexicon.

Foster, M. D., and Matheson, K. (1995). Double relative deprivation: Combining the personal and political. *Personality and Social Psychology Bulletin, 21*, 1167–1177.

Frank, R. H. (1985). *Choosing the right pond: Human behavior and the quest for status*. New York: Oxford.

Franklin, D. (1995, April 11). Co-ops shake up Cloyne Court. *The Daily Californian*, p. 3.

Friedland, N., Thibaut, J., and Walker, L. (1973). Some determinants of the violation of rules. *Journal of Applied Social Psychology, 3*, 103–118.

Frohlich, N., and Oppenheimer, J. A. (1990). Choosing justice in experimental democracies with production. *American Political Science Review, 84*, 461–477.

Fry, W. R., and Cheney, G. (1981, May). *Perceptions of procedural fairness as a function of distributive preferences*. Paper presented at the annual meeting of the Midwestern Psychological Association, Detroit.

Fry, W. R., and Leventhal, G. S. (1979, March). *Cross-situational procedural preferences: A comparison of allocation preferences and equity across different social settings*. Paper presented at the annual meeting of the Southeastern Psychological Association, Washington, DC.

Furnham, A. (1985). Just world beliefs in an unjust society: A cross cultural comparison. *European Journal of Social Psychology, 15*, 363–366.

Furnham, A. (1993). Just world beliefs in twelve societies. *Journal of Social Psychology, 133*, 317–329.

Gaertner, S. L., Rust, M. C., Dovidio, J. F., Bachman, B. A., and Anastasio, P. A. (1994). The contact hypothesis: The role of a common in-group identity on reducing intergroup bias. Special Issue: Social cognition in small groups. *Small Group Research, 25*, 224–249.

Gamson, W. A. (1968). *Power and discontent*. Homewood, IL: Dorsey.

Gartrell, C. D. (1987). Network approaches to social evaluation. *Annual Review of Sociology, 13*, 49–66.

Gergen, K. J., Morse, S. J., and Bode, K. (1974). Overpaid or overworked?: Cognitive and behavioral reactions to inequitable rewards. *Journal of Applied Psychology, 4*, 259–274.

Gergen, K. J., Morse, S. J., and Gergen, M. M. (1980). Behavior exchange in cross-cultural perspective. In H. C. Triandis and R. W. Brislin (Eds.), *Handbook of cross-cultural psychology* (Vol. 5, pp. 121–154). Boston: Allyn and Bacon.

Gibson, J. L. (1987). Homosexuals and the Ku Klux Klan: A contextual analysis of political tolerance. *Western Political Quarterly, 40*, 427–448.

Gibson, J. L., Caldeira, G. A. (1996). The legal cultures of Europe. *Law and Society Review, 30*, 55–85.

Gilliland, S. W. (1994). Effects of procedural and distributive justice on reactions to a selection system. *Journal of Applied Psychology, 79*, 691–701.

Gladwin, T. N., Kennelly, J. J., and Krause, T. S. (1995). Shifting paradigms for sustainable development: Implications for management theory and research. *Academy of Management Review, 20*, 874–907.

Gordon, H. C., and Keyes, W. A. (1983, May). *Fairness II: An executive briefing book*. Washington, DC: White House Office of Policy Information.

Gordon, M. E., and Fryxell, G. E. (1993). The role of interpersonal justice in organizational grievance systems. In R. Cropanzano (Ed.), *Justice in the workplace*. Hillsdale, NJ: Lawrence Erlbaum.

Gray-Little, B. (1980). Race and inequality. *Journal of Applied Social Psychology, 10*, 468–481.

Greenberg, J. (1981). The justice of distributing scarce and abundant resources. In S. Lerner and M. J. Lerner (Eds.), *The justice motive in social behavior*. New York: Plenum.

Greenberg, J. (1982). Approaching equity and avoiding inequity in groups and organizations. In J. Greenberg and R. L. Cohen (Eds.), *Equity and justice in social behavior* (pp. 389–435). New York: Academic Press.

Greenberg, J. (1983). Equity and equality as clues to the relationship between exchange participants. *European Journal of Social Psychology, 13*, 195–196.

Greenberg, J. (1986). Determinants of perceived fairness of performance evaluations. *Journal of Applied Psychology, 71*, 340–342.

Greenberg, J. (1987a). Reactions to procedural injustice in payment distributions: Do the ends justify the means? *Journal of Applied Psychology, 72*, 55–61.

Greenberg, J. (1987b). A taxonomy of organizational justice theories. *Academy of Management Review, 12*, 9–22.

Greenberg, J. (1988). Equity and workplace status: A field experiment. *Journal of Applied Psychology, 73*, 606–613.

Greenberg, J. (1990a). Employee theft as a reaction to underpayment inequity: The hidden cost of pay cuts. *Journal of Applied Psychology, 75*, 561–568.

Greenberg, J. (1990b). Looking fair vs. being fair: Managing impressions of organizational fairness. In B. M. Staw and L. L. Cummings (Eds.), *Research in Organizational Behavior* (Vol. 12, pp. 111–157). Greenwich, CT: JAI.

Greenberg, J. (1990c). Organizational justice: Yesterday, today, and tomorrow. *Journal of Management, 16*, 399–432.

Greenberg, J. (1993). Stealing in the name of justice: Informational and interpersonal moderators of theft reactions to underpayment inequity. *Organizational Behavior and Human Decision Making Processes, 54,* 81–103.

Greenberg, J. (1994). Using socially fair treatment to promote acceptance of a work site smoking ban. *Journal of Applied Psychology, 79,* 288–297.

Greenberg, J., and Folger, R. (1983). Procedural justice, participation, and the fair process effect in groups and organizations. In P. Paulus (Ed.), *Basic Group Processes* (pp. 235–266). New York: Springer-Verlag.

Greenwald, A., and Banaji, M. (1995). Implicit social cognition: Attitudes, self-esteem, and stereotypes. *Psychological Review, 102,* 4–27.

Grossman, D. (1995). *On killing: The psychological cost of learning to kill in war and society.* Boston: Little, Brown.

Guilland, S. W. (1993). The perceived fairness of selection systems: An organizational justice perspective. *Academy of Management Review, 18,* 694–734.

Guinier, L. (1994). *The tyranny of the majority.* New York: Martin Kessler Books.

Gundykunst, W. B. (1988). Culture and intergroup processes. In M. H. Bond (Ed.), *The cross-cultural challenge to social psychology.* Newbury Park, CA: Sage.

Gundykunst, W. B., and Ting-Toomey, S. (1988). Culture and affective communication. *American Behavioral Scientist, 31,* 384–400.

Gurin, P., and Epps, E. (1975). *Black consciousness, identity and achievement: A study of students in historically black colleges.* New York: Wiley.

Gurin, P., and Townsend, A. (1986). Properties of gender identity and their implications for gender consciousness. *American Political Science Review, 67,* 514–539.

Gurney, J., and Tierney, K. (1982). Relative deprivation and social movements: A critical look at twenty years of theory and research. *The Sociological Quarterly, 23,* 33–47.

Gurr, T. R. (1970). *Why men rebel.* Princeton: Princeton University Press.

Guth, W., Schmittberg, R., and Schwartze, B. (1982). An experimental analysis of ultimatum bargaining. *Journal of Economic Behavior and Organizations, 3,* 367–388.

Hafer, C. L., and Olson, J. M. (1989). Beliefs in a just world and reactions to personal deprivation. *Journal of Personality, 57*(4), 799–823.

Hafer, C. L., and Olson, J. M. (1993). Beliefs in a just world, discontent, and assertive actions by working women. *Personality and Social Psychology Bulletin, 19,* 30–38.

Hagiwara, S. (1992). The concept of responsibility and determinants of responsibility judgment in the Japanese context. *International Journal of Psychology, 27*(2), 143–156.

Haidt, J., Koller, S. H., and Dias, M. G. (1993). Affect, culture, and morality, or Is it wrong to eat your dog? *Journal of Personality and Social Psychology, 65,* 613–628.

Halberstam, D. (1972). *The best and the brightest.* New York: Random House.

Hamilton, V. L., and Hagiwara, S. (1992). Roles, responsibility, and accounts across cultures. *International Journal of Psychology, 27*(2), 157–179.

Hamilton, V. L., and Sanders, J. (1988). Punishment and the individual in the United States and Japan. *Law and Society Review, 22,* 301–328.

Hamilton, V. L., and Sanders, J. (1992). *Everyday justice: Responsibility and the individual in Japan and the United States.* New Haven: Yale University Press.

Haney, C. (1991). The Fourteenth Amendment and symbolic legality: Let them eat due process. *Law and Human Behavior, 15,* 183–204.

Hasegawa, K. (1986). *Japanese-style management*. New York: Kondansha International.

Hatfield, E., and Traupmann, J. (1981). Intimate relationships: A perspective from equity theory. In S. Duck and R. Gilmour (Eds.), *Personal relationships*. New York: Academic Press.

Hatfield, E., Traupmann, J., Sprecher, S., Utne, M., and Hay, J. (1985). Equity and intimate relations: Recent research. In W. Ickes (Ed.), *Compatible and incompatible relationships*. New York: Springer-Verlag.

Hatfield, E., Utne, M., and Traupmann, J. (1979). Equity theory and intimate relationships. In R. L. Burgess and T. L. Huston (Eds.), *Social exchange in developing relationships*. New York: Academic Press.

Hayden, R. M., and Anderson, J. K. (1979). On the evaluation of procedural systems in laboratory experiments: A critique of Thibaut and Walker. *Law and Human Behavior, 3*, 21–38.

Hays, R. B. (1985). A longitudinal study of friendship development. *Journal of Personality and Social Psychology, 48*, 909–924.

Heberlein, T. A. (1972). The land ethic realized: Some social psychological explanations for changing environmental attitudes. *Journal of Social Issues, 28* (4), 79–87.

Heider, F. (1958). *The psychology of interpersonal relations*. New York: Wiley.

Helson, H. (1964). *Adaptation-level theory*. New York: Harper and Row.

Herbert, T. B., and Dunkel-Schetter, C. (1992). Negative social reactions to victims: An overview of responses and their determinants. In L. Montada, S. Filipp, and M. J. Lerner (Eds.), *Life crises and experiences of loss in adulthood* (pp. 497–518). Hillsdale, NJ: Lawrence Erlbaum.

Hermkens P., and van Kreveld, D. (1992). Social justice, income distribution and social stratification in the Netherlands: A review. In H. Steensma and R. Vermunt (Eds.), *Social Justice in Human Relations*. New York: Plenum.

Herring, C. (1985). Acquiescence or activism? Political behavior among the politically alienated. *Political Psychology, 10*, 135–161.

Hirschman, A. O. (1970). *Exit, voice, and loyalty: Responses to decline in firms, organizations, and states*. Cambridge, MA: Harvard University Press.

Hochschild, J. L. (1981). *What's fair: American beliefs about distributive justice*. Cambridge, MA: Harvard University Press.

Hofstede, G. (1980). *Culture's consequences: International differences in work related values*. Beverly Hills, CA: Sage.

Hogan, R., Curphy, G., and Hogan, J. (1994). What we know about leadership: Effectiveness and personality. *American Psychologist, 49*, 493–504.

Hogan, R., and Emler, N. P. (1978). The biases in contemporary social psychology. *Social Research, 45*, 478–534.

Hogan, R., and Emler, N. P. (1981). Retributive justice. In M. J. Lerner and S. C. Lerner (Eds.), *The justice motive in social behavior*. New York: Academic Press.

Hogg, M. A., and Abrams, D. (1988). *Social identifications: A social psychology of intergroup relations and group processes*. London and New York: Routledge.

Hogg, M. A., and Abrams, D. (1993). Group motivation: social psychological perspectives. In M. A. Hogg and D. Abrams (Eds.), New York and London: Harvester Wheatsheaf.

Hollander, E. P. (1985). Leadership and power. In G. Lindzey and E. Aronson (Eds.), *The handbook of social psychology*, (Vol. 2, pp. 485–537). New York: Random House.

Horai, J., (1977). Attributional conflict. *Journal of Social Issues, 33* (1), 88–100.

Horai, J., and Bartek, M. (1978). Recommended punishment as a function of injurious intent, actual harm done, and intended consequences. *Personality and Social Psychology Bulletin, 4,* 575–578.

Horan, H. D., and Kaplan, M. F. (1983). Criminal intent and consequence severity: Effects of moral reasoning on punishment. *Personality and Social Psychology Bulletin, 9,* 638–645.

Houlden, P. (1980). The impact of procedural modifications on evaluations of plea bargaining. *Law and Society Review, 15,* 267–292.

Huggins, M. K. (1991). Introduction: Vigilantism and the state—A look south and north. In M. K. Huggins (Ed.), *Vigilantism and the state in modern Latin America: Essays on extralegal violence.* New York: Praeger.

Huo, Y. J. (1995, June). Justice and exclusion: Exploring the boundaries of our justice concerns. In R. Vermunt (Chair), *Procedural fairness and unfairness: Theoretical positions, and effects on judicial treatment and norm violation.* Symposium conducted at the Fifth International Conference on Social Justice Research, Reno, NV.

Huo, Y. J. (1996). *How boundaries are drawn: The psychology of exclusion and inclusion.* Unpublished manuscript, University of California, Berkeley.

Huo, Y. J., Smith, H. J., Tyler, T. R., and Lind, E. A. (1996). Superordinate identification, subgroup identification, and justice concerns: Is separatism the problem, is assimilation the answer. *Psychological Science, 7,* 40–45.

Hyden, R. M., and Anderson, J. K. (1979). On the evaluation of procedural systems in laboratory experiments: A critique of Thibaut and Walker. *Law and Human Behavior, 3,* 21–38.

Hyman, H. H., and Singer, E. (1968). *Readings in reference group theory and research.* New York: Free Press.

Issac, L., Mutran, E. and Stryker, S. (1980). Political protest orientation among black and white adults. *American Sociological Review, 45,* 191–213.

James, K. (1993). The social context of organizational justice: Cultural, intergroup, and structural effects on justice behaviors and perceptions. In R. Cropanzano (Ed.), *Justice in the workplace.* Hillsdale, NJ: Lawrence Erlbaum.

Jones, E. E., and Davis, K. E. (1965). From acts to dispositions: The attribution process in person perception. In L. Berkowitz (Ed.), *Advances in experimental social psychology* (Vol. 2, pp. 220–266). New York: Academic Press.

Jost, J. T., and Banaji, M. R. (1994). The role of stereotyping in system-justification and the production of false consciousness. *British Journal of Social Psychology, 33,* 1–27.

Kabinoff, B. (1991). Equity, equality, power, & conflict. *Academy of Management Review, 16,* 416–441.

Kahneman, D. (1979). Prospect theory: An analysis of decision under risk. *Econometrica, 47,* 263–291.

Kahneman, D. (1992). Reference points, anchors, norms, and mixed feelings. *Organizational Behavior and Human Decision Processes, 51,* 296–312.

Kahneman, D., Knetsch, J. L., and Thaler, R. H. (1986). Fairness and the assumptions of economics. *Journal of Business, 59,* 5285–5300.

Kahneman, D. and Miller, D. T. (1986). Norm theory: Comparing reality to its alternatives. *Psychological Review, 93,* 136–153.

Kahneman, D., and Tversky, A. (1973). On the psychology of prediction. *Psychological Review, 80,* 237–251.

Kahneman, D., and Tversky, A. (1982). The psychology of preferences. *Scientific American, 246*(1), 160–173.

Kanfer, R., Sawyer, J., Earley, P. C., and Lind, E. A. (1987). Participation in task evaluation procedures: The effects of influential opinion expression and knowledge of evaluative criteria on attitudes and performance. *Social Justice Research, 1,* 235–249.

Karlovac, M., and Darley, J. M. (1988). Attribution of responsibility for accidents: A negligence law analogy. *Social Cognition, 6,* 287–318.

Karsh, B., and Cole, R. E. (1968). Industrialization and the convergence hypothesis: Some aspects of contemporary Japan. *Journal of Social Issues, 24* (4), 45–64.

Kashima, Y., Siegal, M., Tanaka, K., and Isaka, H. (1988). Universalism in lay conceptions of distributive justice: A cross-cultural examination. *International Journal of Psychology, 23,* 51–64.

Kawakami, K., and Dion, K. (1993). The impact of salient self-identities on relative deprivation and action intentions. *European Journal of Social Psychology, 23,* 525–540.

Keith, P.M., and Schafer, R. B. (1985). Role Behavior, Relative Deprivation and Depression in One and Two Job Families. *Family Relations, 34,* 227–233.

Kelley, H. H., and Thibaut, J. W. (1978). Interpersonal relations: A theory of interdependence. New York: Wiley.

Kelly, C., and Kelly, J. (1994). Who gets involved in collective action?: Social psychological determinants of individual participation in trade unions. *Human Relations, 47,* 63–88.

Kelman, H. C. (1969). Patterns of personal involvement in the national system: A socio-psychological analysis of political legitimacy. In J. Rosenau (Ed.), *International politics and foreign policy* (Rev. ed.). New York: Free Press.

Kelman, H. C., and Hamilton, V. L. (1989). *Crimes of obedience.* New Haven: Yale University Press.

Kerr, N. (1978). Severity of prescribed penalty and mock jurors' verdicts. *Journal of Personality and Social Psychology, 36,* 1431–1442.

Kerr, N. L., Hymes, R. W., Anderson, A. B., and Weathers, J. E. (1995). Defendant-juror similarity and mock juror judgments. *Law and Human Behavior, 19, 6,* 545–567.

Kidder, L. H., and Muller, S. (1991). What is "fair" in Japan? In R. Vermunt and H. Steensma (Eds.), *Social justice in human relations: Vol. 2. Societal and psychological consequences of justice and injustice* (pp. 139–154). New York: Plenum.

Kitzmann, K. M., and Emery, R. E. (1993). Procedural justice and parents' satisfaction in a field study of child custody dispute resolution. *Law and Human Behavior, 17*(5), 553–567.

Klandermans, B. (1989). Grievance interpretation and success expectancies: The social construction of protest. *Social Behavior, 4,* 113–125.

Klandermans, B. (1993). A theoretical framework for comparisons of social movement participation. *Sociological Forum*, *8*, 383–402.

Klandermans, B., and Oegema, D. (1987). Potentials, networks, motivations and barriers: Steps towards participation in social movements. *American Sociological Review*, *52*, 519–531.

Kleinke, C. H., Wallis, R., and Stalder, K. (1992). Evaluation of a rapist as a function of expressed intent and remorse. *The Journal of Social Psychology*, *132*, 525–537.

Kluegel, J. R., and Smith, E. R. (1986). *Beliefs about inequality: Americans' views of what is and what ought to be*. New York: Adegruyter.

Klugman, P. (1994). *The age of diminished expectations*. Cambridge, MA: MIT Press.

Kohlberg, L. (1969). Stage and sequence: The cognitive-developmental approach to socialization. In D. A. Goslin (Ed.), *Handbook of socialization theory and research*. Chicago: Rand-McNally.

Konovsky, M. A., and Cropanzano, R. (1991). Perceived fairness of employee drug testing as a predictor of employee attitudes and job performance. *Journal of Applied Psychology*, *76*, 698–707.

Koper, G., Van Knippenberg, D., Bouhuijs, F., Vermunt, R., and Wilke, H. (1993). Procedural fairness and self-esteem. *European Journal of Social Psychology*, *23*, 313–325.

Koss, M. P., Goodman, L. A., Browne, A., Fitzgerald, L. F., Keita, G. P., and Russo, N. F. (1994). *No safe haven: Male violence against women at home, at work, and in the community*. Washington, DC: American Psychological Association.

Kramer, R. M., and Brewer, M. (1984). Effects of group identity on resource use in a simulated commons dilemma. *Journal of Personality and Social Psychology*, *46*, 1044–1057.

Kravitz, D. A., and Platania, J. (1993). Attitudes and beliefs about affirmative action: Effects of target and of respondent sex and ethnicity. *Journal of Applied Psychology*, *78*, 928–938.

Kristof, N. (1995, January 22). Kobe's survivors try to adjust. *New York Times*.

Kurosawa, K. (1992). Responsibility and justice: A view across cultures. *International Journal of Psychology*, *27*, 243–256.

Lalonde, R. N., and Cameron, J. E. (1994). Behavioral responses to discrimination: A focus on action. In M. P. Zanna and J. M. Olson (Eds.), *The psychology of prejudice*. Hillsdale, NJ: Lawrence Erlbaum.

Lalonde, R. N., and Silverman, R. A. (1994). Behavioral preferences in response to social injustice: The effects of group permeability and social identity salience. *Journal of Personality and Social Psychology*, *66*, 78–85.

Lamm, H., and Keyser, E. (1978). The allocation of monetary gain and loss following dyadic performance: The weight given to effort and ability under conditions of low and high intra-dyadic attraction. *European Journal of Social Psychology*, *8*, 275–278.

Landy, D., and Aronson, E. (1969). The influence of the character of the criminal and his victim on the decisions of simulated jurors. *Journal of Experimental Social Psychology*, *5*, 141–152.

Lane, R. (1962). *Political ideology*. New York: Free Press.

Lane, R. (1981). Markets and politics: The human product. *British Journal of Political Science*, *11*, 1–16.

Lane, R. (1986). Market justice, political justice. *American Political Science Review*, *80*, 383–402.

Lane, R. (1988). Procedural goods in a democracy: How one is treated vs. what one gets. *Social Justice Research, 2,* 177–192.

Lane, R. (1993). Does money buy happiness? *The Public Interest, 113,* 56–65.

Langer, E. J. (1992). Matters of mind: Mindfulness/mindlessness in perspective. *Consciousness and Cognition: An International Journal, 1,* 289–305.

LaTour, S. (1978). Determinants of participant and observer satisfaction with adversary and inquisitorial modes of adjudication. *Journal of Personality and Social Psychology, 36,* 1531–1545.

LaTour, S., Houlden, P., Walker, L., and Thibaut, J. (1976). Procedure: Transnational perspectives and preferences. *Yale Law Review, 86,* 258–290.

Lau, R. (1989). Individual and contextual influences on group identification. *Social Psychology Quarterly, 52,* 220–231.

Lawler, E. (1968). Equity theory as a predictor of productivity and work quality. *Psychological Bulletin, 70,* 596–610.

Lea, J. A., Smith, H. J., and Tyler, T. R. (1995). *Predicting support for compensatory public policies: Who, why and how.* Unpublished manuscript, University of California, Berkeley.

Leach, C. W., Smith, R. H., and Garonzik, R. (1996). "Reaction to the lot of the other": Theory and measurement. Unpublished Manuscript, Swarthmore College, Swarthmore, PA.

Lee, H. K. (1995, December 6). Black family's home vandalized in Fremont. *San Francisco Chronicle,* pp. A13, A17.

Lerner, M. J. (1977). The justice motive: Some hypotheses as to its origins and forms. *Journal of Personality, 45,* 1–52.

Lerner, M. J. (1980). *The belief in a just world.* New York: Plenum.

Lerner, M. J. (1981). The justice motive in human relations: Some thoughts on what we know and need to know about justice. In M. J. Lerner and S. C. Lerner (Ed.), *The justice motive in social behavior.* New York: Plenum.

Lerner, M. J. (1982). The justice motive in human relations and the economic model of man: A radical analysis of facts and fictions. In V. J. Derlega and J. Grzelak (Eds.), *Cooperation and helping behavior: Theories and research.* New York: Academic Press.

Lerner, M. J., and Lerner, S. C. (1981). The justice motive in social behavior: Adapting to times of scarcity and change. New York: Plenum.

Lerner, M. J., and Mikula, G. (1994). *Entitlement and the affectional bond: Justice in close relationships.* New York: Plenum.

Lerner, M. J., and Simmons, C. H. (1966). Observer's reactions to the "innocent victim": Compassion or rejection? *Journal of Personality and Social Psychology, 4,* 203–210.

Lerner, M. J., Somers, D., Reid, D., Chiriboga, D., and Tierney, M. (1991). Adult children as caregivers: Egocentric biases in judgments of sibling contributions. *Gerontologist, 31,* 746–755.

Leung, K. (1987). Some determinants of reactions to procedural justice models for conflict resolution: A cross-national study. *Journal of Personality and Social Psychology, 51,* 898–908.

Leung, K. (1988). Theoretical advances in justice behavior: Some cross-cultural inputs. In M. H. Bond (Ed.), *The cross-cultural challenge to social psychology* (pp. 218–229). Newbury Park, CA: Sage.

Leung, K. (1989). Cross-cultural differences: Individual-level vs. culture-level analysis. *International Journal of Psychology*, 24, 703–719.

Leung, K., and Bond, M. H. (1982). How Chinese and Americans reward task-related contributions: A preliminary study. *Psychologica*, 25, 32–39.

Leung, K., and Bond, M. H. (1984). The impact of cultural collectivism on reward allocation. *Journal of Personality and Social Psychology*, 47, 793–804.

Leung, K., Chiu, W.-H., and Au, Y.-F. (1993). Sympathy and support for industrial actions: A justice analysis. *Journal of Applied Psychology*, 78, 781–787.

Leung, K., and Lind, E. A. (1986). Procedural justice and culture: Effects of culture, gender, and investigator status on procedural preferences. *Journal of Personality and Social Psychology*, 50, 1134–1140.

Leventhal, G. S. (1976). The distribution of rewards and resources in groups and organizations. In L. Berkowitz and E. Walster (Eds.), *Advances in experimental social psychology* (Vol. 9, pp. 91–131). New York: Academic Press.

Leventhal, G. S. (1980). What should be done with equity theory? New approaches to the study of fairness in social relationships. In K. Gergen, M. Greenberg, and R. Willis (Eds.), *Social exchange* (pp. 27–55). New York: Plenum.

Leventhal, G. S., Karuza, J., and Fry, W. R. (1980). Beyond fairness: A theory of allocation preferences. In G. Mikula, (Ed.), *Justice and social Interaction*. New York: Springer-Verlag.

LeVine, R. A., and Campbell, D. T. (1972). *Ethnocentrism: Theories of conflict, ethnic attitudes, and group behavior.* New York: Wiley.

Levine, J. M., and Moreland, R. L. (1987). Social comparison and outcome evaluation in group contexts. In J. C. Masters and W. P. Smith (Eds.), *Social comparison, social justice and relative deprivation*. Hillsdale, NJ: Lawrence Erlbaum.

Lewin, K., Dembo, T., Festinger, L., and Sears, P. S. (1944). Level of aspiration. In J. Hunt (Ed.), *Personality and behavior disorders*. New York: Ronald Press.

Lewin, K., Lippitt, R., and White, R. K. (1939). Patterns of aggressive behavior in experimentally created "social climates." *Journal of Social Psychology*, 10, 271–299.

Lifton, R. J. (1986). *The Nazi doctors.* New York: Basic Books.

Lind, E. A. (1990, August). Corporate justice: Testing the limits of justice concerns in inter-organizational disputes. Paper presented at the annual meeting of the Academy of Management. San Francisco.

Lind, E. A., Ambrose, M., de Vera Park, M., and Kulik, C. T. (1990). Perspective and procedural justice: Attorney and litigant evaluations of court procedures. *Social Justice Research*, 4, 325–336.

Lind, E. A., and Earley, P. C. (1992). Procedural justice and culture. *International Journal of Psychology*, 27, 227–242.

Lind, E. A., Erickson, B. E., Friedland, N., and Dickenberger, M. (1978). Reactions to procedural models for adjudicative conflict resolution: A cross-national study. *Journal of Conflict Resolution*, 22, 318–341.

Lind, E. A., Huo, Y., and Tyler, T. R. (1994). . . . And justice for all: Ethnicity, gender and preferences for dispute resolution procedures. *Law and Human Behavior*, 18, 269–290.

Lind, E. A., Kanfer, R., and Earley, P. C. (1990). Voice, control, and procedural justice: Instrumental and noninstrumental concerns in fairness judgments. *Journal of Personality and Social Psychology, 59,* 952–959.

Lind, E. A., Kulik, C. A., Ambrose, M., and de Vera Park, M. V. (1993). Individual and corporate dispute resolution: Using procedural fairness as a decision heuristic. *Administrative Science Quarterly, 38,* 224–251.

Lind, E. A., Kurtz, S., Musante, L., Walker, L., and Thibaut, J. (1980). Procedure and outcome effects on reactions to adjudicated resolutions of conflicts of interest. *Journal of Personality and Social Psychology, 39,* 643–653.

Lind, E. A., and Lissak, R. I. (1985). Apparent impropriety and procedural fairness judgments. *Journal of Experimental Social Psychology, 21*(1),19–29.

Lind, E. A., Lissak, R., and Conlon, D. E. (1983). Decision control and process control effects on procedural fairness judgments. *Journal of Applied Social Psychology, 13,* 338–350.

Lind, E. A., MacCoun, R. J., Ebener, P. A., Felstiner, W.L.F., Hensler, D. R., Resnik, J., and Tyler, T. R. (1990). In the eye of the beholder: Tort litigants' evaluations of their experiences in the civil justice system. *Law and Society Review, 24,* 953–996.

Lind, E. A., and Tyler, T. R. (1988). *The social psychology of procedural justice.* New York: Plenum.

Lipkus, I. M., and Siegler, I. C. (1993). The belief in a just world and perceptions of discrimination. *Journal of Psychology, 127,* 465–474.

Lissak, R., and Sheppard, B. H. (1983). Beyond fairness: The criterion problem in research on dispute intervention. *Journal of Applied Social Psychology, 13,* 45–65.

Loewenstein, G. F., Issacharoff, S., Camerer, C., and Babcock, L. (1993). Self-serving assessments of pretrial bargaining. *Journal of Legal Studies, 22,* 135–159.

Loewenstein, G. F., Thompson, L., and Bazerman, M. H. (1989). Social utility and decision making in interpersonal contexts. *Journal of Personality and Social Psychology, 57,* 426–441.

Longworth, R. C., and Stein, S. (1995, September 17). Miseries of the middle class: American dream is endangered, future filled with uncertainty. *San Francisco Examiner,* p. A-17.

Luker, K. (1984). *Abortion and the politics of motherhood.* Berkeley: University of California Press.

MacCoun, R. J. (1993). Drugs and the law: A psychological analysis of drug prohibition. *Psychological Bulletin, 113,* 497–512.

MacCoun, R. J., Lind, E. A., Hensler, D. R., Byrant, D. L., and Ebener, P. A. (1988). *Alternative adjudication: An evaluation of the New Jersey automobile arbitration program.* Santa Monica, CA: Institute for Civil Justice, RAND.

MacCoun, R. J., and Tyler, T. R. (1988). The basis of citizen's preferences for different forms of criminal jury. *Law and Human Behavior, 12,* 333–352.

Mahler, I., Greenberg, L., and Hayashi, H. (1981). A comparative study of rules of justice: Japanese versus Americans. *Psychologica, 24,* 1–8.

Mahoney, T. A. (1987). Understanding comparable worth: A societal and political perspective. *Research in Organizational Behavior, 9,* 209–245.

Major, B. (1994). From social inequality to personal entitlement: The role of social comparisons, legitimacy appraisals and group membership. In M. P. Zanna (Ed.),

Advances in experimental social psychology (Vol. 26, pp. 293–355). New York: Academic Press.

Major, B., and Deaux, K. (1982). Individual differences in justice behavior. In J. Greenberg and R. L. Cohen (Eds.), *Equity and justice in social behavior* (pp. 43–76). New York: Academic Press.

Major, B., and Forcey, B. (1985). Social comparisons and pay evaluations: Preferences for same-sex and same-job wage comparisons. *Journal of Experimental Social Psychology, 21*, 393–405.

Major, B., and Testa, M. (1988). Social comparison processes and judgments of entitlement and satisfaction. *Journal of Experimental Social Psychology, 25*, 101–120.

Marin, G. (1981). Perceived justice across cultures: Equity vs. equality in Columbia and in the United States. *International Journal of Psychology, 16*, 153–159.

Mark, M., and Folger, R. (1984). Response to relative deprivation: A conceptual framework. *Review of Personality and Social Psychology, 5*, 192–218.

Markovsky, B. (1988). Injustice and arousal. *Social Justice Research, 2*, 223–233.

Markus, H. R., and Kitayama, S. (1991). Culture and the self: Implications for cognition, emotion, and motivation. *Psychological Review, 98*, 224–253.

Markus, H. R., and Nuris, P. (1986). Possible selves. *American Psychologist, 41*, 954–969.

Marques, J. M. (1990). The black sheep-effect: Out-group homogeneity in social comparison settings. In D. Abrams and M. A. Hogg (Eds.), *Social identity theory: Constructive and critical advances* (pp. 131–151). New York: Springer-Verlag.

Martin, J. (1981). Relative deprivation: A theory of distributive justice for an era of shrinking resources. In L. L. Cummings and B. M. Straw (Eds.), *Research in Organizational Behavior* (Vol. 3). Greenwich, CT: JAI.

Martin, J. (1986a). The tolerance of injustice. In J. Olson, C. P. Herman, and M. Zanna (Eds.), *Relative deprivation and social comparison: The Ontario symposium*. Hillsdale, NJ: Lawrence Erlbaum.

Martin, J. (1986b). When expectations and justice do not coincide: Blue-collar visions of a just world. In H. Bierhoff, R. Cohen, and J. Greenberg (Eds.), *Justice in social relations*. New York: Plenum.

Martin, J. (1994). Inequality, distributive justice, and organizational illegitimacy. In J. K. Murnighan (Ed.), *Social psychology in organizations*. Englewood Cliffs, NJ: Prentice-Hall.

Martin, J., Brickman, P., and Murray, A. (1984). Moral outrage and pragmatism: Explanations for collective action. *Journal of Experimental Social Psychology, 20*, 484–496.

Martin, J., and Harder, J. W. (1994). Bread and roses: Justice and the distribution of financial and socioemotional rewards in organizations. *Social Justice Research, 7*, 241–264.

Martin, J., Scully, M., and Levitt, B. (1990). Injustice and the legitimation of revolution: Damning the past, excusing the present and neglecting the future. *Journal of Personality and Social Psychology, 59*, 281–290.

Mashaw, J. L. (1985). *Due process in the administrative state*. New Haven: Yale University Press.

Masters, J. C., and Smith, W. P. (1987). *Social comparison, social justice, and relative deprivation*. Hillsdale, NJ: Lawrence Erlbaum.

Masters, K. (1995, December 4–10). The attorney major general. *The Washington Post National Weekly Edition*, p. 10.

McClosky, H., and Brill, A. (1983). *Dimensions of tolerance.* New York: Russell Sage.

McEwen, C. A., and Maiman, R. J. (1984). Mediation in small claims court: Achieving compliance through consent. *Law and Society Review, 18,* 11–49.

McFarlin, D. B., and Sweeney, P. D. (1992). Distributive and procedural justice as predictors of satisfaction with personal and organizational outcomes. *Academy of Management Journal, 35,* 626–637.

McKillip, J., and Riedel, S. L. (1983). External validity of matching on physical attractiveness for same and opposite sex couples. *Journal of Applied Social Psychology, 13,* 328–337.

Mead, G. H. (1934). *Mind, self, and society.* Chicago: University of Chicago Press.

Meindl, J. R., Hunt, R. G., and Cheng, Y. K. (1994). Justice on the road to change in the People's Republic of China. *Social Justice Research, 7,* 197–224.

Merry, S. E., and Silbey, S. S. (1984). What do plaintiffs want? Reexamining the concept of dispute. *The Justice System Journal, 9,* 151–178.

Merton, R. K., and Kitt, A. S. (1950). Contributions to the theory of reference group behavior. In R. K. Merton and P. F. Lazarsfeld (Eds.), *Continuities in social research: Studies in the scope and method of "The American Soldier"* (pp. 40–105). Grencoe, IL: Free Press.

Messe, L. A., Hymes, R. W., and MacCoun, R. J. (1986). Group categorization an distributive justice decisions. In H. W. Bierhoff, R. L. Cohen, and J. Greenberg (Eds.), *Justice in social relations* (pp. 227–248). New York: Plenum.

Messe, L. A., and Watts, B. L. (1983). The complex nature of the sense of fairness: Internal standards and social comparison as bases for reward evaluations. *Journal of Personality and Social Psychology, 45,* 84–93.

Messick, D. M., Bloom, S., Boldizar, J. P., and Samuelson, C. D. (1985). Why we are fairer than others. *Journal of Experimental Social Psychology, 21,* 480–500.

Messick, D. M., and Mackie, D. M (1989). Intergroup relations. *Annual Review of Psychology, 40,* 45–81.

Messick, D. M., and Sentis, K. P. (1985). Estimating social and nonsocial utility functions from ordinal data. *European Journal of Social Psychology, 15,* 389–399.

Messick, D. M., Wilke, H., Brewer, M. B., Kramer, R. M., Zemke, P., and Lui, L. (1983). Individual adaptations and structural change as solutions to social dilemmas. *Journal of Personality and Social Psychology, 44,* 294–309.

Miceli, M. P., (1993). Justice and pay system satisfaction. In R. Cropanzano (Ed.), *Justice in the workplace: Approaching fairness in human resource management. Series in applied psychology* (pp. 257–283). Hillsdale, NJ: Lawrence Erlbaum.

Mikula, G. (1986). The experience of injustice: Toward a better understanding of its phenomenology. In H. W. Bierhoff, R. L. Cohen, and J. Greenberg (Eds.), *Justice in social relations* (pp. 103–124). New York: Plenum.

Mikula, G. (1993). On the experience of injustice. In W. Strobe and M. Hewstone (Eds.), *European review of social psychology* (Vol. 4, pp. 223–244). New York: Wiley.

Mikula, G. (1994). Perspective-related differences in interpretations of injustice by victims and victimizers: A test with close relationships. In M. J. Lerner and G.

Mikula (Eds.), *Entitlement and the affectional bond: Justice in close relationships.* New York: Plenum.

Mikula, G., Petri, B., and Tanzer, N. (1990). What people regard as unjust: Types and structures of everyday experiences of injustice. *European Journal of Social Psychology, 22*, 133–149.

Milgram, S. (1965). *Obedience to authority.* New York: Harper and Row.

Milgram, S. (1974). *Obedience to authority: An experimental view.* New York: Harper and Row.

Miller, D. T., and Ratner, R. K. (in press). The power of the myth of self-interest. Unpublished manuscript, Princeton University.

Miller, D. T., and Vidmar, N. (1981). The Social psychology of punishment reactions. In M. J. Lerner and S. C. Lerner (Eds.), *The Justice motive in social behavior.* New York: Academic Press.

Miller, J. G., and Bersoff, D. M. (1992). Culture and moral judgment: How are conflicts between justice and interpersonal responsibilities resolved? *Journal of Personality and Social Psychology, 62*, 541–554.

Miller, J. L., Rossi, P. H., and Simpson, J. E. (1986). Perceptions of justice: Race and gender differences in judgments of appropriate prison sentences. *Law and Society Review, 20,* 313–334.

Mirowsky, J. (1985). Depression and marital power: An equity model. *American Journal of Sociology, 91*, 557–592.

Mitchell, G., Tetlock, P., Mellers, B., and Ordonez, L. (1993). Judgments of social justice: Compromises between equality and efficiency. *Journal of Personality and Social Psychology, 65,* 629–639.

Monahan, J., and Walker, L. (1994). *Social science in law* (3rd ed.). Westbury, NY: Foundation Press.

Montada, L. (1991). Coping with life stress: Injustice and the question "Who is responsible?" In H. Steensung and R. Vermunt (Eds.), *Social justice in human relations* (Vol. 2, pp. 9–39). New York: Plenum.

Montada, L. (1994). Injustice in harm and loss. *Social Justice Research, 7,* 5–28.

Montada, L., and Kals, E. (1995). Perceived justice of ecological policy and proenvironmental commitments. *Social Justice Research, 8,* 305–327.

Montada, L., and Schneider, A. (1989). Justice and emotional reactions to the disadvantaged. *Social Justice Research, 3,* 313–344.

Moore, B. (1978). *Injustice: The social bases of obedience and revolt.* White Plains, NY: Sharpe.

Moore, D. (1991). Entitlement and justice evaluations: Who should get more, and why? *Social Psychology Quarterly, 54,* 208–223.

Moorman, R. H. (1991). Relationship between organizational justice and organizational citizenship behaviors: Do fairness perceptions influence employee citizenship? *Journal of Applied Psychology, 76,* 845–855.

Moorman, R. H., Neihoff, B. P., and Organ, D. W. (1993). Treating employees fairly and organizational citizenship behavior. *Employee Responsibilities and Rights Journal, 6,* 209–225.

Muller, E. N. (1972). A test of partial theory of potential for political violence. *American Political Science Review, 66,* 928–959.

Muller, E. N. (1979). *Aggressive political participation*. Princeton: Princeton University Press.

Muller, E. N. (1980). The psychology of political protest and violence. In T. R. Gurr (Ed.), *Handbook of Political Conflict*. New York: Free Press.

Muller, E. N., and Jukam. T. (1983). Discontent and aggressive political participation. *British Journal of Political Science, 13,* 159–179.

Mummendey, A., and Otten, S. (1993). Aggression: Interaction between individuals and social groups. In R. B. Pelson and J. T. Tedeschi (Eds.), *Aggression and violence: A social interactionist perspective.* Washington, DC: American Psychological Association.

Murphy, W.F., and Tanenhaus, J. (1969). Public opinion and the United States Supreme Court: A preliminary mapping of some prerequisites for court legitimization of regime changes. In J. B. Grossman and J. Tanenhaus (Eds.), *Frontiers in judicial research*. New York: Wiley.

Murphy-Berman, V., Berman, J. J., Singh, P., Pachauri, A., and Kumar, P. (1984). Factors affecting allocation to needy and meritorious recipients: A cross-cultural comparison. *Journal of Personality and Social Psychology, 46,* 1267–1272.

Musante, L., Gilbert, M. A., and Thibaut, J. (1983). The effects of control on perceived fairness of procedures and outcomes. *Journal of Experimental Social Psychology, 19,* 223–238.

Mydans, S. (1994, July 22). In Simpson case, an issue for everyone. *New York Times,* p. A16.

Mydral, G. (1944). *An American Dilemma* (Vols. 1 and 2). New York: Pantheon.

Myers, D. G. (1992). *The pursuit of happiness: Who is happy—and why*. New York: Marrow.

Nacoste, R. W. (1989). Affirmation action and self-evaluation. In. F. Blanchard and F. Crosby (Eds.), *Affirmation action in perspective*. New York: Springer-Verlag.

Nacoste, R. W. (1990). Sources of stigma: Analyzing the psychology of affirmative action. *Law and Policy, 12,* 175–195.

Nacoste, R. W. (1992). Toward a psychological ecology of affirmation action. *Social Justice Research, 5,* 269–289.

Nacoste, R. W. (1993). Procedural justice and preferential treatment: A brief review and comment. *Current Psychology: Research and Reviews, 12,* 230–235.

Nader, L., and Todd, T. F. (1978). *The disputing process: Law in ten societies.* New York: Columbia University Press.

Nagata, D. K. (1990). The Japanese American internment: Perceptions of moral community, fairness, and redress. *Journal of Social Issues, 46* (1), 133–146.

Nagata, D. K. (1993). *Legacy of injustice: Exploring the cross-generational impact of the Japanese American internment*. New York: Plenum.

Narby, D. J., Cutler, B. L., and Moran, G. (1993). A meta-analysis of the association between authoritarianism and jurors' perception of defendant culpability. *Journal of Applied Psychology, 78,* 34–42.

Niehoff, B. P., and Moorman, R. H. (1993). Justice as a mediator of the relationship between methods of monitoring and organizational citizenship behavior. *Academy of Management Journal, 36,* 527–556.

Nisbett, R. E., and Wilson, T. D. (1977). Telling more than we can know: Verbal reports on mental processes. *Psychological Review, 84,* 231–259.

Oakes, P. J., Haslam, S. A., Turner, J. C. (1994). *Stereotyping and social reality.* Oxford, UK: Blackwell Publishers.

Ochs, J., and Roth, A. E. (1989). An experimental study of sequential bargaining. *American Economic Review, 79,* 335–385.

Ohbuchi, K., Kameda, N., and Agarie, M. (1989). Apology as aggression control: Its role in mediating appraisal of and response to harm. *Journal of Personality and Social Psychology, 56,* 219–227.

Okun, A. M. (1975). *Equality and efficiency: The big tradeoff.* Washington, DC: Brookings.

Olson, J., Hafer, C. L., Couzens, A., and Kramins, I. (1990, August). Self-presentation motives in relative deprivation. Paper presented at the Canadian Psychological Association, Ottawa, Ontario.

Olson, J. M. (1986). Resentment about deprivation: Entitlement and hopefulness as mediators of the effects of qualifications. In J. Olson, C. P. Herman, and M. Zanna, (Eds.), *Relative deprivation and social comparison: The Ontario symposium.* Hillsdale, NJ: Lawrence Erlbaum.

Olson, J. M., and Hafer, C. L. (1996). Affect, motivation and cognition in relative deprivation research. In R. M. Sorrentino and E. T. Higgins (Eds.), *Handbook of Motivation and Cognition* (Vol. 3, pp. 85–117). New York: Guilford Press.

Olson, J. M., Herman, C. P., and Zanna, M. P. (1986). *Relative deprivation and social comparison.* Hillsdale, NJ: Lawrence Erlbaum.

Olson, J. M., Roese, N. J., Meen, J., and Robertson, D. J. (1994). The preconditions and consequences of relative deprivation: Two field studies. *Journal of Applied Social Psychology, 25,* 944–964.

O'Malley, M. N. (1983). Interpersonal and intrapersonal justice: The effect of subject and confederate outcomes on evaluations of fairness. *European Journal of Social Psychology, 13,* 121–128.

Ophuls, W. (1977). *Ecology and the politics of scarcity.* San Francisco: Freeman.

Opotow, S. (1990). Moral exclusion and injustice: An introduction. *Journal of Social Issues, 46* (1), 1–20.

Opotow, S. (1993). Animals and the scope of justice. *Journal of Social Issues, 49* (1), 71–85.

Opotow, S. (1994). Predicting protection: Scope of justice and the natural world. *Journal of Social Issues, 50* (3), 49–63.

Opotow, S. (1995). Drawing the line: Social categorization, moral exclusion, and the scope of justice. In B. B. Bunker and J. Z. Rubin (Eds.), *Conflict, Cooperation, and Justice.* San Francisco: Jossey-Bass.

Ordonez, L. D., and Mellers, B. A. (1993). Trade-offs in fairness and preference judgments. In B. A. Mellers and J. Baron (Eds.), *Psychological perspectives on justice.* Cambridge, UK: Cambridge University Press.

Organ, D. W., and Moorman, R. H. (1993). Fairness and organizational citizenship behavior: What are the connections? *Social Justice Research, 6,* 5–18.

Parker, S., and Kleiner, R. J. (1966). *Mental illness in the urban Negro community.* Toronto, Canada: Free Press.

Parkin, F. (1971). *Class inequality and political order.* New York: Praeger.

Patchen, M. (1958). The effect of reference group Standards on Job Satisfaction. *Human Relations, 11,* 304–314.

Pavlak, T. J., Clark, P. F., and Gallagher, D. G. (1992). Measuring attitudes toward grievance systems: A procedural justice perspective applied to the workplace. *Social Justice Research, 5,* 173–194.

Pepitone, A. (1975). Social psychological perspectives on crime and punishment. *Journal of Social Issues, 31*(4), 197–216.

Pepitone, A. (1976). Toward a normative and comparative bicultural social psychology. *Journal of Personality and Social Psychology, 34,* 641–653.

Petersilia, J., and Deschenes, E. P. (1994). What punishes? Inmates rank the severity of prison vs. intermediate sanctions. *Federal Probation, 58*(1), 3–8.

Peterson, R. S. (1994). The role of values in predicting fairness judgments and support of affirmative action. *Journal of Social Issues, 50*(4), 95–155.

Petta, G., and Walker, I. (1992). Relative deprivation and ethnic identity. *British Journal of Social Psychology, 31,* 285–293.

Pettigrew, T. F. (1964). *A profile of the Negro American.* Princeton: Van Nostrand.

Pettigrew, T. F. (1967). Social evaluation theory. In D. Levine (Ed.,) *Nebraska symposium on motivation.* Lincoln, NE: University of Nebraska Press.

Pettigrew, T. F. (1972). *Racially separate or together.* New York: McGraw-Hill.

Pettigrew, T. F. (1978). Three issues of ethnicity: Boundaries, deprivations, and perceptions. In J. M. Yinger and S. J. Cutler (Eds.), *Major social issues: A multidisciplinary view* (pp. 25–49). New York: Free Press.

Pettigrew, T. F. (1985). New Black-White patterns: How best to conceptualize them? *American Review of Sociology, 11,* 329–346.

Pettigrew, T. F., and Meertons, R. (1993). *Relative deprivation and intergroup prejudice.* Unpublished manuscript, University of California, Santa Cruz.

Petty, R. E., and Cacioppo, J. T. (1986). The elaboration likelihood model of persuasion. In L. Berkowitz (Ed.), *Advances in experimental social psychology* (Vol. 19, pp. 123–205). New York: Academic Press.

Piaget, J. (1948). *The moral judgment of the child.* Glencoe, IL: Free Press.

Plous, S. (1993). Psychological mechanisms in the human use of animals. *Journal of Social Issues, 49*(1), 11–52.

Pontell, H. N., Granite, D., Keenan, C., and Geis, G. (1985). Seriousness of crimes: A survey of the nation's chiefs of police. *Journal of Criminal Justice, 13,* 1–13.

Potter, J., and Reicher, S. (1987). Discourses of community and conflict: The organization of social categories in accounts of a "riot." *British Journal of Social Psychology, 26,* 25–40.

Pratt, C., Schmall, V., Wright, S. (1987). Ethical concerns of family caregivers of dementia patients. *Gerontologist, 27,* 632–638.

Pritchard, D., Dunnette, M. D., and Jorgenson, D. O. (1972). Effects of perceptions of equity and inequity on worker performance and satisfaction. *Journal of Applied Psychology, 56,* 75–94.

Pruitt, D. G., Pierce, R. S., McGillicuddy, N.B., Welton, G. L., and Castrianno, L. M. (1993). Long-term success in mediation. *Law and Human Behavior, 17,* 113–330.

Pruitt, D. G., and Rubin, J. Z. (1986). *Social conflict: Escalation, stalemate, and settlement.* New York: McGraw-Hill.

Putnam, R. D. (1995). Bowling alone: America's declining social capital. *Journal of Democracy, 6*(1), 65–78.

Rabbie, J. M., Schot, J. C., and Visser, L. (1989). Social identity theory: A conceptual and empirical critique from the perspective of a behavioral interaction model. *European Journal of Social Psychology, 18*, 117–123.

Rachlin, V. C. (1987). Fair vs. equal role relations in dual-career and dual-income families: Implications for family interventions. *Family Relations, 36*, 187–192.

Rasinski, K. (1987). What's fair is fair ... or is it? Value differences underlying public views about social justice. *Journal of Personality and Social Psychology, 53*, 201–211.

Rasinski, K. (1992). Preference for decision control in organizational decision making. *Social Justice Research, 5*, 343–358.

Rasinski, K., and Tyler, T. R. (1987). Fairness and vote choice in the 1984 presidential election. *American Politics Quarterly, 16*, 5–24.

Rawls, J. (1971). *A theory of justice.* Cambridge, MA: Harvard University Press.

Rawls, J. (1993). *Political liberalism.* New York: Columbia University Press.

Reicher, S. (1987). The St. Paul's riot: An explanation of the limits of crowd action in terms of a social identity model. *European Journal of Social Psychology, 14*, 1–21.

Reis, H. T. (1986). Levels of interest in the study of interpersonal justice. In H. W. Bierhoff, R. L. Cohen, and J. Greenberg (Eds.), *Justice in social relations.* New York: Plenum.

Reis, H. T. (1987). The nature of the justice motive. In J. C. Masters and W. P. Smith (Eds.), *Social comparison, social justice, and relative deprivation.* Hillsdale, NJ: Lawrence Erlbaum.

Roberts, J. (1992). Public opinion, crime, and criminal justice. In M. Tonry (Ed.), *Crime and justice* (Vol. 16). Chicago: University of Chicago Press.

Robinson, P. H., and Darley, J. M. (1995) *Justice, liability, and blame: Community views and the criminal law.* San Francisco: Westview Press.

Robinson, P. H., and Darley, J. M. (1996). The utility of desert. Unpublished manuscript, Northwestern University School of Law, Chicago.

Rose, P. I. (1993). "Of every hue and caste": Race, immigration, and perceptions of pluralism. *Annals of the American Academy of Political and Social Science, 530*, 187–202.

Ross, H. L. (1980). *Settled out of court.* New York: Aldine.

Ross, M., and Ellard, H. (1986). On winnowing: The impact of scarcity on allocators' evaluations of candidates for a resource. *Journal of Experimental Social Psychology, 22*, 374–388.

Rossi, P. H., Waite, E., Bose, C. E., and Berk, R. E. (1974). The seriousness of crimes: Normative structure and individual differences. *American Sociological Review, 39*, 224–237.

Rousseau, D. M. (1995). *Psychological contracts in organizations.* Thousand Oaks, CA: Sage.

Rousseau, D. M., and Anton, R. J. (1988). Fairness and implied contract: Obligations in job terminations: A policy-capturing study. *Human Performance, 1*, 273–289.

Rousseau, D. M., and Aquino, K. (1993). Fairness and implied contract: Obligations in job terminations: The role of remedies, social accounts, and procedural justice. *Human Performance, 6*, 135–149.

Rousseau, D. M., and Parks, J. M. (1993). The contracts of individuals and organizations. *Research in Organizational Behavior, 15*, 1–43.

Rumsey, M. G. (1976). Effects of defendant background and remorse on sentencing judgments. *Journal of Applied Social Psychology, 6,* 64–68.

Runciman, W. G. (1966). *Relative deprivation and social justice: A study of attitudes to social inequality in twentieth-century England.* Berkeley: University of California Press.

Rusbult, C. (1987). Responses to dissatisfaction in close relationships: The exit-voice-loyalty-neglect model. In D. Perlman and S. Duck (Eds.), *Intimate relationships: Development, dynamics, and deterioration* (pp. 209–237). Newbury Park, CA: Sage.

Sales, S. M. (1973). Threat as a factor in authoritarianism: The analysis of archival data. *Journal of Personality and Social Psychology, 28,* 44–57.

Sampson, E. E. (1975). On justice as equality. *Journal of Social Issues, 31*(3), 45–64.

Sarat, A., and Vidmar, N. (1976). Public opinion, the death penalty, and the Eighth Amendment: Testing the Marshall hypothesis. *Wisconsin Law Review, 1,* 171–206.

Scase, R. (1974). Relative deprivation: A comparison of English and Swedish manual workers. In D. Wedderburn (Ed.), *Poverty, inequality and class structure.* Cambridge, UK: Cambridge University Press.

Schaubroeck, J., May, D. R., and Brown, F. W. (1994). Procedural justice explanations and employee reactions to economic hardship: A field experiment. *Journal of Applied Psychology, 79,* 455–460.

Scheingold, S. A. (1974). *The politics of rights.* New Haven: Yale University Press.

Schlenker, B. R., and Miller, R. S. (1977). Egocentrism in groups. *Journal of Personality and Social Psychology, 35,* 755–764.

Schmidt, G., and Weiner, B. (1988). An attribution-affect-action theory of behavior: Replications of judgments of help-giving. *Personality and Social Psychology Bulletin, 14,* 610–621.

Schmitt, D. R., and Marwell, G. (1972). Withdrawal and reward allocation as responses to inequity. *Journal of Experimental Social Psychology, 8,* 207–221.

Schwartz, G. S., Kane, T. R., Joseph, J. M., and Tedeschi, J. T. (1978). The effects of post-transgression remorse on perceived aggression, attributions of intent, and level of punishment. *British Journal of Social and Clinical Psychology, 17,* 293–297.

Schwinger, T. (1986). The need principle in distributive justice. In H. W. Bierhoff, R. L. Cohen, and J. Greenberg (Eds.), *Justice in Social Relations.* New York: Plenum.

Senchak, M., and Reis, H. (1988). The fair process effect and procedural criteria in the resolution of disputes between intimate same-sex friends. *Social Justice Research, 2,* 263–287.

Shapiro, D. L. (1993). Reconciling theoretical differences among procedural justice researchers by reevaluating what it means to have one's views "considered": Implications for third-party managers. In R. Cropanzano (Ed.), *Justice in the workplace.* Hillsdale, NJ: Lawrence Erlbaum.

Shapiro, D. L., and Brett, J. M. (1993). Comparing three processes underlying judgments of procedural justice. *Journal of Personality and Social Psychology, 65,* 1167–1177.

Shaver, K. G. (1970). Defensive attribution: Effects of severity and relevance on the responsibility assigned for accidents. *Journal of Personality and Social Psychology. 14,* 101–113.

Shaver, K. G. (1985). *The attribution of blame.* New York: Springer-Verlag.

Shaver, P., Schwartz, J., Kirson, D., and O'Connor, C. (1987). Emotion knowledge: Further exploration of a prototype approach. *Journal of Personality and Social Psychology, 52,* 1061–1086.

Shepelak, N. J. (1987). The role of self-explanations and self-evaluations in legitimating inequality. *American Sociological Review, 52,* 495–503.

Sheppard, B. H., and Lewicki, R. J. (1987). Toward general principles of managerial fairness. *Social Justice Research, 1,* 161–176.

Sheppard, B. H., Lewicki, R. J., and Minton, J. W. (1992). *Organizational justice: The search for fairness in the workplace.* New York: Lexington.

Sherif, M., Harvey, O. J., White, B. J., Hood, W. R., and Sherif, C. W. (1961). *Intergroup conflict and cooperation: The Robber's Cave experiment.* Norman, OK: University of Oklahoma Book Exchange.

Shotland, R. L. (1976). Spontaneous vigilantism: A bystander response to criminal behavior. In H. J. Rosenbaum and D. C. Sederberg (Eds.), *Vigilante Politics.* Philadelphia: University of Pennsylvania Press.

Shotland, R. L., and Goodstein, L. I. (1984) The Role of Bystanders in Crime Control. *Journal of Social Issues, 40,* 9–26.

Shultz, T. R., and Darley, J. M. (1991). An information processing model of retributive justice based on "legal reasoning." In W. M. Kurtiness and J. L. Gewirtz (Eds.), *Handbook of Moral Behavior and Development*: *Vol. 2. Research.* Hillsdale, NJ: Lawrence Erlbaum.

Shultz, T. R., Scheleifer, M., and Altman, I. (1981). Judgments of causation, responsibility, and punishment in cases of harm-doing. *Canadian Journal of Behavioral Science, 13,* 238–253.

Shultz, T. R., and Wright, K. (1985). Concepts of negligence and intention in the assignment of moral responsibility. *Canadian Journal of Behavioral Science, 17,* 97–108.

Siegal, M., and Schwalb, D. (1985). Economic justice in adolescence: An Australian-Japanese comparison. *Journal of Economic Psychology, 6,* 313–326.

Silver, E., Cirincione, C., and Steadman, H. J. (1994). Demythologizing inaccurate perceptions of the insanity defense. *Law and Human Behavior, 18*(1), 63–70.

Sinclair, R. C., and Mark, M. M. (1991). Mood and the endorsement of egalitarian macrojustice versus equity-based microjustice principles. *Personality and Social Psychology Bulletin, 17,* 369–375.

Singer, E. (1981). Reference Group and Social Evaluations. In M. Rosenberg and R. Turner (Eds.), *Social psychology: Sociological perspectives.* New York: Basic Books.

Skitka, L. J. (1996) Setting limits and living with them: Ideological reactions to scarcity and change. Unpublished manuscript, University of Chicago.

Skitka, L. J., and Tetlock, P. E. (1992). Allocation of scarce resources: A contingency model of distributive justice. *Journal of Experimental Social Psychology, 28,* 491–522.

Skitka, L. J., and Tetlock, P. E. (1993). Of ants and grasshoppers: The political psychology of allocating public assistance. In B. A. Mellers and J. Baron (Eds.), *Psychological perspectives on justice* (pp. 205–233). New York: Cambridge University Press.

Smith, H. J., Pettigrew, T. F. and Vega, L. (1994, August). *Measures of Relative Deprivation: A Conceptual Critique and Meta-analysis.* Paper presented at the annual meeting of the American Psychological Association, Los Angeles, California.

Smith, H. J., and Spears, R. (1996). Ability and outcome evaluations as a function of personal and collective (dis)advantage: A group escape from individual bias. *Personality and Social Psychology Bulletin, 22, 690–704.*

Smith, H. J., Spears, R., and Oyen, M. (1994). The influence of personal deprivation and salience of group membership on justice evaluations. *Journal of Experimental Social Psychology, 30, 277–299.*

Smith, H. J., and Tyler, T. R. (1996). Justice and power. *European Journal of Social Psychology, 26, 171–200.*

Smith, R. E., Parrott, W. G., Ozer, D., and Moniz, A. (1994). Subjective injustice and inferiority as predictors of hostile and depressive feelings in envy. *Personality and Social Psychology Bulletin, 20, 705–711.*

Snell, W. E., Jr., and Belk, S. S. (1985). On assessing "equity" in intimate relationships. *Representative Research in Social Psychology, 15, 16–24.*

Snyder, D., and Tilly, C. (1972). Hardship and collective violence in France, 1930–1960. *American Sociological Review, 37, 520–532.*

Somer, K., and Williams, K. (1994). *Working with people who ignore you: The impact of social ostracism and gender on social loafing.* Unpublished manuscript, University of Toledo, OH.

Sondak, H., and Sheppard, B. (1995, August). Evaluating alternative models for allocating scarce resources: A relational approach to procedural justice and social structure. Paper presented at annual meeting of the Academy of Management, Vancouver, British Columbia, Canada.

Steil, J. (1983). The response to injustice: Effects of varying levels of social support and position of advantage or disadvantage. *Journal of Experimental Social Psychology, 19, 239–253.*

Steil, J. M. (1994). Equality and entitlement in marriage: Benefits and barriers. In M. J. Lerner and G. Mikula (Eds.), *Entitlement and the affectional bond: Justice in close relationships.* New York: Plenum.

Steil, J. M., and Turetsky, B. A. (1987). Is equal better? The relationship between marital equality and psychological symptomatology. In S. Oskamp (Ed.), *Family processes and problems: Social psychological aspects.* Beverly Hills, CA: Sage.

Stenner, P., and Marshall, H. (1995). A Q methodology study of rebelliousness. *European Journal of Social Psychology, 25, 621–636.*

Stinchcombe, A. L., Adams, R., Heimer, C. A., Scheppele, K. L., Smith, T. W., and Taylor, D. G. (1980). *Crime and punishment—Changing attitudes in America.* San Francisco: Jossey-Bass.

Stouffer, S. A., Suchman, E. A., DeVinney, L. C., Star, S. A., and Williams, R. A., Jr. (1949). *The American soldier: Adjustments during army life* (Vol. 1). Princeton: Princeton University Press.

Stringer, M., and Lavery, C. (1987). The acquisition of ethnic categorization ability by British university students in Northern Ireland. *Social Behavior, 2, 157–164.*

Strumpel, B. (1976). *Economic means for human needs: Social indicators of well-being and discontent.* Ann Arbor, MI.: Institute for Social Research.

Sugawara, I., and Huo, Y. J. (1994). Disputes in Japan: A cross-cultural test of the procedural justice model. *Social Justice Research, 7*, 129–144.

Sullivan, J. L., Piereson, J., and Marcus, G. E. (1979). An alternative conceptualization of political tolerance: Illusory increases 1950s–1970s. *American Political Science Review, 73*, 781–794.

Sullivan, J. L., Piereson, J., and Marcus, G. E. (1982). *Political tolerance and American democracy.* Chicago: University of Chicago Press.

Suls, J., and Wills, T. A. (1991). *Social comparison: Contemporary theory and research.* Hillsdale, NJ: Lawrence Erlbaum.

Sweeney, P. D., and McFarlin, D. B. (1993). Workers' evaluations of the "ends" and "means": An examination of four models of distributive and procedural justice. *Organizational Behavior and Human Decision Processes, 55*, 23–40.

Tajfel, H. (1982). *Human groups and social categories.* New York: Cambridge University Press.

Tajfel, H., and Turner, J. (1979). An integrative theory of intergroup conflict. In W. G. Austin and S. Worchel (Eds.), *The social psychology of intergroup relations* (pp. 33–47). Monterey, CA: Brooks/Cole.

Tajfel, H., and Turner, J. (1986). The social identity theory of intergroup behavior. In S. Worchel (Ed.), *Psychology of intergroup relations.* Chicago: Nelson Hall.

Takenishi, A., and Takenishi, M. (1992). Does commitment affect the meaning of fairness?: Commonality and stability of fairness criteria in a political setting. *Social Justice Research, 5*, 415–429.

Tansky, J. W. (1993). Justice and organizational citizenship behavior: What is the relationship? Organizational justice-citizenship behavior [Special issue]. *Employee Responsibilities and Rights Journal, 6*(3), 195–207.

Taylor, C., and Kleinke, C. L., (1992). Effects of severity of accident, history of drunk driving, intent, and remorse on judgments of a drunk driver. *Journal of Applied Psychology, 22*, 1641–1655.

Taylor, D. M., and McKirnan, D. J. (1984). A five stage model of intergroup relations. *British Journal of Social Psychology, 23*, 291–300.

Taylor, D. M., and Moghaddam, F. M. (1994). *Theories of intergroup relations.* New York: Praeger.

Taylor, D. M., Moghaddam, F. M. and Bellerose, J. (1989). Social comparison in an intergroup context. *Journal of Social Psychology, 129*, 499–515.

Taylor, D. M., Watson, G., and Wong-Reiger, D. (1985) Social categorization, justice, and socioeconomic status. *Journal of Social Psychology, 125*, 89–109.

Taylor, D. M., Wright, S., Moghaddam, F., and Lalonde, R. (1990). The personal/group discrepancy: Perceiving my group, but not myself, to be a target for discrimination. *Personality and Social Psychology Bulletin, 16*, 254–262.

Taylor, D. M., Wright, S. C., and Porter, L. (1994). Dimensions of perceived discrimination: The personal/group discrimination discrepancy. In M. P. Zanna and J. M. Olson (Eds.), *The psychology of prejudice.* Hillsdale, NJ: Lawrence Erlbaum.

Taylor, M. C. (1982). Improved conditions, rising expectations and dissatisfaction: A test of the past/present relative deprivation hypothesis. *Social Psychology Quarterly, 45*, 24–33.

Taylor, S. E., and Brown, J. (1988). Illusion and well-being: A social psychological perspective on mental health. *Psychological Bulletin, 103*, 193–210.

Taylor, S. E., and Lobel, M. (1989) Social comparison activity under threat: Downward evaluation and upward contacts. *Psychological Review, 96,* 569–575.

Tedeschi, J. T., and Nesler, M. S. (1994). Grievances: Development and reactions. In R. B. Felson and J. T. Tedeschi (Eds.), *Aggression and violence: Social interactionist perspectives.* Washington, DC: American Psychological Association.

Terrill, R. (1996, April 1–7). China's savage secret. *Washington Post National Weekly Edition,* p. 25.

Terry, D. (1995, October 2). Distrust fuels racial divide on justice for Simpson. *New York Times,* p. B9.

Thibaut, J., and Faucheux, C. (1965). The development of contractual norms in a bargaining situation under two types of stress. *Journal of Experimental Social Psychology, 1,* 89–102.

Thibaut, J., Friedland, N., and Walker, L. (1974). Compliance with rules: Some social determinants. *Journal of Personality and Social Psychology, 30,* 792–801.

Thibaut, J., and Kelley, H. H. (1959). *The social psychology of groups.* New York: Wiley.

Thibaut, J., and Walker, L. (1975). *Procedural justice: A psychological analysis.* Hillsdale, NJ: Lawrence Erlbaum.

Thibaut, J., and Walker, L. (1978). A theory of procedure. *California Law Review, 66,* 541–566.

Thompson, L., and Loewenstein, G. (1992). Egocentric interpretations of fairness and interpersonal conflict. *Organizational Behavior and Human Decision Processes, 51,* 176–197.

Thurow, L. (1995, November 19). Why their world might crumble: How much inequality can a democracy take? *New York Times Magazine,* pp. 78–79.

Toch, H., (1993). Good violence and bad violence: Self presentations of aggressors through accounts and war stories. In R. B. Felson and J. T. Tedeschi (Eds.), *Aggression and violence: Social interactionist perspectives.* Washington, DC: American Psychological Association.

Tornblom, K. Y., and Foa, U. G. (1983). Choice of distributive principle: Cross-cultural evidence on the effects of resources. *Acta Sociologica, 26,* 161–173.

Tougas, F., and Veilleux, F. (1988). The influence of identification, collective relative deprivation, and procedure of implementation on women's response to affirmative action: A causal modeling approach. *Canadian Journal of Behavioral Science, 20,* 15–27.

Towson, S. M., Lerner, M. J., and DeCarufel, A. (1981). Justice rules or in-group loyalties: The effects of competition on children's allocation behavior. *Personality and Social Psychology Bulletin, 7,* 696–700.

Triandis, H. C. (1972). *The analysis of subjective culture.* New York: Wiley.

Triandis, H. C. (1989). The self and social behavior in differing cultural contexts. *Psychological Review, 96,* 506–520.

Turner, J. C. (1991). *Social Influence.* London, Milton Keynes: Open University Press.

Turner, J. C., Hogg, M. A., Oakes, P. J., Reicher, S., and Wetherell, M. S. (1987). *Rediscovering the social group: A self-categorization theory.* Oxford, UK: Blackwell.

Tyler, T. R. (1984). The role of perceived injustice in defendant's evaluations of their courtroom experience. *Law and Society Review, 18,* 51–74.

Tyler, T. R. (1985). Justice in the political arena. In R. Folger (Ed.), *The sense of injustice*. New York: Plenum.

Tyler, T. R. (1987). Conditions leading to value expressive effects in judgments of procedural justice: A test of four models. *Journal of Personality and Social Psychology, 52,* 333–344.

Tyler, T. R. (1988). What is procedural justice?: Criteria used by citizens to assess the fairness of legal procedures. *Law and Society Review, 22,* 301–355.

Tyler, T. R. (1989) The psychology of procedural justice: A test of the group value model. *Journal of Personality and Social Psychology, 57,* 850–863.

Tyler, T. R. (1990). *Why people obey the law: Procedural justice, legitimacy, and compliance.* New Haven: Yale University Press.

Tyler, T. R. (1991). Using procedures to justify outcomes: Testing the validity of a procedural justice strategy for managing conflict and allocating resources in work organizations. *Basic and Applied Social Psychology, 12,* 259–279.

Tyler, T. R. (1994a). Governing amid diversity. *Law and Society Review, 28,* 701–722.

Tyler, T. R. (1994b). Psychological models of the justice motive. *Journal of Personality and Social Psychology, 67,* 850–863.

Tyler, T. R. (1995*). The psychology of legitimacy.* Unpublished manuscript, University of California, Berkeley.

Tyler, T. R. (1996). The relationship of outcome and procedural fairness: How does knowing the outcome influence judgments about the procedure? Paper prepared for a special issue of *Social Justice Research.*

Tyler, T. R., and Belliveau, M. (1996). Dealing with tradeoffs among justice principles: The motivational antecedents of definitions of fairness. In J. Rubin and B. Bunker (Eds.), *Conflict, cooperation, and justice: Essays in honor of Morton Deutsch.* San Francisco: Jossey-Bass.

Tyler, T. R., and Bies, R. J. (1990). Interpersonal aspects of procedural justice. In J. S. Carroll (Ed.), *Applied social psychology in business settings.* Hillsdale, NJ: Lawrence Erlbaum.

Tyler, T. R., and Boeckmann, R. J. (in press) Three strikes and you are out, but why?: The psychology of public support for punishing rule breakers. *Law and Society Review.*

Tyler, T. R., and Caine, A. (1981). The role of distributional and procedural fairness in the endorsement of formal leaders. *Journal of Personality and Social Psychology, 41,* 642–655.

Tyler, T. R., Casper, J. D., and Fisher, B. (1989). Maintaining allegiance toward political authorities: The role of prior attitudes and the use of fair procedures. *American Journal of Political Science, 33,* 629–652.

Tyler, T. R., and Dawes, R. M. (1993). Fairness in groups: Comparing the self-interest and social identity perspectives. In B. A. Mellers and J. Baron (Eds.), *Psychological perspectives on justice: Theory and applications.* New York: Cambridge University Press.

Tyler, T. R., and Degoey, P. (1995). Collective restraint in social dilemmas: Procedural justice and social identification effects on support for authorities. *Journal of Personality and Social Psychology, 69,* 482–497.

Tyler, T. R., Degoey, P., and Smith, H. J. (1996). Understanding why the justice of group procedures matters. *Journal of Personality and Social Psychology, 70,* 913–930.

Tyler, T. R., and Folger, R. (1980). Distributional and procedural aspects of satisfaction with citizen-police encounters. *Basic and Applied Social Psychology, 1,* 281–292.

Tyler, T. R., and Hastie, R. (1991). Social psychology and negotiation: The social consequences of cognitive illusions. In R. Lewicki, B. Sheppard, and M. H. Bazerman (Eds.), *Handbook of research on negotiation in organizations.* Greenwich, CT: JAI.

Tyler, T. R., Huo, Y. J., and Smith, H. J. (1995). *Relative and absolute evaluations as a basis for self-esteem and group oriented behavior: Do we have to be better than others to feel good about ourselves?* Unpublished manuscript, University of California, Berkeley.

Tyler, T. R., and Kramer, R. (1996). *Trust in organizations.* Thousand Oaks, CA: Sage.

Tyler, T. R., and Lind, E. A. (1990). Intrinsic versus community-based justice models: When does group membership matter? *Journal of Social Issues, 46* (1), 83–94.

Tyler, T. R., and Lind, E. A. (1992). A relational model of authority in groups. In M. Zanna (Ed.), *Advances in experimental social psychology* (Vol. 25, pp. 115–191). New York: Academic Press.

Tyler, T. R, Lind, E. A., and Huo, Y. J. (1994). *Culture, ethnicity, and authority: Social categorization and social orientation effects on the psychology of legitimacy.* Unpublished manuscript, University of California, Berkeley.

Tyler, T. R., Lind, E. A., Ohbuchi, K. Sugawara, I., and Huo, Y. J. (1995). *Conflict with outsiders: Disputing within and across cultural boundaries.* Unpublished manuscript, University of California, Berkeley.

Tyler, T. R., McGraw, K. M. (1986). Ideology and the interpretation of personal experience: Procedural justice and political quiescence. *Journal of Social Issues, 42*(2), 115–128.

Tyler, T. R., and Mitchell, G. (1994). Legitimacy and the empowerment of discretionary legal authority. *Duke Law Journal, 43,* 703–814.

Tyler, T. R., Rasinski, K., and McGraw, K. (1985). The influence of perceived injustice on support for political authorities. *Journal of Applied Social Psychology, 15,* 700–725.

Tyler, T. R., Rasinski, K., and Spodick, N. (1985). The influence of voice on satisfaction with leaders: Exploring the meaning of process control. *Journal of Personality and Social Psychology, 48,* 72–81.

Tyler, T. R., and Weber, R. (1983). Support for the death penalty. *Law and Society Review, 17,* 201–224.

Umbreit, M. S. (1989). Crime victims seeking fairness, not revenge: Toward restorative justice. *Federal Probation, 53*(3), 52–57.

United States Catholic Bishops. (1986, November). *Economic justice for all* [Pastoral Letter]. Washington, DC: National Catholic News Service.

Valenzi, E. R., and Andrews, I. R. (1971). Effect of hourly overpay and underpay inequity when tested with a new induction procedure. *Journal of Applied Psychology, 55,* 22–27.

Vanderslice, V. J. (1995). Cooperation within a competitive context: Lessons from worker cooperatives. In B. Bunker, and J. Z. Rubin (Eds.), *Conflict, cooperation and justice*. San Francisco: Jossey-Bass.

van Knippenberg, A. (1989). Strategies of identity management. In J. P. Van Oudenhoven and T. M. Wilemsen (Eds.), *Ethnic minorities: Social psychological perspectives*. Amsterdam: Swets and Zeitlinger.

van Knippenberg, A., and van Oers, H. (1984). Social identity and equity concerns in intergroup perceptions. *British Journal of Social Psychology*, 23, 351–361.

VanYperen, N. W., and Buunk, B. P. (1994). Social comparison and social exchange in marital relationships. In M. J. Lerner and G. Mikula (Eds.), *Entitlement and the affectionate bond: Justice in close relationships*. New York: Plenum.

Vanneman, R. D., and Pettigrew, T. F. (1972). Race and relative deprivation. *Race, 13*, 461–486.

Vaughan, D. (1996). *The Challenger launch decision: Risky technology, culture, and deviance at NASA*. Chicago: University of Chicago Press.

Veilleux, F., and Tougas, F. (1989). Male acceptance of affirmative action programs for women: The results of altruistic or egoistical motives? *International Journal of Psychology, 24*, 485–496.

Vermunt, R., van den Bos, K., Lind, A. (1993). The effect of inaccurate procedure on protest: The mediating role of perceived unfairness and situational self-esteem. Submitted for publication.

Vidmar, N. (1974). Retributive and utilitarian motives and other correlates of Canadian attitudes toward the death penalty. *The Canadian Psychologist, 15*, 337–356.

Vidmar, N., and Miller, D. T. (1980). The social psychology of punishment. *Law and Society Review, 14*, 565–602.

Walker, I., and Mann, L. (1987). Unemployment, relative deprivation and social protest. *Personality and Social Psychology Bulletin, 13*, 275–283.

Walker , I., and Pettigrew, T. F. (1984). Relative deprivation theory: An overview and conceptual critique. *British Journal of Social Psychology, 23*, 301–310.

Walker, L., LaTour, S., Lind, E. A., and Thibaut, J. (1974). Reactions of participants and observers to modes of adjudication. *Journal of Applied Social Psychology, 4*, 295–310.

Walster, E. (1966). Assignment of responsibility for an accident. *Journal of Personality and Social Psychology, 3*, 73–79.

Walster, E., Berscheid, E., and Walster, G. W. (1973). New directions in equity research. *Journal of Personality and Social Psychology, 25*, 151–176.

Walster, E., and Walster, G. W. (1975). Equity and social justice. *Journal of Social Issues, 31*, 21–43.

Walster, E., Walster, G. W., and Berscheid, E. (1978). *Equity: Theory and research*. Boston: Allyn and Bacon.

Walzer, M. (1983). *Spheres of justice: A defence of pluralism and equality*. Oxford, UK: M. Robertson.

Warr, M., Meier, R. F., and Erickson, M. L. (1983). Norms, theories of punishment, and publicly preferred penalties for crimes. *Sociological Quarterly, 24*, 75–91.

Whatley, M. A., and Riggio, R. E. (1993). Gender differences in attribution of blame for male rape victims. *Journal of Interpersonal Violence, 8*, 502–511.

Whitney, C. (1995, December 6). For French, it's not 1968. *New York Times*, p. A12.

Williams, R. M. (1975). Relative deprivation. In L. A. Coser (Ed.), *The idea of social structure*. New York: Harcourt Brace Jaovanovich.

Wills, T. A. (1991). Similarity and self-esteem in downward comparison. In J. Suls and T. A. Wills (Eds.), *Social comparison: Contemporary theory and research*. Hillsdale, NJ: Lawrence Erlbaum.

Wish, M., Deutsch, M., and Kaplan, S. J. (1976). Perceived dimensions of interpersonal relations. *Journal of Personality and Social Psychology, 33*, 409–420.

Wish, M., and Kaplan, S. J. (1977). Toward an implicit theory of interpersonal communication. *Sociometry, 40*, 234–246.

Wood, J. (1989). Theory and research concerning social comparisons of personal attributes. *Psychological Bulletin, 106*, 231–248.

Wood, J., and Taylor, K. L. (1991). Serving self-relevant goals through social comparison. In J. Suls and T. A. Wills (Eds.), *Social comparison: Contemporary theory and research*. Hillsdale, NJ: Lawrence Erlbaum.

Wright, R. (1994). *The moral animal: Why we are the way we are: The new science of evolutionary psychology*. New York: Pantheon.

Wright, S. C., Ropp, S. A., Jenson, J., Blucher, S., and Darrow, P. (1996, August). *Violent acts as intergroup versus interpersonal events: Perceptions of sexual assault.* Paper presented at the annual meeting of the American Psychological Society, San Francisco.

Wright, S. C., Taylor, D. M, and Moghaddam, F. M. (1990). The relationship of perceptions and emotions to behavior in the face of collective inequality. *Social Justice Research, 4*, 229–250.

Wright, S. C., Taylor, D. M., and Moghaddam, F. M. (1990). Responding to membership in a disadvantaged group: From acceptance to collective protest. *Journal of Personality and Social Psychology, 58*, 994–1003.

Zamble, E., and Kalm, K. L. (1990). General and specific measures of public attitudes towards sentencing. *Canadian Journal of Behavioral Science, 22*, 327–337.

Zanna, M., Crosby, F., and Loewenstein, G. (1987). Male reference groups and discontent among female professionals. In B. Gutek and L. Larwood (Eds.), *Women's career development*. Newbury Park, CA: Sage.

ABOUT THE BOOK AND AUTHORS

For this unique text focused on the social psychology of justice, the authors have assembled the most current information relating to five major questions. These questions look specifically at how justice is defined, how it influences individuals' thoughts and actions and shapes their behavior, and when and why it matters. The underlying unifying theme is that individuals do care about issues of fairness in their interactions with others, with groups, and with institutions they support or oppose.

Using this theme as their guidepost, the authors explore research on relative deprivation, distributive justice, procedural justice, and retributive justice. Extensive use of examples drawn from contemporary culture make this book an informative and engaging collection of the most current thinking about topics such as diversity, gender, equal pay, personal satisfaction, third-party dispute management, crime, cultural preservation, and scarcity theory.

This text will be a valuable source for advanced courses on social justice, interpersonal relations, negotiation, intergroup conflict, and group processes in social psychology, political science, sociology, and legal studies.

Tom R. Tyler is a professor of psychology at the University of California at Berkeley. **Robert J. Boeckmann** is a visiting assistant professor at Mills College. **Heather J. Smith** is a visiting assistant professor at Saint Mary's College. **Yuen J. Huo** is a research fellow at the Public Policy Institute of California.

INDEX